STAGES OF CAPITAL

RITU BIRLA

STAGES OF CAPITAL

Law, Culture, and Market Governance

in Late Colonial India

Duke University Press

Durham and London

2009

© 2009 Duke University Press

All rights reserved

Designed by C. H. Westmoreland

Typeset in Warnock by Keystone Typesetting, Inc.

Printed in the United States of America on

acid-free paper ∞

Library of Congress Cataloging-in-Publication

Data appear on the last printed page of this book.

For my family, and especially
in memory of Dadaji, Badema,
Nanaji, and Naniji

Contents

ACKNOWLEDGMENTS ix
INTRODUCTION 1

PART 1   A Non-Negotiable Sovereignty?

1   THE PROPER SWINDLE: *Commercial and Financial Legislation of the 1880s* 33

2   CAPITALISM'S IDOLATRY: *The Law of Charitable Trusts, Mortmain, and the Firm as Family, c. 1870–1920* 67

3   FOR GENERAL PUBLIC UTILITY: *Sovereignty, Philanthropy, and Market Governance, 1890–1920* 103

PART 2   Negotiating Subjects

4   HEDGING BETS: *Speculation, Gambling, and Market Ethics, 1890–1930* 143

5   ECONOMIC AGENTS, CULTURAL SUBJECTS: *Gender, the Joint Family, and the Making of Capitalist Subjects, 1900–1940* 199

CONCLUSION: *Colonial Modernity and the Social Worlds of Capital* 232

NOTES 239
REFERENCES 307
INDEX 329

Acknowledgments

THIS BOOK IS THE PRODUCT of an extended network of intellectual and creative kinship. I am blessed with visionaries, pragmatists, critics, and charmers that link my worlds across New York, Toronto, London, and all about India. Many teachers and interlocutors have contributed to the genealogy of the ideas in this book, from Brearley, to Columbia, to Cambridge and beyond. It would be impossible to name them all here, but I hope that this book conveys a respect for historical depth that keeps them present.

In its early stages, this book was nurtured at Columbia University, where I had the benefit of engaging with a wealth of scholars in the fields of history and South Asian and colonial/postcolonial studies. The unmatchable experience of teaching Contemporary Civilization in the Columbia Core enlivened my engagement with political and social theory and the history of ideas. The University of Toronto has supported me generously and offered many fertile opportunities to discuss and fine-tune the research with colleagues in the Department of History, and through the Centre for South Asian Studies; the Centre for the Study of Ethics; and the Markets and Modernities Project at the Asian Institute. Recent presentations and invited lectures, most especially at the American Society of Legal History, the University of Chicago, Columbia University, Delhi University, Harvard University, the University of Hawaii, the New School for Social Research, the University of Oregon, the Yale University Center for International and Area Studies, the North American Conference on British Studies, PUKAR Mumbai, and the University of Toronto School of Law have fueled revisions and elaborations. The various stages of this project have been supported by the Columbia University Traveling Fellowship, the American Institute for Indian Studies, the Whiting Foundation, and the University of Toronto Connaught Fund, Start-Up and Matching Grants.

At Duke, infinite thanks are due to my editor, Ken Wissoker, for his time, vision, and patience. He offered invaluable comments and helped immensely in visualizing my audience. Great thanks also go to Courtney Berger, who read my drafts with care and managed the process both warmly and impeccably, and to Molly Balikov for tending expertly to all the details of production. The two anonymous readers for Duke University Press have contributed significantly to the final product with their lucid, precise, and motivating comments.

I am indebted to mentors, friends, and colleagues for their generosity, humor, and intellectual company. Since its early stages, Sugata Bose, David Cannadine, Victoria de Grazia, Ayesha Jalal, and Gayatri Chakravorty Spivak have offered this project their insightful critiques and enthusiasm. From its inception, Gayatri Spivak has sparked my critical imagination and inspired me to push on, push on. Lively exchanges, both formal and informal, with them and with Arjun Appadurai, Carol Breckinridge, Dipesh Chakrabarty, Faisal Devji, David Ludden, Uday Mehta, and Natalie Zemon-Davis have especially informed the conceptual and organizational contours of this book. I thank them immensely for their time and support. I must also thank many inquiring minds for thought-provoking and even intoxicating conversations across disciplines, methods, and regions: Anjali Arondekar, Himani Bannerji, Angela Blake, Marcus Boon, Elspeth Brown, Michael Cobb, Lawrence Cohen, Gina Dent, David Eng, David Garrett, Kanishka Goonewardena, Harry Harootunian, Sean Hawkins, Linda Hutcheon, Nasser Hussain, Fatima Imam, Kajri Jain, Eric Jennings, David Johnston, Louis Kaplan, Farhad Karim, Ken Kawashima, Tom Keenan, Christiana Killian, Tong Lam, Sanda Lwin, Margaret MacMillan, Rochona Majumdar, Dilip Menon, Susette Min, Michelle Murphy, Kunal Parker, Derek Penslar, Rashmi Poddar, Katharine Rankin, Teemu Ruskola, Rashmi Sandana, Melissa Shiff, Ajay Skaria, Michael Stanislawski, Lynne Viola, and Leti Volpp, among many others. My students at Columbia and Toronto have also made the classroom a most stimulating arena for developing thoughts; many thanks go to them for their enthusiasm and spirit, especially to those who have continued to be in touch with their own research projects.

I consider myself exceptionally lucky to enjoy the robust support of old friends, some of over two decades, who have indulged me in confabulation, inquiry, and the art of living. Foremost among them, structuring my NY-TO shuttle with the richest of affective networks, are Adrienne FitzGerald, David Garrett, Jill Jonas, Chad Kia, Mark Landsman, Jessica Monaco, Nicholas Noyes, Zoe Pappas, Alexander Platt, Elizabeth Rubin, Nermeen Shaikh, Jake Short, Jennifer Weisberg, and Lynn Whitehead. Robert McIntosh, all *sprezzatura*, cheered me on from our time at Cambridge. Ever-generous friends in London have welcomed me back and hosted me grandly over the years, most especially Edwina Ashton, Merrie Ashton, Frances Harrison, Laura Knowles-Cutler, Vanessa Letts, Douglas Mackie, Clare McCaldin, Tom Price, Steven Rickard, and Brian Skeet.

In India, the greatest of gratitude goes to all my vast family, which since my departure with adventurous parents at the tender age of three has kept many homes there for me. Special thanks go to my *Bhuas* and *Phuphajis* who helped me uncover account books, trust deeds, and the world of Burrabazaar. I also send my warmest thanks to friends in India who have taken great care of me and enthusiastically supported my research, especially Ruchira Gupta and Samta Gupta, and their wonderful, generous parents. Between the start and the publication of this project, a generation of my family has been lost. My grandparents, Radhakrishna and Kamla Devi Birla (*Dadaji* and *Badema*) and Moolchand and Laxmi Lalchandani (*Nanaji* and *Naniji*), were channels to unknown worlds, and unconditionally enthusiastic about my endeavors. Key aspects of the research were uncovered with the insight and inspiration of my grandfather, Radhakrishna Birla, who brought his keen intelligence, joie de vivre, and all his admiring fans to my project. Finally, and most importantly, my parents, Drs. Rajendra and Savitri Birla, and my sister, Belu Birla, have taken the long ride with me. I thank them for always being there, for distracting me with brilliant questions and grand comforts, and for being models of independence of mind.

Introduction

INDIA'S CELEBRATED TITLE, "the world's largest democracy," functions prominently today as a corporate logo for a vast market society bustling with entrepreneurs. As neoliberalism decorates political democracy in the subcontinent, India's long history with the rule of law takes center stage in discussions about its incarnation as capitalist powerhouse. The spirit of capitalism and the stability of markets, analysts argue, have been enabled by a well-developed legal infrastructure. Experts in the global business pages explain, for example, that because India has already paid "the sunk fixed costs of democracy," it has a sophisticated civil infrastructure, most especially an "effective legal system to protect contracts" and secure markets.[1]

Narratives about India's colonial history (which exacted the "sunk fixed costs of democracy") and its culture undergird the contemporary public discussion. In the immediate postindependence development decades, India's poverty had evoked colonial economic exploitation alongside stereotypes of its other-worldly spirituality, the mark of a culture inclined towards enduring, rather than alleviating, material deprivation. Now, the story seems to have changed. Colonialism gifted the rule of law, which synchronized entrepreneurial instincts, cultural habits, and democratic practice, so building the ethical and political foundations for a modern Indian capitalism.[2] Today, corporate gurus pose the ascetic Mahatma Gandhi as the "master strategist" of a homegrown, "follower-centric" management style, and new-agey philosophies of "karma capitalism" sell the *Bhagavad Gita* as manual for a holistic corporate ethics.[3] The colonial legal inheritance evinces India's assimilation into modernity, and its ancient culture appears now to enable capitalism and the proliferation of capitalist subjects.

But at the beginning of the twentieth century, during a previous great era of globalizing capital under imperialism, figurations of the indigenous or "native" capitalist stood in stark contrast to the contemporary corporate yogi. At the government-sponsored Indian Industrial Conference of 1912, for example, colonial administrators and nationalist intelligentsia contemplated the state of "Indian Economic Man," articulating an ongoing interest in reforming the ways of indigenous merchant-capitalists, who operated through ties of kinship, clan, and caste. These *vernacular practitioners of capitalism* were universally recognized as key actors in the colonial economy, for their extensive credit networks had fueled commodity production, exchange, and consumption since the early days of the East India Company. But according to early twentieth-century modernizers, Indian Economic Man required a radical makeover. Donned in "ragged dress," he was burdened by family and caught in tangled customary webs regulating partnerships and the "division of parental property." The assessment was dire: Indian Economic Man evinced "no economic ambition, only longing for nirvana."[4] Policymakers, both colonial and nationalist, who sought to promote economic development, especially *swadeshi* or home industry, argued that the "indigenous system of banking and other business" posed a challenge for India's progress, for "men trained under it are generally incapable of taking broad views of things or rising above their traditions."[5]

Such assessments of the indigenous merchant-capitalist had been reiterated in legal discourse throughout the late nineteenth century, a period marked by an unprecedented governmental interest in standardizing market practice and organization. The "problem" of the indigenous capitalist and his age-old cultural constraints exposes broader historical shifts under colonialism, particularly the legal casting of Indian society as a market of economic men. But even as current accounts assert that Indian capitalism owes much to its long history with the rule of law, these stories—of the problematic native capitalist, and of law governing market ethics more broadly—remain untold. Law and jurisprudence on economy open rich genealogies of market society and the modern capitalist in India and draw attention to the production of cultural discourses that legitimize both.

This book is a history of the colonial rule of law that governed market practice, and in particular, the governing and hegemonic assertions of its key targets, indigenous merchant-capitalists. Presenting a new archive for the history of capitalism and colonialism, it charts three interrelated processes: the legal production of "the market" as a supra-local object of governance, as an abstract model for the public, and as a stage for cultural politics. These processes are illuminated through the analysis of indigenous capitalism, and especially the attempts of vernacular capitalists—understood as insiders in the colonial economy but outsiders to modern market ethics—to legitimize themselves as modern subjects. Colonial law on economy, I argue, distinguished between legitimate forms of capitalism and local ones embedded in kinship, between practices that directed capital to circulate for the benefit of the public or to be hoarded in what were considered "private" extended family networks. In the chapters to follow, the legal histories opened by the inside/outside status of the indigenous capitalist, histories marked by the advocacy of formal relations of contract over and above customary norms, evince a defining feature of Indian modernity and its capitalist genealogy: the staging of the distinction between public and private as a distinction between economy and culture.

In the latter half of the eighteenth century, perhaps the most prominent ancestor of the modern joint-stock corporation, the East India Company, launched a political government in the subcontinent. Equipped with a mercenary army, its officers reaped profits like today's pirate hedge-fund managers. We know that by the early nineteenth century, this joint-stock-corporation-turned-sovereign-power sought to legitimize itself through projects of civilizing improvement, putting missionary convictions and utilitarian visions of good government to work.[6] But it was only after the rebellions of 1857, when the Company was dissolved and the Crown assumed authority over India that colonial sovereignty sought aggressively to standardize market practice and organization. Significantly, at the very time that the Government of India launched this legal regime directed at the free circulation of capital, it pushed a postrebellion policy of so-called noninterference to preserve indigenous culture, which was governed as a "private" realm under personal law. At the interstice of the two projects stood indigenous merchant-capitalists. Through them, this book investigates a defining dynamic of colonial liberalism: the utilitarian call to economic progress on the one hand, and the paternalist imperative of cultural preservation on the other. Historians have addressed this dynamic as a tension in the aims of sovereignty, a contradiction in law that manifested itself as a failure to implement economic modernization.[7] This book approaches this sovereign tension differently, as a central feature of colonial modernity and its capitalist forms of governing, which produced economy and culture as exclusive, a priori ethico-political arenas.

By the late nineteenth century, economic development had become the centerpiece of colonialism's civilizing mission, articulated most pithily in the official mantra calling for "moral and material progress." After 1870, declining agricultural revenues and a fall in the value of India's silver currency reinforced an ongoing interest in making the colony more profitable. As fiscal burdens deepened, colonial authorities directed their energies to systematizing law and jurisprudence that governed economic relations. By about 1870, three decades of law commissions had already established the basic infrastructure of modern India's legal system: the civil and criminal procedure codes, based on British law and principles of contract, alongside the personal laws that regulated matters of religion, caste, family, inheritance—in short, all arenas that were understood to constitute indigenous culture. In this setting, processes of political representation began a long and slow devolution from the imperial center to provincial, local, and municipal councils, while regimes of market governance rapidly accelerated.

A barrage of novel and foundational legal measures, spanning companies law, negotiable instruments, income tax, charitable giving, pension funds, and procedures distinguishing gambling from speculation and futures trading, among many finer matters, were implemented in the period from about 1870 to 1930. All were promoted with the ubiquitous call to "general public utility." This understudied legal infrastructure for colonialism's development regime, I argue, institutionalized a new object of sovereign management, the market, as a *public* venture.[8] As the following chapters demonstrate, market governance ushered in a modern and colonial concept of the public. Jurisprudence, case law, and statute all enforced an abstract or, to use Karl Polanyi's term, "disembedded" vision of society as a public of exchanging, contracting actors.[9] In legal discourse on economic matters, the idea of the public functioned as a shorthand for the supra-local terrain of market exchange: colonial sovereignty claimed to pursue the interests of the public, defining benefit to it as capitalist productivity, rather than as political representation. Moreover, the installation of contractual market relations delineated a public of subjects for whom modern civic association would be modeled on market organization.

The legal histories to follow chart how the categories of public and private infiltrated colonial law on economy, establishing distinct worlds for economic and cultural practice, and challenging the worldviews and market ethics of indigenous capitalism. In colonial India, where an ideology of free trade legitimized an economic system intended to profit Britain, law directed at the free circulation of capital referred first and foremost to the releasing of capital from the binds of tradition and ancient customary codes. But despite these concerns, new legal measures, I illustrate, did not simply render indigenous market norms unilaterally illegal by abolishing them summarily. Even as statutes and jurisprudence established universal models for modern market practice, they regularly insisted on establishing *exceptions* for vernacular capitalism. It is the nature of these exceptions that are the focus of the legal analysis to come. Again and again, kinship-based firms were placed under the purview of the personal law that governed what were considered "private" concerns.

Histories of Indian capitalism have argued that indigenous merchant groups were therefore protected from new regulations by the umbrella of personal law. This book, in contrast, argues that colonial authorities regulated vernacular capitalism exactly by coding it as a rarefied cultural formation. Kinship-based enterprises were governed first and foremost as what were called "joint families," that is, as ancient cultural institutions that threatened to lock capital in complicated rules of extended family inheritance, rather than as commercial firms with extensive networks and flexible channels for the circulation of capital. As vernacular capitalists were governed as cultural actors, they were rendered illegitimate as economic agents. The transformation from ragged bazaar merchant to ideal Indian Economic Man, I emphasize, required that indigenous economic actors legitimize themselves as modern subjects. They did so in the period between 1870 and 1930, challenging and then deploying the categories of culture that regulated them. The chapters that follow recount this transformation as an active process of translation across hegemonies: between vernacular systems of valuation, both moral and material, and colonial ones.[10] This history of subject-formation, I argue, preceded and informed a period much studied by historians of capitalism: that is, the period after 1930, when key sectors of the emergent capitalist class consolidated themselves as an industrial bourgeoisie and asserted claims to the economic management of the nation. These claims to sovereignty were informed by a half-century of negotiation with sovereignty, both colonial and emergent national. In this half-century, vernacular market actors challenged the law's standardizing impulses—its investment in the universal transition from *gemeinschaft* to *gesellschaft*—even as they folded their bazaar idioms into new languages of capitalist development.[11] The stories in this book elaborate by detailing the negotiations of a group that constituted a powerful core of the indigenous capitalist class, the Marwaris, whose social and economic geography is introduced below.

The questions about market governance and the production of culture explored here emerge by bringing together two fields that are rarely in conversation: economic and social histories of Indian capitalism, and colonial/postcolonial studies. To histories of capitalism this book brings greater attention to dynamics of sovereignty, governmentality, and subject formation; and to colonial/postcolonial studies, the complicated texture of market cultures and mercantile practice on the ground.[12] To both I bring a new archive, law on economy, which foregrounds the indigenous capitalist as a colonial subject, an actor produced by and participating in hegemonic discourses. The figure of the colonial subject most often evokes a Shakespeare-quoting member of the English-educated native elite, as in Macaulay's famous "Minute on Education."[13] Here, I consider the colonial subject as an economic actor subject to new market disciplines. Our attention to vernacular capitalists' key contests with colonial governance draws especially on postcolonial approaches that engage the double meaning of the term *subject*, as in the concept of a legal subject: the subject *of* authority and *with* will and agency.[14] Addressing the indigenous capitalist in this way, as a complicit figure "folded into" new discourses of modernity, opens new ways of narrating the history of colonial capitalism.[15] In this analysis, the rise of an indigenous capitalist class is considered part of a history of negotiation with forms of governing that enforced the parameters of public/private as economy/culture.

Mapping this colonial refraction of the public/private distinction into a distinction between economy/culture, this book demonstrates how discourses on culture coded vernacular capitalism as "pre-modern" gemeinschaft even as modern economic subjects were made. Through an interdisciplinary historical method, the chapters enact a critique of a universal history of capital: that is, of any master evolutionary logic of capitalist development.[16] As such, they elaborate a common concern of histories of capitalism, as well as colonial/postcolonial studies. Both are critical of the concept of a universal logic of capital, though in different ways. The stories to follow are written, as I call it, *between histories of world capitalism and the world history of capital*. Studies of world capitalism, conducted largely by social and economic historians, have challenged master narratives of capitalist transition by emphasizing the historicity, as well as the diverse terrains, of markets and systems of production, exchange, and consumption. They detail the localized empirical contexts of capital flows to guard against overdetermined globalizing schemas.[17] Scholars in colonial and postcolonial studies, on the other hand, have been concerned with the operations of hegemony, that is, the ways in which colonial discourses staged, institutionalized, and naturalized what we can call a world history of capital: a universal transition from gemeinschaft to gesellschaft, extraeconomic to economic coercion, status to contract.[18] The myriad historical trajectories that constitute the empirical ground of world capitalism certainly throw into question any universal model for capitalist transformation. At the same time, hegemonic actors and institutions translate, though never perfectly, the specificities of practice on the ground into universalizing discourses of modernity. Indigenous capitalists were such actors. Our attention to their subject formation seeks neither to celebrate a "native" voice for capital nor to rehearse ethnographic scripts directed at codifying indigenous identities. Rather, this kind of colonial subject, first classified in colonial discourses as "native commerce," brings into focus the translation of local market cultures into a universalizing logic of capital, into a market ethic structured by the economy/culture distinction.

Contributing to a colonial genealogy of modernity, our conversation across fields and between history and theory foregrounds the relationship between capitalism and modern forms of governing. As such, this study revitalizes the specific genealogy of the Foucauldian term *governmentality*, too often deployed as a catchall phrase for knowledge/power. Remembering that the term emerges in his lectures on economic liberalism and early twentieth-century neoliberal philosophy, this book historicizes, via a "circuitous colonial route" notoriously unexamined by Foucault, his interest in economy as an object and practice of government.[19] My term *market governance* resonates with

Foucault's robust ethico-political meaning of government or governing, that is, the continuum across technologies of state and processes of subject formation. The analysis of colonial market governance supplements Foucault's critique of liberalism, which poses "civil society [as] the concrete ensemble within which ... abstract points, *economic men*, need to be positioned in order to be made adequately manageable."[20]

At the same time, our attention to vernacular capitalists' subject formation takes a cue from Marx's famous figuration of Economic Man, of the capitalist as the "bearer of capital." For Marx, the agency of the capitalist—identifiable in his "subjective purpose," which is the "valorization of value"—slips into instrumentality for a higher power, capital: "It is only in so far as the appropriation of ever more wealth *in the abstract* is the sole driving force behind his operations that he functions as a capitalist, i.e., as capital personified and endowed with a consciousness and a will."[21] As conceived by modernizers, Indian Economic Man would become such a bearer of capital in the abstract, the bearer of a world-historical script of capitalist development. Interested in how the name "culture" is given to capitalist practices that do not follow this script, this analysis asks: what kind of cultural subject accompanied the bearer of capital in India?

In its broadest gesture, this book charts the stages of capital that ordered new colonial mappings of the political and the social—"stages" being understood in two distinct senses: temporal and spatial. It is concerned especially with the ways in which the temporal stages of capitalist development so central to the logic of late colonial governance correspond to stages or theaters of political performance. Temporally, colonial law installed evolutionary stages of capitalist development, distinguishing between premodern relations of status and those of contract, between gemeinschaft and gesellschaft. Spatially, these stages constituted platforms for the performance of culture and economy, for scenes of private and public community. By historicizing these categories, this book challenges an ongoing formulation of development discourses and discussions of non-Western capitalisms: whether a thing called "culture" enables or is a deterrent for "the economy." The expanding literature on corporate governance and "Asian values," for example, now rehashes older debates over ethnicity as an economic variable, evoked in terms such as "the Hindu rate of growth."[22] In contrast, this book asks: in what ways does the institutionalization of an abstract ethico-political universe, the market, produce discourses on culture?

The following sections of this introduction provide the background necessary for responding to this question. The first two further locate this project within histories of South Asian capitalism and colonial/postcolonial studies, detailing its interventions in both. The next two sections present an introduction to key legal terms and concepts that governed vernacular capitalism; followed by an overview of the social and economic geography of the groups that were targeted by policymakers as "native commerce," in particular the Marwaris, the group on which we focus. The last three sections outline interventions in history and theory that frame the study of colonial market governance. The first two elaborate recent work historicizing "the economy" by posing economy as both an object *and* a practice of governing, and colonial law on market practice as a "conduct of conduct."[23] The third section employs a broad notion of the corporate to build on established critiques of the public/private and capital/community distinctions.

The Historiography of Vernacular Capitalism in India: Inside/Outside Capital Logic

This is not an economic history, but rather a story of market governance, brought into focus through the lens of a significant and signifying group within vernacular capitalism, the Marwaris. It builds on the work of historians who have detailed the social and material networks of kinship-based capitalism and have long challenged the gemeinschaft/gesellschaft distinction. The idealized opposition between the bazaar, a premodern arena of personalized exchange, and the market, a site of rationalized and impersonal transactions, has been put to rest especially by studies of indigenous merchant and industrial capitalists. As economic historians have argued, the Indian bazaar, the material domain of indigenous commerce and finance, was not peripheral, but central to the world system of the late nineteenth century; it was a vast intermediate network enabling the deep local penetration and extensive global reach of colonial capitalism.[24] Studies on South Asian merchant groups have detailed the symbiosis of material and social capital that structured the expansion of markets within India, and in interregional trade across the Indian Ocean and Bay of Bengal. Research on the period after 1750 in particular has delved into the role of extended family ties and marriage in the production of status, an element crucial to merchants' commercial and financial operations. Economic and social histories, then, have demonstrated how ties of kinship and idioms of clan and caste fueled the colonial economy via vast networks of credit, wholesale and retail trade, and the financing of commodity production.[25] In this way, South Asian history has been at the vanguard of alternative histories of capitalism that demand attention to embedded forms of exchange and exploitation within modernizing economies and social texts.[26]

However, even in the process of mapping vernacular capitalism's diverse terrains and instruments, the presentation of evidence challenging the gemeinschaft/gesellschaft distinction can fall prey to the telos of economic rationality. A functionalist logic often undergirds analysis: many histories of indigenous capitalism detail culturally specific idioms of market practice in order to reclaim merchants' economic rationality.[27] In so rectifying misperceptions about culture as a burden for economic development, they assume a universal bearer of capital, a rational actor garbed in ethnic wardrobe. Here, *culture* and *economy* are presupposed as distinct systems, shown, via the rational indigenous actor, to be consistent. In the process, the affirmation of an authentic "*Indian* capitalism" repeats the structural logic of the economy/culture distinction, validating culture on the grounds of its consistency with capitalist economic rationality.[28] In this way, attention to the difference of local capitalisms reproduces the master historical agency of Capital; the operations of indigenous commerce become its Indian enactment. Here, the very necessary attention to different forms of market organization and practice overrides, rather than engages, the politics of difference that initiates the inquiry. The "peculiar history of Indian capitalism," as manifest in the peculiar history of Indian capitalists, has reproduced a universal subject, an economically rational agent of capitalism and an instrument of Capital, even as it elaborates a particularist history.[29]

It is important to note that social histories informed by anthropological approaches have been less mechanistic. As Natalie Zemon Davis has put it, historical research may be directed at "understanding economics as a cultural activity," elaborating the textures of meaning that constitute market practices, rather than privileging the functional role of "rational calculation."[30] The study of market cultures investigates economy as culture, and "culture" as a way of being, as the shifting meanings attending lived practice, as ethos and as ethics. Keeping this notion of culture alive by reading law and jurisprudence against the grain, this book follows a different path of inquiry, asking what happens to market cultures when "the market" becomes a stage for colonial governance. To get this problem, it is necessary to supplement the detailing of mercantile, entrepreneurial, and market practices with attention to the cultural politics of colonial political economy. Drawing on the thick description of economic activity, this analysis considers the way it was translated into the legal archive and the mechanics of colonial sovereignty.[31] How did late colonial sovereignty know and regulate indigenous commerce? And how did this history inform Indian capitalists' nationalist and postcolonial politics, their strategies for dominance and exploitation?

Studies of South Asian merchant communities have elided such questions, as evinced by a chronological gap in research on merchants' negotiations with the state and with colonial sovereignty, research that concentrates on the period before 1860, and then again on the period after the First World War. For the pre-1860 period, narratives of the British conquest at Plassey have enshrined the figure of the indigenous merchant as crucial political agent and instrument: Jagat Seth, the leader of a powerful banking clan who allied with the British to overthrow the Nawab of Bengal in 1757, remains a popular personification of indigenous capitalists' comprador and catalyzing qualities.[32] More extensively, the economic history of the Company Raj has detailed merchants' broadening of internal credit markets and their crucial role in the expansion of the colonial export trade.[33] Research on this period has also mapped the installation of a trading company as political authority by identifying a mercantile moral economy and its symbolic exchanges with sovereignty, particularly through the performance of gifting and tribute.[34] Up to about 1860, then, merchants appear in economic histories as agents of market expansion and financiers of the Company and princely states; they also figure in studies of the culture and discourse of early colonial sovereignty.

Histories that address indigenous commerce and its relations with sovereignty then leap to the period between the First and Second World Wars, drawing attention to the political economy of nationalism. Studies of the interwar period highlight indigenous capitalists' contributions to and manipulations of nationalist politics, and particularly their support of Gandhi and the Indian National Congress.[35] Here the ghost of Jagat Seth is reincarnated as the voice of industrial capital and its Gandhian devotees. If merchant-sovereignty relations garner attention for the period before 1860 and then after 1920, the historiography overlooks the crucial period in which the legal standardization of market practice and organization was concentrated. The gap is indicative of a turn away from the investigation of market discourse as source of sovereign legitimacy, a concern motivating studies of East India Company rule but abandoned in the study of the late nineteenth century; indeed, it is as if historians have taken too seriously the nominal shift from Company Raj to formal empire. Moreover, this chronological gap betrays a predetermined logic of capital underlying the historiography, the effect of which is to present a seamless shift from mercantile to industrial capitalism. By the second decade of the twentieth century, indigenous merchant-capitalists emerge in modern Indian history as triumphant entrepreneurs, or as comprador-collaborators, and in either case, *Homo economici* par excellence.

How were earlier mercantile negotiations with sovereignty reconfigured after 1860? Studies that do concern themselves with market practice in the late nineteenth and early twentieth centuries have been interested in mapping the worlds of marketplaces, elaborating on merchants' multifarious material roles and more generally, on intermediary capitalists as engines of commodity production and peasant indebtedness.[36] Still, while scholars have demonstrated the importance of kinship and caste as idioms for market practice, there has been little research on the ways in which late colonial sovereignty accommodated and redefined that idiom. The impact of law and the public/private distinction has been minimized, even as the material gains and political interests of the emerging capitalist class have been emphasized. The historiography thus precludes the possibility of historicizing the modern Indian capitalist as an *effect* of market governance. In contrast, this study examines the indigenous merchant as a colonial subject involved in a process of negotiation, contestation, and appropriation of new technologies of rule that presented capitalist development as a sovereign imperative. It thus charts the negotiations that made the historical transition from mercantile to industrial capitalism appear seamless.

Market Governance and Colonial/Postcolonial Studies

If sparingly addressed in economic and social histories, sovereignty and technologies of rule between 1860 and 1930 have been much engaged by interdisciplinary historical writing within the field of South Asian colonial studies and in postcolonial studies more broadly. Elaborating the fields of ethnohistory, subaltern studies, as well as critical and feminist theory, interdisciplinary research on colonialism in India has explored previously unrecognized sites of cultural contestation and transformation.[37] Colonial studies have been concerned, broadly speaking, with modes of governing/ knowing, with the government/mentality of colonial rule, and with the making of colonial modernities, as well as with the formation of the subject of rule, with both subjecthood and subjectivity. Scholars interested in law and the genealogy of postcolonial citizenship, and those concerned with the cultural politics of postcoloniality and globalization, have delved especially into the constitution of the colonial subject, the politics of political and discursive representation, and the dynamics of mimesis and difference. And joining with feminist methodology, studies of the gendering of colonial power have mapped new and intimate terrains of politics, problematizing the production of collective agency as nation, community, and woman.[38] These interdisciplinary approaches and themes inform the broad gestures of this book, which supplements social and economic history with attention to sovereignty and governmentality. At the same time, the argument here also uncovers a new archive, mapping a new terrain for colonial studies by investigating the law on economy and market practice as a site of cultural contestation.

In the burgeoning industry within colonial studies that is the study of law, remarkably little attention has been paid to the concentrated impetus of market standardization. Uncovering this process, this analysis extends the reach of established research on colonial legal knowledges. Work on the codification of civil and criminal law, and especially on the misrecognition and reification of culture in the compilation of Hindu and Muslim personal laws, has emphasized the contrapuntal logic of colonial administration: legislators mediated any direct application of British legal principles by actively engaging a politics of culture, manifest in the legal ossification of Indian tradition. Studies of India's dual legal system have exposed cultural protectionism as benignly performed discipline and regulation, a crucial point for our reading of law and its mistranslation of kinship-based market practices. As Bernard Cohn has outlined, the gradual compilation of personal law was tied to the Orientalist discovery of Indian "culture" as ancient artifact in the late eighteenth century, when British officials sought to revive the authority of what were deemed originary Hindu and Muslim legal texts. Indigenous norms of arbitration and jurisprudence, on the other hand, had modulated these textual sources, themselves varied and vast, with the shifting and situated conventions of local and customary practices.[39] By the 1860s, personal law reflected a selected set of principles from ancient written sources, applied as universal guidelines for the assessment of a wide array of customs and conventions.[40] These fixed prescriptions, which regulated matters of marriage, inheritance, and caste-based community relations, overrode attention to the flexibility and contingency of local usages with new notions of legal precedent.[41] This history of fixing had potent effects on what was called the indigenous "lex mercatoria," or mercantile law, a term that British and Roman jurisprudence had defined as the largely autonomous sphere of common law governing trade and finance.

Reinventing living practices as petrified mandates, the "private" domain thus emerged, not as a site of cultural protection, but rather as a space that enabled new techniques of sovereign regulation. An extensive body of work in women's rights, gender, and the law in India has illustrated this point by exploring the fortification of patriarchal consensus in personal law, and more broadly, the gendered production of tradition and community in colonial and postcolonial legal regimes.[42] At the same time, the very division of law into public and private spheres enabled the exercise of British sovereignty in matters that had heretofore been settled through community arbitration. Anthropological and historical research on the management of temples, indigenous endowments, and other such sites of local authority has revealed the active and pervasive role of British courts in the adjudication of community disputes among temple managers.[43] Again, such work has demonstrated that the public/private distinction did not maintain an undisturbed and autonomous realm of indigenous authority. However, while feminist and anthrohistorical approaches to the law have elaborated this point, scant research has been conducted on the infiltration of these categories into the regulations intended to modernize market exchange.

As the categories of public and private were deployed in civil law, new pressures emerged for kinship-based commerce. In India, the indigenous *lex mercatoria* had consisted of sets of shifting and flexible conventions, subject to the jurisdiction of *mahajans*, caste and community-based councils of informal arbitration. The rule of law, I argue, challenged the authority of these conventions in two ways: first, by rendering them directly subject to personal law, fetishizing their characteristic negotiability of social and material capital as ancient ritual, and second, by imposing contractual models on practices not easily relegated to personal law. In both processes, the law as a systematized logic—either civil, criminal, or personal—increasingly commanded mercantile conventions, customs, and practices. Moreover, the public/private divide also established a distinction between *legitimate and illegitimate* trade. As the chapters illustrate, vernacular market practices either were tolerated as alternatives to modern market ethics, or were criminalized. Thus anxieties about kinship as an idiom of market organization were articulated as concerns about hoarding and about "secret" networks of information that distorted supply and demand and promoted gambling.

The "Hindu Undivided Family": Personal Law to Manage Kinship-Based Capitalism

Vernacular capitalism was ubiquitously understood as operating through what were called "family firms." The law governed these via an Anglo-Indian legal construct, the Hindu Undivided Family, or HUF, which referred broadly to the variety of joint property relations in the subcontinent. Contributing to new research on the historical meanings of family in India, this book addresses a significant discourse on the joint family, one emerging not in debates on domesticity, but in an archive on economy.[44] A brief background on the kinship networks of the family firms and the category of the HUF will be useful here as preface for the remaining chapters. First, it is important to note that though this study highlights Hindu trading castes that constituted the core of India's industrial class, the analysis of the HUF is also relevant for non-Hindus engaged in kinship-based commerce, including Jain and Muslim commercial groups (for example, the Ismailis of western India), exactly because colonial legislation deployed the Hindu Undivided Family as the universal model for the customary organization of trade. Privy Council decisions on inheritance and succession had established as early as the 1860s that "persons who do not profess Hinduism may, nevertheless, adopt Hindu law and usage."[45]

The activities of the family firm defied categorization into public trading affairs and private household concerns in two broad ways. First, there were porous boundaries between kinship as a symbolic logic and commerce as a material one.[46] Resilient webs of credit operated through unwritten notions of trust, a symbolic currency secured by ties of consanguinity, marriage, and lineage. Marriage secured affinal networks that could bring a firm's activities into new cities, towns, and hinterlands.[47] Second, the very notion of *family* extended beyond the household and encompassed a variety of patriarchal relations. The commercial joint family household—father, wife, sons and their wives, and unmarried daughters—existed within a much broader context, the nexus of extended relations harnessed by the firm. These networks were constituted spatially across villages, bazaars, and even global regions, and temporally through descent from ancestors. Commercial "trust" could be established on the basis of lineage, that is, mutual descent from a common male ancestor dating back as many as five or more generations. Lines of descent arranged as *gotres*, or exogamous clans within a particular endogamous caste, constituted yet another barometer for degrees of affinity. Women, understood as carriers of the moral substance of their households and patrilineal decent, bound together affinal relations of family, commerce, and finance.

The family firm, then, was not simply a discrete institution tied to a single or perhaps a few households. Its successful operation depended upon extensive networks that were as much public in their material import as they were private and personal in their selective construction. Still, colonial regulations coded indigenous commercial organization narrowly, as the HUF. This term referred specifically to the joint property relations of the household, and it was understood in a concrete way as of a group of people living together, rather than as a vast network. Our legal story demonstrates how the classification of the family firm as HUF viewed the firm's extended kinship relations through the narrow framework of co-residence, that is, the shared living arrangements characterized by joint estate.[48] This limited view defined kinship primarily through access to ancestral property, and not by the extensive webs of consanguinity and affinity that structured commerce. For joint families who conducted businesses, the capital and profits of the firm constituted joint family property. This fact rendered family firms subject to personal law, and distinct from civil partnerships constituted by legal contracts. Regulating the family firm's broad and fluid activities of exchange via the HUF, I argue, meant governing the firm through a personal law that was directed at inheritance and succession and that emphasized the rigid nature of "jointness." The privatizing of the firm as household reflected the governing of kinship as a religio-cultural code, a process that reflected the systematizing of caste more broadly.[49]

In the personal law, two systems regulated the property relations of the HUF: the *Mitakshara*, which governed virtually all the commercial castes and most of British India, and the *Dhayabhaga*, which was predominant in Bengal and Assam.[50] Under the *Mitakshara*, the household's ancestral property and any additions to it were held jointly by fathers and sons, and the question of distinct shares emerged only at the rare event of formal partition. Succession to the joint property occurred at a son's birth, rather than at the death of a father. Daughters and wives had rights to maintenance, and daughters to their marriage portion, or *stridan*. Management of joint property was the responsibility of the father. Despite earlier practices and jurisprudence allowing for the father's right to alienate any property acquired on his own, Anglo-Indian personal law emphasized the *inalienable* nature of the joint family property, which was defined legally as a "coparcenary unit," an arrangement of collective property composed of "coparcenors," that is, partners with a priori distinct shares. The following chapters detail how Anglo-Indian law at once reduced the extended family firm into joint household, making it suspect as market actor, *and* abstracted it in a mimesis of individuated contractual relations. By reduction and abstraction, the gendered lifeworlds of mercantile kinship were translated into culture and economy.

Geographies of Vernacular Capitalism and the Marwaris

A broad array of influential commercial castes informed the gemeinschaft visions of the colonial legal imaginary and ultimately constituted the core of India's industrial class. These included the Gujerati bankers and traders in western India, particularly in the Bombay cotton market and the Indian Ocean trade; the *bania* moneylenders and traders of north India who originated in the United Provinces; Punjabi Khattris who managed the grain, textile, and timber trade of northwest India; the Chettiar trader-bankers of Madras, who were tied to the Southeast Asian and China trade; Sindhis, whose networks extended from Hong Kong to East Africa; and the Marwaris, a powerful core of the industrial bourgeoisie, who came primarily from the western princely states of Bikaner, Marwar (or Jodhpur), and Jaipur in Rajputana (contemporary Rajasthan), settling in large numbers in Bombay, Calcutta, and central India beginning in the 1880s. Social and economic histories have mapped the range of activities encompassed by these and other groups, from extensive banking operations, to small industry (such as cotton spinning), to local moneylending and trading in hinterlands. Typically, influential firms combined moneylending, brokerage, wholesale and retail trade, and, later, speculation and industry, expanding earlier models of "portfolio capitalism" by diversifying their commercial and financial concerns and adapting to spatial and sectoral changes in the late colonial economy.[51]

To elaborate on the major legal developments that affected what colonial authorities referred to as "native commerce," and to foreground important vernacular capitalist strategies for negotiating new governmental regulations, the later chapters of this book illustrate the story through Marwari merchant-capitalists, ubiquitous signifiers of "native commerce" in official discourse and in popular folklore. Their capitalist trajectory, as a material conquest and as a self-fashioning of hegemonic status, operates even today as an emblematic tale of Indian Economic Man. Marwaris have been the subjects of economic histories on the one hand and ethnographic analyses on the other. The analysis here enacts a deconstruction of this disciplinary economy/culture distinction.[52] The later chapters of this book thus elaborate Marwari charitable gifting, gambling, and social reform discourses by placing them within the context of market governance and its legal history.

The term *Marwari* referred broadly to merchants from Marwar and the surrounding princely states of Rajputana. Denoting a region of origin, the term was popularized as merchants from these Rajasthani states immigrated throughout India. *Marwari* encompassed two distinct endogamous kinship groups, Agarwals and Maheshwaris. The latter traced their origins almost exclusively to the northeastern Shekhawati region of Jaipur state, and the former, far more populous, to

Shekhawati and across Rajputana. More broadly, in the late colonial period, the term also referred to two other endogamous groups, Hindu Khandelwals and Jains, also predominantly from the states of Jaipur and Bikaner. Unlike diasporic groups trading across oceanic and overland trade networks, Marwari merchants sustained a pervasive presence in the internal economy and, by the 1920s began to represent themselves as spokespersons for "native commerce." In the subcontinent, their spheres of influence were less localized than those of other commercial groups, so that their geography of immigration and trade reflected the production of a supralocal market terrain. Though merchants from Rajputana were found in small numbers throughout the subcontinent from the beginnings of the East India Company trade, the period particularly from 1880 to 1910 saw a vast immigration of Marwaris to the major markets of Bombay and Calcutta and to market centers throughout India as bankers, traders of grain, cloth, and a variety of local agricultural commodities ranging from oil seeds to sugar to jute, and as brokers and commission agents to British firms.[53] In Calcutta, Marwaris entered the textile trade as clerks or agents for British interests; after the First World War, they began to finance them. Marwari speculation markets fueled the group's financing potential, and after 1900, the accelerated rise in the world's demand for jute saw them become financiers of crop production and jute balers; later, they became owners of factories for finished products. In Bombay, they speculated in the cotton market, serving as financiers and agents in the export trade. Moreover, they came to dominate trade and finance in important market towns and entrepôts such as Kanpur (United Provinces), Nagpur (Central Provinces), and Indore and Gwalior (in the princely states of west central India, and connected to opium production). In the south, they had established a community of traders in Hyderabad as early as 1850, and later they migrated to Madras. In western India and in the east in Bihar and Assam, Marwaris combined merchandising with purchasing on commission and the financing of local agricultural crops.[54]

This burgeoning entrepreneurship and conquest of markets also brought with it the dispossession and impoverishment of nonmercantile classes. Marwaris have long been infamous for their extraction from and exploitation of noncommercial groups, of both the rural and urban laboring classes. Their control of internal credit depended upon cycles of enforced indebtedness for the smallholding and landless peasantry and below-subsistence wages for factory workers. Long represented in popular mythology as rapacious and miserly, Marwaris consolidated their capitalist dominance by reinforcing traditional material and social hierarchies, reinventing their own origin myths and caste histories, and performing charity and philanthropy.[55] This study builds on the history of mercantile, and more specifically, Marwari relations with laboring groups and landholders, both of which have been well elaborated by labor and agrarian historians.[56] Concerned with the reproduction of traditional hegemonies within capitalist modernity, it follows the politicization of culturalist discourses that legitimize processes of expropriation.

Historicizing Economy as Object and Practice of Government

This book's interweaving of histories of capitalism and colonial/postcolonial studies furthers the burgeoning project of historicizing that modern phenomenon called "the economy."[57] In his analysis of modernity and techno-politics, Timothy Mitchell has called for rigorous attention to distinct phases in the making of "the economy," emphasizing the inextricable role of colonialism in the process: "Certain forms of social exchange, contract law, disposition of property, corporate powers, methods of calculation, dispossession of labor, relationship between public and private, organization of information and government regulation that were formalized in western Europe in the nineteenth century as 'market exchange' were abstracted by economics as a social science [in the twentieth]. The new science ignored the importance of a larger structure of empire in making possible these domestic arrangements."[58] The present book works in this spirit, emphasizing the chronology from nineteenth-century "market exchange" to twentieth-century "economic science." In India, new law governing commerce and finance enacted the classical concept of economy as a practice—of arranging and managing exchange—and informed the modern production of the economy as an object of governance.[59] As the following chapters detail, the formalization of market exchange in the late nineteenth and first decades of the twentieth century coincided with, and indeed informed, such formalization in Britain, most clearly in the legal acrobatics that installed the public/private distinction and a market ethics grounded in contractual relations. As Mitchell highlights, beginning in the 1870s in Europe, earlier traditions of political economy were reinterpreted by a new academic economics that instituted a "locationless notion of exchange"; this vision informed new applications of contract law in India.[60] In the late nineteenth century, legal disciplines of written contract regulated embedded or vernacular forms of market exchange by distinguishing between transactions that demarcated a supra-local or locationless arena for the free circulation of capital—the public—and transactions that benefited only private, familial interests. Colonial law sought to restrict what I call the *extensive negotiability* that characterized vernacular practices: an extensive negotiability between the symbolic capital of kinship, caste, and lineage, and the capital flows of market exchange and production.[61] New forms of contractual association and exchange—the company, the trust, the pension fund, the futures trade—all produced a bifurcation between the material logics governing the public and the cultural logics governing the private.[62] Analyzing the regulation of vernacular capitalisms, largely overlooked in recent research that historicizes the making of the economy, foregrounds the integral role of cultural discourses in its production.[63]

By the time economic science took hold in the twentieth century, the term *political economy* referred to an objective method of analysis of a priori categories: that is, the state and market. Studies of colonial political economy in South Asia often work in this framework, addressing state and market as already constituted categories. This book, in contrast, engages the term *political economy* in its classic sense, as a discourse of governing, one that, as Foucault has famously articulated, structures a historical process that "isolates the economy as a specific sector of reality" and becomes "the science and the technique of intervention of the government in that field of reality."[64] I highlight the relation between the concept of economy as a model for governing and the economy as an object of governance that underlies Foucault's 1977–1979 lectures at the Collège de France, only one of which is the much-cited essay on "Governmentality." Compiled in two volumes, *Sécurité, territoire, population* and *La naissance de la biopolitique*, these lectures, only recently published in full, consider theories of political economy, the economic "subjects of interest" (as distinct from subjects of law/rights) they produce, and their manifestation in apparatuses of security.[65] At the same time, these investigations expose a slippage in Foucault: the term *economy* is often used loosely, at times referring to a practice of managing, at others to an abstract arrangement (as in an economy of power, also evoked in the lectures on *Power/Knowledge*), and at others to a specific sector of reality.[66] Moreover, the 1978–1979 lectures move from the political economy of the French Physiocrats; to a reading of the totality of economic processes figured in the invisibility of Adam Smith's invisible hand; to the economic science of U.S. and German schools in the 1920s and 1930s.[67] This gesture towards charting a genealogy results in a historical leap that too easily links the social space carved out by eighteenth-century political economy with the disembedded mid-twentieth-century thing called "the economy."[68] The gap calls for historicizing, and is telling especially of Foucault's now-infamous lack of engagement with nineteenth-century colonialisms.

Colonialism in India, for example, offers a rich genealogy of political economy as a modern discourse of governing. The East India Company enacted a range of theories of political economy in eighteenth- and early nineteenth-century India. As Ranajit Guha's classic study has shown, the permanent settlement of Bengal drew on physiocratic models of wealth vested in land. At the same time, the regulation of bazaars and marketplaces saw a Smithian emphasis on exchange and circulation.[69] In the late eighteenth and early nineteenth centuries, as Sudipta Sen has demonstrated, the Company deployed free-trade ideology to assume the authority held previously by *zamindars* (landlords) over places of exchange, seeking to control "local sites of production, passage and distribution."[70] Particularly after the Charter Act of 1813, which dismantled the Company's monopoly in India, free trade promoted the theoretical fiction of the equilibrium of supply and demand, the very impossibility of which legitimized the regulation of production and the flow of commodities.[71] In the period before the rebellions of 1857, the Company had conducted localized interventions in arenas of trade and exchange, challenging the customary rights and practices of a variety of indigenous authorities, kings, landlords, and other notables.[72] By the 1870s, the rule of law, with all its standardizing impetus, was put to work in unprecedented fashion for the free circulation of capital.

Marking a new phase in political economy as a practice of sovereignty, late colonial law on economy is an untapped archive of what I refer to as "market governance" in India. In this study, *market governance* denotes the production of "the economy" as an object of governance, but also the utopic production of "the market" as an ethico-political sovereign: that is, as a model for social relations. Recent studies have broken ground on the former, examining the development regime of the late-colonial/nationalist period and postcolonial economic planning. But little attention has been paid to law and its casting of the market as the ultimate authority, ethical ground, and template for the social.[73] This was a process introduced under colonial liberalism and now pursued in India's neoliberal enthusiasms.

Economy as a Problem of Law: Contract and the Conduct of Bazaar Conduct

Despite slippages in the analysis, Foucault's concept of government remains useful for unpacking the ethical concerns of colonial market governance, which posed economy as a problem of law. For Foucault, liberal governmentality has a strong relation to the idea of economy in its most formal definition, rooted in the greek *oikonomia*, which refers to the conventions/laws (*nomos*) for arranging, distributing, and managing the household (*oikos*).[74] This idea of economy as arranging and managing is revitalized with the emergence of political economy as a knowledge form, which marks a shift in government from "imposing law on men" to "disposing things" and "using laws themselves as tactics to arrange things in such a way that . . . such and such ends may be achieved."[75] The legal standardization of market practice in India marks an important phase in the history of liberal governmentality, for it exemplifies techniques of governing enacted in a language of facilitating, enabling, and managing (*gérer*), a civilizing mission dissimulated as laissez-faire.[76] In the late nineteenth century, the brute coercive power of colonial law, manifest in what has been called a "despotism of law" and a "jurisprudence of emergency," was consolidated alongside the institutionalization of a new kind of legal subject, the free-willing, contracting subject of market governance.[77]

As an analytical lens, governmentality draws attention to the directing of conduct, or the "conduct of conduct," a concept that I elaborate rigorously through the legal archive.[78] It is important to note that in the Collège de France lectures, the term conduct, *conduite*, has many resonances that pose the subject as both agent and instrument, complicating the notion of the autonomous legal subject. *Conduite* refers to "the activity of directing, conducting, but equally the manner in which one conducts oneself, the manner in which one lets oneself be directed, the manner in which one is directed, and finally how one comports oneself [*on se trouve se comporter*] under the effect of directing or conducting, which would be the acting out of the direction or conduct."[79] In addition, the term *conduct* encompasses distinct concepts of law: systematized rules that serve to conduct, and the conventions *of* conduct, that is, of everyday practice. This distinction and its incarnations occupy the legal analysis here. The chapters investigate the relationship between law as a systematized logic (or *logos*, as in the Benthamite vision) and as convention (*nomos*) especially through the implementation of contract and its a priori, rational, intending subject.[80]

In the half century after 1880 especially, market ethics emerged as a legal problem of governing conduct. The regulation of conduct, a matter previously reserved for criminal law, thus opened to the civil law governing contracts. Jurists were particularly concerned to clarify the relationship between mercantile conventions, cultural norms as codified in personal law, and written contracts. The chapters to come chart this important colonial chapter in the standardizing of contract law by British and U.S. jurists in the late nineteenth and early twentieth centuries.[81] They highlight especially the ways in which the installation of a gesellschaft, a public arena inscribed by contracts, coded vernacular capitalism as premodern gemeinschaft. The enforcement of written contracts, with its focus on individual a priori intentionality, I argue, classified indigenous market ethics as the commands of culture, or, to use Max Weber's words, the "unreflective habituation to a regularity of life that has engraved itself as custom."[82] The principle of contract and its conduct of bazaar conduct illustrate a disembedding of "the market," one that incites a disembedding of "culture" into a name for difference and a politicized script.[83]

Public/Private: Corporate Life and Its Colonial Refraction

In its attention to new discourses on culture and kinship as effects of market governance, this analysis revisits classic investigations of law, economy, and community. By *community* I mean the full range of corporate or group life—from family to customary mercantile guild or *mahajan* to the contractual associations of the joint-stock company and trust, to the idea of society itself. As such, I return critically to a concern of nineteenth- and twentieth-century theorists of law and society such as Henry Sumner Maine, Max Weber, and F. W. Maitland: the history of corporate life and its temporization from gemeinschaft to gesellschaft, status to contract.[84] Deploying the idea of the corporate against this master evolutionary narrative, the book demonstrates how the legal standardization of market practice and the concomitant regulation of vernacular conventions ushered in new imaginings of community and corporate life, both public and private. The joint-stock corporation impinged upon a variety of corporate forms, becoming a model for public association, both for profit and for charity. At the same time, colonial law sought to privatize the corporate life of vernacular capitalism, that is, its world of extended kinship, into narrow notions of family.

Detailing the dissection of forms of indigenous corporate life into public and private, this analysis is informed especially by Marx's well-known critique of the sophistry of the bourgeois liberal-secular state, one engaged by feminist and postcolonial studies.[85] For Marx, we will remember, sovereignty in the name of the public sustains capitalist subjects and the subjects of capitalism, for it monopolizes the terrain of the political and renders its effect—the private, acquisitive individual—as a natural, a priori origin of the social.[86] The stories here view this modern monopoly of the political through a colonial lens. In India, precolonial practices of layered, negotiated sovereignty, as manifest in merchants' customary practices of tribute to kings, were challenged, I argue, by the emergent nonnegotiable sovereignty of the market.[87] As law posed "the market" as sovereign, *cultural* subjects emerged as "natural" *and* a priori. As is well established, feminist methodology has elaborated on the production of the private as natural and therefore depoliticized. With its attention to the regulatory operations of the public/private distinction, as well as its robust understanding of the public as mapping *both* political and economic relations, feminist political theory particularly informs this study. The overarching thematic of this inquiry—the economy/culture distinction—refracts the feminist critique of the public/private distinction through a postcolonial lens.[88]

For Marx, the liberal state laid claim to the public, divesting civil society of political life, but other influential social theorists have addressed the public as a political arena that is exactly not the state, an arena of active citizenship (rooted in the Aristotelian model), collective discussion, and decision making, as in the thought of Hannah Arendt and Jürgen Habermas.[89] Habermas's "public sphere" has been particularly influential in studies of the caste, religious, and communal identities that constituted the public in late colonial India. Drawing on European studies of nationalism, public performance, and popular culture, such research has highlighted the various forms of collective participation informing the emergence of South Asian nation-states; it has thus been interested in locating indigenous idioms within the colonial framework for political exchange.[90] Still, the adoption of Habermas's model requires caution, for as feminist and postcolonial approaches have emphasized, his account of the public sphere as space of rational-critical discourse presents a universal template for the bourgeois transition to modernity, one that lacks an account of rationalities and technologies of governing.[91] Expanding these critiques, I emphasize two points. First, the public in colonial India was as much "an arrangement of economic men" as it was a site of political performance: the law's re-presentation of the public as the market must be examined alongside the devolution of political representation.[92] Second, law on economy installed the public by *privatizing* indigenous forms of corporate life, a process that in turn produced hegemonic public assertions of community. Studies of the colonial public sphere have focused on the historical recovery of indigenous political agency. In contrast, the analysis here addresses collective participation as a "folding in" to hegemony.[93]

The attention to the colonial refraction of public/private as economy/culture in this book thus challenges state/civil society and state/market binaries. In this spirit, it revisits Partha Chatterjee's interest in the problem of capital and community, through which he theorizes the anticolonial nation-state.[94] For Chatterjee, "the narrative of capital seeks to suppress the other narrative of community and produce in the course of its journey both the normalized individual and the modern regime of disciplinary power."[95] Capital's universalizing logic illuminates the postcolonial nation's sameness with "modular" European forms, since the nation is the only form of community, "single, determinate and demographically enumerable," that capital allows.[96] Performing difference, anticolonial nationalism thus operates through a distinction between an "outer" realm of statecraft and economy, where the *nation-state* is embedded *inside* capital's social logic; and an "inner" realm of national culture and unconquered sovereignty, where the *nation* asserts itself as *outside* this logic. The inner realm, Chatterjee argues, "was neither coextensive with nor coincidental to the field constituted by the public/private distinction."[97]

Delving into the operations of the public/private, this study works on the other side of Chatterjee's analysis, exploring how the capital/community distinction is managed on the terrain of capitalist practice itself. I magnify an inside and integral part of world capitalism that is nevertheless posed as outside the logic of capitalist modernity. The late colonial staging of capital, in contact with vernacular capitalism, at once delegitimized community as "natural, prepolitical and primordial" and reproduced it, particularly in the form of the Hindu Undivided Family.[98] In colonial discourse, these various premodern connotations of community marked the difference of indigenous capitalisms. Hegemonic capitalist groups legitimized their economic agency, and their claims to nation building, I argue, through a language of community as ancient culture. Highlighting the making of the distinction between contract and kinship, this analysis emphasizes the ways in which market governance produced and managed two general modes of community: state, civil society, and market, on the one hand (as gesellschaft), and family, caste, and culture on the other (as gemeinschaft). I thus shift the analytical focus from the tensions between capital and nation to an attention to the discourses of community that enable and are reproduced by capitalist relations and forms of governing.

Chapters

Part 1, "A Non-Negotiable Sovereignty?" opens with a focus on market governance and its legal framework, which occupies the first three chapters. The last of these introduces a theme developed in greater detail in part 2: the colonial subject as economic agent. Part 1 charts the story of contract and its public/private distinction, which is elaborated in part 2, "Negotiating Subjects," through the negotiations of Marwari commercial groups.

Chapter 1, "The Proper Swindle," examines foundational statutes in the standardization of commercial, fiscal, and financial procedures in

India. Charting the construction of official public versus unofficial private or kinship-based market activity, it analyzes the 1882 Indian Companies Act, the 1886 Indian Income Tax Act, and the 1881 Negotiable Instruments Act, exposing in the genealogy of each the production of the Hindu Undivided Family and the concomitant delegitimizing of vernacular capitalism. The Companies Act crafts a legal fiction of the corporation as a public person and the limited liability contract as associational template for civil society, while the Indian Income Tax Act exposes anxieties about the family firm and highlights its classification as the HUF. Moreover, the Negotiable Instruments Act reveals that customary credit mechanisms, though protected as cultural "local usages," nevertheless became subject to new contractual procedures.

Chapters 2 and 3 turn to the standardization of the law on charitable endowments as a central feature of market governance. Charity and philanthropy were defined specifically as gifting for the benefit of "the public," a transformation in governance that introduced and enforced a novel legal mechanism, the trust contract. Chapter 2, "Capitalism's Idolatry," focuses on case law and the jurisprudential machinations which introduced the law of mortmain. The only category of property allowed to exist in perpetuity—as a charitable gift—mortmain represented the logical *exception* to the free circulation of property. The chapter maps the regulatory capacities of the public/private distinction, which reconfigured the symbolic and material economies of vernacular capitalism's customary social welfare practices. It does so through a legal story in which deities, to whom customary gifts were consecrated, became juridical subjects, even as the HUF was criticized as an abyss of perpetual property-holding. These legal confabulations inform the larger point, that Anglo-Indian law recoded all customary gifting as a contractual trust relation: that is, as a permanent gift to the deity. The analysis details two key effects: First, as colonial law insisted on gifts given in perpetuity, it restricted the material fluidity between profitable and charitable ventures that characterized vernacular capitalism. Secondly, new definitions of charity as public benefit challenged the symbolic status of indigenous gifts for social welfare, which were dedicated to ancestors and coded as private ventures.

Drawing attention to the period between the groundbreaking Charitable Endowments Acts of 1890 and its revision in 1920, chapter 3, "For General Public Utility," focuses on mercantile negotiations with sovereignty. It begins by mapping the uneven application of the criterion of "general public utility" to customary social welfare practices and then elaborates on the recasting of mercantile social gifting as irrelevant to public, civic benefit. The uneven sovereign affirmation of customary gifting, dependent on analogies to contract, exposes tactics of modern market governance. Precolonial, layered sovereignties had acknowledged merchants' gifts by granting local autonomy to commercial groups and, indeed, by allowing localized performances of sovereignty. This chapter reveals the unraveling of this bargain after 1890: it charts a shift from precolonial shared sovereignty to new models of *shares in* sovereignty through public philanthropy. The shift was accompanied by the production of a new category of trust, the "private" family trust, which encompassed a variety of indigenous social welfare practices and which, in turn, became a site for discourses of cultural protectionism.

Building on the arguments in Part 1 that demonstrated how indigenous capitalism's family firms were delegitimized, chapter 4, "Hedging Bets," illustrates that by the early twentieth century, family firms became subjects of criminal investigation. This chapter begins by detailing indigenous speculative practices never before examined, outlining varieties of futures trading and speculation akin to transactions that were being discussed and legitimized in formal stock and commodities exchanges in the West. The problem of the legality of vernacular forms of futures trading is investigated through a major public discourse of the period, the moral problem of gambling. Criminal law on gambling in late nineteenth-century India was intimately tied to the new publicizing of the market and to the making of a rational, contracting subject. At the interstices of civil and criminal law, the gambling story opens with controversies in Bombay and Calcutta in the 1880s and 1890s over "rain gambling," a recreation involving betting on rainfall, popularized by Marwaris. Public scandals over the moral degradation of this innocuous leisure practice, it argues, exposed concerns over vernacular capitalism and its aleatory inclinations. Then, surveying an unexamined archive of provincial legislative measures and local police surveys of indigenous futures markets in cotton, jute, silver, opium, and grain—all key commodities in the colonial economy—the analysis demonstrates that new regulations categorized these markets as gambling enterprises rigged by personalized ties. Marwaris rigorously and publicly contested this coding. Investigating these public performances as moments in the making of economic *and* cultural subjects, the chapter tracks a new governmental interest in identifying economic crimes and fraudulent trading practices and in establishing the written contract as the legal criterion for ethical and legitimate market practice and organization. More broadly, by highlighting the gendering of the market in public morality discourses, the chapter charts anxieties concerning the virtuality of capital (as speculation), reflected in the burgeoning of legal instruments and fictions to manage it.[99]

Chapter 5, "Economic Agents, Cultural Subjects," returns to the Hindu Undivided Family to elaborate questions of colonial subject formation. Here, the problem of the making of modern economic subjects is read through gendered discourses on culture. As such, the chapter provides a new lens through which to examine the emergence of the family as a subject of public contestation in the 1920s. In this period, as Marwaris became increasingly involved in civic institutions and nationalist politics, they actively legitimized the joint family and its patriarchical authority, especially over the exchange of women in marriage. Resisting any easy inscription of social-reform movements into modernization narratives, our analysis locates Marwari social-reform debates within the long history of their negotiations with colonial market governance. It charts how *both* the modernizing and orthodox wings of the Marwari community deployed the category of the HUF to promote the institution of the joint family. Attempts to protect joint kinship mediated the intensified and expanding regulation of vernacular capitalists' market practices and informed their new hegemonic claims as national economic experts. Completing the approach to economy as a problem of culture, and to capital as constitutive of community in its many forms, the analysis maps how the female subject was managed as an instrument of indigenous male economic agency: how governing the household was integral to governing the market.

PART ONE

※

A Non-Negotiable Sovereignty?

1

The Proper Swindle

Commercial and Financial Legislation of the 1880s

> It was not my own fault that, like those who first hatched me, I was conceived in sin and shapen in iniquity, and became almost immediately the means of demoralising every one who came into contact with me, of deceiving those who trusted in me, and of crushing those who opposed me, until my own turn came and I fizzled out in a gutter of fraud.—LAURENCE OLIPHANT, "The Autobiography of a Joint-Stock Company (Limited)," 1876

IN THE LATE NINETEENTH CENTURY, literary texts such as Laurence Oliphant's "The Autobiography of a Joint-Stock Company (Limited)" enacted the new legal world of Victorian England, populated by fictitious persons and societies, and capturing, as Mary Poovey has called it, the "virtual and embodied states" of capital proliferating at this time.[1] Novel legal fictions that coded the limited liability joint-stock company as a public person, for example, accompanied the unprecedented global reach of finance capital in this period. Performing the legal selfhood of this public person, Oliphant's literary confession personifies the spurious origins of modern forms of market association, manifest in their colonial histories. As British territorial colonialism carved out new global markets, new legal instruments enabled capital to move globally, to discover new resources, and to settle and collect in corporate bodies such as the joint-stock company. Legal developments in Britain informed a barrage of commercial, financial, and fiscal legislation that was enacted during the 1880s in India. Marking a new era in India's development regime, these measures conveyed greater concern over the customary commercial and financial practices of "native commerce." This chapter elaborates key debates surrounding the Indian Companies Act of 1882, the Indian Income Tax Act of 1886, and the Negotiable Instruments Act of 1881. These foundational statutes reflected the complicated history of Britain's financial system throughout the nineteenth century, whose contradictions and anxieties were magnified in the Indian colonial context.

Crowning confirmations of the disembedding of the market, these measures introduced almost at once procedures and principles evolved from long legal histories in the British context: the concept of generalized limited liability, the expansion of the fiscal system, and the standardization of currency.[2] Directed at new sites of surveillance, the nonagricultural classes, these statutes represented novel strategies for the regulation and assessment of vernacular merchant capitalists and the promotion of contractual models for trade and association. The fluid relationship between indigenous credit, the export trade of British merchants, and the sovereignty of the East India Company before 1858 was, in the latter half of the nineteenth century, increasingly codified in legal controls that sought to administer the ideals of free trade and allow "capital's ability to generate wealth through circulation."[3] Reflecting concerns about the material profitability of the Indian empire, these regulations emerged in the period after major processes of legal codification and the compilation of Hindu and Muslim personal law, bringing the public/private distinction to questions within commercial civil law and common law, also known as the *lex mercatoria*, law merchant or mercantile law.[4]

In the British-Indian imperial social formation of the 1880s and 1890s, the burgeoning of new financial instruments enabled the free spirit of capital *and* sought to capture it through the disciplines of law. In Britain, the eighteenth and nineteenth centuries had marked a shift away from land as the primary register of personal wealth; by the late nineteenth century, the growing dominance of finance capital in Britain's economy had produced new social imaginaries. As Poovey explains, "Even as they occupied an everyday world increasingly filled with objects from all over the globe, more Britons measured their worth not simply by the acres (or square feet) that surrounded them, but by immaterial [representations] . . . of value that [were] always deferred."[5] The virtuality of capital, manifest in the stories of the new financial press as well as in the intricate plots of Victorian novels, had been enabled by the theoretical fictions of the law. Legal developments that spanned the nineteenth century reflected scandals concerning financial and commercial practice and the stabilization of new forms of capitalist value. Certainly, important components of modern business—such as the joint-stock association, the idea of the national debt, and share trading—had histories reaching back to the early seventeenth century. But legal historians acknowledge that the pace of legal change after the 1840s was much accelerated. They highlight a general discrepancy between the innovations of eighteenth- and early nineteenth-century commercial and financial practice and the "stagnant legal framework" of the same period.[6] Early twentieth-century jurists such as F. W. Maitland, for example, bemoaned measures such as the "Bubble Act" of 1720, repealed only in 1824, which had managed speculation mania through excessive restrictions on pioneering commercial practice, strictly enforcing the express authority of Parliament and royal charters to incorporate joint-stock companies.[7] In Britain, the shift from law as an arm of sovereignty to a tactic of laissez-faire built momentum in the nineteenth century and was evinced in legal innovations that enabled new vehicles of investment, savings, debt remittance, and credit, as well as the standardization of tax law. Significant markers included the formal establishment of the London Stock Exchange in 1801; the repeal of the "Bubble Act" in 1824; the recasting of companies law beginning in 1844; the introduction of bankruptcy legislation in 1831 (revised in 1869 and 1883); the revision and expansion of the tax law, which had been primarily directed at land, in order to thoroughly cover trade, business, investment, and salaried income; the revision of trust law starting in the 1830s and its standardization beginning in the 1890s; and the amalgamation of the English banking system in the 1880s and 1890s.[8]

In India, the pace of such developments was even more accelerated, and their impact more jolting, as the statutory changes and jurisprudential debates of much of the nineteenth century in Britain were concentrated in India in the period after 1875, following the passage of the Indian Evidence Act and Indian Contract Act, both in 1872. These measures standardized rules of evidence and defined the rules of contract as well as the competency to contract, establishing the figure of the rational contracting subject as legal subject.[9] In the Contract Act especially, the interested subject, the template for the market agent, was consolidated as a subject of law. Elaborating the incarnations of this generalized legal subject, the foundational statutes of the 1880s (which coincided with concerns about declining agricultural productivity) confirmed a century-long shift from a physiocratic model of political economy focused on land as a source of revenue and wealth, to the taxation of income and investments. Here, the order of Adam Smith's market offered a model for sovereignty itself—as governing justly by managing, arranging, distributing.[10] Two general trends in economic policy in the 1870s exemplify the affirmation of free trade alongside the development of technologies of extraction that characterized colonial liberalism in this period: the lowering and abolition of customs duties and the expansion of the fiscal system. Beginning in 1870s, the high import duties (as much as 20 percent) established by the Government of India immediately after the rebellions of 1857 were reduced substantially. In 1875, they were taken down to 5 percent, and in 1882, the year of the Indian Companies Act, import duties were eliminated entirely except for those on special articles (opium, salt, ammunition, and liquor). Export duties were also largely done away with (except for on rice), and in a perfect enactment of the move from landed wealth to finance capital and its virtuality, the Inland Customs hedge—an actual organic hedge that was carefully patrolled and that stretched from the Indus River to the Bay of Bengal —was, according to the *Imperial Gazetteer of India*, "practically abandoned" in 1879.[11] At the same time, negotiations were conducted with princely states to abolish their customs duties. Fiscally, 1873 began a twenty-year period in the decline of the value of silver, the standard currency of India, with respect to gold; this substantially increased the burden that the Government of India faced in paying Home Charges and interest on its debt to Britain.[12] In particular, the year 1885 saw an extreme and sudden decline in the exchange rate, and for the next decade, the Government of India sought out new sources of extraction. Most notably, it identified the urban population as a source of tax revenues, as manifest in the 1886 Indian Income Tax Act.[13]

After the famine of 1876–1878, a new department of Land Revenue and Agriculture was distinguished from the Finance Department, and between 1875 and 1905, when the Department of Commerce and

Industry was established, the government directed itself consciously at the collection and standardization of commercial information, a trend evinced by the debates surrounding the Negotiable Instruments Act of 1881.[14] Indeed the statutory changes of the 1880s evinced the opening of new channels of information after 1870—the modern postal system, newspapers, printed books and pamphlets, and the electric telegraph —information that in its circulation carved out a civic public and produced knowledges of public import.[15] Indian historiography has documented well the expanding civic arena of the late nineteenth century, an arena buzzing with political publicists and early nationalist associations, and facilitated by the Indian Councils Acts of 1861 and 1892 as well as measures for municipal government. Alongside the production of a new political public by corporate bodies like the Indian National Congress (established 1885), the law formalized models of public association and exchange that institutionalized another version of the public which was the corollary of the emergent nation: the market.

Before turning to the statutes themselves, it is important to note that our approach to the law, as outlined in the introduction, addresses contradictions presented in the social and economic history of Indian capitalism. Broadly speaking, these arguments have posed colonial law on economy as undermining itself and therefore ineffective. Perhaps the most well known example is David Washbrook's argument on law and agrarian society in this period, which asserts that "if the rule of law were meant to provide the social and political force driving the market economy, the raj was doing its best to see that it had little power."[16] Here, free market liberalism, as manifested in the rule of law, confronted the Raj as a colonial power, with its interest in propping up conservative forces for social stability; this confrontation ultimately limited capitalist transformation. As an empirical statement about the mechanics of colonial governmentality, the assessment is sound, but as a reading of law, it is too literal. Washbrook reads the rule of law as a failure, as not able to accomplish its liberal vision; he thus assesses the law on the basis of its own criteria of success and its own modernizing propositions, a perspective that presupposes and reiterates a universal narrative of capitalist development.

This casting of the law as ineffective is echoed more broadly in histories of Indian merchant-capitalists that argue that while commercial and financial law called for the regulation of market exchange, the peculiarities of indigenous market practice were protected under the personal law. As such, the public/private distinction is understood from within its own logic, as ensuring an arena of autonomy for indigenous practices. David Rudner's study of the Nattukottai Chettiars, for example, emphasizes that while banking legislation sought to control customary exchange through restrictions on indigenous negotiable instruments, the vast material accumulations of this caste of merchant-bankers evinces the failure of colonial law in regulating this group. This argument tells us quite a bit about the material agency of indigenous capitalists and the continuity of Chettiar banking and trading activity, but less about the ways in which law produced boundaries for the operation of that activity.[17] More broadly, studies often rightly emphasize the concomitant operation and porous boundaries between the informal bazaar economy and the official sector, but say little about the law. While it is important to remember that British and Indian systems worked side by side and, indeed, were intimately connected to one another in a "mutually recognized division of spheres," as Amiya Kumar Bagchi has put it, our attention to law allows us to investigate the politics of the reproduction of these spheres.[18]

Whether presented as a failure, or as a benign distinction between public/private, formal/informal, law is under-researched in the history of Indian capitalism. Rather than assessing the rule of law based on the criteria it sets up for itself, or reproducing its claims, this analysis investigates the operation, rather than just intention, of colonial law: its production of subjects and parameters of legality and legitimacy. As such, it considers processes by which the law, as a language of sovereignty, suppresses and transforms local knowledges and conventions, even in benign or benevolent performance. As critical legal theorists have asserted, legal systems exploit the difference between "legitimacy and illegitimacies," a central concern of this analysis, manifest especially in our attention to the deployment of the public/private distinction.[19] If we assess the law from within its own logic and claims, then the private arena will be understood as space of indigenous autonomy; informed by feminist approaches, we investigate the distinction as one between legitimate and illegitimate arenas for economy and modernity.

As framed in the introduction, the approach here attends to the difference between a juristic understanding of the law as a logically coherent system of meaning (*logos*) and law as the range of social meanings manifest in convention/conduct (*nomos*).[20] The analysis examines the tensions between the rationalizing process of law as a logic and the contingencies of local conventions and practices. At the same time, drawing on Foucault, it also engages the concept of economy as a model of governing—as management and arrangement, as in *oikonomia*—that is, the conventions that regulate and manage the household.[21] Late colonial sovereignty performed itself as economy in this sense—as a management and naming of the household, in its various senses as family, society, nation, nature. Highlighting the ethical register of market governance, and the tropes of community at play within it, this chapter poses two guiding questions. First, what legal processes rendered the situatedness of mercantile conventions commensurate with the universalizing logic of civil law, and *at the same time* utterly incommensurate with modern market ethics? Secondly, how did colonial sovereignty manage market relations as a problem of community: that is, how did it name the households it governed?[22] Speaking rhetorically, we might say that colonial authority, as a paternal authority, indeed, as a *despot* (a word which is descended from the ancient Greek *despotes* and akin to the Sanskrit *dampati*, both referring to lord of the house/household), and speaking through the rule of law, named its household in two ways: as public and private. In commercial and financial law, the household understood as society, as an abstract public of subjects and as market, was posed in contrast to household as family. Framed by kinship, the family nexus mapped the realm of indigenous culture and the unofficial, private bazaar exchange of indigenous merchant-capitalists. The categories of public and private distinguished between those economic practices rendered legal by statute and those tolerated as legal by operation of law, that is, mercantile custom. Examining this supposedly benign distinction in legality, between the universe of the rule of law and the realm of the customary, this chapter charts their production as arenas that are framed as legitimate and illegitimate, and in other circumstances as licit and illicit.

White-Gloved Swindlers:
Limited Liability and the Companies Act, 1882

The Indian Companies Act of 1882 was a revision of the earlier Act X of 1866, passed in India as an adaptation of the English law on joint stocks, whose long history had been transformed by the repeal of the "Bubble Act" in 1824 and, more significantly, by the passage of the English Companies Acts of 1844 and 1856. In Britain, the 1844 "Act for the Registration, Incorporation and Regulation of Joint-Stock Companies" marked the first time that joint stocks could be incorporated without the specific permission of the state (by act of Parliament or royal charter). Procedures for registration were generalized under law, but it was not until the 1856 act that limited liability became generalized. That is, until 1856, joint-stocks in Britain enjoyed limited liability only with state permission; the 1856 statute enabled joint stocks to incorporate as limited-liability associations by following strict procedures governed by law. The nine years after the introduction of general limited liability saw a huge burst in the registration of limited liability companies—at least 4,800 in London alone.[23] Revisions to these foundational statutes continued through the 1860s and later. The 1882 Indian act for the "incorporation, regulation and winding up of trading companies" was rewritten ostensibly in order to extend statutory amendments that had been passed in England since 1860 to the Indian context. The Statement of Objects and Reasons for the 1882 Indian bill argued that the amendments should be incorporated not only because "they are good in themselves," but because "it is desirable that the laws relating to such a subject as mercantile Companies should be as nearly as possible the same in India as in England."[24] This manufactured consonance was to encourage British investment in India through the joint-stock company, a supposedly familiar framework for English entrepreneurs.

In addition to its homogenizing concerns, the Indian Companies Act of 1882 was also a product of the volatile boom and bust of the cotton market in western India during the 1860s and 1870s. Echoing concerns over the corruption and ostentation of the "nabobs" or governors of the East India Company that surrounded the trial of Warren Hastings a hundred years before, the debates concerning the 1882 Act grappled with the question of how to promote profit while managing piracy. The heightened demand for Indian cotton in the 1860s due to the American Civil War had created a new landscape of joint-stock concerns, particularly in the Bombay Presidency, but the fall in cotton prices after the war soon rendered them highly unstable. British merchants who had invested their capital in the cotton export trade in the

1860s redeployed their energies in the 1870s by starting up spinning and weaving mills in Bombay. While historians are quick to point out the rise in the number of mills in operation in Bombay in the 1870s, these statistics overshadow the perceived climate of instability that surrounded the 1882 Companies Act.[25]

Despite the codification of British companies procedure in the Indian Act of 1866, the brief lifespans of many of the joint-stock concerns floated in this period, especially those in and around Bombay, threw into question the principle of limited liability enshrined in the 1866 act. In England, limited liability had been promoted, especially since the eighteenth century, as a form of contract and a doctrine of legal protection for associations engaged in trade. At its most basic, the principle asserted that shareholders and directors were liable only to the extent of their share capital. Participants in joint-stock concerns could not incur, in other words, any *personal* liability in the case of debts. In India in the 1870s, British merchants who established joint-stock companies in both trade and manufacture had lured investment in shares from wealthy landowning groups, as well as indigenous merchants, moneylending and trading groups like Gujarati *banias*, and the increasingly itinerant Marwaris, who migrated to Bombay in the 1870s and then to Calcutta in the 1880s.

But shareholders who financed the new joint stocks did not seem to experience *protection* as the characteristic principle of joint-stock investment. As the official responses to the Companies Bill elaborated, British directors and managing agents speculated on invested share capital, transferred shares between a variety of companies they controlled, and in the process produced a chain of bankruptcies that financed new concerns. As bankruptcies became common, directors absconded with the share capital of populations of largely "native" shareholders. The amendments introduced to the 1882 Companies Act sought to manage this volatile climate with provisions directed primarily at the procedures for dissolving or "winding-up" companies and at enforcing new models of contractually based governing. Amidst rampant material speculation, the principle of limited liability became a subject of public debate and moral speculation. At stake was the future of limited liability as the contractual basis for commercial and industrial organization in India. The hundreds of pages of opinions gathered before the passage of the new act speak to the challenges to, and ultimate affirmation of, the limited liability principle. While the act of 1866 had simply ordered the principle into existence, by 1882, government officials had gathered long testimonies concerning the inefficacy of the companies procedure. These memorials and opinions from the diverse interests of local officials, commercial associations, and emergent Indian nationalist organizations all spoke to the necessity of joint-stock organization, even as many opinions exposed the unethical practices it harbored and protected.

The critique of limited liability had begun with the Indian Companies Act of 1866. By 1882, local officials lamented that British-run companies, while displaying great feats of financial wizardry, were unable to transform the legal rules for companies procedure into everyday habit: that is, into legitimate market ethics. Included in the papers of the 1882 act were several letters relating the history of noncompliance by British directors in India. Definitive evidence came from an official at the center of the Bombay cotton boom, the acting registrar of joint stock companies in Bombay, J. B. Peile. In 1866, the Government of Bombay had solicited from him the number of companies that had complied with registration procedures in the six months since the 1866 act. He wrote that of the 172 companies registered in Bombay at the time, 71 had not submitted a list of members and summary capital, 66 had not submitted balance sheets, and 62 had not given notice of the location of their registered offices. Peile admitted that there were companies that had probably never "sent a single document since the day they were incorporated," despite their likelihood of "having ... called up capital, [which had probably] disappeared while no accounts whatever [had] been published."[26]

Despite his enumeration of British directors' extralegal operations, the registrar was unwilling to question the principle of limited liability, which had protected the "disappearance" of called-up capital he himself had recounted. Responding to complaints he had received from indigenous shareholders, he argued confidently that limited liability should not be at issue, but rather the customs and indeed ethics of indigenous commerce:

> The evils incidental to limited liability have been exaggerated in Bombay by peculiarities in Native character. The money ... diffused after the Russian [Crimean] War, and in a much greater degree during the American [Civil] War, naturally collected itself into joint-stock concerns with

limited liability. There was no possible means of employing healthily the enormous seam of capital thus collected, and there came to be a competition among the companies as to who should lend on the worst security. It is doubtful if the extremest prudence and candour could have preserved a healthy tone in business. But the mass of Native shareholders, profoundly ignorant, and placing blind confidence in the new discovery in "finance" placed no watch on their Directors and Managers. The latter only wanted to profit from the sale of shares, and cared nothing for the regular transaction of business. The shareholders have now changed the blindness of confidence for the blindness of terror, and it appears that they are generally quite ready to get out of the concern at any cost without calling the responsible parties to account.[27]

Here, even as the swindling of British directors was acknowledged, the blame for the instability of the joint-stock principle in India lay squarely on the shoulders of native shareholders. The registrar's main complaint was that these shareholders "appear[ed] to consider it [the registrar's] business to undertake the entire duty of rectifying their affairs."[28] Instead, native shareholders ought to have taken more responsibility, embracing and exercising the rights of the contract into which they had engaged. The criticism focused not on the question of whether limited liability ought to be rethought, but rather on the passiveness of native shareholders, who had to learn to be active citizens in the affairs of their companies. They had to attend meetings, keep watch, and call responsible parties to account, both figuratively and literally: by enforcing the responsibility of directors through the use of legal channels and by insisting upon the written, numerical account, the balance sheet, established by companies procedure. The registrar did not question the legitimacy of the companies law itself. Rather, he presented a diagnosis of indigenous commercial ethics in which the central malady was the preponderance of "blindness," a blind confidence rather than the clarity of contract. The virtues of contractual obligation seemed lost on the absconding directors, but these transgressions were excused in an account of the market as a feminine agent of desire. The "extremest prudence and candour" could not have repelled the seduction of the market during the cotton boom. Indeed, such a seductive force presented ever more the necessity for the enforcement of the contract. And given the "naturally" desirous disposition of British director-adventurers, the responsibility for such enforcement fell upon shareholders, who, coded as naive children, were neither amenable to sexualized market temptations nor mature enough to manage them.

This assessment of commercial organization in the 1860s, then, drew boundaries of legitimate and illegitimate activity. The swindling of British directors, while openly accounted for as illegal, did not present itself as *illegitimate* in the registrar's complaints. The passivity of native shareholders, on the other hand, was clearly not illegal, but was narrated as illegitimate in an ethical sense. This account seemed to neutralize the official or "visible" boundaries between legal and illegal established by the law and replace them with new invisible ones distinguishing legitimate from illegitimate activity. These boundaries were not written in the law explicitly, and yet were operational: they outlined the spaces in which activities were to be understood and validated as commercial practice. The act of speculation was not to be understood as in itself unethical; if speculation operated within the contractual framework of the managing agency, it was a legitimate kind of investment banking, but when conducted through the framework of kinship, it threatened social order and morality.[29]

By the 1880s, new opinions on companies procedure solicited by the Government of India turned to unequivocal enumerations of the illegal activities of joint-stock concerns. Many of the opinions came from local officials and the publicists of emerging Indian political associations. These were not voices of an anticapitalist project, nor did they necessarily represent the on-the-ground interests of vernacular merchant-capitalists. In particular, native officials that were part of the growing administration for the regulation of commerce and industry were key contributors to the emerging public discussion on capitalist development at this time. Such educated elites argued for the incorporation of English law into Indian civil law in order to "encourage the native public to enter into associations for the healthy and useful employment of capital."[30] Despite this loyalty to capitalist progress, such officials and political spokespeople did not excuse the fraudulent activities of largely British-run joint stocks, as evinced in their opinions on the Companies Bill of 1882.[31] Indeed, they challenged the efficacy of limited liability to protect shareholders and so to produce an ethics suitable for the progress of capital and industry.

In these critical opinions, British directors were repeatedly represented as a sort of elite club of white-gloved swindlers, engaging in illegitimate activity all the while made respectable by the law itself. Thus, unlike the Bombay registrar's opinion of 1866, in which the illegal activities of directors had been pronounced legitimate, native opinions argued that the legal principle of limited liability protected illegitimate practices. For example, in an unsolicited memorial sent to the Legislative Council of India in 1882, the retired government translator of the North-Western Provinces and Oudh pleaded that the "powers which the existing law [the Act of 1866] confer[red] on the Directors of such [joint-stock] Companies were too exorbitant as regards the circumstances of the people of the country."[32] Interpreting the protection of limited liability as a kind of buttress for arbitrary power, the petition presented directors as agents of fraud and deception, rather than victims of market seduction:

> In this part of the country, there have been two instances in which native capitalists contributed to a business undertaken by a corporation. In one of these instances the Directors, by an abuse of their power, involved the company into debts, and at last contrived to purchase the whole concern of large value for a comparatively small price, *depriving the shareholders of their rights*. . . . The occurrence . . . of such examples was highly discouraging and a great drawback to the development of the native capitalist enterprize [sic] in a jointed concern; and to guard against such public frauds, it is hoped that the Hon'ble Members will make some provision before the Bill is passed into law.[33]

In this opinion, the law promoted neither stable commercial organization nor indigenous capitalism, but in fact only suspicion in modern methods of arranging and managing capital. Embracing modernity as moral and material progress by distinguishing it from the irresponsible activities of British directors, native opinions such as this one cast the colonial subject as willing but constrained exerciser of legal rights. Many testimonies promoted a risk-averse, indigenous contracting subject as market agent, contrasting this figure with the pirate joint-stock floater. Indeed, according to another petition, "if popular testimony is to be accepted, . . . [joint stocks] are generally no better than huge superstructures of fraud, erected to inveigle the unwary and imprudent."[34] If in 1866 the Bombay registrar had bemoaned the naive blind confidence of native capitalists, by 1882, critics of limited liability spoke of the blindness effected by the law in order to deceive, rather than educate, those uninitiated in the ways of the market game.

Still, native critics resisted a wholesale denial of joint-stock organization as blueprint for India's material progress, instead reinforcing the force of law. The laws introduced for public organization of companies were "good in themselves," and therefore activity that did not correspond to their strictures—morally illegitimate activity—had to be labeled as such: that is, it had to be pronounced illegal. The condemnation of companies procedure thus demanded a consistency between law and market ethics: the law was to protect only legitimate practices. In the process, critics reinforced the power of civil law to designate new categories of legitimate and illegitimate commercial practice.

In this vein, Protap Chandra Ghosh, Calcutta's registrar of joint-stock companies, wrote in a solicited opinion to the undersecretary to the Government of Bengal in 1881 that "the limited liability principle, for the advancement of trade or industry, was unknown in this country until the advent of British capital, energy and spirit; even now it has not received the adequate appreciation from native capitalists."[35] The remedy, he said, was to encourage such enterprise with an improvement in the law in order to "impart new impetus to the cause of material progress in this country."[36] Ghosh charted in detail the process of fraud and its main agents, directors and managing agencies. Here again his analysis focused on the calculated manipulations enabled by the established companies legislation. The spiral of bankruptcy and reinvestment would begin as the "joint-stock company is started as a speculation; a few speculators club together to raise the wine; they fix upon a stock and block, set a nominal value upon them, and fill their pockets by sending forth glowing prospects of the projected company." After the memorandum of association is set and share capital goes into the purchase of a capital investment, usually a mill, the mill's owner-directors pocket the mill's profits, speculate with those profits, run up the value of shares, and sell them at high rates. Then the directors become managing agents for the company in order to transfer share capital into other concerns, then become liquidators, "and thus go on building one house of cards upon another. Then the smash comes, the innocent and credulous public, represented in the shareholders and creditors, suffer." The Calcutta registrar thus concluded that this process, the de facto companies procedure, was simply "reckless and immoral speculation."[37]

What held together these "houses of cards," these precarious, though huge, "superstructures of fraud"? The secretary of the British Indian Association, Kristodas Pal, argued that while the joint stock seemed from the outside to be a structure fortified by registration procedures, it revealed itself upon closer inspection as only a facade of fluid, personalized relations. Pal's argument for rectifying the situation again demanded the enforcement of the letter of the law: to assert forcefully the principle of contract. Thus he argued that the Memorandum of Association, a legally binding contract for procedure among directors and shareholders through which companies were registered, generally contained no limitations for curbing the powers of directors, and in fact provided the opportunity to create, under the heading of "association," an organization which had little public responsibility. The flaws of the joint stock began at its inception:

> The manner in which such companies are floated is not always aboveboard. Two to three persons may own some property; they may assess it at their own valuation, and then induce a few others to join them in converting the concern into a company. They frame a Memorandum of Association, and register it. In that memorandum they may prescribe conditions which the outside public have no means of knowing, but which will be binding upon shareholders; and the law gives them facility to commit abuse and fraud, by declaring that any alterations that may be made in the regulations of the Company by a special resolution at a general meeting, must be subject to the conditions contained in the Memorandum of Association.[38]

The secret nature of the memorandum of association produced a situation in which the private decisions of a few directors were able to regulate, through a supposedly public framework, the activities of the company. According to this opinion, the Companies Act of 1866 had allowed public responsibility to become subject to private and personal connections.[39] This was a kind of despotic, arbitrary power that had to be rectified. Public organization, Pal argued, had to be exactly that: "above board" and visible, and so able to be accounted for by the public of shareholders. Again, the criticisms offered by the British Indian Association, an organization publicizing the interests of indigenous landholders entering the commercial sphere, enforced a model of contractual civil society; indeed, they enforced a very literal interpretation of it, in order to counteract the potential despotism of the joint-stock organization.

To summarize, critics of limited liability in the early 1880s reiterated the validity of this form of contract as the basis for public commercial association. Directors' performance of accountability to the public of shareholders was absolutely necessary for the proper organization of trade and finance. If early spokespeople for companies law had argued that the irregularities of companies procedure were due at least partially to the inability of natives to perform their duties as shareholders, later Indian opinions argued that the law had not protected these shareholders' rights. These were the very rights that enabled active citizenship in the joint-stock association. Buttressing this discourse of citizenship as shareholding was an affirmation of the public nature of the limited liability contract. Only activity that was public or publicly accountable would guarantee the legitimacy of a commercial or financial organization. The criticism of limited liability ultimately called for its rigorous enforcement, legitimizing the principle and the kind of organization that it was meant to establish and manage: the public contract of the joint-stock association.[40] This process also coincided with the de-legitimizing of indigenous mercantile organization in the form of the family firm, codified in personal law as the coparcenary Hindu Undivided Family (HUF).

Thus despite a broad array of concerns, the principle of limited liability was re-enshrined in the 1882 Companies Act. The Legislative Council inserted amendments to ensure the public procedures for debt and bankruptcy, in addition to requiring public announcements for potential shareholders of any contracts made previously by a company's directors or promoters.[41] Moreover, Section 26 of the 1882 Companies Act introduced a new form of public association that was modeled on and extracted from the contractual basis of joint-stock organization. This section allowed for "associations not engaged in mercantile pursuits" to become "incorporated" under the act, but without "annexing to their names the inappropriate term 'limited.'"[42] Indeed, the public framework for association enshrined in the act, a framework which ensured status as a legal person and the right to sue as a corporate organization, became a standard for civic association, both profit and nonprofit, and the template for modern associative community.

The Legitimacy of Public Association

The reassessment and final reinscription of the limited-liability principle in the early 1880s depended upon the application of the categories of public and private. As reformers of companies procedure insisted upon limited liability as the model for public commercial association, the Hindu family firm, in the framework of the joint *Mitakshara* household, was posed as a problem for those interested in encouraging the "healthy and useful employment of capital" by native merchants.[43] Most opinions on the 1881 bill ignored the question of the caste-based trading firm on the grounds that companies procedure referred de facto mainly to British mercantile interests in India and to joint-stock organization; the family firm, they therefore argued, need not be addressed as a relevant object of regulation.[44] As the judicial commissioner of Oudh explained in his opinion, "The subject matter [of the Companies Bill] is not known to native law, but is the offspring of western civilization."[45] The Companies Bill introduced in 1881 was a "bill for the incorporation, regulation, and winding-up of Trading Companies and Associations" and yet did not set out to address, in any specific way, the family firm as a trading firm. This avoidance was perhaps an effect of the debates surrounding the Negotiable Instruments Act the year before, which had evinced the difficulty in assessing or codifying customary commercial operations. But more significantly, the attitude of nonengagement—of laissez-faire, even—operated by *excluding* the family firm from the category of proper trading concerns. Legislators understood the family firm as a family above all else, a "private" concern, rather than as a mechanism for trade or moneylending. Because the family defined the firm (and not vice versa, as one might expect from legislation interested in regulating trade), its commercial organization could be considered neither public nor a legitimate model for trade and finance.[46]

Certain critics of the Companies Bill asserted that if the legislation was to be consistent, Hindu family firms, understood as unincorporated partnerships without limited liability, ought to be subject to the act. Sreenath Roy, the judge of the Small Case Court in Howrah, had adjudicated at the local level on cases involving such firms, addressing the question of their regulation directly. Even as he produced an analogy between the contractual partnership and the joint family firm, the judge also drew a distinction between the partnership, understood legally as an association of unlimited liability, and the Hindu Undivided Family, also an organization with a kind of unlimited liability due to its jointness. This double bind—of the family as a mimesis of a contractual relation, and as its difference—captured the inside/outside place of the HUF in the debate. Roy asserted that Hindu families conducting business, like the firms of the traditional mercantile castes, ought to be considered legal partnerships and therefore subject to companies regulations. However, given this, it was also very important to make certain that not *all* Hindu Undivided Families would become, under a slippery definition of partnership, subject to regulation, particularly in the case of debt:

> The word partnership used in section 243 of the Bill may, unless a specific exemption is allowed, include a joint Hindu family. But considering the laws and usages applicable to such families, it is desirable that they should be specifically exempted from the operation of the bill in question. . . . If the legislature intend to include the affairs of such families as partnership business within the purview of the Bill, numerous would be the difficulty, and delay in causing separation on those families. Almost all Hindu families are abnormally joint and as soon as occasion arises they square their accounts either amicably or through the intervention of the court, and thus cause separation without any risk or inconvenience to the common creditors, to whom the members of the family are jointly and severally liable in spite of separation. The case however, would be different where several members of such family carry on a mercantile business in the shape of partnership business. In such cases the provisions of the Bill must apply, without, however, interfering with the general affairs of the family in other respects.[47]

This opinion sought to distinguish the Hindu family firm as *a firm* from its role as a family, which would governed by Hindu personal law. But a key Bombay High Court decision of 1880 had confirmed that the joint family firm was to be understood legally as a creation of the "operation of law"—that is, custom—and thus under the jurisdiction of the Hindu personal law.[48] Contrary to this juridical definition of the family firm as a family first, Roy attempted to characterize the joint family firm as a trading partnership. As the citation above betrays, in India, the definition of a "partnership" was extremely slippery and indeed not settled upon until 1935, though it had been codified in England by the Partnership Act of 1890.[49] Because of the flexibility of the term in India, Roy argued it was possible to regulate the family firm as a partnership in the case of its trading activities. He thus pushed for legal mechanisms that would distinguish between the private family affairs of the joint family firm, and its public commercial engagements.

Similarly, the Bengal Chamber of Commerce, an association of British business interests based in Calcutta, wrote that while the HUF in general could not be viewed as a company, indigenous mercantile partnerships ought to be specifically regulated under the Companies Act.[50] The act, of course, sought to control the groups represented by the chamber, and its members thus demanded the same surveillance for the indigenous merchants with whom they dealt. Both the chamber and the opinion from Howrah argued that if the family firm was to be understood first as a Hindu Undivided Family, only personal law would apply to its affairs. If, as they advocated, the family firm was to be understood as a trading partnership to be regulated by the Companies Act, the wording of the act would have to state specifically that the companies legislation would override personal law in the regulation of trade and moneylending.

But the 1882 Companies Act ultimately demanded, without any qualification, the registration of all trading partnerships of more than twenty persons, as well as banking partnerships of more than ten. This was an equivocal regulation, because the act did not, as the above opinions had requested, specifically identify the Hindu family firm as a trading or banking partnership. Moreover, the very definition of "partnership" was unstable at this time. The 1880 judicial precedent had established the Hindu family firm as customary: that is, produced through the operation of law. "Partnership" was commonly understood as an association resulting from contract, but that definition was not written into statute in India until 1935. In the 1880s, "partnership" might have been interpreted as a contractual association, but also as an association created by the operation of law and regulated by mercantile convention. So that in a broad sense, the act might be understood as a direct control of family firms, since they could be subject to definition as customary partnerships. The legal refuge from such regulation was to claim that only personal law regulated the affairs of the family firm, which would mean defining the firm *via* the family and its household property. To evade the controls of registration, submission of balance sheets, and debt procedure, which challenged the unwritten kinship-based trust of vernacular commercial organization, the family firm could claim to operate in the autonomous, private arena of the HUF. By not specifically identifying the Hindu family firm as an object of its jurisdiction, then, the 1882 Companies Act opened an entrance to evasion: the "autonomous" arena of family. This "recentering of the theme of economy on a different plane from that of the family" was not simply a contradiction in the regulatory intentions of the Companies Act.[51] Rather than positively define objects of regulation, the new legislation applied the categories of public and private to market activity and asserted a distinction between economic enterprise accountable to the public and that accountable only to the customs of family and indigenous culture.

After over a decade of criticism, the reaffirmation of limited liability and the benefits of joint-stock association for public welfare suggested an ordering of the public and private as arenas of legitimate and, if not yet illegitimate, then tolerated, but extralegitimate activity. Again, it is important to remember that these categories produced as naturally private and domestic an institution that was neither. The family firm defied the public/private dichotomy in its very liminality as an institution that produced a public exchange of credit and goods based on marriage and kinship, and predicated marriage and kinship on the necessities of credit and trade.[52] Therefore, the representation of the firm as either a trading partnership with unlimited liability, or as a jointly and severally liable Hindu Undivided Family, would necessarily misrepresent it. While the category of the partnership abstracted unlimited liability from the kinship and status ties of the family firm, that of the HUF reduced the material activities of the firm to a domestic economy, identified through the procedures of personal law concerning inheritance and succession. The political articulations of the Hindu commercial groups to be explored in the following chapters reflected attempts to negotiate this abstraction and reduction.

The commercial activities of the Hindu family firm, in its various regional, caste, and kinship incarnations, were, after the Companies Act, officially understood to operate in a private and customary arena. In fact, the Companies Act inaugurated two economies that named two households: an official household of a public of subjects, and the unofficial household, the family, which stood in for the nexus of indigenous trade through family firms. Commercial activities might then be divided into those that benefited the public and produced the wealth of the colony (and proto-nation), and those that produced wealth for private consumption. While the Companies Act equivocated on the definition of the family firm, other foundational commercial legislation of this period revealed that the family firm was ultimately understood via its reduction into the family, and so was willfully interpreted through the lens of a legal construct, the HUF. The Indian Income Tax Act of 1886 made clear that despite the so-called autonomy afforded by the protection under personal law, commercial legislation used the HUF to control and assess indigenous merchant-capitalists. This new interest in direct control articulated itself in anxieties concerning the family and kinship-based organization of indigenous commerce, anxieties that emerged in debates concerning the introduction of a permanent tax on nonagricultural incomes.

Secret Treasure: The Indian Income Tax Act and the Illegitimacy of the Private

According to government officials, the Indian Income Tax Act of 1886 was brought into being by the pressures of an unmanageable fiscal environment. Passed in a period of increased trade that brought town and city merchants into new and more intricate nexuses of agriculture, credit, and commerce, the Act directed itself specifically at urban incomes. An untenable fiscal gap had been precipitated by the decline in the gold value of silver beginning in the early 1870s.[53] In fact, earlier temporary tax measures had been passed in 1871 and then again in 1872. The decline in the exchange rate had helped agricultural prices in the world market and so contributed to an increase in agricultural revenue, despite famines in western India in the late 1870s. But agricultural revenue was nevertheless declining as a portion of total tax revenue in the two decades from 1873 to 1893. Over one-third of the increase in government tax revenue in this period came from nonagricultural sources: most significantly from income tax.[54] In addition to the pressure of military expenditures from the first and second Afghan Wars, the implementation of free-trade policies in the late nineteenth century meant declining revenues from customs duties and a greater reliance on the identification of new sources of income.[55]

The Indian Income Tax Act of 1886 thus sought to extract in service of laissez-faire. Asserting the sovereign authority to distribute and manage material affairs through new methods of assessment, it inaugurated a permanent assessment on nonagricultural incomes, codifying in particular a concern over indigenous family firms and their secret arts of evasion.[56] The drafters' attention to merchant groups as key targets of the measure challenges any unqualified picture of their autonomy in the private arena. More importantly, the Income Tax Bill debates evince a governmental rationality that depended on the public/private distinction to justify new forms of extraction. Building the emergent discourse on vernacular capitalists' market ethics as it enacted the market as an abstract space of exchange, and indeed as exchangeable with the public, the act drew a distinction between public and private/customary spaces of capital accumulation, between productive and unproductive circuits of exchange.

Like the Companies Act, the 1886 Income Tax Act had only ineffectual precedents in the 1860s and 1870s, decades which produced many attempts to fill fiscal gaps temporarily. The first Indian Income Tax Act had been passed in 1860 (ACT XXXII), a general tax on all "profits arising from property, professions, trades and offices."[57] Making no distinction between agricultural and nonagricultural profits, this measure lapsed in 1865. The 1860 act had called for a general notice of tax schedules and voluntary returns to be channeled through newly appointed commissioners in the presidency towns and through land revenue mechanisms elsewhere. Still, it was silent on the question of the Hindu Undivided Family as a category subject to tax assessment. Rather, it assessed only two components of capitalist enterprise: the person and the company. A "person" referred to an individual, but also loosely included "any corporation," that is, any *customary* corporate body, including the HUF. "Company," on the other hand, referred both to a legally constituted person, and to "any Society, Association, Fraternity, or Partnership of any kind whatever, of or carried on by more than six persons."[58] It is important to note that while the distinction between a corporation and company implied a difference between customary and legal contractual relations, this distinction was not yet drawn along the axis of public and private.

Just as there was only an implied distinction between customary and legal ties, so too did this early legislation leave unspoken any standardized distinction between profitable and charitable associations. In 1860, charitable associations were either wholly or partially tax exempt, but the exemption depended on the executive discretion of the local government, and all exemptions required the prior approval of the governor-general.[59] "Charity" was yet an unstable category in legal discourse, to be understood through the particularities of the transaction, and not naturalized as the corrective of profit. This distinction between profit-making companies and charitable ones remained unelaborated, and again, this early legislation defined assessees based only on their *forms* of social and commercial organization rather than on the location of their activities within a map of material relations. As the next chapter elaborates, the more specific delineation of the profitable and the charitable emerged only later in the 1880s, after the public/private distinction entered tax legislation.

In 1867, a license tax was imposed on trades and professions, followed by yearly certificate taxes in 1868 and 1869.[60] The lineaments of the 1886 act emerged in temporary legislation enacted between 1870 and 1872. While these earlier measures likewise taxed all income and did not address nonagricultural income specifically, they did clarify the distinction between a company and a person. In them, a company was defined as "an association carrying on business in British India whose stock or funds are divided into shares and are transferable, whether such Company be incorporated or not." A person included both "a firm and a Hindu Undivided Family."[61]

The 1886 act inherited these definitions, and by this time, the Companies Act had also given legal status to the incorporated company as a public legal person. "Person," in the 1886 Income Tax act, thus referred specifically to the *private* conglomeration of the firm and the HUF, as well as to individuals. In addition, the act modified the voluntary return policy by strengthening the prerogatives of tax commissioners, who were given discretion to determine persons and companies liable to tax and to make lists of assessees. It also enumerated, for the first time, income categories that were *not* taxable under its provisions: most significantly, income derived from agriculture, as well as "any income derived from property solely employed for religious or public charitable purposes" and "any income which a person enjoys as a member of a company or of a firm or of a Hindu undivided family when the company or the firm or the family is liable to the tax."[62]

This elaboration of exemptions marked a change in the operation of tax law by the 1880s. By this time, the mapping of material exchange into public and private arenas not only identified legal-contractual, as opposed to customary, forms of commercial organization, but also colored the very definitions of profitable and charitable activity. Exemption from taxation would now only go to those activities that performed a *public* charitable purpose: that is, those that were deemed beneficial to the public.[63] At the same time, the public/private distinction also enabled analogies between HUF/family firm, on the one hand, and the public limited liability company on the other. The 1886 legislation inaugurated a comprehensive taxation policy that brought together an interest in permanent assessment, a focus on nonagricultural income, a concern over the status of the Hindu Undivided Family as a private arena, and, finally, the delineation of activities that were tax exempt.

The statute targeted the profits of commerce and the professions. According to Auckland Colvin, finance member of the Legislative Council of India, the "great blot on the administration" had been the failure to extract this profit from these beneficiaries of British sovereignty: "The mercantile and professional classes, for whom this time of sunshine has brought such abundant harvest, are precisely those who contribute least toward the support of the Government in the light of whose power they bask."[64] While the professional classes constituted important targets, in many areas, it would be commercial income, and indigenous commerce in particular, that was directly hit. A member of the Viceroy's Council thus pleaded, "How much longer . . . are we to tolerate the fact that non-agricultural wealth, though considerable and daily increasing, pays very little, in proportion to its means, for the protection and great advantages it enjoys under British rule—to which the very existence of the bulk of it is attributable?"[65] As C. P. Ilbert, the law member of the Viceroy's Council best known for his Criminal Jurisdiction Bill of 1883, wrote in a confidential note responding to the question of taxing merchants in newly annexed Upper Burma, "The wealthy merchants and the traders of the towns are the *only* class whom we wish to hit."[66] That this was an overriding concern was clear even in arguments that opposed the permanent assessment of income. Those who argued against it asserted that as an alternative, the reimposition of taxes on imported piece goods, along with the established license taxes on trades, would adequately cover most of the fiscal gap and would hit merchants specifically, especially members of the native princely states, the very population that had most benefited from and contributed least to British India's economy.[67]

The 1886 legislation did indeed target trade, but not without the permanent assessment of income. It called for taxation of *all profits* made in British India, without regard to the territorial origin of the earner. Many indigenous merchants trading in British India maintained ancestral domiciles in the princely states, whose territorial sovereignties were recognized by the Crown. Members of these commercial groups could not, however, claim tax exemption from the British treasury because of their status as subjects of sovereign native kingdoms. Thus, the act claimed for the public the necessary extraction from groups who had hitherto been "exempt from their due share of the public burden."[68] Indeed, the long relationship of taxation and political subjecthood was manifest here in the making of economic, as *opposed to* territorial, subjects.[69] Extraction via taxation thus delineated a market arena distinct from traditional territorial boundaries.

To define these delinquent groups in the most profitable manner, legislators enthusiastically appropriated the legal construct of the HUF. Echoing the interpretation of kinship-based indigenous commerce found in the Companies Act, the family firm was understood narrowly as a family first, as a joint coparcenary unit cut off from the broader kinship ties of lineage and marriage. As stated above, companies were to be taxed as wholes, so that the income of the company as a unit would be assessable, and individual members could not be taxed again on their shares of company profit. In a mirror of this picture, the firm and the HUF were deemed categorically inseparable, so that the individual members of a firm could not be assessed separately but only as a coparcenary whole. This collapsing in effect precluded the possibility of the firm being assessed as a partnership of individuals, for which there was legal precedent at this time.[70] It meant a larger population of taxpayers, as whole firms and families were more likely to surpass income threshold necessary for taxation, five hundred rupees per year. The result was that the coparcenary status of the HUF was read into the family firm, and the profit incentive of the firm was read into the HUF.

In a utilitarian attention to the differences of "culture," the government's insistence on the coparcenary unity of the HUF, necessary for the profitable assessment of firms as indivisible units, was written into law despite the claims of modernizing native political associations like the Indian Union, who argued that it was better to assess individual members of Hindu Undivided Families *as individuals*.[71] These groups made it clear that material concerns overrode the sanctity of the HUF as a cultural artifact. The Executive Council of the Indian Union argued, for example, that clubbing the small incomes of members of a joint family was unfair, as "exempting small income is applicable as much to persons who live jointly or carry on a joint business as to those who live or carry on business separately."[72] Other groups argued that if the Hindu joint family was to be affirmed as a culturally constituted collectivity, its cultural and moral economy ought to be taken seriously. Thus, as the British Indian Association argued, the collective ethos and material exigencies of the HUF rendered it a kind of social welfare organization, with the pressure of feeding many "unproductive" members exacerbated by the "the expenses of marriages and other rites."[73] The law, however, wrote the HUF as a private mechanism of culture, the norms of which distorted market ethics. The Indian Income Tax Act insisted that the Hindu joint family was to be more accurately described as a profit-oriented vacuum for capital. Indeed, the legal mapping of material relations into public and private determined the very definitions of legitimately profitable and legitimately charitable activity. Like a magnetic field, the ethical cartography of private and public could invisibly distort the meaning of material relations, recasting household economy into a collective club of profit and transforming extraction into capitalist productivity.

The HUF played a key role in the Indian Income Tax Act, a shift from its cameo appearances in the exception clauses of earlier civil legislation associated with codification. If Anglo-Indian civil law had generally coded the HUF as private and so protected by personal law, this measure of market governance rendered that private arena visible as a collective person and stock of income, and so subject to taxation. At the same time, this need to make income visible, especially in the case of the family firm, was expressed through the reproach of its secrecy. Secrecy distorted the privacy of the private by contesting rather than complementing the authority of the public. The act thus marked the emerging illegitimacy of the private as a space for economic transactions: in the question of revenue and its assessment, the private space of family, as site of indigenous culture more broadly, was a *secret* arena that hoarded income and profit. With its concern for public accounting and permanent assessment, the 1886 act formalized ongoing characterizations of the secrecy of indigenous accounting. Legislators and other public officials argued that indigenous merchants betrayed a particular propensity to conceal accounts. In the words of one Legislative Department opinion, "It is almost impossible to get the traders of an Eastern country like India to make anything like a correct return of the . . . yearly profits of their trade. This arises from the old fixed idea . . . that self-preservation requires that they should conceal their profits from Government and all outsiders."[74] Spokespeople for native concerns, on the other hand, responded that written accounts were of "priceless value" for merchants, who only feared "compulsory proclamation to the world of their pecuniary position."[75] Such comments pointed to both the detailed written conventions of indigenous accounting practices, as well as the family firm's performance of value in status-producing spending (in marriage and social gifting), rather than in rituals of enumeration. Through the lens of the private, this economy of extensive negotiability between commercial practice and symbolic capital, with its emphasis on the performance, rather than the public accounting of worth, was recognized as secretive, occluded, and evasive.

The argument for the imposition of a permanent tax on urban income, then, had been presented as a necessary extraction. The Finance member's summary of the bill outlined an impossible fiscal situation, which had to be rectified by extraction, a last resort. Drawing an analogy between public and private life, and casting model governance as the very practice of economy in its classical sense, he argued that economy, the most prudent channel, had been exhausted:

> Now there are several ways open to us to obtain the funds which we require. The first and most obvious method is *economy*, and no one can be more conscious than the Government of India . . . how urgent it is . . . to carry out . . . all *economies* which are practicable. . . . We have been told that if *economy* is a good dog, borrowing is better. [But there is] "no remedy against the consumption of the purse. . . ." In public as well as private life . . . the approach of money difficulties is the signal for retrenchment; and if we do not at the present moment look to *economies* to fill the void which threatens in the coming year, it is . . . because they are not . . . immediately attainable. The arrangement by which the Government of India has assigned to Provincial Governments the disposal of a large part of public revenues has had for its aim, and has achieved, *economy* and good administration. . . . Hence, if those contracts are not to be disturbed, the Government of India can *economise* only on the margin left for its own administration, . . . which [is] not susceptible of instant reduction. . . . What is needed is as much an increase of existing revenue as a repartition of those which are already available.[76]

This admission of the intent to extract betrays the currency of the idea of economy as model of sovereign practice and as a public venture. The accumulation of the family firm in particular, and the HUF in general, was to be taxed because, as many argued, it had been heretofore exempted from its share of the public burden. In other words, profit accumulated in the boundaries of the private, in the family and more broadly in the kinship-based networks of indigenous culture, remained out of circulation in *political* economy, that is, out of circulation in the public household. Private profit was thus to be legitimized through its contribution to public wealth.[77] Moreover, the finance minister's obsessive justification for the abandonment of "economy" underlines the authority of the very idea of economy as a totalizing ideal of good governance—of perfect distribution and management of resources. The imposition of the income tax required the expansion of governmental machinery, an expansion that spoke in the name of a sovereignty modeled on economy and at the same time evinced the impossibility of governing so totally.[78]

The Negotiable Instruments Act, 1881: Contract and Early Attempts at the Standardization of Customary Mercantile Practice

Shortly before the standardized templates of the Companies Act and the Indian Income Tax Act were passed into law, the Government of India grappled with establishing uniform rules for the circulation of negotiable instruments. The burgeoning of British joint-stock banks by the mid–nineteenth century, and their domination of foreign exchange, depended on transactions with the indigenous credit market, which financed agriculture and British managing agencies.[79] Concerns about procedures for negotiable instruments reflected this growing institutionalization of British banking within the Indian economy. The indigenous banking sector, whose varied "personalized" and multi-regional conventions for borrowing, lending, and investing were understood as "unorganized," posed problems for legislation aimed at rationalizing flows of credit and forms of paper currency.[80] Unlike the companies and income tax measures, the Negotiable Instruments Act of 1881 resisted entanglements with personal law and made no reference to the HUF. On the other hand, following the familiar policy of noninterference in indigenous culture, legislators also restricted the statute's purview over native commerce and finance. The Negotiable Instruments Act offers evidence of another trend in the regulation of indigenous mercantile procedures: the gradual and informal assimilation of customary market practices into the law of contract. As key statutes in the 1880s rendered the family firm a cultural mechanism, other debates associated with negotiable instruments argued that customary mercantile practices could be assimilated into modern market conventions.

Codified personal laws, which focused on the regulation of joint succession and inheritance, were often silent on the intricacies of trade. Personal law could not wholly subsume the commercial affairs of joint family firms into its authority. In fact, Anglo-Indian jurisprudence recognized a separate arena labeled the indigenous mercantile law, a common law regulating activities specific to trade and finance.[81] But the acknowledgment of a customary mercantile realm did not mean that its conventions were free from regulation. The debates around the Negotiable Instruments Acts demonstrate especially how public and private mapped the distinction between law and customary practices, *logos* and *nomos*. This act provides an important introduction to the ways in which public civil law encroached on the indigenous law merchant, even as its autonomy was recognized and affirmed.

Indigenous negotiable instruments functioned as bills of exchange, promissory notes, letters of credit, interest-bearing certificates of deposit, and forms of insurance such as bills of lading. Broadly known as *hundis* (bills of exchange) and *chittis* (letters or documents extending credit to known persons or calling in debts), these instruments' types, functions, rates of interest, and rules for discount varied according to commercial community and local customs. Among the *hundis* drafted against the deposits of a firm, for example, were those payable on sight to a named bearer (*darshani hundi*), or only to a respectable banker known to both parties (*shajog hundi*), or only to persons specifically named and accounted for by at least two other trustworthy traders (*namjog hundi*). The conditions for payment were settled by the merchants conducting the transaction and were specific to a particular time and location. Often re-endorsed multiple times, these written instruments carried with them an extensive negotiability sustained by status and carried through community-based networks.[82]

In 1866, the first Indian Law Commission, guided by the famed legal modernizers Henry Sumner Maine and James Fitzjames Stephen, introduced the question of standardized rules for negotiable instruments. Intended to be one of the chapters of the Indian Civil Code, an inaugural bill on the subject was introduced in 1867 and referred to a Select Committee.[83] The mercantile members of the Legislative Council, all representatives of British trading interests, had unanimously objected to the bill because of its numerous deviations from English law. On the other hand, other members had strongly criticized it for not including a clause saving the customs of native merchants. From the bill's inception, then, the question of preserving indigenous customs, and so sustaining the official policy of noninterference, conflicted with arguments for their assimilation into British legal models. This debate was driven by the ambiguous place of the native law mercantile, which did not fall under the purview of personal law within the Anglo-Indian legal system. The debate continued for a decade, and in 1877, the Select Committee finally circulated the bill for opinion to all local administrations. This time, the draft legislation included a clause rendering it specifically inapplicable to "local usages" regarding *hundis*.[84]

Opinions from British trade and finance, as well as legal experts on finance, then insisted that the bill had gone too far in protecting native customs. Most argued that indigenous negotiable instruments were in function analogous to their European counterparts, and that therefore no protection was necessary. Such arguments posited the assimilation of indigenous commercial practice as the underlying cause, rather than the effect, of legal standardization. Thus the Madras Chamber of Commerce, for example, argued that "a law relating to Promissory Notes, Bills of Exchange, and Cheques should apply to the instruments termed 'hundis' in use among Natives, which presumably, represent among the Native community the separately specified instruments employed by Europeans in financial and mercantile transactions." Even still, this opinion emphasized legal standardization as an important tool for effecting this already discovered assimilation, positing that "it should be an advantage to assimilate Native commercial practices to English usages."[85] Similarly, a legal expert representing British trade in Burma explained in the Rangoon *Recorder* that protection of native customs was unnecessary, as in practice they were in effect no different from British mechanisms:

The omission of hundis may have arisen from a reluctance to interfere with the trading laws and customs of the country; but if that objection were to have in all cases weight, no reformation or amendment of the law would take place. . . . I have had both at the Bar and judicially frequently to deal with questions respecting [*hundis*]; and . . . judging from the opinions I have received from bankers and Native merchants, I should say there is but a trifling difference in the law of hundis and that respecting our own bills of exchange and that, with a slight alteration in the definition of a bill of exchange, the present Bill might very well be extended as it stands to hundis.[86]

Such assertions claimed that civil law would simply reflect the de facto operations of negotiable instruments in India. Rather than pointing to the similarity of conventions between British and Indian merchants as evidence for maintaining the customary status quo, they supported the extension of the rule of law over commercial and financial matters. Thus, customary mercantile practices that were outside the purview of family law ought to be, with "slight alteration," accommodated by universal principles for contracts. Promoting the classification of "local usages" as a natural and noncoercive policy, such opinions banked upon the shortcomings of codified Hindu and Muslim law. Because personal law did not have authority over *hundis*, British mercantile interests insisted that a clause saving local usages would be at best a redundant provision and therefore advocated the ultimate authority of the civil law over affairs of trade.

The interest in assimilating the indigenous law mercantile to the rule of law was not exclusive to British commerce. While government officials grappled with the policy of noninterference, their investigations into the operation of *hundis* revealed new concerns over variations in custom. As early as the late 1860s, legislators drafting the bill began collecting accounts of native procedures; in the process, they encountered irregularities of practice, slippery informal contracts, and the extensive negotiability of indigenous bills of exchange. In 1867, the manager of the Agra Savings Bank had, for example, highlighted difficulties with proposals for the contractual enforcement of notices of dishonor, that is, of official notices announcing that a bill of exchange had been declined by nonpayment or nonacceptance. Recounting the travels of *hundis* in Marwari-dominated areas of Central and Western India, he remarked,

It is customary for a usance hundi to change holders ten or twelve times before its date of maturity arrives. This instrument is never endorsed in full according to Native custom, but passes from merchant to merchant, or from banker to banker, by an endorsement in blank of the name only of the endorser; and it may have been drawn at Nagpore, travel to Hinganghat [30 miles away], thence to Akola in Berar, thence to Hyderabad, thence to Indore or Ajmir, thence to Jeypur, thence to Mattra or Agra, and thence to Bombay, the place of residence of the drawee; and there, on presentation for payment at maturity, it may at last be dishonored. It will be most difficult, if not almost impossible, for a Native, the holder of such a dishonored hundi, to give notice of its dishonour to every endorser, as he may not know who or what they are or where they reside, their names only being affixed to the instrument. The difficulty in the case of a European being the holder of such a hundi is still greater.[87]

Such descriptions contributed to the expanding discourse on native procedures, a discourse that at once emphasized the need for a local usages clause as well as the necessity for uniformity under civil law. Central to this equivocation was the incompatibility of *hundi* exchange with European conventions, a recurrent theme in government investigations. This was particularly true in opinions from Punjab, where customary law held more sway than in other provinces of British India. Officials from the Punjab administration and its courts consistently reiterated the particularities of the *hundi* arrangements in that region.[88]

Legislators continued to gather information on indigenous finance throughout the late 1870s for the second revision of the bill. This involved examining manuals on native banking and soliciting opinions from native experts, a process that confirmed the irregularities of usages and the need for standardization. One such pamphlet, which was translated from Hindustani and circulated among the members of the council, attested to the futility of compiling a rulebook of *hundi* procedures. Offering examples of various kinds of *hundis*, it elaborated fifteen categories of rules. Each category included several subcategories; as a rulebook, it offered no standard principles, but rather elaborated specificity of circumstance. Indeed, the translator complained of its overwhelming irregularity: "It is written with such inaccuracy of expression . . . that I was obliged to call in the aid of a Native banker to assist me, and he was himself frequently at a loss to understand the meaning of the author; and he, moreover, states that the rules therein given are subject to the variations of local custom and not at all applicable in Calcutta."[89]

In 1880, the final version of the Negotiable Instruments Bill amended the absolute authority of local usages found in earlier drafts. In order to "facilitate the assimilation of the practice of Native shroffs [bankers] to that of European merchants," its preamble now explained that the act would extend "to the whole of British India; but nothing herein" would affect "any local usage relating to any instrument in an oriental language: Provided that such usage may be excluded by any words in the body of the instrument which indicate an intention that the legal relations of the parties thereto shall be governed by this Act."[90] Local usages could thus be overruled if *hundis* were written to accommodate the practices of British bankers and merchants. While not directly affecting relations among indigenous merchants, this provision was particularly important for the increasing transactions between British and indigenous interests conducted through burgeoning joint-stock banks. The Select Committee in 1879 defended the new provision as one which would not "stereotype and perpetuate these [indigenous] usages," but rather "induce the Native mercantile community gradually to discard them for the corresponding rules contained in the Bill." Changing the conduct of bazaar conduct, and so arguing that "the desirable uniformity of mercantile usage will thus be brought about without any risk of causing hardship to Native bankers and merchants," the Committee pointed to evidence offered by the Bank of Bengal, "that the native usages as to negotiable paper have of recent years been greatly changing, and that the tendency is to assimilate them more and more to the European custom."[91] The Negotiable Instruments Act thus merely reflected "European custom," which was, as custom per se, understood as analogous to indigenous customs of written credit.

Moreover, the act governed instances in which no customary law could be found to apply. This was an important principle buttressing the ultimate authority of the new statute. Indeed, trends in Anglo-Indian jurisprudence on mercantile law affirmed the act's assimilative potential by defining *usages* in an extremely flexible manner and therefore making them more difficult to identify. As early as 1858, the Privy Council had held that "local usages," in the case of trade, were not necessarily to be confined to time-honored conventions.[92] By 1902, new precedents emphasized that customary norms for credit and trade ought to be of *recent* origin, rather than ancient, which departed significantly from the standard rules of precedent established for adjudicating the authority of indigenous customs.[93] Citing a 1902 judgment, a canonical early twentieth-century digest on negotiable instruments thus explained,

> Local usages ... need not necessarily be those existing at the time when the [Negotiable Instruments] Act came into force; they may come into existence later on. Under the ordinary law, any usage to be recognised by a Court of Justice must be ancient, uniform, and certain; but in the case of negotiable instruments, however, that the custom should be ancient will not be insisted upon by the courts with the same strictness as in other cases, for the very fact that the ways of commerce have so widened and the number of transactions in every department of the trade so greatly multiplied has led inevitable to new customs and usages being more speedily devised, more speedily adopted, and more speedily recognised, than in times past.[94]

In the case of *hundis*, then, the courts reversed the predominant policy of cultural preservation that recognized customs by ancient status and operation since "time immemorial." Rather than invent tradition, as was the case with personal law and customs governing family and religion, juridical trends read mercantile law governing the circulation of capital as inherently progressive and flexible. The speed of its shifting norms reflected the pace of legal change in the 1880s, which institutionalized a new governmental rationality with new parameters and rules for market practice. Jurisprudence that asserted that the *lex mercatoria* tended toward assimilation into the most current practices in turn legitimized increased surveillance to classify current vernacular conventions, and served to promote their assumption by the codified and universal principles for negotiable instruments. As the family firm was interpreted as a family, and so rendered the subject of static culture and a suspect mechanism for trade, its mercantile practices—that is, those outside the purview of the Hindu Undivided Family—were slowly to be assumed by the rule of law and the principles of contract.

2

Capitalism's Idolatry

The Law of Charitable Trusts, Mortmain, and the Firm as Family, c. 1870–1920

> The Trust . . . impose[s] itself upon all wielders of political power, upon all organs of the body politic. Open an English newspaper, and you will be unlucky if you do not see the word "trustee" applied to "the Crown" or to some high and mighty body. . . . When a Statute declared that the *Herrschaft* [lordship] which the East India Company had acquired in India was held "in trust" for the Crown of Great Britain, that was no idle proposition but the settlement of a great dispute. It is only the other day that American judges were saying that the United States acquired the sovereignty of Cuba upon trust for the Cubans.—F. W. MAITLAND, *State, Trust and Corporation*, 1904

AT THE TURN OF THE TWENTIETH CENTURY, the prominent jurist and legal historian F. W. Maitland, Downing professor of English Law at Cambridge, delivered a series of lectures addressing the concept of the trust. A sibling of the joint-stock corporation, it encapsulated the rocky legal history of corporate bodies and collective *persona ficta* (fictitious persons) since Roman times. If, he asserted, "the march of progressive societies, as we all know, is from status to contract," now "that forlorn title [contract] is wont to introduce us to ever new species and new genera of persons."[1] Contract enabled the "vivacious controversy" and "teeming life" of a legal jungle of associative forms, and the burgeoning popularity of the trust at this time was perhaps the best example.[2] A tripartite contract between a donor, a beneficiary (of the donor's gift), and a trustee (who acts on behalf of the beneficiary and administers the gift), the trust, according to Maitland, had taken on myriad applications in Victorian England: "It is a big affair our Trust. . . . It has all the elasticity of Contract. Anyone who wishes to know England . . . should know a little of our Trust."[3] And if England had nurtured the trust, he asserted, "out in America the mightiest trading corporations that the world has ever seen are known by the name of 'Trusts.'"[4] By the end of the nineteenth century, the elasticity of the trust extended to the polar limits—or, said differently, to the logical ends of capitalist enterprise, to both charity as well as monopoly, enabling both benevolence and cartel.

The colonial history of the trust is an unwritten chapter in this narrative of modernity seen through group association, status to contract, and beyond. In India, colonialism's development regime, implementing the market as a model for social relations, enforced a distinction between status and contract. To illustrate this, this chapter pursues the charitable trust as object and instrument of market governance. It maps an uncharted legal history in which the introduction of the trust contract wrenches open the distinction between legitimate market ethics and cultural practice, between economy and culture. Legal debates in India at the end of the nineteenth century evinced the intimate connection between concepts of charitable trust and the modern limited liability corporation. If the 1880s statutes had confirmed the role of law in buttressing the free circulation of capital, concomitant developments in jurisprudence and case law began to delineate conditions for the logical *exception* to this circulation: the charitable gift.

Beginning in 1890, a gift for charitable purposes was defined in statute as a gift for public benefit, for "general public utility." But preceding this statutory definition, two decades of acrobatic jurisprudence had slowly introduced into India the British law of mortmain. This term referred to an exceptional category of property—the only category of property that was allowed to exist in perpetuity, outside capitalist exchange. Mortmain, a principle derived from Roman law, came from the Latin *manus mortus*, or the dead hand, which eerily conveyed the influence of a testator on the future use of his property.[5] In this chapter, we follow the spectral life of the "the dead hand," which, marking property for charitable purposes, affirmed the workings of its cousin, the invisible hand.

In Victorian England, the trust concept encompassed both "private trusts," designed for the benefit of dependants such as widows and children, as well as "public charitable trusts." The distinction between private and public charitable trusts was imported into India beginning in the 1880s, in the same period that the distinction was being codified in England. At the same time, the Indian context, informed by the Government of India's role as adjudicator on personal law and its concerns over the spurious nature of smaller joint family endowments, resonated in British discourses on the uses and abuses of trusts. In England, the particular definition of charity as a gift benefiting the public, and so the very category of the public trust, was clarified in a series of statutes beginning in midcentury with the Charitable Trusts Act of 1853. Revisions and new statutes were concentrated first in the 1860s, and again in the period from 1887 to 1894, and then in 1914 and 1925. The legal definition of charity was descended from an Elizabethan statute of 1601, which had outlined a variety of practices encompassed by charity in its popular sense, as well as a general notion of purposes beneficial to the community. Though jurists from the late colonial period make little mention of it, the legal genealogies they present mark a shift from a broad notion of community to the more specific and abstract concept of the public, a trajectory charted by case law from the late eighteenth century.[6]

In 1888, the Mortmain and Charitable Uses Act repealed the Georgian Mortmain Act of 1736, a measure that had been directed specifically at the explosion of "mischief" of "improvident alienations or dispositions made by languishing or dying persons . . . to uses called charitable uses."[7] Such deathbed alienations were usually designed to transfer property away from lawful heirs. The interest in clearly defining charitable uses, and so public benefit, thus began as a control mechanism for the legitimate transfer of property across generations, and the legitimate reproduction of wealth—questions that would plague case law in India. Indeed, the Indian context speaks particularly to a major concern of the 1888 Mortmain Act, a section of which was devoted to defining illegitimate gifts for "superstitious purposes," such as instruments to support priests for prayers and masses for deceased testators, reflecting nineteenth-century anxieties about "Popish" idolatries.[8] At the same time, the Charitable Trusts Act of 1887, amended in 1891, clarified procedures for the public charitable trust, including the jurisdiction of courts and the charity commissioners, which were first established in 1853 to monitor and enforce the provisions of charitable trusts. By the late 1880s then, the legal definition of charity in England referred specifically to the gift given with clear intention of public benefit. As a contemporary digest for the legal profession summarized, "If the intention of the donor is merely to benefit specific individuals, the gift is not charitable, even though the motive of their gift may be to relieve their poverty . . . on the other hand, if the donor's object is to accomplish the *abstract purpose* of relieving poverty, advancing education or religion or other purpose . . . without giving any particular individuals the right to claim the funds, the gift is charitable."[9] This emphasis on the intentionality of the donor in distinguishing between public charitable trusts and private trusts directed at specific individuals would refract into India and distort customary social welfare practices that defied the public/private distinction.

In Britain, the standardization of procedures for public trusts also reflected the growing popularity of forms of private trust and, indeed, the trust itself as a legal concept. As Maitland had asserted, the trust was a quintessential English institution, and it had become so in the Victorian period. Reflecting changing class demographics, forms of private trust were also elaborated and codified in law, especially after 1850.[10] As a mechanism for the reproduction of wealth across generations, the private trust had been almost exclusively the domain of the landed classes during the eighteenth century; it was in the next century that it came to be appropriated by the burgeoning middle class, especially the commercially astute and upwardly mobile business and professional sectors. Trusts for family dependents marked social status in an environment where the expansion of wealth was increasingly expressed through money rather than land. They also encapsulated the gender regime of the Victorian middle class. Building fortresses for family security in an era before the social welfare state, trusts institutionalized economic ethics associated with thrift and self-reliance alongside paternal moral duty to family. Provisions for relatives such as orphaned children, widows, and single women, and for the education of sons (and later, daughters), among other concerns, confirmed the trust as an insurance mechanism and as a moral compass serving a broad range of beneficiaries.[11]

The popularizing of the trust reflected the growing public exchange about finance, investment, and wealth in Victorian England and the concomitant legalization of social relations. After midcentury, legislators standardized procedures for the private trustee.[12] By the 1880s, being a trustee was increasingly seen as a burden, requiring time and expert knowledge of business, finance, and law. Beginning in late 1888, lawyers actively involved in trust administration instigated a series of acts that consolidated provisions relating to private trustees found in thirty previous acts; an 1895 Parliamentary Select Committee on Trusts Administration furthered the standardization process.[13] These measures mark a concern not only for the efficient administration of trusts, but also a reinvention of the trustee from voluntary administrator of moral duty to professional business manager, reliant on a variety of experts to whom he would delegate responsibilities. By the turn of the century, the trustee had become perhaps the quintessential figure of the ethical subject *as* economic subject, a household manager required to be an entrepreneur and financier. The conjuring of the trustee as Economic Man, as it were, was also reflected in a long discussion beginning in the late 1880s and throughout the 1890s over proposals to create the office of public trustee, finally established in 1906, to monitor neglect and fraud, and ensure that beneficiaries received benefits as intended.[14] In India, the trustee as ethical economic subject structured suspicions about indigenous endowments, especially those established by increasingly prosperous merchant-capitalist groups. In the subcontinent, the legal distinction between public charitable trusts and private trusts actively (mis)translated customary social welfare practices that were traditionally directed at both families and broader communities—practices, again, that defied the public/private distinction.

The chapter begins with an overview of the historiography on charitable endowments and mercantile gifting in India and then follows with a section on the ethical and political meanings of the gift for dharma. It then proceeds through details of British Indian statute and case law on charitable endowments. This legal history weaves the story of four broad shifts: First, the argument maps the translation of customary Hindu endowments into modern legal trust contracts—especially those established by merchant groups, which simultaneously provided for social welfare and family benefit. This move from endowment to trust was encapsulated in a masterful turn of legal idolatry. The deity, to which Hindu endowments were consecrated, was rendered a legal subject and thus the beneficiary in the trusts' tripartite contract. Second, I will elaborate how this translation from convention to contract introduced the principle of mortmain and new categories of trusts for public, as opposed to private, benefit. These categories were distinguished by the legal emphasis on contractual intention, rather than on social import. Mortmain, which established a rigorous rule against perpetual holdings *except* in the case of charitable gifts, posed questions about the administration of social welfare by joint families. As such, the Hindu Undivided Family, and legal conceptions of it as an institution of perpetual holding/hoarding, informed the introduction of the principle of mortmain. Third, the argument maps throughout the delegitimizing of customary endowments, reading trusts as a register of economic ethics. It addresses the ways in which the public/private distinction regulated and restricted the extensive negotiability of material and symbolic economies that characterized vernacular market practice.[15] This chapter and the next chart how new juridical trends redefined social gift giving, thus affecting the status production and the material flows of indigenous capitalisms. As was customary, merchants often used earnings from gifted property to fund commercial ventures, to invest in new enterprises, or to defray debts; profits regained would then revert back to gifted property. As we shall see, the trust regulated this fluidity. Fourth, the distinction between public charitable trusts and private trusts is explored through the way it recoded customary social welfare as a purely religio-cultural ritual, divesting the vernacular production of status of its ethical and political claims and rendering it subject to taxation.

    The regulation of charitable and religious endowments in India began with developments in case law in the 1870s. These produced the Charitable Endowments Act of 1890. This statute broadened local government's direct control over endowments for public benefit. At the same time, it remained inapplicable to any indigenous endowments, whether great temple complexes or small family institutions, due to the official policy of noninterference in native culture. The act incited debates over the inadequate regulation of indigenous religious endowments, which ultimately culminated in the Charitable and Religious Trusts Act of 1920. The 1920 measure was itself rigorously debated in the succeeding decade. In this chapter, we focus especially on the period from 1870 to 1890, outlining the ramifications of case law through the 1920s. The following chapter, focusing on the period from 1890 to 1930, explores the public charitable trust as a site for contestation and negotiation between commercial groups, and colonial as well as emerging national sovereignty.

The Historiography of Sovereignty, Endowments, and Mercantile Gifting

Considering the public/private distinction as governmental technology, this chapter returns to two established areas of South Asian historiography rarely considered together. First, speaking to the social history and ethnography of merchant groups, it examines the symbolic roles of mercantile gifting, including the performance of market dominance and of local sovereignty. Secondly, it elaborates on anthropological and historical work on kingship and sovereignty, which has highlighted the significance of the distributive role of gifting for the performance of sovereign authority. Focusing on south India, such studies have highlighted the temple complex as a site for sovereign performance, collective pilgrimage, and social welfare.[16] In this context, the anthropological and historical literature has exposed the juridical regulation of these temples and so problematized the Government of India's claims of nonintervention in indigenous culture. Deemed of public value due to their historical association with centers of kingship, these seats of political, social, and spiritual authority came under the purview of the colonial courts by the 1890s. While claiming noninterference in Hindu institutions, the courts assumed authority in adjudicating battles over south Indian temple management. Scholarship has therefore emphasized the dissimulations of colonial sovereignty, which by resisting direct regulation over indigenous institutions performed its control benignly and circuitously.[17]

However, there has been little examination of the effect of juridical changes on endowments not associated with local rulers, such as those of the increasingly prosperous Hindu commercial castes. Mercantile family firms rarely established temples and other institutions on the large scale associated with kings; most often they endowed deities with property that was managed by single joint families. After 1850, mercantile wealth cultivated a burgeoning landscape of informal indigenous institutions for religious and social welfare. Marwaris, for example, established endowments throughout northern and western India in this period, and especially after about 1880, in the Central Provinces, Bengal, and Assam. Indigenous endowments, grand and ascetic, included sites such as temples, *dharmshalas* (rest houses for travelers), stepwells and freshwater wells, *panjrapols* (shelter for animals), *gaushalas* (shelters for cows), and *mathas* (centers of instruction in Hindu philosophy and Sanskrit literature). For mobile commercial groups like the Marwaris, making a gift for dharma, whether it be a local temple, *dharmshala*, or other form of social welfare, was a way to negotiate their entry as immigrants to a new social world, performing both ritual purity and material conquest. The institutions endowed by these groups did not command the broad political authority of age-old centers of worship associated with political rulers; rather, they mapped the localized market dominance of business families and performed a kind of localized sovereignty. That merchants saw themselves as local rajas is perhaps most convincingly expressed in the grand elaborately painted *havelis* (multiple-courtyard houses) they built as ancestral homes, adorned with frescoes of episodes from the *Ramayana* alongside images of trains, British Sahibs, and the world of the bazaar.

Historiography on the colonial administration of endowments has addressed kingship and public temples in late nineteenth-century India but has not addressed the emergence of a legal private arena for most native endowments, one which came to circumscribe a vast array of indigenous gifting practices. On the other hand, merchant ethnographies have highlighted the importance of social gifting in negotiations with sovereignty, but they have not considered the effects of the colonial coding of traditional endowments as private gifts. Instead, arguments have emphasized the continuity of traditional forms rather than the changing parameters in which those practices operated. Haynes's study of the shift from "tribute to philanthropy," for example, demonstrates that even as Gujerati *mahajans* (merchant-bankers) engaged in "modern" forms of gifting that reflected a Victorian "humanitarian" ethic—hospitals, colleges for liberal and scientific education, libraries, institutions for poverty relief—they continued funding traditional endowments.[18] Similarly, Rudner's study of the Chettiars refers to the new colonial distinction between public and private trusts, "a significant difference from the precolonial distinction between *individual* and *collective* worship," but again asserts the continuity of indigenous forms in the "myriad 'private' temples that fill the Indian landscape."[19] In contrast, I am interested in the construction of the public/private distinction as a new mapping of "the social" itself. Asserting the persistence of a precolonial merchant gemeinshaft without contemplating the recasting of social welfare as private leaves unchallenged the claims of colonial sovereignty: that the private was, indeed, a natural and protected space of cultural autonomy.

Like work on mercantile gifting, legal research on religious and charitable endowments has resisted historicizing the categories of public and private. Legal histories narrate from within the logic of the law and its propositions, detailing the workings of the public/private distinction, but are less concerned with its introduction as an asymmetrical framework for local practices.[20] This is true for the study of Hindu endowments, as well as Muslim endowments, or *waqfs*. One significant study of colonial *waqf* administration, for example, summarily states that court decisions "actually bore little relation to the ways Muslims lived" by creating "a distinction between 'public' and 'private' endowments," but the author does not pursue the implications of this point.[21] In contrast, my analysis focuses on the mad maneuvers—sometimes legal flights of fancy—necessary to establish and normalize the distinction between private and public endowments, presented here by considering the activities of Hindu merchant groups. More specifically, for the case of *waqfs*, the shifts outlined here for the Hindu joint family were relevant for prominent Muslim mercantile groups like Ismailis, whose joint family firms continued to be adjudicated in this period through the category of the HUF and who were, in late nineteenth- and early twentieth-century legal language, referred to as "anomalous Muslims." These groups were not the primary demographic targets of the late nineteenth- and early twentieth-century legislation on *waqfs*, which were informed by the colonial state's concerns about Muslim landed classes.[22]

The Gift for Dharma and Intention in the Law

For Hindu commercial groups, the socially beneficial and ritually pure gift came under the broad and flexible category of the gift for dharma. The philosophical concept of *dharma* is very difficult to translate, let alone its myriad customary embodiments, and it became a problem for jurisprudence interested in the distinct intents and functions of charitable institutions. In the classical Sanskrit texts, "dharma" conveyed an ethics of duty and right conduct, and not just "religion" as belief or devotion. It represented an ethics of practice in which the intention of an act was understood as embedded within its performance and not as premeditated and a priori. Hindu jurisprudence divided the gift for dharma into two general types: *istha*, or the gift for ritual sacrifice, and the vast category of *purutta*, the support of mankind.[23] The latter covered a broad array of gifts that included the construction of temples, works for the storage of water, the gift of food, the relief of the sick, and the "bestowal of learning."[24] These aims defied categorization as either public or private, and by the colonial period they fell under the more common umbrella expression *jagat-hitaya*, or the benefit or welfare (*hitaya*) of the world (*jagat*).[25] Based upon a reading of Shastric texts on *dana*, or gifting, the legal scholar J. D. M. Derrett has emphasized that "nowhere do we find the requirement of a 'public element'" in Hindu gifting. Certain gifts, such as "shelters and tanks, obviously enure for the benefit of the public. But the conception is that every *act* of dedication is for the benefit of the world (*jagat-hitaya*), since every act of *dharma*, whether obligatory or optional, contributes to the welfare of mankind."[26] If the "benefit of the world" resisted classification in terms of public or private import, the performance of the gift for dharma also posed a problem for the question of intention, the crux of the emerging legal distinction between public and private benefit.

In the ethics of mercantile gift giving, the variety of practices encompassed by *jagat-hitaya* was matched by a multiplicity of symbolic and material functions within any single act of gifting. Anthropological research has emphasized the complex overlapping meanings of gifts, meanings that are manifest only in the specific contexts of performance. As a study of Jain merchants in Jaipur elaborates, categories of gifts which regulate the lay ethics of *len-den*, or give-and-take/exchange, are distinguished by intention, but also overlap: *anukampa-dan*, a gift given out of compassion; *ucit-dan*, a gift given out of duty; *kirti-dan*, a gift given to earn fame; *abhay-dan*, a gift of fearlessness; *supatra-dan*, a gift for religion. The shifting classification of *dan* underlines the importance of the context and situation of the gift itself.[27] Here, the gift cannot be classified *solely* by a priori, unmediated intention. Rather, reflecting the broader worldview of Hindu and Islamic jurisprudence in India, the intention of any act of gift giving is interpreted through the circumstances of its performance.[28]

If the public/private lens cannot accurately focus the multifaceted character of social gifting, it also distorts negotiations of power between merchant gift givers and their sovereigns established in the two centuries preceding formal British rule. For South Asian merchants, gifting for the "welfare of the mankind" marked a participation in a layered and shared precolonial sovereignty.[29] Gifts for social welfare, if recognized by kingly authority, had traditionally secured merchants' participation in sovereignty, as well as their *autonomy* from it. Indeed, kingly recognition of social gifts confirmed prominent merchant groups' local authority even as they performed subjection in tribute to a greater sovereignty. The legitimacy of the endowment for *jagat-hitaya* was not, before the mid–nineteenth century, dependent upon the distinction between public and private welfare. As the next chapter will elaborate, with the new category of public charity, the layered formula of *participation* in sovereign authority alongside *autonomy* from sovereign regulation was reconstituted.

Patterns of sovereignty in the seventeenth and eighteenth centuries protected merchants materially and symbolically. Tribute, whether paid in coin or as *peshkash* (in-kind) not only performed loyalty and subordination to a ruler; it also functioned as an investment in protection. Tribute brought, in return, commercial privileges such as monopolies in the sale of particular commodities, the protection of trade routes, and exemption from duties.[30] In the eighteenth century, the East India Company, competing with prominent merchants for privileges, also offered tribute to local rajas, though records reveal that they perceived tribute as bribery pure and simple.[31] In addition to tribute, the sovereign offered status and legitimacy to prominent merchants by protecting temples and other merchant endowments. Rulers protected such institutions when they could be deemed important for social welfare. Significantly, an endowment was so legitimated not solely on the criterion of its intention, but rather, on its *import*: the "pre-British king was not primarily concerned with the intention of the founder, which might be expressed to be 'for the merit of me and my parents and elder sister and brother' but with the *employment* of the dedicated property. . . ."[32] In contrast, late colonial sovereignty focused only on the intention of the gift. By asking the question of public or private intent, colonial authorities sought to identify charitable projects from those tied to family benefit, and thus to the family firm's profitable ventures. This juridical process privileged the a priori intentionality of contract and so recognized the purpose of customary gifts by reading their ritual dedications as contracts and interpreting them literally.

Statutory Definitions of Charity before 1890

Trends in case law in the 1870s and 1880s reflected the slippery statutory definitions of charity in this period. As early as 1860, the Government of India had passed the Societies Registration Act, "an act for the registration of literary, scientific and charitable societies." It enabled societies of more then seven persons to combine officially through a memorandum of association. Concerned primarily with promoting new forms of civic association, the act created the post of the registrar of societies.[33] In 1860, charitable activities had not yet been standardized as endeavors on behalf of the public, although they were associated with contractual organization, and the production and exchange of "modern" and "useful" forms of knowledge and information. Modern notions of charity were, however, rendered legally distinct from religion in the 1860s. The Religious Endowments Act of 1863, for example, dealt with all religious endowments of a public nature, including Muslim and Hindu institutions, and came largely to dominate the disputes in south Indian temple complexes.[34] Up until the mid-1880s, public religious endowments were still legally distinct from charitable endowments, and the only indigenous religious endowments addressed in statute were those that had been associated with traditional sites of pilgrimage and sovereignty.

In the 1880s, the Indian Income Tax and Companies Acts enforced new definitions of charity as activity *exclusively* for public benefit. Section 26 of the Indian Companies Act provided a framework for the not-for-profit limited liability corporation as distinct from the public charitable organization. It was the product of questions concerning the Calcutta Trades Association, which had campaigned for legal status as a public association in order to sue on behalf of creditors it represented. Section 26 produced a distinction between charity in its lay and legal senses by allowing for registration of not-for-profit associations that promoted "art, science, charity, or any other useful object." Such institutions were not charitable in the legal sense, because benefits were directed only at their members—as in, for example, mutual assistance societies that pooled funds to be distributed in times of need, or chambers of commerce—and *not* at an abstract "public." In establishing the category of the nonprofit limited liability corporation, then, the Companies Act thus reinforced the notion of charity as a gift to a supralocal public of subjects.[35]

Moreover, the Indian Income Tax Act offered a new incentive for claiming charitable status: exemption from taxation. But the debates during the 1886 Income Tax Bill reflected confusion around the distinction between public charitable versus religious purposes. The draft of the bill had exempted "any income solely employed for religious or public charitable purposes," producing a flurry of questions around the difference between the legal abstractions of public charity, religious purposes, and private charity, terms which were themselves being worked out at this time in England.[36] Significantly, despite the confusion, legislators did emphasize that exemptions applied only to gifts "*solely employed* for religious or public charitable purposes," stating clearly that "colorable gifts to idols" would not be tolerated.[37] The rules for exemption thus emphasized the criterion of sole employment for religious or charitable ends and did not cover, as it were, multitasking forms of endowment, revealing concerns about family-managed gifts to deities that operated simultaneously as social gifts and commercial investments.

The 1870s and 1880s marked the beginning of a long debate over the charitable status of indigenous endowments large and small, which were understood, first and foremost, as religious institutions. Questions concerning social gifting brought dharmic notions of right conduct to colonial law's conduct of conduct: were the great Hindu temple complexes that had been understood as public religious endowments now to be understood as charitable institutions? An even greater dilemma concerned endowments that did not carry the weight of traditional kingship and were managed by families: were these to be considered charitable endowments? While they were not public sites in the sense that pilgrimage centers were, legislators and jurists debated whether family endowments could be deemed publicly beneficial in some ways, or whether they were simply instruments for private family benefit masquerading as social welfare.

From Endowment to Trust:
Fetishizing the Idol as Legal Subject

From 1870 to 1890, the question of direct government regulation of religious and charitable endowments appeared in the courts. Judges contemplated both the managerial rites of large temple complexes, as well as the status of what was referred to as the family idol. The two decades before the passage of the first Charitable Endowments Act of 1890 produced a complex body of case law in which the endowment of a deity was recast as trust property. Case law introduced the model of the trust held in mortmain, a category of property to exist in perpetuity, and irrevocable. Once established, parts of its corpus could be alienated only in order to serve and reproduce the purpose of the trust. With an inalienable purpose that could not revert to activity for gain, the trust in mortmain became the logical exception to the free circulation of capital. In the late nineteenth century, jurists sought to distinguish between property that existed in perpetuity legitimately, that is, in trust as mortmain, and that which existed as such illegitimately, that is, the joint family property of the Hindu Undivided Family. The HUF's perceived propensity towards jointness and hoarding was thought to be the end, in the double sense of the aim and the undoing, of its gifting practices; jurists questioned whether anything, a gift or otherwise, could ever be completely alienated from it. Anxieties about the excessively inalienable nature of the Hindu joint family property were confirmed in a wholly new development: legal status for the Hindu deity as proprietor of endowed property. This new juristic avatar, available to the whole of the Hindu pantheon, enabled the endowment to be cast as modern trust. This process then opened up questions about the distinction between, first, public charitable and private trusts and, second, between public religious and private religious trusts; these distinctions came to predominate Indian legislative and judicial measures after 1890.

These developments fill volumes of late nineteenth-century legal digests dedicated to the subject of religious and charitable endowments in Hindu and Muslim law. It is important to highlight the key cases and statutes in this two-decade trajectory from endowment to trust, especially since the terms are used synonymously in postindependence legal texts, though primary texts from the late nineteenth and early twentieth centuries offer evidence for an evolving endowment-trust analogy that later became an identification.[38] As mentioned earlier, the trust was a contractual relation involving three legal actors: person(s) A (donor) vests property in person(s) B (trustee) for the benefit of person(s) C (beneficiary).[39] Colonial jurists' analogies between the indigenous endowment and the trust emphasized that a more general definition of trust did not require ownership of the property by the trustee; it was enough for the trustee to control the property to hold that title. Postindependence legal scholars have agreed. Thus, in the 1951 Tagore Law Lectures on Hindu religious and charitable endowments, B. K. Mukherjea, the Indian Supreme Court justice, outlined the applicability of Hindu gifting practices to the more general definition of the trust. The Hindu endowment constituted "fiduciary relations under which a person in possession of *or* having control over any property is bound to use that property for the benefit of certain persons, or specified objects."[40] Thus, the *shebait* (the manager of a deity, *devata*, and its shrine or temple, *devottaram or debuttar*) and the *mahant* (the superior or leader of a religious order or educational institution, *matha*) came to qualify as trustees, or controllers of property, in the general sense described above.[41] In an attempt to "see how far elements of trust could be discovered" in "the legal ideas underlying various types of Hindu religious and charitable endowments," Justice Mukherjea echoed earlier legal scholars. He argued that one must invent an analogy with British contract and property law, as Hindu legal texts told the reader very little about "how the intention of the donor ... was given effect to."[42] The trust paradigm emphasized the intention of the donor as the crucial variable in determining its function and charitable status, while Hindu legal traditions, both written and customary, said little on intention as a priori foundation for the gift.[43] The endowment-trust equation, a palimpsest of late nineteenth-century statute and case law, veils the shift from import to intention.

The history of the charitable and religious trust might begin in 1882, with the Indian Trusts Act. Passed in the same year as the companies legislation, it defined the law relating to secular private trusts and trustees at time when uniform procedures for the private trustee were being contemplated in Britain.[44] It introduced the property relations of the private secular trust as elaborated in English law: a "trust" was an "obligation attached to the ownership of property which arise[s] out of a confidence reposed in and accepted by the owner for the benefit of another."[45] But like most Government of India statutes concerned with noninterference in indigenous culture, it also argued that this notion of trust was *unknown* to both the Hindu and Muslim legal systems. Section 1 of the act specifically excluded all public and private religious trusts, which included all types of traditional indigenous endowments.[46] However, in the legislative debates preceding enactment, the Privy Council asserted that while Hindu and Muslim law did not offer any concept of "trust" in the English sense, managers of indigenous endowments could be understood to be trustees in the more general sense adopted by the act.[47] Thus, while indigenous endowments did not fall under the scope of the act, the legislation in effect established them as trusts for future legal reference.

This equivocal stance was the logical conclusion of trends in case law in the decade prior, in which the courts had repeatedly affirmed the role of the *shebait*, *mahant*, and, in the case of Muslim endowments, the *mutawalli* as effective trustees. In the case of Hindu gifting, the legal trajectory from endowment to trust reflected concerns about the charitable claims of family endowments to deities and whether these "religious" institutions could be classified as gifts for public benefit. The Indian Income Tax Act had left open the definition and status of a religious trust. But by the time this statute was passed in 1886, judicial decisions had already delineated a separate set of precedents for family endowments dedicated to deities, including religious educational institutions, and other customary forms of gifting. Case law in the 1870s had begun to carve out the category of the private religious trust, applicable to a broad range of indigenous gifting practices that could not easily be classed as public. The majority of endowments created by newly emergent merchant-capitalists fell under this private category. Like contemporary statutes that classified the extended commercial nexus of the family firm as private, late nineteenth-century case law on religious endowments began to circumscribe the symbolic and material import of its gifting. The gift was read by jurists as religio-cultural ritual, but not as part of an economy.[48]

First, jurists had to sort out the status of the deity, and the alienability of the trust itself. The inaugural landmark case in this process dealt with the question of whether the *shebait* of land endowed "in favor of an idol" had the right to create and alienate derivative tenures from that land. In *Maharani Shibessouree v. Mothooranath Acharjo*, the Privy Council decided in 1869 that the *shebait* could act only as the manager and trustee of the deity, who was the proprietor of the endowed lands.[49] The plaintiff, Mothooranath, had claimed that he had purchased fixed tenures which had been created by the *shebait* for him. The Privy Council argued that the purchase was not valid, as the *shebait* could not grant tenures on a deity's property for purposes that were not directly beneficial to the deity. The case defined the *shebait*'s position as one of manager and trustee of the deity's property and, more importantly, inaugurated the status of the deity as the *owner* of that property.

This judgment offered an interpretation and reification of customary practice that superseded a dominant school of Hindu jurisprudence on the question of the proprietorship of the deity. Popular belief, expressed in everyday practices of devotion, certainly embodied the notion that "gifts please the deity, that the deity can accept them, and that the fruit of such gifts is the merit of the donor."[50] Historically, the flourishing of *bhakti* devotionalism brought the details of the deity's *oikonomia* into prominence. As Derrett has explained, colonial authorities came to understand that the "idol has his house, his attendants, his hours of audience, his repose.... Payment for the buildings and their upkeep, the idol's meals and entertainment, baths, clothing and so forth, must be found somewhere.... The idol requires, from this point of view, an establishment, and lastly a business manager."[51] Mirroring the notion of the joint family as a private mechanism outside the legitimate circulation of goods and credit in the public, this colonial understanding of the "idol's house" saw it as a self-contained private estate, rather than as a nodal point for a broader web of merit and status exchange. Colonial jurisprudence abstracted and fixed the customary conventions of the deity's household within a contractual property relation. At the same time, it cast the *shebait* as economic subject, as business manager.

Furthermore, the decision in *Maharani Shebessourie v. Moothoranath* overrode the predominant view of orthodox Hindu jurisprudence. The widespread perception, and indeed acceptance, that the temple priest often lived on the offerings of the deity had been legitimated by the *mimamsa* system of Hindu philosophy.[52] Codified in the Gupta period in the sixth and seventh centuries, *mimamsa* emphasized the Vedas, the sources of Brahminical ritual power, and contested the universalist challenges of post-Vedic thought.[53] The orthodox Hindu jurisprudence of the colonial period appropriated the tenets of the *mimamsa* system and buttressed the principle of Brahminical authority over the deity in this world. Indeed, many colonial jurists asserted that idols "could not accept, for they could form no intention.... The gift therefore did not vest in the deity at all" and instead "shebaits, or other receiving ministrants accepting the gift, constituted it as a fund which was available to them according to custom."[54] In the 1870s then, the deity's ability to hold property was by no means an accepted legal concept or, indeed, an accurate reflection of the meanings of ritual convention.

Still, the Privy Council precedent set in 1869 arguing for the ultimate authority of the deity informed two succeeding landmark decisions. In another foundational case in 1875, *Prosonna Kumari Debya and another v. Golab Chand Babu*, the Privy Council echoed the 1869 decision by arguing that the *shebait*, as a trustee but *not* an owner of gifted property, could not alienate the property of the deity: "'As a general rule of Hindu Law, property given for the maintenance of religious worship and of charities connected with it, is inalienable.'"[55] At the same time, the judgment also clarified the extent of the *shebait*'s powers. Here, the managerial rights of the *shebait* were likened to those of a trustee responsible for the property of an "infant heir."[56] The Privy Council reaffirmed that the ownership of the endowment rested in the deity, but as a sort of juvenile entity devoid of economic acumen. "'It is only in an ideal sense that property can be said to belong to an idol,'" it explained, thus concluding that the trustee "must of *necessity* be *empowered to do whatever may be required* for the service of the idol and for the benefit and preservation of its property, at least to as great a degree as the manager of an infant heir. If this were not so, the estate of the idol might be destroyed or wasted, and its worship discontinued, for want of necessary funds to preserve and maintain them."[57]

An exquisite equivocation, the decision offered contradictory perspectives on the proprietary status of the idol and status of its property. The endowment vested absolutely in the deity, but as a legal entity disabled by its minority. The deity's property rights were to exist inalienably and in perpetuity, but to maintain this perpetuity the endowment became partially alienable. The judgment argued that "notwithstanding" the authority of Hindu law, the *shebait* could incur debts and borrow money for maintaining religious worship.[58] The impetus of *mimamsa* philosophy, which gave precedence to the managerial rights of the *shebait* to the extent that the deity's property became his property, was here both limited and reconfirmed. The *shebait*'s prerogative to alienate property reiterated the precedent of the orthodox jurists; alternatively, the role of the *shebait* as merely a trustee demanded that alienations only be made in favor of the deity. This limited right of alienation, in turn, presupposed the ultimate inalienability of the corpus of the endowment: a gift to a deity, it was implied, was to be made irrevocably and in perpetuity.[59] This challenged commercial groups' gifting practices.

The final clarification of the proprietary authority of the trustee versus the deity arrived with another landmark judgment made by the Bombay High Court in 1887, the year after the Indian Income Tax Act hazily provided exemption for "income derived from property solely employed for religious or public charitable purposes." *Manohar Ganesh Tambekar v. Lakhmiram Govindram*, or, as it is colloquially referred to, the Dakor Temple case, elaborated the precedents of 1869 and 1875 by establishing the deity as a *juristic entity*.[60] The case involved a battle over the managerial rights of the Sri Ranchodrai Temple, a Vaishnavite pilgrimage site located in Dakor, a village near Baroda. Located in inland Gujarat, the temple's Krishna worship attracted large numbers of Hindus, often on their way to the larger and more ancient holy sites of Dwarka and Somnath on the coast of Kutch. The existence of the deity at Dakor could be traced back about seven hundred years, and at the time of the court case it was estimated that the shrine received gifts worth an enormous 1 lakh (100,000) rupees per annum.

The dispute occurred between the family that managed and oversaw the activities of the temple, the temple managers, and a group of Brahmin *sevaks* (literally, "those who serve"), who ministered to the deity. The temple managers had accepted a written agreement from the *sevaks*. The agreement confirmed that the *sevaks* would observe certain rules in the performance of daily services and distribution of donations. The plaintiff and temple manager alleged that the defendants, the *sevaks*, had frequently ignored these rules, deciding among themselves how donations were to be distributed. The *sevaks* defended themselves by arguing that they had a proprietary right to the deity's income and in the temple itself. Reflecting the tenor of Brahminic jurisprudence, they contended in their written statement that they "'were not the servants of the temple but the *owners of the idol* and its property.'"[61] In response to this daring defense, the judges argued that the proprietary right, as established by precedent, vested in the deity and not in any trustee, manager, or priest. In order to reinforce this proprietary right, this judgment went further than its predecessors and argued that the "Hindu idol is a juridical subject and the pious idea that it embodies is given the status of a legal person and is deemed capable in law of holding property in the same way as a natural person."[62] Further, the deity's property could not, under the claimed authority of custom, transfer to any trustee, as it was inalienable.[63] Again, while the trustee had a duty to serve the endowment, and while that duty did allow for partial alienations in favor of the deity, the intention and perpetual existence of the endowment itself depended on keeping the deity's rights to proprietorship outside the circulation of property exchange. As one prominent authority on endowments, Prannath Saraswati, summarized it in his 1892 Tagore law lectures, according to the precedent established by judges of the Bombay High Court in this case, "property dedicated to pious purpose is, by the Hindu as well as by the Roman law, placed *extra commercium*."[64]

Again, the courts spoke in a contrapuntal manner. The making of deities into legal persons with the power to sue, be sued, and hold property reflected the slow transformation of the Hindu endowment into a form of contractual private property.[65] Many other forms of Hindu gifting, all classified as broadly religious, including the *matha*, the *dharmshala*, and other gifts for dharma, also fell under this under this category. However, such forms of private property were not to be thrown into unrestricted free-market circulation. Understood in a limited way as transfers of property for purely religious purposes, *debuttar* estates could be partially alienated only for the benefit of the deity or in the case of "legal necessity."[66] Thus, the courts began to enforce religion as a sphere outside of commerce; the charitable import of religion had to remain outside the commercial circuit of profitability. The making of the juristic personality encapsulated this process of boundary drawing. In the trajectory of case law charted above, the courts imbued the deity with an essentially religious identity. The trust reduced dharma to religion, as piety or devotion. The purpose of the trust, to exist perpetually, defined the property rights of this new juristic avatar and circumscribed the import of the gift to dharma. Here again intention defined the trust and religious intention endowed the property with an absolute value, a non-negotiable value that was to protect it from becoming incarnate as a market commodity. The process of imbuing the Hindu deity with a juristic personality reinvented the deity *as* idol (deities were indeed consistently called "idols" in legal discourse)—as a purely religious fetish distinguished from the commodity. Market exchange for profit became explicitly distinguished from a charitable transfer of property.

Still, despite the courts' alignment of Hindu law with Roman law, it had never been clear that indigenous gifting necessarily existed *extra commercium*. The Dakor Temple case had addressed one of the most ubiquitous forms of the ritual devotional gift, the donation to the deity at a temple, which served as a ritual offering but also as property to be distributed by the priest at his discretion. The judges had asserted that this customary discretionary prerogative did not imply the transfer and vesting of that property to the priest.[67] However, as Derrett has argued, "if one thing is certain it is that making a personal profit out of possessing an idol is as old as the Vedic age, and perfectly legitimate."[68] This dynamism between gifted material compensation and the ritual labor of the priest was often read by British administrators as an immoral traffic in the sacred, much like the Papal indulgences of the fifteenth and sixteenth centuries. But, as anthropologists have emphasized, unlike the Christian or classical Greek traditions, which equate money with sin or denounce all profit as usury, "in Hinduism it is by no means easy to find parallels for such Biblical notions as the love of money being the 'root of all evil,' or as camels having an easier time getting through needles' eyes than rich men getting to heaven."[69] Among noncommercial castes, the necessary suspicion of the moneylender-trader, manifest in proverbs like "if you meet a snake and a Marwari . . . kill the Marwari," did not express a condemnation of trade itself as an immoral activity.[70]

Hindu commercial groups did not exorcise the material interests of trade from their devotional practices. Perhaps the most significant symbol of this dynamism of devotion and materiality were the rituals performed on Diwali, the beginning of the accounting year, when old account books (*bahis*) were tied up for safekeeping and new ones opened and ritually blessed in a worship of Lakshmi, the goddess of wealth.[71] Gifts to dharma performed wealth and status, promoted hierarchies both material and ritual, and enacted social welfare. And the renowned asceticism (also known as miserliness) associated with mercantile castes—including practices such as vegetarianism, sobriety, plain dress, and restricted spending on household consumption—enabled lavish spending on traditional forms of social welfare.[72]

The Hindu family firm depended on a fluid relationship between charity—that is, gifts towards social welfare—and profit. The endowment or its income might at times operate as a capital reserve, or as credit. The capital or income of gifts for dharma might be used temporarily as loans for the firm's business, to be reimbursed in time. Thus, the gift to a deity did not *always* operate in service of the deity or temple; part of the income of the temple could be used to finance debt, for example. Customary practice and Hindu legal traditions "by no means required that the capital and income [of an endowment] should be spent on the deity's needs, and on these only."[73] Alternatively, family endowments also mediated commercial and financial relations between family firms. A gift payment by one firm to another firm's family endowment might operate as interest on a loan, or insurance for a loan, or as payment on a debt.[74]

The endowment for dharma or social welfare constituted an integral part of the material and symbolic portfolio of the family firm. Perhaps the best example of the integration of dharma into the fabric of business itself was the institution of the *dharmada khata*, or dharma account, often overlooked in studies of commercial groups. These offer a picture of the multiple forms of charity and their embeddedness within the procedures and practices of business. Among Marwaris, the *dharmada* account was summarized in the first page of a firm's ledger, or *pakka khata*, and also detailed in its own *khata*, or account book, which registered the expenses from funds collected on *dharmada* profits. These were generated by an invisible tax of usually between 0.25 and 0.5 percent on retail sales. In effect, *dharmada* funds were collected as a sort of value-added tax and were thus not simply transfers of capital from accumulated profits but rather profits made in the service of dharma itself.[75] This was a standard practice in the markets specializing in particular commodities, such as cotton or grain. The retailers of each commodity sector would pool their donations and then determine the allocation of the funds, sometimes through a formal meeting of the caste *mahajan*, or guild, but also informally.

Usually funds were donated to temples, *dharmshalas*, and other institutions associated culturally with social welfare and geographically with the marketplace. Reflecting the spatial and commercial landscape of the bazaar, and collected in effect as a sort of sales tax, *dharmada* funds constituted capital to be distributed at merchants' discretion. Thus, in addition to traditional gifting from net earnings or ancestral capital, Marwari family firms, much like the government as tax collector, assumed an allocative prerogative and performed a distributive local sovereignty. For example, in the 1907–1908 account books of a Marwari retail cloth concern I examined, *dharmada* accounts revealed claims to various levels of local status and sovereignty. The firm had three *dharmada khatas*: one for *Sri Ganesh*, the firm's safekeeper and a family deity; one for *Sri Ram*, donated to the local Ram temple in the center of town, run by another prominent Marwari family; and another, created in 1907, called the *Sri Congress ka dharmada khata*, the account for the emerging secular deity, the Indian National Congress. In 1907, it showed Rs. 317 and 10 annas that was to be carried forward to the next year. An ongoing collection to which the firm itself contributed, the Congress account was to be spent in opportune political circumstances.[76]

Commercial groups' gifts to dharma, then, carried with them multiple functions and intentions. Like *hundis*, the multifarious indigenous bills of exchange that operated as promissory notes, certificates of deposit, letters of insurance, and, broadly, as documents of social and financial credit, gifts to dharma were diverse and carried with them a very extensive negotiability. Like the standardization instituted by the Negotiable Instruments Act of 1881, the impact of case law in the 1870s and 1880s limited the negotiability of these gifts.

The Invisible Hand Plays Dead: Mortmain, the HUF, and the Question of Perpetuities

As statutes in the 1880s began to delineate the market, case law on trusts carved out a distinct space for charity *extra-commercium*. The "dead hand" of mortmain marked the privilege of perpetuity allowed in this extracommercial space. The invisible hand thus worked through its lifeless cousin; conveying control of the present by the past, mortmain is an appropriate emblem for colonial law's reification of culture as ancient tradition, even as its morbid symbolics evoke a prominent characterization of capital itself.[77]

By the late 1880s, legal decisions enforced the separation of profitable versus charitable or religious pursuits. The permissibility of holding property in perpetuity marked the boundary between social welfare and profit-oriented activity. In mapping these distinctions throughout the 1870s and 1880s, jurists confronted the question of perpetuities within the property relations of the Hindu joint family. If perpetual holdings were to be understood as *exceptions* for charitable purposes only, then the joint family's normative inheritance procedures would necessarily have to prohibit perpetuities. However, British Indian law, which had invented the legal creature called the HUF, was reticent on its rules for perpetual tenure, a principle foreign to the logic of the joint family system, even in its textually biased representation in nineteenth-century Hindu law. The problem of perpetuities in the HUF bespoke a concern for its resistance to alienation, its propensity towards hoarding, and its preoccupation with profit. Jurists asked whether joint family coparcenary property was *inherently* a form of perpetual holding. If so, could the Hindu endowment be a legitimate alienation from joint family property, or was it simply part of its perpetual holdings? That is, were Hindu endowments revocable? If so, then how were they to be considered gifts to charity or religion, since they remained, in effect, part of coparcenary property, to be used potentially for other purposes?

In nineteenth-century British jurisprudence, mortmain for religious and charitable purposes stood as the *exception* to what was termed the general "rule limiting perpetuities," which supported the unrestricted circulation of capital. In Britain, this general rule limited the future vesting of property by a testator to "lives in being" and up to twenty-one years after their deaths, or one generation plus twenty-one years.[78] In India, the question of perpetuities was necessarily woven into the case law on customary endowments. This question informed two important features of case law: first, the recoding of such endowments as forms of private property in trust, and second, the assertion of the excessive jointness of the Hindu Undivided Family.

The translation of the medieval Sanskrit commentaries on joint family property by Colebrooke first published in 1810 established the central point of reference for inheritance in Hindu law. Colebrooke had translated the texts of the *Dhayabaga* system, predominant in Bengal and Assam, and the *Mitakshara*, which governed most of the rest of British India, including commercial castes.[79] The *Dhayabhaga* asserted the discretion of the father, governed by moral considerations, in the management of moveable and immoveable property; at the father's renunciation or death, sons inherited the ancestral property and the property of the father in undivided shares of fixed proportion. But in the *Mitakshara* system, sons were considered joint owners, along with their father, of the ancestral property and of anything that the father had inherited from his father. The emphasis in *Mitakshara* was that inheritance occurred not, as in the Western context, upon death, but rather upon the birth of a new son.[80] As Colebrooke's much-cited translation of the *Mitakshara* recounts, "It is a settled point that property in the paternal or ancestral estate is by birth, although the father have independent power in the disposal of effects other than immoveables for indispensable acts of duty and for purposes prescribed by the text of law, as gifts through affection, support of the family, relief from distress."[81]

The inheritance and succession procedures of the *Mitakshara* were translated into Anglo-Indian law through analogy to contract. First, jurisprudence described these forms of joint ownership as "coparcenary," a notion of jointness in which distinct individual shares constituted a joint whole, even though in the *Mitakshara* context such "shares" did not emerge until after legal partition. Second, the contractual relation called "survivorship," which was derived from English law, was adopted as an analogy for the rules of succession and inheritance in the HUF.[82] Survivorship regulated the devolution of rights and liabilities in joint contracts; if one member of the joint contract died, then the rest of the contracting members inherited that person's rights and liabilities. Hindu coparcenors were understood to have "a community of interest and of possession" that was "comparable with joint-tenants [in] English law with benefit of survivorship." As Derrett explains, the difference was that joint tenants in English law became so by a legal transfer of property, while in the joint family, "individual rights commence independently and by operation of law, not by transfer between parties. . . . *No one can create a coparcenary interest, no more than he can create, with a stranger, a joint Hindu family.*"[83] As such, the HUF was the site of both manageable similarity and slippery difference; in its originary jointness, the customary operation of the joint family only ever approximated the principle of contractual survivorship. In the 1870s and 1880s, the problem of *Mitakshara* inheritance at birth, understood as coparcenary survivorship, opened questions about whether a rule limiting perpetuities could be gleaned from or, said differently, read into the laws of the HUF.

In 1865, the Indian Succession act established a rule limiting the vesting of property in the future to one generation plus eighteen years. The rule limiting perpetuities was thus introduced by statute, but it was not made applicable to Hindu or Muslim personal law. In 1870, the Hindu Wills Act applied this limit to the HUF, but it was left unenforced, and a debate ensued in the courts. Prominent jurists argued that such a rule limiting perpetuities could not apply to the procedures of joint Hindu inheritance.[84] In 1871, two years after *Maharani Shibessouree v. Mothooranath* had established the proprietorship of the deity, a Privy Council case, *Jagat Mohini Dossee v. Sokheemony Dossee*, reasserted that a gift to a deity was valid in Hindu law and, more importantly, added that the rule prohibiting perpetuities was not applicable to "idols."[85] Defendants in the case argued that the dedication of lands for the worship of ancestral deities was revocable: that such property could revert to other uses as the family saw fit. An irrevocable dedication of land to a deity, they pleaded, could only be secured with the assent of the state. Only the state's recognition of certain shrines as important and incontestable arms of sovereignty would establish them in perpetuity. However, the Judicial Committee of the Privy Council refused to recognize the authority of "ancient" custom, a force often willingly reverted to in Anglo-Indian jurisprudence, and asserted definitively that " 'a *family* trust of this nature has never, in modern times, at least, been held to require such an assent.' "[86]

The import of the judgment was threefold. First, in asserting that such indigenous endowments were "family trusts," the judges reinforced that they were purely private concerns. Second, this point was underlined by the argument that sovereigns, "in modern times at least," had not adjudicated on the revocable or irrevocable nature of the family trust. This reading of customary precedent denied any broader public significance that the state might previously have recognized in family-founded Hindu endowments. Third, exactly because the judges deemed state assent unnecessary in establishing the irrevocability of a family trust, the judgment viewed irrevocability and perpetuity as normative for all such forms of family gifting, with one qualification: the trust had to be real and bona fide. A bona fide dedication for religious trust was identified by the original *intention* of transfer of property for religious purposes. If such intention could be discovered, or perhaps invented, as it was in this case, a trust was deemed "valid and irrevocable" and so could not legally be deployed by the joint family for uses other than its original purpose. The customary use of the land for purposes other than the original dedication, the judges argued, did not revoke the validity of its original dedication.[87] Thus, the decision both enforced the private nature of the trust managed by the joint family, and at the same time instituted a safeguard to prevent the property from being tied up within the HUF: the criterion of valid dedication. If a trust reverted to other uses than that to which it was dedicated, it was not valid, and considered revoked. Irrevocable and perpetual religious or charitable gifts were made distinct and separate from invalid trusts for potentially profitable purposes.

A year later, in 1872, another precedent-setting case concerning the principles of Hindu inheritance confirmed this concern over the hoarding potential of the joint family. In a Calcutta High Court decision that asserted that the English law of wills was to be introduced through analogy with the Hindu law of gifts, *G. M. Tagore v. U. M. Tagore*, it was argued that "a person capable of taking under a will, gift, or settlement must . . . be in existence at the death of the testator, or the date of the gift, as the case may be."[88] The prohibition of a gift to a nonexistent being meant that in effect, the Hindu joint family was to be understood as harboring an extreme rule *against* any perpetuity, since joint family property could only be transferred to a living person. This radical interpretation of Hindu law envisioned the HUF as such an excessively joint mechanism that it eschewed any future vesting of property. A decade later, the Transfer of Property Act of 1882, passed the same year as the Companies Act, instituted a rule limiting perpetuities similar to that found in Britain and restricted the vesting of property in the future for up to one generation plus eighteen years. However, the statute included a "saving clause" that left it inapplicable to the HUF, for which the vesting of property in the future remained prohibited.

This trend in case law prohibiting the transfer of property to a nonexistent being posed a problem for concomitant decisions that were arguing for the perpetual existence of a gift to a deity. The quandary was partially resolved through the vehicle of the deity's juristic personality, which qualified it as a being "in existence" (albeit a legal existence, with the limited capabilities of a minor). Property could thus be transferred to the deity, which, given its special religious status, could hold property in perpetuity. The perpetual transfer of property to a deity was confirmed in a 1910 decision. It asserted that the absolute prohibition of perpetuities established in the 1872 *Tagore v. Tagore* case did not apply to "gifts to idols" or to other Hindu religious trusts.[89] In the next decade, the trends in jurisprudence leaned towards a tempering of the *Tagore v. Tagore* precedent and expressed a new view that this ruling had established an excessive restriction on the free disposition of property. This perspective materialized in 1921 in the Hindu Disposition of Property Act. This measure reiterated the rule on the future vesting of property found in the by-then-obsolete 1870 Hindu Wills Act and the 1882 Transfer of Property Act, codifying for the HUF a rule that limited but did not wholly prohibit perpetuities; it allowed the vesting of property in the future to one generation plus eighteen years.[90] Again, the perpetual and irrevocable character of the valid religious trust stood as the only exception to this limit. Fifty years prior, the perpetuity and irrevocability of the Hindu endowment had been a contested principle. By 1921, perpetual holding came to define the valid indigenous religious trust, and indeed marked its privileged and exceptional status as mortmain. In this process, the exception delineated the rule. Thus, concomitantly, the HUF was ascribed a normative status as an institution governed by a rule limiting perpetuities, a principle which ultimately wove the logic of succession into a mechanism distinguished by its jointness.

The legal history of perpetuities from approximately 1870 through 1920 thus betrays the growing anxiety over the tying up of land and capital in the HUF. Emerging in the wake of the Deccan riots, which brought into focus the role of usurious indigenous credit in peasant indebtedness, the question of perpetuities reflected a particular concern over the HUF as the commercial and banking family firm.[91] These anxieties were confirmed by the Punjab Land Alienation Act of 1901, which prohibited the sale of agricultural lands to nonagricultural classes; it was directed specifically at mercantile and moneylending groups who had been rapidly acquiring the land of dispossessed peasants.[92] Gifts to deities marked the self-proclaimed auspicious entry of immigrant commercial groups like Marwaris into the social and material economies of their new locales. The legal queries regarding the holdings of the joint family and its capacity for perpetual transfer to endowments held particular significance for such networks of gifting and commerce. As a mechanism of a peculiar sort of survivorship, which in its customary operation mimicked the de jure joint contract, and yet by that very customary existence also eluded it, the HUF was thought inherently to resist alienation of family property, immoveable or otherwise. Legal decisions on perpetuities reveal a consistent effort to manage this resistance.[93] In 1872, *Tagore v. Tagore* interpreted survivorship not as a principle ensuring, but rather prohibiting, the passing on of any property into the future: only birth enabled the vesting of coparcenary property. But by the 1920s, a juridical about-face instituted a rule limiting perpetuities—a middle ground—for an institution that was first conceived as rendering all property perpetual in survivorship, and then perceived as prohibiting all perpetual holdings. Despite see-sawing, the juridical and legislative management of perpetuities sought consistently to prevent unproductive accumulation in the joint family. In the process, judicial decisions restricted the temporal continuity of ancestral property, just as commercial and fiscal statute contained the spatial nexus of commerce and kinship within the private space of the household. Jurists understood the generational continuity of the joint family as meaningful *only* in birth, and not in any memorializing of ancestors that might inform the endowing of temples and other institutions. Families endowed temples, *dharmshalas*, and the like by blessing them in the name of a deity, but they also performed debt and respect to ancestors, a focus of the foundation ceremonies of such institutions, at whose entrances names of family members would be inscribed.

Moreover, the working out of the rules for the future and perpetual vesting of property established the irrevocable nature of the indigenous religious trust, a significant development for commercial family firms. The irrevocable condition of the trust ensured that charitable or religious aims could not assume commercial interests. In the late 1880s, the Hindu family endowment, reconstituted as the religious trust, which implied a public or social import, was enforced as a form of mortmain. But at the same time, it was managed by joint-family trustees. Concerns remained about the use of such property for profit-oriented purposes. These suspicions were most clearly manifest in the unspoken dilemma over the tax status of the indigenous religious trust, which itself informed the eventual classification of different kinds of indigenous trusts via the criterion of their public import.

The most concrete marker of charitable status arrived in 1886 with the Indian Income Tax Act, which, to reiterate, exempted from its purview "any income derived from property solely employed for religious or public charitable purposes." As highlighted above, the Legislative Council resisted defining religious purposes, and it refused to clarify whether all religious trusts were exempt. While it was clear that exempted charitable purposes included only those which offered public benefit, the drafters of the bill refused also to divide the category of religious purpose along the axis of public and private. Rather, the Select Committee of the Legislative Council simply insisted that the act, as worded, would not encourage "colorable gifts to idols or any like device." This confidence stemmed perhaps from the particular qualification that income be used *solely* for religious purposes. This criterion reflected concerns of case law: that many indigenous endowments were indeed part of family and firm economies, and thus had the potential to be "colorable gifts," tainted by profitable motives. While in the 1880s the exemption status of the family endowment was unclear, by 1939 statute explicitly identified such gifts as liable to tax. As we shall see, they came to be defined as private religious trusts, classified in contrast to the religious trust for public benefit. A brief examination of the categories of exemption in income tax legislation will reveal that private religious trusts' religious purposes did not protect them from the tax collector; rather, their private characters rendered them unquestionably taxable.

The Deity Is Liable

The trajectory of case law from 1870 to 1890 set the stage for the rather idiosyncratic measure of the taxation of the deity. This is best evinced by the postindependence citations of legal precedent on the taxable status of the private religious trust. In a section on private trusts subtitled "God Not Beyond IT Act," a recently compiled legal digest on the taxation of charity refers to a 1974 decision that confirmed that a deity could hold property and be in receipt of income. Asserting that the deity, as a juristic entity, was assessable through its manager, the author invoked foundational legal precedents, including the Dakor Temple case, the 1869 Privy Council judgment in *Maharani Shibessouree v. Mothooranath*, and the 1875 case which established the analogy of the deity as an infant heir, in addition to the major postindependence revision of tax law.[94] The 1961 Income Tax Act had affirmed that *person* referred also to "every artificial juridical person" and clearly elaborated procedures for the taxation of private trusts, religious or secular.[95] In 1969, the Indian Supreme Court furthered the intention of income tax legislation by offering a subtle but important distinction between spiritual purpose and material means: "In the spiritual sense God is untaxable, but . . . the organization and therefore accumulation and exploitation of wealth for such [spiritual] purposes are secular manifestations which are as liable to taxation as any other source of wealth."[96] This postindependence attitude made explicit the extractive intent buried in the logic of earlier colonial legislation: the 1886 act and its major revision, the Indian Income Tax Act of 1922. While both measures left unspoken the exemption of religious trusts endowed and managed by family firms and joint families, their liability was implicit in sections that specifically addressed the taxation of trust property.

Incorporating the trust as a new category of property in India, the Indian Income Tax Act of 1886 codified for the first time the revenue collection procedure for "trustees, agents, managers, and incapacitated persons."[97] It demanded that "a person being the trustee, guardian, curator or committee of any infant . . . lunatic or idiot" be assessable and responsible for the beneficiary's tax liability. The deity, then, which had already been deemed by 1875 an infant heir and beneficiary of trust property, became open to tax liability through its manager. Thus, while the act did not elaborate on the exemption status of "property employed for religious . . . purposes," it provided legal ammunition for the courts in cases where such trusts might be sued for tax evasion. This fiscal supervision opened the possibility of taxing indigenous trusts, particularly those with large endowments and income managed by influential commercial families.

The revised act of 1922, which included new provisions for "supertax," or tax on high profits, directed specifically at indigenous capitalists profiting from the jute and cotton boom during the First World War, was more explicit on exemptions.[98] These now included (i) "any income derived from property held under trust or other legal obligation wholly for religious or charitable purposes" and (ii) "any income of a religious or charitable institution derived from voluntary contributions and applicable solely to religious or charitable purposes."[99] In addition, while "religious purposes" remained vague, "charitable purposes" referred specifically to "relief of the poor, education, medical relief, and the advancement of any other object of general public utility."[100] This act confirmed the codification of the trust as the normative form of endowment; reiterated the earlier concern for the use of income for "solely religious purposes" while leaving them undefined; and elaborated charity as public benefit, clearly linking it to "general public utility," a concept first introduced in the 1882 Companies Act. Like its predecessor of 1886, the 1922 Income Tax Act included a section titled "Liability in Special Cases," which demanded compliance from "any guardian, trustee or agent." Again, the act silently incorporated the taxation of private trusts endowed and managed by families and firms.[101] This circuitous control was enabled by the comprehensive Charitable and Religious Trusts Act of 1920. This legislation will be discussed in the next chapter, but its import for income tax lay in the codification of a new category of religious trust, the public religious trust, which was deemed a subset of the charitable trust due to its public character. Emerging in the first two decades of the twentieth century, this category of the public religious trust helped to specify the function and indeed delegitimize the status of the private religious trust.

Case law in the 1920s and 1930s furthered the implicit intention of taxing the private trust, which was finally confirmed in Amendment Act VII of 1939, a fine-tuning of the 1922 statute. A 1926 suit by the Madras commissioner of income tax against a Chettiar business family which had established a *patshala* (an educational institution for religious teaching in Tamil) was a case in point. Here, a partitioning joint Hindu family had agreed to set aside Rs. 15,000 from the ancestral property in order to found a *patshala* "for teaching Hindu Tamil hymns." The balance on the cost of building the *patshala* was to be invested in land, which would provide income for its maintenance. But rather than investing the balance in land, the family deployed these resources in rice mills. The commissioner of income tax assessed the family on this income, and in response, they pleaded exemption, arguing that the income of the invested funds had been used for the maintenance of religious trust property. However, the Madras High Court held that "the income [derived] not from [trust] property but from business and as such it was liable to income tax, in the name of the manager of the Patshala."[102] By the mid-1920s, private religious trusts, legally circumspect as potentially profitable institutions, gradually became liable to tax. These developments reflected the greater visibility and influence of indigenous capital, particularly after the First World War. Indeed, a 1936 decision of the Patna High Court argued that the "proper construction of the words 'religious and charitable purposes' in the Income Tax Act [of 1922] is to be judged *not by the personal law of the assessees* but according to the general principles . . . applying to statutes."[103]

In 1939, an amendment to the income tax provisions secured the logic of preceding statute and case law. Qualifying the criteria for exemption, the amendment proclaimed that "nothing contained" in the clauses explaining the application of the Income Tax Act "shall operate to exempt from the provisions of this Act that part of income of a private religious trust which does not enure for the benefit of the public."[104] This finessing of the issue of tax liability for religious trusts revealed that by the late 1930s, Anglo-Indian jurisprudence had divided the umbrella category of the religious trust into public and private, labels which marked their import and indeed legitimacy. The 1939 act also provided a new qualification: that some privately managed trusts could be construed as having public purposes. These would qualify for exemption, but by this period, the provisions of the 1920 Charitable and Religious Trusts Act rendered all public trusts subject to administrative regulation. The history of the Hindu family endowment's tax status thus reflects the initially hazy but ultimately concrete mapping of the categories of charitable and profitable along the axis of public and private. Like the case law on the irrevocability of the indigenous religious trust, income tax legislation attempted to arrest the traffic between profit and gift sustained by the family firm.

The Charitable Endowments Act of 1890:
Sovereignty as Trusteeship of "The Public"

The mapping of charitable and religious purposes into public and private had begun in the 1880s. Beginning in the 1890s, new legislation designed to address concerns over the mismanagement of charitable trusts clarified this distinction. In 1890, a new statute defined the charitable trust as that specifically for public purposes. This, in turn, initiated a process of legal mitosis that eventually divided the public religious trust from the private religious trust. The Charitable Endowments Act of 1890 pointed to new trends in the regulation of public charities.

The act propagated the model of the trust contract by creating a new species of manager: the Government of India. It created the office of official trustee, in whom charitable trust property could be vested.[105] In addition, the measure outlined the definition of charity more specifically than any preceding statute: "In this Act 'charitable purpose' includes relief of the poor, education, medical relief, and the advancement of any other object of general public utility, but does not include a purpose which relates exclusively to religious teaching or worship."[106] Here, "charitable purpose" was specifically linked to an abstract public of beneficiaries. British-inspired notions of charity as philanthropy, informed by an ethics of utility, were explicitly distinguished from indigenous gifts for dharma, which, if valid, were classified as institutions devoted "exclusively to religious teaching or worship." Like the Companies Act, the Indian Trusts Act, and other legislation passed in the 1880s regulating property and commercial exchange, the Charitable Endowments Act vowed not to tamper, at least directly, with indigenous practices. Enacted in response to a growing number of cases in which charitable institutions had not provided for trustees or had been vested temporarily in local officials, the measure sought to codify a general procedure for the operation of charitable institutions outside the authority of customary practice. Thus, the Governor General in Council was to appoint an officer as the treasurer of charitable endowments, subject to the authority of local governments.

According to one legal informant, "in India, where the European population is ever shifting, it is often difficult to form a board of trustees... of a permanent nature.... Added to this difficulty... there is in India a distinct repugnance on the part of many to enroll themselves as members of a legally-constituted society or company, with duties and responsibilities and powers stereotyped by law."[107] The opinion highlighted several cases of charitable endowments in the United Provinces including an alms house and leper asylum in Moradabad, a dispensary in Bareilly, a "female hospital" in Romna Gulzar Bagh, and the Committee of High Schools in Allahabad, all with no trust deeds and thus no legal protection for their property.[108] The statute guaranteed the viability of these local efforts and legitimated them as public and humanitarian endeavors. The choice of activities that counted as public efforts reflected the emerging distinction between modern methods of relief and "traditional" ones, which were not to be interfered with. The invention of an official government trustee underlined that only support of the civic public would be validated as humanitarian. As the law linked charitable endeavors exclusively with public benefit and, indeed, with benefit as utility, it began to carve out a space for philanthropy, a new and modern terrain of gifting. In the process, legislators reinscribed the distinction between charitable and profitable, and public and private, that had also marked the commercial and financial law. Colonial sovereignty, manifest in philanthropy, also performed itself as political economy: as the distribution and management of the public.

Here, the Government of India assumed trusteeship for its public of subjects, *producing colonial sovereignty itself as a benevolent trust relation*, with "the public" as its object and effect. At the same time, the measure claimed nonintervention in indigenous gifting practices, virtually all categorized as religious. In this way, the act was emblematic of the colonial fracture between the diverse multitude of subjects and the ubiquitous metonym of the civic public. This particular configuration of sovereignty circumscribed the import of the gifting practices of indigenous commerce, which, by 1890, were normatively constituted as religious. What made an indigenous religious trust "public" and therefore a legitimate subset of charitable activity?[109] How did the working out of these categories reconstitute the indigenous endowment's status, intentions, and performance of sovereignty? For commercial family firms whose activities were symbolically articulated through so-called religious gifts, the settling in of the categories of public and private demanded new strategies of negotiation with colonial sovereignty.

The period from 1870 to 1890 saw the recoding of the endowment as a form of private property in perpetuity, a mistranslation that enforced the distinction between the irrevocably charitable and potentially profitable use of property. The fluidity of charitable and profitable purposes in the gift for dharma had been remapped along the axis of public and private. Moreover, by restricting customary endowments' negotiability of material and symbolic capital, colonial jurisprudence recoded them as religious institutions and sites of purely religio-cultural ritual. The next chapter examines a similar sort of remapping that became visible after 1890, marking the new relationship of commercial gifting with sovereignty. In the period from 1890 to 1920, the participation within, and autonomy from, sovereignty which had been secure in earlier patterns of merchant tribute and gifting was also remapped along the axis of public and private; participation came to mean charitable support of the public, while autonomy came to mean freedom to profit in the private. The 1920s offer a picture of the robust appropriation of this logic, illuminated by the legal negotiations of a financially prominent and politically influential sector of indigenous commerce.

3

For General Public Utility

Sovereignty, Philanthropy, and Market Governance, 1890–1920

> Those who own money now are asked to behave like trustees, holding their riches on behalf of the poor. Your may say that trusteeship is a legal fiction. But if people meditate over it constantly and try to act up to it, then life on earth would be governed far more by love than it is at present.—M. K. GANDHI, interview in *Modern Review*, 1935

IN THE 1920S, MOHANDAS K. GANDHI, a lawyer by training, posed the concept of trusteeship as the ethical ground for India's rapidly expanding industrial bourgeoisie.[1] After a half century of preening by jurists in Britain and in India, the trust emerged in public discourse via Gandhi as he grappled with the asymmetrical relationship of indigenous capitalism and Indian nationalism. Trusteeship cast Indian Economic Man not as a profit-oriented and self-interested capitalist, but as a philanthropic trustee, a figure both paternal and entrepreneurial, managing his wealth as the nation's wealth, in service of beneficiaries, the nation, and the poor, the public and the population. To live by this legal fiction meant embracing the universality of law as ethical self-discipline, in service of social relations *"governed* by . . . love." Redirecting private interest to public benefit, Gandhi's notion of trusteeship appropriated a distinctively British legal concept, one that constituted a model for governing itself. If for Maitland, the renowned legal philosopher with whom we began the last chapter, the trust captured a distinctly English ethos, it did so perhaps most significantly as figuration of colonial paternalism. In a 1904 essay entitled "Trust and Corporation," Maitland remarked that in the early years of empire, India was understood legally to be held in trust by the East India Company as an agent of the Crown.[2] In this example, the trust captured the relationship of proxy between the Company and the Crown, but more significantly, it provided a model for colonial sovereignty itself. As legal allegory, the trust staged the fiduciary relations between the Government of India and its public of subjects, a public posed as beneficiaries, not yet mature, on whose behalf colonial sovereignty, as trustee, exercised its benevolent authority.

It is perhaps no wonder, then, that the legal institution of the trust—both public and private—was so rigorously thought through at the height of the British Empire. Gandhi's theory of trusteeship called upon benevolence to regulate capitalism's concentration of wealth, evoking the disciplines of contract—that is, legal obligations to beneficiaries—as the moral duty of capitalists. As public discourse, Gandhian trusteeship reflected the prominence of legal concepts in colonial modernity's social imaginary, where the charitable trust and the joint-stock company institutionalized the public as alibi for the market. Drawing attention to the new category of public trust as a site for participation in and affirmation by sovereignty, this chapter follows developments after the Charitable Endowments Act of 1890. The public trust, a contractual relation that cast the public as a beneficiary, challenged the local authority and status production of customary mercantile endowments. This chapter is especially concerned with a new legal category, the public religious trust, which after 1890 referred to indigenous endowments that were deemed broadly socially relevant, and therefore charitable in the legal sense. As colonial authorities determined which vernacular endowments contributed to general public utility (and thus qualified for tax exemption), they also challenged the social and political authority claimed by mercantile social gifting. A site where local capitalisms negotiated and contested sovereign power, the public trust offers evidence of a historical shift in idioms of access to sovereignty. When precolonial rulers had acknowledged socially beneficial gifts, they had affirmed forms of shared and layered sovereignty. By the turn of the twentieth century, participation in the sovereign responsibility of social welfare was reconstituted as a philanthropic investment in an abstract public. This recoding of customary social gifting into a contractual relation with the public reflected broader transformations into liberalism's political modernity: a move from forms of negotiable and shared sovereignty to shares in a non-negotiable sovereignty.[3] In fact, as elaborated here, vernacular capitalists' contests with modern, non-negotiable sovereignty remained at play and even intensified as nationalists began to speak on behalf of the public.

This chapter, like the previous one, also approaches law as lived fiction and social text, posing the trust as a metonym for colonial market governance. As codified in late nineteenth-century Britain, the trust was a legal form that took relations associated with a gemeinschaft worlding—status, hierarchy, paternal authority—and translated them into the contractual worlding of gesellschaft.[4] Formalizing conventions of faith and duty, it evokes the modern staging of capital (status to contract). An important story in casting of the social by nineteenth-century capitalism was the legal codification of corporate life—into the limited liability corporation, the nonprofit association, the registered society, the charitable trust. It is a story which comes to the fore in the Indian context, where forms of corporate life—most significantly, the joint family—did not quite fit contractual paradigms. The legal coding of the mercantile firm as Hindu Undivided Family, and so as site of radical difference from modern relations of contract, was one important effect of this asymmetry. Concomitantly, the standardization of trusts procedure saw attempts to align the family firm and other forms of customary association with contractual models. Case law that had coded the endowment as a trust opened new possibilities for governing custom as analogous with the contract, and the social relations of indigenous culture as analogous with the social relations of the market. In this vein, this chapter highlights two sites of public discussion: debates concerning joint contracts and the family firm preceding the 1890 Charitable Endowments Act, and the classification of caste-based mutual assistance as nonprofit associations on the model of the Companies Act.

Beginning with an overview of shifts in the meaning of charitable and religious purposes after 1890 and an outline of trends in mercantile gifting, the argument turns first to the above stories concerning the alignment of kinship with contract. These present two themes are woven through the rest of the chapter: first, indigenous capitalists' interests in autonomy from sovereign regulation, and second, the emergence of a new form of public status, the charitable trust, conferred only by sovereignty and subject to its regulations. Highlighting Marwari voices, the chapter then charts legal developments that enabled officials to validate certain customary endowments as beneficial to the public, shifts that brought new forms of regulation. This recognition/regulation is illustrated through legal debates on the charitable status of the *dharmshala* (or *dharmsala*), a rest house for travelers and a popular form of customary endowment. Even as some *dharmshalas* were validated as social welfare, others were subject to surveillance, as our evidence on the deployment of the *Sarais* Act of 1867 attests. The act was a police measure that sought to monitor *dharmshalas*, addressing them as sites of popular disorder rather than as welfare for the public. In conclusion, the question of the charitable status of the customary mercantile endowment, and its symbolic participation in sovereignty, is pursued in the initiatives of nationalist public figures, who sought to elaborate regulatory procedures and were contested by vernacular capitalists.

Charitable and Religious Purposes after 1890: From Shared Sovereignty to Shares in Sovereignty

Spanning an era of limited but expanding political representation that included the 1892 Indian Councils Act and the reforms of 1909 and 1919, the period between the Charitable Endowments Act of 1890 and the Charitable and Religious Trusts Act of 1920 saw the emergence of "native commerce" in public discussion.[5] In the four decades following the foundational market statutes of the 1880s, the growth in the collection of information on commerce and industry confirmed that "trade" had become a distinct category of representation in the emerging civic public. At the turn of the century, it referred mostly to chambers of commerce dominated by British agencies. In 1905, a new Department of Commerce and Industry took over the commercial purview of the older Finance and Commerce Department of the Government of India, and a Commercial Exhibitions Branch was founded in 1906, a year after the first Indian Industrial Conference. In 1917, largely out of an effort to locate and tax the rapidly growing profits of indigenous capitalists during the First World War, the government established a Commercial

Intelligence Department. C. W. E. Cottons's popular manual, the *Handbook of Commercial Information for India*, compiled beginning in 1917, was a product of this department.[6] By the First World War, prosperous indigenous merchants themselves attempted such information-collecting efforts to assert the leverage of Indian industry in imperial trade. For example, in 1917, Laximichand Dossabhai and Bros., a prominent Gujarati textile firm based in Bombay, wrote to the Commercial Intelligence Branch proposing to start a "Commercial Museum and Intelligence Bureau," which would "undertake to furnish every possible information about the Indian and British manufactured goods and raw materials and give all facilities to promote . . . the increased Indo-British trade relation."[7] Examples such as this speak as much to the new public presence of vernacular merchant-capitalists as to their entrepreneurial ambitions. After 1890, service to an abstract public offered a new social welfare model for a variety of modernizing elites, who supported a host of public charitable purposes: philanthropic concerns for education, scientific and economic progress, and the health and order of the civic body.[8] These included hospitals, colleges of higher education, libraries, institutions for the promotion of scientific and commercial knowledge, and museums. Indigenous capitalists began to support such institutions especially after the First World War, after their earlier patterns of negotiation with sovereignty had shifted significantly.

As we noted at the end of the last chapter, by codifying two decades of case law and establishing the trust contract as the bona fide channel for gifts for social welfare, the Charitable Endowments Act of 1890 opened up new questions for the classification of charitable gifts. This statute had also excluded all religious institutions from the category of charitable trusts. Transfers of property for exclusively religious purposes had not been considered public charitable institutions for two reasons. First, since indigenous culture was understood fundamentally as bound by religion, so religious purposes were understood as cultural norms, to be governed by the private realm of personal law, and so irrelevant to the public in general. The disjuncture between the multitude of indigenous subjects and the new abstract category of the public was patently clear in the governmental distinction between religion and charity. Second, the classification of indigenous gifting as religious and private, rather than charitable and public, reflected a concern over the gifting practices of the Hindu joint family, and particularly the Hindu family firm, which, as outlined in the last chapter, allowed for flows of capital between social gifts and profitable endeavors. These practices informed broader concerns about whether a gift given by an HUF, with its vacuum of jointness, could ever be completely alienated to the public.

Reflecting the slow devolution of colonial sovereignty after 1890, the next comprehensive statute on trusts, The Charitable and Religious Trusts Act of 1920, established that religious trusts deemed of public import would also be eligible for classification as charitable trusts, and thus be classified as tax exempt. As such this new legislation made explicit juridical trends that were only implicit in the 1890 Charitable Endowments Act. A major juridical development came as a ramification of the 1887 Privy Council judgment in the Dakor Temple case, which had confirmed the status of the Hindu deity as a juristic entity. This case had also set the precedent for the application of section 539 of the Civil Procedure Code to indigenous trusts. Section 539, as written in the 1882 code, dealt with "suits relating to public charities" and elaborated procedures for the interference of the court "in case of any alleged breach of ... trusts."[9] The judgment in the Dakor Temple case held that some Hindu religious trusts might be construed as public charitable trusts under this section for the purposes of settling the claims of competing parties to trusteeship.[10] The decision thus asserted that Hindu religious trusts might be construed as public institutions in the case of mismanagement, in order to enable court intervention and regulation of their affairs. Here, the regulation of indigenous trusts and the construction of their public status were allowed in exceptional cases. The courts expanded their authority over indigenous endowments through this circuitous mechanism. The 1890 Charitable Endowments Act expressed the equivocations of case law by codifying indigenous trusts' normative status as religious and private, while at the same time buttressing section 539 of the Civil Procedure Code by providing for an official trustee. By 1920, the Charitable and Religious Trusts Act had codified the juridical precedent of the Dakor Temple case: it established the category of the "public religious trust" and standardized measures for its regulation.

In the period from 1890 to 1920, the distinction between the public religious trust and the private religious trust was popularized in debates on the proper management of indigenous institutions. Beginning in the 1890s, all forms of indigenous endowments, from the great temple of the precolonial sovereign to the family shrine, became open to classification as either public or private.[11] With the 1920 statute, the Government of India expanded the regulatory powers of local governments and courts over public religious and charitable trusts. These new regulations elaborated procedures for publicizing trust finances and accounts and so quite literally enforced an ethics of public accountability. They reflected growing concerns over the mismanagement of larger temples and mosques, especially those with histories as sites of collective pilgrimage and centers of precolonial kingship. Battles between groups competing for trusteeship rights over these sites incited public debates on the management of public trusts in the 1890s.[12] Increasing "native" demands for the responsible management of these influential sites, emerging largely from south India, provided impetus for government intervention in indigenous trusts in general.

These developments, in turn, had a particularly problematic effect on the influential social gifting of wealthy merchants. The increased visibility of mercantile gifting beginning in the 1890s, as exemplified in the burst of Marwari endowments in this period, reflected the commercial and geographic expansion of commercial castes.[13] The diversification and growth of mercantile social investment coincided with greater legal regulation of indigenous trusts. Unlike the temple sites of the south, large temples or other institutions endowed by commercial groups were managed either by family members or close business associates. Such tight managerial organization, which reflected the close-knit kinship ties of business, protected merchants' endowments from the problems of competing claimants to trusteeship found in large temple complexes, especially those in south India. Nevertheless, merchant endowments became open to the same standards of regulation as the great historical temples, mosques, and pilgrimage sites.

Beginning in the 1900s, and certainly after the act of 1920, influential family-managed endowments came to qualify as public ventures. Case law slowly began to recognize as public trusts the large temples and *dharmshalas* built near markets by single families. By the 1930s, judicial decisions held that while the definition of public religious and charitable purposes was not to be judged by personal law or customary practice, even private family trusts might claim a public component.[14] Many such shrines earned public status beginning in the second decade of the twentieth century, especially as they supplemented their traditional endeavors with charitable ventures such as libraries and medical dispensaries.[15] Commercial towns throughout the subcontinent burgeoned with these hybrids of customary hierarchies and modern public performance. Spatially, such endowments marked both the boundary and the overlap between the lived space of the bazaar and the abstraction of the public. One representative and still-functioning example from a growing provincial commercial town of the period was the Poddar *Dharmshala* and Ram Temple in Nagpur. Both were founded by a powerful Marwari family in the center of Nagpur city, opposite the railroad station that served as a central junction for the major lines crossing India from north to south and east to west. This branch of the family had migrated to Nagpur from the Shekhawati region of Rajputana in 1875 as commission agents for Empress Mills, the great industrial concern owned by Jamshedji Tata. By the late nineteenth century they had become its sole selling agents, and in 1915 they established the *dharmshala* next to Nagpur's famous orange market. The temple, a center of orthodox Hindu activity, standing adjacent to the *dharmshala* and opposite Mayo Hospital, a civil institution, was completed in 1923. In 1926, a new public charitable trust was founded, with funds from the temple trust, for adding a modern library to the premises, which was opened at the festival of Dassera in 1929. The legal history of the public trust and the *dharmshala* in the late nineteenth and early twentieth centuries was manifest in the local histories of endowments such as this one.[16]

The Trust, the Joint Contract, and the Joint Family Firm

Beginning in the 1880s, legislation and jurisprudence on customary endowments grappled especially with the purview and authority of personal law over the indigenous *lex mercatoria* or law merchant. The Companies Act, we will remember, had asserted that the property relations of the family firm were to be governed by Hindu personal law. In this way, the firm was understood first as a Hindu Undivided Family. But as debates surrounding the Negotiable Instruments Act revealed, indigenous commercial practices were also understood to constitute a special kind of common law outside the purview of Hindu personal law: a relatively autonomous Indian mercantile law, understood by British administrators, jurists, and traders as a set of flexible conventions that regulated exchange among firms, and that could be rendered analogous to formal relations of contract. Beginning in the 1890s, legislators focused on mercantile law as an instrument for bringing the customs of the HUF into alignment with contractual procedures. The trust was a key site in this endeavor.

In 1888, when the Charitable Endowments Bill was circulating for opinion, questions concerning the trust as a joint contract articulated anxieties about the perpetual jointness of the HUF and the family firm. The bill posed the possibility of establishing an official trustee to monitor charitable institutions. This required the clarification of the trust as a joint contract and so as distinct from the customary institutions governed by personal law. While case law had established an analogy between the customary operations of the endowment and the contractual relations of the trust, statute had yet to enforce that analogy. If the trustees of an endowment were to be given the option to vest trust property in the official trustee on the occasion of their deaths, the law had to be clear on the question of the devolution of their joint rights and liabilities. More broadly, if endowments were to be understood legally as trusts, their procedures would have to be clarified according to the laws of joint contracts, as the trust was a legal relation between donors, trustees, and beneficiaries.

This posed an interesting dilemma for the analogy between the contractual model of survivorship—that is, the rules for the devolution of rights and liabilities within the joint contract—and the customary inheritance of the Hindu Undivided Family. The joint inheritance of the HUF was interpreted through an analogy with the contractual notion of what was called coparcenary survivorship. Just as the endowment was not exactly the trust, contractual survivorship only ever approximated the joint inheritance of the HUF.[17] The attempt to assert the precedence of contractual succession over customary inheritance was tied to the concern that endowments funded by families might revert to the family property on the death of a trustee. Again, it is important to remember that in this period the courts were grappling with the question of the revocability of the indigenous endowment and the possibility that capital gifted to social welfare might be reclaimed by the family firm for profitable enterprise. Could the authority of the trust contract be asserted over the claims of members of joint families?[18]

Beginning in April 1888, the Judicial Branch of the Home Department solicited opinions on whether, at the death of a trustee managing a trust jointly with other trustees, the management rights of the trust would continue among the *survivors* of the contract (a term that despite its organic implication referred specifically to legal contractees, that is, the other trustees or the deceased's appointed legal successor) or whether a *representative* of the family of the deceased might also claim rights to trusteeship and so influence the purpose of the endowment. The relationship between contractual *survivor* and joint family *representative* had a long history dating back to the Indian Contract Act of 1872. Section 45 of the Indian Contract Act had asserted that upon the death of a member of a joint contract, the representatives of that deceased member's joint family had equal claims with the survivors of the joint contract. This meant, for example, that in the case of a trust with three trustees, A, B, and C, when A died, representatives of A's family could influence trust management along with the contract's survivors, B and C.[19] However, in 1886, the Indian Securities Act amended this section of the Indian Contract Act and produced an exception to its rule of joint succession.[20] Interested in limiting the government's liability in jointly held government securities, it established that upon the death of a shareholder, the survivors of the joint securities contract had first and immediate claim to the deceased's share. The act did allow for suits to be brought against contractual survivors by family representatives, but only after the survivors had secured possession of the legal rights of the deceased. Thus the Securities Act gave clear precedence to members of the joint contract and not to customary claims.[21]

Beginning in April 1888, the Judicial Branch of the Home Department debated the laws of joint contracts and their devolution in the case of trusts. Confronting the opposing precedents of the Indian Contract Act and the Indian Securities Act, C. P. Ilbert, then finance member of the Legislative Council of India, proposed to standardize the devolution of joint rights and liabilities for trusts on the model of the Indian Securities Act. Here, market governance called for extending the purview of civil law: as one opinion summarized, "an exception" to the Indian Contract Act's equity between survivors and representatives had "already been made in the case of Government securities, and the expediency of making further exceptions in the case of partnerships, trusts, and shares in companies ha[d] been advocated."[22] Still, invoking the example of the family firm, many opinions argued that the precedence of the joint contract over customary claims would be difficult to enforce. Indeed, the mercantile family firm stood in for the HUF in this discussion. Anxiety over the firm was clear in the Judicial Branch opinions, which considered the impact of changes in the devolution of joint rights and liabilities on "native partnerships" and their extensive networks of credit and trade.[23] The question of the trust as joint contract thus opened immediately to questions concerning the amenability of mercantile usage to contractual procedure. If indigenous negotiable instruments could be aligned with contractual procedures, could customary mercantile practice accommodate the joint contract as a model for succession and inheritance? Would it be possible to modernize the HUF through vernacular capitalism?

Insisting that the authority of the joint contract would be difficult to enforce over customary claims, many opinions asserted that mercantile custom seemed to be particularly resistant to codification of any sort, whether by civil or personal law. This argument was strongly articulated by opinions coming from the Central Provinces, a center of Marwari banking and commercial power.[24] Two major Marwari firms located there, the firm of Raja Gokul Das in Jabbalpur, and that of Seth Kasturchand Daga in Nagpur, had been longtime financiers of the Government of India; indeed, they were the among the earliest to be recognized with honorary titles. The control of credit in the districts of Jabbalpur and Nagpur lay in these "great firms," which by the mid-1880s were expanding their commercial activities into industries such as cotton spinning, wheat processing, and tile manufacturing.[25]

The government of the Central Provinces solicited opinions from Gokul Das and Daga, citing them as spokespersons for native commerce. Both asserted the rights of the family representative and indeed suggested the precedence of customary authority over the rule of survivorship. The opinion of Seth Gokul Dass Rai Bahadur offered these correctives:

> The surviving partner [to a commercial joint contract] will be bound to complete the transaction, but some provision should be made to protect the rights of the heirs of the deceased partner . . . :
>
> (1) The fear of criminal prosecution will be a great safeguard to protect the rights of heirs.
>
> (2) When there are two or more persons jointly entitled to the benefit of a contract . . . and one of them dies, the right to enforce the contract shall vest in the survivor or survivors, but the right shall not affect any

claim which the heirs of the deceased person may have against the survivors in respect of the contract.

(3) In the event of fraud being suspected, the heir may proceed against the survivor either by a civil action or by prosecuting him criminally.[26]

Gokul Das's opinion respected the contractual devolution of joint rights but sought protection for joint family heirs. His suggestion of criminal prosecution against contractual survivors revealed a suspicion that civil law served as an instrument for protecting fraud; such a view reflected earlier critiques of the principle of limited liability. Similarly, speaking on behalf of the "native mercantile community," Seth Kastur Chand Daga argued that "according to mercantile usage, it would be better . . . if [section 45 of the Indian Contract Act] is allowed to stand . . . as it is," and he asked that "no further exceptions be made to this rule."[27]

Both opinions from these government-selected native informants expressed concern that the proposed legal regulation of trusts had ramifications for indigenous mercantile practice. If trusts were to be governed primarily as joint contracts, they argued, native firms would become open to interpretation and regulation as contractual partnerships, impeding on the authority of indigenous mercantile usage, as Daga emphasized. It is important to note that neither opinion evoked the sanctity of the Hindu Undivided Family; both articulated the legitimacy of the indigenous *lex mercatoria*, rather than asserting the Hindu joint family's cultural orthodoxy. By the 1920s, as we shall see, the call of cultural protectionism had taken hold, not least because of the challenges to mercantile status and sovereignty outlined here.

Local opinions from officials dealing directly with mercantile firms insisted, for the most part, that indigenous firms' customary arrangements, charitable and commercial, would be difficult to regulate through the rules of joint contracts. Ultimately, these potential difficulties proved too complicated to clarify in statute, and the provisions of the Indian Contract Act remained intact, allowing family representatives equity with contractual survivors in the management of trusts.[28] However, the Charitable Endowments Act of 1890 did carve out a space for the unqualified purview of the law of contract: the public charitable trust. Public charitable trusts came under the authority of official trustees assigned to local governments. Customary authority might have claim in cases involving private and religious trusts, but public charitable trusts were to be enforced as corporate, contractual entities with the power to sue and be sued in civil courts.[29] On the one hand, the import of the law of contract was restricted to charitable trusts, which were by definition gifts to the public. On the other, the status of the charitable gift came only through entry into a public contract, regulated by statute and civil procedure.

Pension Funds and the Uneven Application of Charitable Status

The Charitable Endowments Act of 1890 established a new basis for deciding charitable purpose: general public utility. In addition, the 1886 Indian Income Tax Act had assured that institutions that fulfilled this criterion would be exempt from taxation. But the criteria for determining public benefit were still being worked out in the three decades after the 1890 act. In this period, a variety of customary institutions of social welfare approached the Government of India for public charitable status, only to be repeatedly denied. In the 1890s, the colonial administration addressed the ongoing issue of indigenous pension funds: contractual associations that formalized customary practices of mutual relief, such as caste-based arrangements for the support of widows, orphans, and the needy. They reflected the ethos of the extended family, a mechanism of insurance for commercial and noncommercial families alike.[30] These new cooperative associations were attempts to broaden the impact of kinship-based social welfare through civic organization and reflected modern models of the economic subject who saves and invests in the future. But despite their investment in modern contractual association, these pension funds were considered to be private, customary bodies rather than associations with public relevance. In this period, a series of discussions in the Home and Finance Departments on the taxability of pension payments articulated the growing gap in status between indigenous notions of social welfare and the standards of the modern public charity. Indeed, the decisions of colonial administrators and the advocate general demonstrated how public charitable status could be deployed both to regulate customary practice and to expand civic association by contract.

In January of 1886, while the Indian Income Tax Bill circulated through the Legislative Department, the directors of five pension funds sent a collective memorial to the viceroy, Lord Dufferin, to ask for tax exemption for the pensions paid to "widows and orphans and other helpless defendants of deceased subscribers." The Income Tax Bill had allowed for the deduction of subscription payments to pension funds, but pension payments had not been granted the same exemption. The directors of the General Family Pension Fund thus asked for exemption, emphasizing that it was "the object of the Government to encourage and facilitate the prudent arrangements rendered possible by these Funds."[31] In effect, the letter called for government recognition of organizations promoting patterns of productive saving. This request was reiterated in a memorial to the viceroy sent by the directors of the Uncovenanted Service Family Pension Fund, the General Family and Bengal Christian Family Pension Funds, and the Hindu Family Annuity Fund on January 29.[32] A note from the private secretary to the viceroy a few days later stated simply, "It is not perhaps the intention of the Government to exempt such pensions or allowances as referred to from the payment of Income Tax," an assertion then affirmed by the Department of Finance and Commerce.[33]

In 1895, the question of pension funds re-emerged as the Charitable Endowments Act extended the regulatory arm of the Government of India. The Sind (Hindu) Mutual Family Relief Fund sent a memorial to the Revenue Department asking for permission to be registered under Act XXI of 1860, the Societies Registration Act. This statute had contained procedures for the registration of "literary, scientific and charitable societies" and was established in an era when, in both Britain and India, legal notions of charity were more flexible and reflected the term's broad popular usage.[34] The fund's secretary explained that the association sought legal recognition as a charitable institution, a logical step towards tax-exempt status. The registrar of Joint-Stock Companies for the Bombay Presidency, who had purview over this request, had declined to register the fund under the 1860 act, arguing that its purposes were clearly not charitable. The fund then sent a petition to the Government of Bombay, which again refused to recognize it as a charitable society. As a final resort, its secretary submitted its memorial to the Government of India asking for a ruling on the issue, asserting its charitable intent and distinguishing it from profit-oriented practices of actuarial enumeration:

> The main object of our society is to give relief to middle class families. Our society does not act upon the principle of Insurance Companies.

> We do not take into consideration the average duration of life, or charge any granted premium. We ask each of our members to pay Rs. 1.8 for his annual subscription, whether he is 50 or merely 18 years old. We further call upon him to pay a rupee extra when any member dies. . . . He is thus . . . promised a certain amount . . . on his death, for when any of our member dies [sic], all the rest come out with their contributions for the relief of the family. This is the only benefit promised. The society does not work for profit. . . . We submit that a society acting on these principles is a society formed for a charitable purpose, and is not a mercantile company.[35]

Emphasizing that other such organizations had been allowed to register as charitable societies under the 1860 act by the registrars of Lahore, Calcutta, Allahabad, and Madras, the memorial reflected the slippery definitions of charitable purpose since that time.[36] The fund asserted its status as a civic association that formalized and broadly applied customary ethics and practices of social welfare:

> Our rules and the rules of societies like ours merely give body and shape to a well known charitable custom prevailing among the Hindus as well as Mahomedans. The custom is for the members of caste[s] and tribes to contribute each a small amount on the occasions of marriage or death in the family of a member. We extend the scope of that custom and allow all Hindus in Sind to become members of our society and to give relief on a larger scale. . . . Those who know native society fully understand the difficulties which middle class families experience on the death of their bread-winners. The women of such families would rather die than beg. To give any money to them in the form of a donation is to ensure its rejection. The custom mentioned above was therefore invented to give an appearance of social equality to the members of castes and tribes, and thus to facilitate the reception of relief. There is no doubt that according to Hindu and Mussalman ideals, societies like ours are societies for a charitable purpose, and the fact that the Registrars at Calcutta and Lahore have taken the same view ought . . . to . . . induce [the government] to allow our society to be registered under Act XXI of 1860.[37]

For the directors of this fund, the proof of their charitable purpose lay in their broad application of long-held conventions associated with social welfare, rather than self-interest. At the same time, they claimed that it was modern middle-class status, as vested in the honor of middle-class women, which prevented the reproduction of customary aid practices, since the very self-help ethos of the middle class eschewed donations. This pension fund thus sought to manage a conundrum of colonial modernity, allowing especially for donations to widows in the formal guise of law and insurance. On the one hand, the directors of the fund embraced the legality of contract, and on the other, their very definition of charity as social welfare, rather than gifting to an abstract public, channeled customary worldviews.

Though the solicitor to the government explained that the term *charitable societies* as used in the Societies Registration Act had been "differently construed in different presidencies," the advocate general held that the Sind Fund "is not a Society for a charitable purpose within the meaning of... Act XXI." Furthermore, he characterized the fund as "more in the nature of a Provident Fund," one which "is no doubt an Association formed for the purpose of promoting an useful object, and can be registered under Section 26 of the Indian Companies Act, 1882."[38] Section 26 of the Companies Act had provided for the registration of nonprofit associations on the model of joint-stock companies. The provision gave legal status to associations "formed for the purpose of promoting commerce, art, science, charity, or any other useful object."[39] This section had in 1882 created a new category of civic association: the corporate legal person which mirrored the company in its organization, but not in its profitable intention. Societies registered under this section were not considered charitable because while they promoted "useful objects," their benefits were directed exclusively at their members—as was the case with chambers of commerce and professional associations—and not the public in general. Furthermore, registration under section 26 required a payment of Rs. 400 and did not exempt such associations from tax. Indigenous pension funds (some of which were organized specifically around caste relations, such as the Kshatriya Assurance Fund) willfully translated customary social welfare into contractual procedures but were coded legally through economic models of self-help rather than as charitable organizations; again, the universality of the abstraction of "the public" outweighed customary claims to social welfare.

The advocate general's decision had immediate and expansive administrative effect: by 1897, all such funds which had been registered as charitable societies under the 1860 act were deprived of that status, regardless of the varying opinions of the different local governments.

The decision thus helped to specify the definition of charitable endeavor and standardize its implementation. In the process, it also furthered civic association on the model of the joint-stock company. If indigenous pension funds were to maintain their legal status, they had no choice but to register under section 26 of the Companies Act, a procedure which brought with it obligations of public accounting and taxation while denying recognition of charitable status.[40] In 1897, when the government advocate for Punjab received the advocate general's notice on this issue, four funds in that province were struck off the register of charitable societies. The Punjab government advocate even argued that not only were they not charitable; in fact, "money-making [was] the *sole object* of the four societies referred to."[41]

The decisions on the status of pension funds reflected the more detailed classification of public and charitable endeavors in the 1890s. In the three decades after the Charitable Endowments Act, the courts reassessed the private status of customary institutions like temples and *dharmshalas* that served large local populations. These institutions' claims to social welfare forced the colonial administration to address activities that did not easily fit into its public/private distinction. The issue of indigenous pension funds was one early example of such piecemeal decision making. With every particular assessment of indigenous cases, the Government of India asserted a new kind of sovereign prerogative: the right to confer status by deciding which endowments could be classified as public and charitable ventures. After 1890, then, the categories of public and private were applied more specifically to the variety of indigenous practices for social welfare. In the process, the endowment dedicated to ancestors or in the family name, predominant in mercantile gifting, came under closer government scrutiny.

Customary Mercantile Gifting and Public Status, 1890–1914: The Illegitimate Gift for Dharma and the Legitimate *Dharmshala*

Legal opinion after 1890 followed two trends: on the one hand, the courts affirmed the illegitimacy of gifts dedicated to dharma in general, while on the other, they created exceptions to this rule by acknowledging as public various indigenous institutions with broad social welfare intentions. Both trends involved a fine-tuning of the public/private distinction, and reaffirmed civil law, and not personal law, as having the authority to define and validate charitable endeavors. By 1936, a Patna High Court decision on the tax status of a family trust could state without exception that "the words 'religious and charitable purposes' in the Income Tax Act are to be judged not by the personal law of the assessees but according to the general principles of construction applying to statutes."[42] This decision confirmed trends in case law in the first three decades of the twentieth century, which emphasized the private and potentially illegitimate arrangements of family endowments, particularly those founded by commercial groups. One important criterion used as early as 1870 to classify mercantile gifting as private was the spatial location of the trust: the intention of the trust was thought to be manifest in its physical location. According to a Calcutta High Court decision in 1875, "where the deity is installed in the house of the family, or where the temple has been built on land belonging to the family, the [endowment qualifies as] a private trust."[43] Such assessments posed problems for endowments on the premises of commercial families in particular. The *haveli* (home) of the *mahajan* (the wealthy banker-trader) mimicked the kingly palace, and was not conceived only as a private household. Marwari families, for example, maintained palatial homes in their ancestral villages in Rajasthan and, increasingly in the late nineteenth century, at the centers of their business activities. These houses included both outside rooms for receiving clients and conducting business and inner rooms and courtyards that served as domestic space dominated by women. Often a *godown* (warehouse) might be found at entrances. A spatial representation of the firm as kinship structure and commercial mechanism, the *mahajan*'s house accommodated the world of the bazaar and the everyday life of the household. Public and private did not accurately reflect this spatial universe. Indigenous gifting's private legal status coded the home as a purely domestic space. Indeed, the emphasis on the private location of family endowments reinforced the notion of the mercantile firm as HUF rather than as economic mechanism.

In 1899, a Privy Council decision on appeal from the Bombay High Court affirmed that gifts for dharma "simpliciter" were not valid charitable trusts. This decision reiterated that the Hindu notion of dharma did not necessarily imply public benefit. Rather, dharma was a vague term that referred to a wide variety of practices, many of which did not accurately reflect the legal definition of charity as the provision of general public utility. The judgment of the Judicial Committee referred to the broad meaning of the word "dharam [dharma]" as "law, virtue, legal or moral duty" and held that these objects were too uncertain to be placed under administrative control.[44] Indeed, the private and noncharitable status of such gifts rendered them outside the purview of sovereign regulation, as they constituted an arena of indigenous religio-cultural practice. This decision established an influential legal precedent that reflected the longtime official policy of the administration: indigenous culture was not to be tampered with. In the 1890s and later, however, certain customary gifting activities were recognized piecemeal as publicly beneficial, particularly the *dharmshala*.

Dharmshalas, or rest houses for travelers, were, next to temples, and alongside wells and cisterns, the most common form of traditional mercantile gifting. Located centrally, in bazaar areas, near railroad and trade junctions, and often attached to temples, *dharmshalas* exemplified the imbrication of commercial concerns and gifting practices. They offered free room and board and catered largely to merchant travelers. Rooms would also be open to religious mendicants and others with pure caste status. Most *dharmshalas* rejected entry to lower castes and *dalits* (untouchables), enforcing social and material hierarchies. Nevertheless, as courts offered decisions on the public nature of indigenous endowments beginning in the 1890s, the question of public benefit came to rest less on equal access to *all* potential beneficiaries and became instead one of serving more than just the family or trustees. In the context of indigenous trusts, then, public benefit was defined negatively: the term included all trusts that were *not* dedicated for the use of specific, named beneficiaries. Evidence of a broader spectrum of donees might be found in the deed of dedication. But it might also be discovered in the wide-ranging import of an endowment that had been dedicated to a specific family. Colonial jurisprudence thus began to consider the usage of trust property in greater detail.

This shift in juridical emphasis from intention to usage began in the 1890s, as the courts assessed the legal and political status of indigenous institutions like *dharmshalas*. Judicial decisions since the 1880s had held that *dharmshalas* were valid trusts, but in the 1890s they were still considered to be valid *religious* but not public *charitable* trusts.[45] In 1899, the same year that the Privy Council had declared the "gift to dharma" not a valid form of charity, the Bombay High Court heard a case concerning a temple with a *dharmshala*, a dining area for feeding travelers, and a place for giving alms to the poor. The temple had been built and managed privately by its founder until his death, when his son, Jugalkishore, assumed these responsibilities. In 1891, the officiating priest at the temple and five other worshippers of the deity filed suit under section 539 of the Civil Procedure Code asking for the removal of Jugalkishore. In order to remove him under section 539, the Court had to find evidence to support the plaintiff's claim that the temple and *dharmshala* constituted a public charitable trust. The judges received evidence that members of the local population had regularly used the temple and that the resultant surplus funds offered to the deity went towards providing room and board for travelers. Taking account of this usage, the judges held that

> (1) having regard to the fact that a certain number of the public had always used the temple, that there was attached to it a *dharmshala*, and that the surplus funds not required for the service of the temple were to be applied to feeding travellers and maintaining a *sadavart* [dining area], the intention of the founder was to devote the property to public, religious and charitable purposes;
>
> (2) that although the defendant was not appointed a trustee, yet by taking charge of the endowment, and purporting to manage it as temple property, he made himself a trustee, and was liable as such, to the beneficiaries.[46]

Emphasizing the contractual obligation to beneficiaries, the opinions elaborated that if the temple had been dedicated specifically to the family house of the deity, that is, to his ancestors or relations, neither it nor the *dharmshala* could have been construed as a public trust. But the temple had been dedicated directly to the deity, and not to any persons specifically. In addition, neither temple nor *dharmshala* had been reserved for the exclusive use of specific persons. The court thus recognized both as public institutions.[47] This case laid the groundwork for the emerging distinction between the public religious trust, to be understood as subset of the public charitable trust, and the private religious (or family) trust.

By 1908, it had become clear that *dharmshalas* were considered institutions of public benefit. In that year, the Allahabad High Court considered a case concerning a *dharmshala* at Benares.[48] It had been established by an Agra zamindar, Rai Jyoti Prasad, who wanted to apply up to Rs. 500 a month from the net profits of seven villages towards *pun*. A Sanskrit word referring to virtue as meritorious acts, this *pun* would support the *dharmshala*. The judges deemed *pun* or *punya* as too vague a term to have legal relevance and not analogous to English notions of charity. Nevertheless, they held that the gift of Rs. 500 per month to the *dharmshala* was a charitable transaction, despite the vagueness of the object of *pun*. Indeed, the fact that the funds would be applied towards the maintenance and activities of the *dharmshala* was deemed sufficient to prove that such transfer of resources would benefit the public. The court also asserted that if the object of the gift to *pun* remained vague or became contested, it had the authority to intervene to "settle a scheme for its proper administration."[49] Once the *dharmshala* had been established as a public religious trust for charitable purposes, it became open to the growing influence of the courts in matters concerning public religious institutions, a development that would be codified in the Charitable and Religious Trusts Act of 1920.

Status with Regulation: *Dharmshalas* and the *Sarais* Act

Especially with regard to *dharmshalas*, local governments and the police supplemented judicial intervention in indigenous endowments, particularly after 1910. This was due largely to the stricter application of the *Sarais* Act of 1867 (Act XXII of 1867) in this period. The *Sarais* Act became an issue of contention in the same period in which the courts were beginning to recognize *dharmshalas* as charitable institutions. *Sarais* referred to inns or rest houses for public dwelling, many of which were privately owned and charged fees for their facilities. Others might be established as charitable rest houses by *maulvis*, Muslim religious leaders, or as *dharmshalas*. Construed largely as a remedy to a growing anxiety over crime and infectious disease, the act had originated in policing concerns in the North-Western Provinces, a focal point for the attack on dacoity, or banditry. The *Sarais* Act had been drafted to apply broadly to the variety of inns and rest houses. According to the inspector general of police of the North-Western Provinces:

> *Serais* and *puraos* [shelters for carriages and beasts of burden] belong either to Government, or to private individuals who had built them either for their own gain or for the public weal. After construction they

are generally made over to certain *Bhuttiaras* [innkeepers], or to contractors, who are nominally responsible for keeping them clean and in good repair; and . . . there is no law obliging them to do what is required [for their upkeep]. The consequence is that the buildings, their gates and wells, are very often in great disrepair, affording every opportunity for the operations of thieves and robbers, and the Magistrate is powerless to enforce his orders for repairs. . . . Instances of travellers being robbed in *serais* and *puraos* with redress of any kind are innumerable, and very many cases have occurred of travellers being poisoned in *serais* . . . and of their being followed up and poisoned on the road.[50]

The most prominent feature of the act was its demand for the registration of all *sarais* with the local police. In addition, it asked all *sarai*-keepers to maintain lists of travelers, with the date of arrival, names, father's names, caste, age, profession, name of previous place of rest, and "remarks on suspicious character & c" for police inspection.[51]

In 1912, the Advocate General received a request for an opinion on whether the *Sarais* Act could be applied to *dharmshalas* and other charitable rest houses throughout India. While the Act had included them implicitly, it had not enforced registration of such institutions, and indeed opinions on the *Sarais* Bill revealed that they might be construed as exceptions. In 1866, the inspector general of police of the North-Western Provinces had suggested that in the case of *sarais* established by "charitable moulvees," the penalty "for opposition or neglect on the part of the owner, or person in charge, [be rendered] as light as possible."[52] The situation had changed by 1910. In that year, the district magistrate of Gorakpur district in the United Provinces received a petition from Suraj Mal and Bajrang Lal, the Marwari merchant managers of a *dharmshala* in Deoria *tahsil* (township). They complained that the *Sarais* Act had been applied to their rest house, a public charitable institution that did not require such surveillance. The act had been strictly enforced in response to an incident involving the manager of another *dharmshala* in the district, Babu Dhela Singh. He had been convicted for obstructing police procedure after refusing to give information to a constable for a register of travelers. The district officer of Gorakpur reversed the conviction on the grounds that, first, Babu Singh's *dharmshala* had not been registered under the *Sarais* Act, so that its rules did not technically apply; and, second, that under that act, the list of travelers was to be maintained by the *sarai*-

keeper, and not the police constable. To remedy this situation, he issued a notice demanding that *all sarais and dharmshalas* in the district register themselves under the act. The incident had thus produced a universal enforcement of a statute heretofore applied only in the case of inns and other fee-charging facilities.

On May 12 and then again on July 4, 1910, "Suraj Mal, Marwari" and Bajrang Lal were served with notices from the district magistrate of Gorakpur demanding registration of their *dharmshala* under the *Sarais* Act. On September 9, 1910, the two submitted a petition claiming that: "the said building is a *dharmshala*, which means a building for the accommodation of pilgrims and travellers free of any charge whatever.... Your petitioners therefore venture to submit their case does not come within the Act XXII of 1867 ... and beg therefore ... that the *dharmshala* may be exempted from registration."[53]

In November 1910, faced with noncompliance, the district magistrate again sent a notice to the managers stating that their *dharmshala* "should not receive any travellers ... unless and until it was registered and that in the case of non-compliance ... [they] would be dealt with under the penal sections of the said Act."[54] To avoid such prosecution, the managers, in their words, were "obliged to close the said *dharmsala* to the great inconvenience of the Hindu public and travellers."[55] In February of 1912, Suraj Mal and Bajrang Lal sent another petition to the lieutenant-governor of the United Provinces, asking that their *dharmshala* be kept open without registration and that "legislation might be undertaken to amend that Act so as to exclude *dharmsalas* and similar institutions."[56] After outlining the above sequence of events, the petition emphasized that their institution, which had been established exclusively for charity with rooms offered free of charge, could not possibly be meant for the indignity of registration or police intervention. It recounted the history of the institution, its function as a debt to ancestors and as a channel for the family's public obligations:

Most respectfully sheweth:

(1) That about ten years ago Lachmichand, grandfather of your humble petitioners, built a *dharmsala* known as Lachmichand Lalji Mal Dharmsala in Bazar Bharouli, Deoria ... and dedicated it to the public out of purely religious and charitable motive for the use and temporary accommodation of Hindu *sadhus*, pilgrims, and travellers who might happen to pass by it.

(2) That since its dedication hundreds of Hindu *sadhus*, pilgrims and travellers used to put up in the said *dharmsala without any charge for the use thereof.*

(3) That since its dedication the said *dharmsala* has been used for purely public charitable purposes and in order to meet the expenses of its maintenance and up-keep the out-houses [outer buildings] have been let out for shops. Your humble petitioners have no private ownership in the said *dharmsala* but they are interested in it so far as . . . being the descendants of the original dedicator they keep the management thereof in their own hands in order that [the] primary object of the endowment may be faithfully carried out.[57]

The statement asserted that gifts for public welfare and charity ought to be synonymous with *autonomy* from regulation of any kind, particularly that of the police. Citing the 1867 *Gazette of India*, the petition referenced the introduction of the *Sarais* Bill in the Legislative Assembly, which according to the introducing legislative council member, concerned itself with the "regulation of *places of public entertainment kept by private persons* and especially of common lodging houses frequented by the poorer classes." The petitioners argued that *sarais* were for-profit institutions and cited another member's concerns over the "keeper of the sarai and his customers," concluding that "Act 22 of 1867 applies only to buildings and places of public entertainment for the use of which some charge is made and which are owned by private individuals for the purposes of gain."[58] *Dharmshalas* were obviously not of this category: registration and potential police regulation compromised the status of the *dharmshala* as an honorable institution in the service of the public. The petition emphasized that primary object of the act had been to assure that keepers of *sarais* "be respectable persons and not such as would be likely to harbour thieves and evil characters." This concern alone ought to have exempted *dharmshalas* and their managers, as "such a contingency," the possibility of evil characters, "cannot arise in the case of persons who build *dharmshalas* and dedicate them to the public without any motive for personal gain, because it is only persons of respectability and position that make such a dedication." Indeed, the "heirs and representatives of those who constructed" such *dharmshalas* "regard it as humiliating to be classed with *bhathiaras* [innkeepers] and subjected to the police regulations applicable to them." In closing, Suraj Mal and

Bajrang Lal argued that "it was never the intention of the Government of India to bring Hindu *dharmsalas*, such as the one constructed by [their] ancestor, under the scope of Act XXII of 1867" and asked that the law be amended to exempt *dharmshalas* and other such endowments. In this connection, they pointed out that accommodation for "*fakirs* and *durveshes*" in mosques had also not been previously subject to the act.[59]

On the one hand, then, the petition deployed new notions of public charity, while on the other, it evoked the status produced by gifting and its role in negotiating sovereign authority. Speaking in the imported language of civil law, the managers of the Lachmichand Lalji Mal *dharmshala* insisted that their institution was a public charitable enterprise, with no taint of profit-making intention. They associated this status, in turn, with the honor and respect due to benefactors. Here, Suraj Mal and Bajrang Lal translated legal definitions of public charity into an earlier idiom of mercantile gifting and its bargains with sovereignty. Insisting on the nonprofit aims of the *dharmshala*, they asserted compliance with legal definitions of charitable activity and, at the same time, called for the benefits traditionally granted to respectable donors. The social capital of the gift was to be confirmed in its autonomy from government regulation, whether that take the form of simply registration or the watchful eye of the magistrate. The respectability of gift giving implied the entitlement of self-regulation, a validation of the ethics and principles of its founders. The petitioners thus aligned the new legal categories of charity with older customary arrangements between kings and merchants. Suraj Mal and Bajrang Lal's insistence on the charitable nature of the *dharmshala* communicated a fundamental assumption about merchants' relations with sovereignty: that direct sovereign control over honorable gifts for social welfare occurred only in the exceptional instance of their mismanagement.

The petition articulated long-held understandings about the terms of the merchant-king bargain: that status brought autonomy. But the terms of this ethico-political bargain were shifting by the early 1900s. The petitioners' demand for an amendment excluding *dharmshalas* from the *Sarais* Act was taken up in the March 1912 meeting of the Provincial Legislative Council, which refused to address the issue, stating that the local government was not competent to pass legislation amending an "Act of the Supreme Legislature."[60] Ultimately, the question was sent to the advocate general, who maintained that "the definition of 'Sarai'... in the *Sarais* Act XXII of 1867 includes a *dharmsala* or building erected for the accommodation free of charge of pilgrims and travellers. . . . The mischief aimed at by the legislation is the evil resulting from insanitation. This, obviously, is a matter to which the question of paid or gratuitous accommodation is immaterial."[61]

Thus the very focus on the question of profitable or charitable intent, a predominant legal logic appropriated by the petitioners to explain their situation, was ultimately deemed irrelevant in the face of the governmental demands of managing bodies: the problem of the ethics of the giver, and his claims to the political, was simply overridden by the call to security. This decision standardized the regulation of *dharmshalas* and other indigenous meeting places with claims to charitable status. In effect, as the courts began to recognize gifts like *dharmshalas* as public religious trusts, they also became subject to greater governmental and legal regulation. Indeed, it seemed that for indigenous religious trusts like *dharmshalas*, founded by local benefactors, public stature only implied the illicitness and disorder associated with the bazaar, rather than the virtue of the public civic association. In the case of merchant gifting, the universal application of the *Sarais* Act presupposed the potential criminal activity in all *dharmshalas* and local meeting places. In this way, it also reflected the emergent use of criminal law to regulate mercantile custom in this period, a development to be elaborated on in the next chapter.

At the same time, the period from 1890 to 1920 saw the widening purview of civil law over the control of public religious trusts, culminating in the Charitable and Religious Endowments Act of 1920. The greater recognition of indigenous trusts as public ventures coincided with the stricter enforcement of the public trust contract, which borrowed its regulatory procedures from laws concerning joint-stock companies. Officials and influential reformers attempted to clarify the rights of beneficiaries in the trust contract beginning in the 1890s, and their demands often evoked the model of the rights of the joint-stock shareholder. Public discourse thus began to associate beneficiaries' rights specifically with the procedures used to protect shareholders, most especially those connected to the publication of accounts and procedures for audit.

1900–1920: The Codification of the Public Trust Contract and Public Accountability

Beginning in the late 1880s, representatives for important temple sites called upon the colonial administration to enforce procedures for the better management of religious trusts with broad public import. After 1900, a series of private members' bills submitted by nationalist publicists to the Imperial and Provincial Legislative Councils called for the clarification of public trust procedures, and in particular the rights of beneficiaries. The Religious Endowments Bill, for example, was introduced as early as 1897 by Ananda Charlu, a nonofficial member of the Indian Legislative Council. Its object was to correct "certain defects in the management of religious and charitable endowments under the law . . . in force."[62] Applicable to all "non-Christian Institutions," it called for trustees to maintain accounts and submit them to central or district committees, boards maintained by local administrations, either monthly or quarterly.[63] Local governments received the measure unfavorably, reiterating that it called for intervention in areas protected by personal law. In 1903, a member of the Madras council, Mr. Srinivasa Rao, called for the standardized publication of trust accounts in that province.[64] In 1908 Dr. Rash Behari Ghose, another nonofficial member of the Legislative Council and a liberal Congress nationalist from Bengal, submitted a Public Charities Bill, which more specifically provided a "simple procedure to enable the public to obtain inspection of the accounts of public charities."[65] Introducing the bill, he insisted that he was "not going to invite the Council to take away any single right or privilege now possessed by the heads of our religious and charitable institutions or to interfere in the slightest degree in their management. *All that [is asked] is that the public, who are the real beneficiaries*, should be able to obtain under proper safeguards an inspection of the trust accounts."[66] The bill was dropped soon after its introduction and publication, as the framer ceased to be a member of the Legislative Council. However, like its two predecessors, it did point to a new nationalist interest in the protection of beneficiaries (the public claimed by nationalism) and greater surveillance of trust finances.

In 1911, a private bill introduced in the Bombay Provincial Legislative Council reiterated these concerns. Ibrahim Rahimtoola, a nationalist and commercial man, submitted the bill, which called for the registration of all charitable trusts, except for exclusively religious trusts, and the regular publication of audited accounts.[67] Directed at secular charities in the modern philanthropic model, the bill became a reference point for debates on procedures for public trusts, whether charitable in the secular sense, or religious.[68] Introducing the bill, Rahimtoola produced a potent analogy with the joint-stock company:

> It occurred to me as rather strange, that while Government had passed the Indian Companies Act for the protection of Shareholders of Joint Stock Companies, nothing of practical value had been done to protect the beneficiaries under charitable endowments. I will invite the attention of the Council to the provisions of the Indian Companies Act. . . . The State lays down provision to give the fullest publicity to the terms, conditions and particulars, with periodical audited accounts, in the case of private business concerns. . . . Far from regarding this measure as an undue interference with trade, it is universally recognised as a whole and necessary provision for the protection of shareholders. . . . It appears to me that there is much greater need for the State to provide by legislation for the protection of beneficiaries under charitable endowments. . . . The shareholder requires to be protected from . . . personnel of his own choice whom he has entrusted with a certain amount of his capital for the purposes of profit, while a beneficiary requires to be protected from the person or persons in whom the donor reposes confidence . . . for the benefit of such a beneficiary. The State has provided elaborate machinery by means of a special Act to protect the former, while the latter goes practically unprotected.[69]

Rahimtoola offered a model that had by this time seemed obvious to many a reformer. The Companies Act had become the paradigm for government regulation of civic associations, and its lead should be followed in the case of charitable endowments. A year after Rahimtoola's bill was introduced, two Madras Legislative Council members, Seshagiri Iyer and Govindharagava Iyer, introduced a bill in that province for the publication of audited accounts of public temple sites. For them, accounting would enforce the ethics and disciplines of modern civic relations: "The misapplication and misappropriation of trust funds is sapping the foundations of honest citizenship, and the fact that peccant and erring men have so long remained uncondemned and unpunished is creating and encouraging the impression that these men can handle trust money to their own advantage."[70] These legislative interventions were supplemented by a growing number of memorials by local officials from southern India calling for a "clear idea as to the income and expenditure" of charities.[71]

None of these bills were passed, as the Government of India remained cautious about transgressing its policy of noninterference in indigenous culture and religion. However, it did accommodate the growing native demand for the proper management of religious trusts by convening an all-India Religious Endowments Conference in Delhi on March 16, 1914. Its delegates offered a predominantly modern and reformist stance favoring all-India legislation; representatives of orthodox Hindu and Muslim associations and sects were few.[72] Hindu mercantile groups, significantly, were represented only by spokespersons from south India, whose concerns reflected the problems particular to large temples with competing claimants to trusteeship. Increasingly in the late nineteenth century, influential commercial castes in the south offered large gifts to traditional temple sites in addition to establishing ancestral village temples.[73] These practices stood in contrast with the charitable activities of merchant-capitalists in other regions, whose material gains were manifest in local temples, *dharmshalas*, and the like, which were dedicated to ancestors. As an important Chettiar merchant representative to the conference, Diwan Bahadur Ramaswamy Chetty, explained, his community's great investments of "many lakhs and lakhs of rupees for . . . a number of famous temples" were fraught with factional disputes. He, like other delegates from Madras Presidency, asked for an "adequate statutory remedy and fairly easy resort to civil courts," as well as for investigation at the local level of differences in "the history and usages of these institutions."[74]

The 1914 Religious Endowments Conference focused on large, historic temple complexes, and members insisted that—despite a distinction in gifting practice between north and south India—the questions of improper management in the influential complexes in the south were applicable universally. Seshagiri Iyer and Govindaraghava Iyer, in their "Historical Summary (Unofficial) from the Madras Point of View," which was distributed to the delegates, thus contended, "The belief of the Government of India as expressed in their letter to the Government of Madras dated 7th September 1894, that the demand for reform proceeds only from a few educated men and that the public is likely to resent it even, is probably based upon the impression derivable from the state of public feeling in some of the northern parts of India, where the conditions of religious institutions are different owing to many of them being either private or attached to religious houses or mutts [*mathas*]."⁷⁵ The distinction between the largely private or family gifting of the north and the public gifting of the south was reiterated in a 1915 Madras High Court decision, which held that "it is very unusual in Southern India for a Hindu to construct a temple outside his dwelling house for private worship and the general presumption is that temples in the Southern states are public temples unless the contrary is proved."⁷⁶ This distinction between the endowments popular in the north, still construed as private due to their family-based management, and the public gifting of the south had to be managed in any all-India statute.

In its press communique preceding the conference, the Government of India summarized the opinions on the question of all-India legislation regulating charitable and religious endowments. The major policy questions focused on whether the Government of India should adjust its policy of noninterference in all religious endowments that had been articulated in the Religious Endowments Act of 1863, and if so, whether this should be an all-India measure that would call for registration and regular publication of accounts, or should simply maintain resort to the courts. More broadly, the delegates were asked whether it was possible to "differentiate between religious and secular endowments in respect of the control exercised over them."⁷⁷ In this way, the official discussion questioned the categories put forth in the Charitable Endowments Act of 1890: that of the public charitable trust, understood as secular, as opposed to all other trusts, considered religious and broadly construed as private. The query reflected the confusion that had emerged in the courts in the two decades since that foundational statute. The distinction between public and private had not coincided in practice with the secular/religious dichotomy posed in the 1890 act. The courts had since deemed many indigenous religious trusts of public import, from the obvious pilgrimage sites of the south to the family-managed *dharmshala*. Indeed, the majority of conference delegates held the view that differentiation between secular and religious trusts "would frequently be impracticable and that the treatment of all should be uniform."⁷⁸ Opinions varied, however, on the procedures for regulation, with some calling for registration, others for public accounting procedures, still others for the expanded jurisdiction of the courts over these issues. But all agreed, as in the bills which had preceded the conference, that the rights of the beneficiary ought to be protected, and the trust contract enforced. As nationalist critics, particularly those concerned with the obvious and broad social import of large temple complexes, highlighted the asymmetry between the liberal public/private distinction and the geography of social welfare, they animated "the public" as holder of legal rights.

By 1915, war efforts increasingly occupied the Government of India, and the question of legislation was postponed.[79] In May of 1919, a draft Charitable and Religious Trusts Bill was circulated by the Legislative Department, and it passed as statute the next year. The act resisted universal regulations for registration and submission of audited accounts on the model of the Companies Act. Instead, it emphasized the *rights of beneficiaries* of public trusts, who could obtain court orders to enforce the examination and audit of trust accounts. Trustees could also be required to make public information on the object of the trust—its "value, condition, [and] management."[80] Via its procedures for summary proceedings, the act opened the possibility of litigation.[81] At the same time, it codified trusts along the axis of public and private, now establishing two kinds of public trusts: the secular/charitable versus the public religious trust, the latter encompassing customary endowments deemed publicly beneficial by the courts. The statute did not address the matter of private gifting, which referred to indigenous family endowments and private secular trusts.

As an articulation of sovereignty, the Charitable and Religious Trusts Act of 1920 challenged the autonomy of customary mercantile gifting, as well as mercantile performances of authority and hierarchy. While the emphasis on the beneficiaries' right to demand the publication of accounts suited merchant-capitalist combatants in temple management battles in southern India, rituals of public enumeration also challenged the status production of family firms' gifting practices. The paternal and feudal duty performed in making gifts for social welfare was, at least in the case of the public religious trust, reframed as a legal relation to be monitored by the government. The act thus codified legal trends from the 1890s, first by legitimizing the charitable and public nature of many indigenous activities, and second, by enforcing this legitimacy through the public trust contract. For merchant groups, this constituted a new relationship with sovereignty, since the sovereign recognition of gifts for the public empowered beneficiaries rather than donors. The donor's participation in the sovereign prerogative of social welfare was at once recognized as public gifting, and regulated through notions of public rights.

As codified in 1920, the discourse on charitable endowments established both a rights-based script for benevolence and reinforced the notion of the sovereign as trustee in service to an abstract public. Because the question of charity was a question of market governance, the codification of charitable trust procedures map the emergent asymmetry between capitalists and the claims of modern sovereignty, both colonial and national. On the one hand, the making of the modern capitalist subject in India depended on the prominence of the native expert in governmental projects, the expert who claimed authority over managing the economy in the name of the public. As we shall see, modernizers of the industrial bourgeoisie learned to speak on behalf of the public. But at the same time, merchant-capitalists also called upon discourses of cultural protectionism to resist the infringement of the public (especially national) sovereignty on their local authority and customary practices, publicizing orthodoxy.

By 1920, the law on charitable and religious endowments had transformed traditional patterns of merchants' negotiation with sovereigns. Previously, gifting had implied participation in authority, which had been recognized with the entitlement of autonomy, or self-regulation. By the early twentieth century, the terms of the bargain had shifted against gift givers; public status brought public regulation, while private efforts, not legitimated as publicly useful, remained, at least in theory, protected from government intervention (though even they became subject to taxation after 1922).[82] Over the half-century from 1870 to 1920, then, the application of the categories of public and private to charitable and religious endowments produced a disjuncture between the political and social status of gifting, on the one hand, and the entitlement of autonomy, on the other.

The Cultural Orthodoxy of Economic Subjects: The Public Trust, Nationalist Claims, and Vernacular Capitalists in the 1920s

The 1920 Charitable and Religious Trusts Act raised new questions about the degree of public regulation of indigenous trusts, and indeed their public nature. The spread of nationalist politics saw the appropriation of the idea of the civic public by communities, castes, and classes.

Amidst these competing and multiple publics, nationalist reformers considered expanding the regulation of public trusts in order to claim a wide variety of customary endowments as national symbols. The hegemonic claims of national culture, and the governmental authority of the emerging nation-state, were robustly performed in nationalist demands for the greater regulation of public trusts in the 1920s. One telling and influential measure, discussed extensively in the Legislative Assembly from 1924 to 1926, was initiated by one of its most well-known reformists, the legal maverick Hari Singh Gour. Gour drafted the Hindu Religious and Charitable Trusts Bill in response to the 1923 Mussulman Waqf Act, which had provided procedures for the direct regulation and administration of all public *waqfs*, or Islamic charitable endowments. Gour's bill followed the words of this act almost exactly, calling for the registration and submission of accounts from *all* Hindu trusts: "In this Act . . . 'trust' means the permanent dedication by a person professing the Hindu faith of any property for any purpose recognized by the Hindu law as religious, pious, or charitable."[83]

The bill detailed information to be submitted to the Court of the District Judge, the High Court, or other local courts designated by the local governments. This included a description of trust property and its gross annual income; the amount of government revenue and cesses payable annually, as well as an annual estimate of expenses incurred; and, significantly, the detailing of the amount of the trust set apart for "the salary of the trustee," for "purely religious purposes," for "charitable purposes," and for "any other purposes."[84] In his statement of Objects and Reasons, Gour explained, "This Bill is intended to make better provision for the management of Hindu Trust properties throughout India. It closely follows the language of the Mussalman Waqf Act of 1923, which makes a similar provision for the management of Mussalman Waqfs. The reasons which have led the legislature to pass the Mussulman Wakf Act apply *a fortiori* to Hindu religious and charitable trusts, and as the Central Legislature has protected the trusts of one community, it is necessary that it should also protect the trusts of the other community."[85]

Presenting the nation as a site of communal equity, the bill not only presupposed Hindu and Muslim as political categories, it rendered them commensurate, nominally challenging a majority/minority logic.[86] At the same time, it followed most literally the logic of legislation on charitable endowments, appropriating and redefining the legal categories of public and private. Building on the 1920 Charitable and Religious Trusts Act, Gour attempted to resolve the contradiction that customary Hindu endowments had by default been understood as religious and private trusts, even though the courts had legitimized certain exceptions as public religious trusts. In a classic nativist/nationalist and modernizing move, Gour claimed that the criteria of Hindu law confirmed the public charitable nature of *all* Hindu trusts, thus requiring their governmental regulation. He thus tried to transform that which colonial jurisprudence had deemed generally to be religious, and so private, activity into normatively public. In the process, he reproduced an essentialized Hindu culture via secular nationalist rhetoric, and indeed as a template for the public itself. This expansive claim to regulate customary Hindu trusts (or endowments) evinced the nationalist appropriation and aggressive extension of the public of colonial market governance. As the minutes of the Legislative Assembly recount, Gour pushed for this nationalist appropriation by affirming customary endowments' status as participants in the constitution of sovereignty, even as he called for their enumeration and monitoring:

> From time immemorial Hindu trusts which were created and endowed by a succession of pious donors have been managed . . . by bodies who do not recognize their trust character, and if I were to ask any Hindu to make an inventory of all the Hindu public trusts in this country, would he be able to do so? My measure wishes to place upon the register for the benefit of posterity a list of all public endowments which are trust property and the profits of which *must be utilised for a public purpose.* Is that an ignoble desire? Can any Hindu here think that public trusts do not require public supervision?
> (*A Voice*: 'Not personal.')[87]

The records of the Legislative Assembly debates do not identify the interrupting voice in the debate, but it represented a broad opposition to the bill on the part of orthodox Hindu groups to the unprecedented supervision contained in the bill. Orthodox opinions opposed the prominent nationalist leaders who enthusiastically supported the measure, including Motilal Nehru, M. A. Jinnah, and the Gujarati merchant and member for Indian commerce, Sir Purshotamdas Thakurdas.[88] Thakurdas's support is relevant for understanding the emerging double voice of indigenous commerce, which on the one hand articulated economic nationalism, industrial progress, and cultural reform, and on the other spoke cultural and religious orthodoxy. In contrast to Tharkurdas, most representatives or spokespersons for commercial groups argued that the bill created unnecessary intervention in the cultural realm of the private family trust. As a de facto spokesperson for conservative elements, especially among prominent mercantile castes, Madan Mohan Malaviya asserted, "This is a measure which is being introduced for the first time in a community which has never known legislative interference with religious and charitable trusts."[89] He pointed to the unprecedented demand for the inspection of accounts as a transgression of private rights: "One of our colleagues . . . thinks that these temples [i.e., private temples dedicated to families] are national assets and therefore anybody who is interested in the nation might be given an opportunity to make a petition for accounts or further particulars of the trust. I . . . do not agree with this view."[90]

Many reformist opinions also reiterated this concern over surveillance, asserting that the bill would create undo interference in family trusts. The Secretary of the Delhi Bar Association, for example, supported the bill, but pointed out that the measure did not "expressly state whether [it was] confined to public trusts only," and some provision had to be made to protect family deities and their managers within households.[91] Gour had perhaps foreseen this discomfort with regulation, for he had also proposed a Hindu Trusts (Validating) Bill in 1924, which was refused sanction and not put forward for discussion; it tried to apply the provisions of the Mussalman Waqf Validating Act of 1913 to Hindus. The 1913 Waqf Act had allowed for the creation of private trusts in perpetuity for the benefit of family members, a practice that was held to be in accordance with Muslim law. Gour argued that such trusts were also allowed in Hindu law. But the Government of India, echoing a half-century of jurisprudence on mortmain and anxieties about the HUF as hoarding mechanism, argued that such perpetuities were never allowed by Hindu law, thus affirming the general rule against perpetuities: "The foundation of the rule against perpetuities in English law is based upon the axiom . . . that property best answers the purposes of civil life, especially in commercial countries, when its transfer and circulation are totally free and unrestrained."[92]

Gour had thus tried to insist at once on the public validity and regulation of all Hindu charitable trusts, *and* on the autonomy and privileges of private trusts, thus attempting to fit older bargains with sovereignty into the public/private distinction. As his Religions and Charitable Trusts Bill went forward, mercantile opinions argued stringently that other small endowments, such as wells and *dharmshalas*, or temples dedicated to family ancestors, be exempted even as Hindu law recognized them as socially beneficial.[93] The Government of India solicited the opinion of the Marwari Association of Calcutta, an organization founded in the late nineteenth century that by the 1920s represented the most powerful and publicly active members of that community, which was itself an influential sector of vernacular capitalism by this time. It offered recommendations on the wording of the bill and emphasized particularly that the regulation of accounts was acceptable in the case of public, but not private, trusts:

> In view of the fact that Marwaris give away their money very freely for religious and charitable purposes, my Committee are deeply interested in the question of the management of religious and charitable trusts and institutions. . . . They do not think that the object of securing the better management of such Trusts can be fully attained merely by ensuring the keeping and publication of accounts. In many cases it is likely to mean trouble to Trustees and unnecessary expenditure to the Trusts and institutions without serving any useful purpose. . . . Trusts ought to be divided into two classes, private and public. By private trusts my Committee mean Trusts that are for the benefit of private persons or established by an individual or a family or a firm and such trusts should be excluded from the purview of any legislative enactment. Regarding the public Trusts, such as public temples, orphanages, etc., my Committee are of opinion that the small ones having an annual income of not more that Rs. 5,000 should be excluded.[94]

The Marwari Association was particularly sensitive to the financial intrusions of such potential legislation, asking that the auditing of accounts of public institutions with executive committees be conducted not, as the bill provided, by "qualified auditors," but "by a person selected by the members of such institution to be the auditor thereof."[95] This opinion challenged emerging concepts of the rights of beneficiaries and voiced histories of mercantile financial autonomy. Rather than celebrate the potential public status of their trusts, many Marwaris embraced the protection of private cultural autonomy and resisted regulation.

This strategy can be understood less as an articulation of an age-old orthodoxy than the vigorous protection, in culturalist mode, of the social text of the bazaar. Here, the Marwari appropriation of the category of the private trust sought to legitimize family firm's forms of customary gifting, and its symbolic and material economies. Even as they accepted the legitimacy of new definitions of public gifting, Marwaris reinforced and indeed invigorated their traditional forms of gifting and commercial arrangements under the guise of private cultural practice. Customary practices remained so popular that one reformist Marwari newspaper, extolling the virtues of "social reform and national progress" [samaj-sudhar aur deshunnati], complained that traditional forms of welfare detracted from investment in the nation: "In our country it's become a 'fashion' to build temples and *dharmshalas*" [hamare desh me mandir aur dharmshala banane ka "fashion" nikul gya he].[96] While Gour's bill was rejected by the Select Committee of the Legislative Assembly, the generally critical Marwari reaction to it did confirm that by the 1920s, the law of contract, supporting the rights of public beneficiaries, was understood as a potential regulation of emergent vernacular capitalists. In response, they appropriated the restricted colonial (and indeed nationalist) definition of cultural autonomy as protection from regulation.

As the next chapter discusses in the context of Marwari groups, customary economic practices came increasingly into conflict with new governmental disciplines for modern market ethics and became subject to direct criminal regulation in the first two decades of the twentieth century. In order to negotiate new regulations, capitalists followed two strategies that furthered the public/private distinction and served their interests: first, they sought the refuge of private cultural autonomy, coding commercial practice as "culture"; second, they attempted to align the indigenous mercantile law with public, contractual, and legitimate commercial activity. As we shall see, the private space of culture reproduced the idioms and hegemonies of local capitalisms, while the public space of economy offered a place to legitimize them. And as the last chapter elaborates, by the 1930s, the rights of the public (as beneficiaries of the national trust) began to be recoded by capitalists as governance of the public (as market), a totalizing governance enabled by the politicization of the family as site of religio-cultural orthodoxy.

PART TWO

*

Negotiating Subjects

4

Hedging Bets

Speculation, Gambling, and Market Ethics, 1890–1930

> A highly . . . pernicious feature of our present system of trade is the rapid growth of the *Satta* or *Badai* [speculation]. . . . Government paper, grain, opium and silver are the great objects of *Sattas*, which are made under the names of *Souda* or contracts. Neither the seller has or expects to have the goods he professes to sell, nor does the buyer buy nor can he afford to buy the goods he pretends to buy. They are all imaginary goods bought and sold at prospective rates. . . . It is nothing but gambling pure and simple.—RAI BAHADUR LALA BAIJ NATH, "The Indian System of Banking and Other Business," 1908

BY THE END OF THE NINETEENTH CENTURY in India and in Britain, the fictions of law had conjured new vehicles and instruments for trade, finance, and charity, orchestrating new incarnations of capital as they enforced the distinction between the market and the bazaar. Serving the unprecedented global extension and integration of finance capital in this period, law confronted the fertile power of its own sorcery, a new world of imaginary goods traded in futures markets through ever-deferred "time bargains." Precursors to hedge-fund piracy at the turn of the twenty-first century, futures trades were exchanges premised on an extensive temporal negotiability. They evinced a new "valorization of value" and the abstraction of market exchange, even as they tested disciplines of contract. In India, this trade in imaginary goods instigated rigorous debate on the market ethics of local capitalisms, confirming and intensifying anxieties that had been expressed in legal discourse over almost a half century.

Lingering concerns over the slipperiness of indigenous market practice informed a rapidly growing surveillance of what was labeled gambling and disorder in the bazaar, especially in the major commercial centers of Bombay and Calcutta, and in the market towns and entrepôts of the United Provinces and the Punjab. In the period from 1895 to 1914, when brute imperialism and sophisticated finance heralded a new global staging of capital, criminal law directed itself at vernacular forms of hedging and speculation. Associated for the first time with the dangerous habit of gambling, these practices had until this time been free of regulation, civil or criminal. According to government officials and social reformists, burgeoning informal futures markets were driven by irrational habits and offered evidence of a commercial ethics gone awry. Indeed, among certain commercial groups, risk taking betrayed a troubling sort of genetic predisposition that threatened to destabilize the natural forces of supply and demand. Mapping the public discourse on gambling with reference to earlier concerns over indigenous trading practices, this chapter elaborates a debate over market ethics and the possibility of a modern capitalist subject in India. Were capitalist ethics, grounded in the ideals of saving and investment, to be undermined by an unrestrained instinct for fast and furious accumulation, sustained by the private and secret tendencies of community-based commerce? To address these questions, Anglo-Indian criminal law delved for the first time into the subtle distinctions between exchange and theft, skill and chance, interested investment and irrational desire.[1]

This new concern over the broad social and economic effects of gambling followed the standardization of companies procedure in the 1880s and the first comprehensive legislation on charitable gifting in the 1890s. The first statutes directed at gambling in India had been passed separately in the different presidencies and provinces in 1867 and 1868 and focused specifically on locating the gathering places of the criminal classes. In Britain also, gambling laws had been first directed at public disorder and were slowly codified in Victoria Acts 16, 17, 18, and 19 in 1853 and 1854, and then in the Vagrant Act of 1868 and its succeeding amendments, which asserted that any person gambling in public "shall be deemed a rogue and a vagabond." These together made gambling illegal in streets, public places, and in gaming houses open to the public.[2]

In India, the criminal legislation on gambling in the two decades before 1914 became increasingly interested in economic crimes, especially those which threatened to spread unhealthy ethics of accumulation and expenditure not only among commercial groups, but to the public in general. Indigenous futures markets, which were wholly identified with risk taking, were thought to promise fast windfall profits to an unsuspecting and ill-educated public. Furthermore, the very speculative nature of these markets depended on kinship and caste-based information networks which extended from major city bazaars, to towns, to up-country trader-moneylenders who were in direct contact with primary producers. These so-called private and elusive channels carried information that was thought to distort spot prices and predictions for supply and demand.[3] Between 1890 and 1930, the Government of India debated the nature, extent, and criminality of gambling in major commodities whose prices were intimately tied to the fluctuations of the world market: grain, cotton, opium (the potential prohibition of which offered fertile opportunities for speculation), jute, and silver. Beginning with an overview of questions concerning ethics of speculation in the late nineteenth century, and an outline of indigenous futures and speculation practices, this chapter charts governmental anxieties through scandals and criminal investigations in Bombay in the 1880s, Calcutta in 1897, Punjab Province and the City of Delhi in 1898 through 1900, the United Provinces in 1905 through 1911, and in Bengal in 1911–1912 and in the 1920s. At the same time, it charts the emergent public voices of vernacular capitalists, who by the 1920s sought to validate their practices and perform respectability.

The Debate over Market Speculation in Britain and Abroad

The public discussion on economic crime and the swindle in its various incarnations had also reached a new height in Britain and America by the late 1890s and early years of the twentieth century. In order to highlight the specificities of the debate in the subcontinent, it is important to take note of this Euro-American context. The 1890s marked the beginning of a public debate in Britain on market speculation and its potential dangers, both material and moral. The distinction between gambling and speculation remained confused, but two questions in British public discourse informed the criteria for the regulation of indigenous futures markets in India. The first concerned transactions among merchants themselves, and the legality of the futures contract settled without delivery. The second was the broader question of the nonmercantile public's engagement with the market. This was informed by anxieties about gamblers, mimicking traders and commission agents, who might dupe the uninformed general public by at once popularizing and distorting investment practices.

Futures markets in agricultural produce, which involved both hedging and speculation—that is, activities associated with risk minimizing and risk taking respectively—remained largely informal and unregulated in Britain and Europe in the late nineteenth century.[4] Information on the variety of forms of futures trading in these markets was sparse, but by the 1890s, British legislators sought to establish rules for bringing them under the rule of law. In 1895, a Parliamentary Select Committee solicited information from British representatives in Belgium, Germany, and the United States on "Legislative Measures for Suppressing Gambling in Fictitious Wheat Contracts."[5] In May of 1898, more comprehensive reports were sent to Parliament on "Legislative Measures Respecting Gambling in 'Option' and 'Future' Contracts" from representatives in Vienna, St. Petersburg, Washington, Brussels, Athens, Stockholm, Berne, Buenos Aries, and Budapest.[6]

The 1895 investigations addressed new practices of futures trading, those which did not result in delivery of wheat or grain. This was a common method of concluding contracts for future delivery, which would be hedged by traders against other such contracts. Such trades would be settled through payment of price differences and without the exchange of goods. The British government sought information on these practices as a first step in ensuring price stability in the world markets for grain. The prevailing British opinion asserted that such stability might be secured by invalidating contracts that did not perform their original intent of delivery. But Belgium, Germany, and the United States remained less concerned about penalizing such settlements.[7]

In 1898, a more exhaustive inquiry into penalties for gambling in options and futures contracts revealed a broad array of responses to these market practices. Options contracts, broadly, provided for the buying and selling of commodities (including stock shares) at fixed prices over given periods of time. Similarly, futures contracts allowed for the buying and selling of commodities against anticipated rises and falls in spot prices. Almost always understood as purely speculative ventures despite their potential for managing risk, futures and options trades proliferated with the greater integration of the world economy by 1900, and indeed the standardization of commercial information, sent with unprecedented speed through the telegraph. This standardization powered Britain's dominant role in world finance and helped to sustain the free-trade faith even while it increasingly came under attack after 1900. Especially for British devotees of free trade, this new level of global integration also fueled the fear of destabilizing speculative ventures. However, according to the 1898 parliamentary inquiry, no general international consensus yet existed on the forms or even necessity for regulating or penalizing these types of speculation.

The Argentine commercial code, for example, allowed options and futures trades, but made losses on these contracts irrecoverable by law and made "gambling in stocks"—that is, the settling of differences in prices with no delivery of goods—an "illicit" transaction with "no legal effect."[8] Austria-Hungary promoted de jure but not de facto regulation; speculating and gambling were understood as mutually inclusive, and were illegal except in the case of merchants settling differences in prices among themselves (which, in fact, constituted the majority of futures trades).[9] In Belgium, contracts for agricultural goods that did not result in delivery were illegal, but trading in the rise and fall of securities prices was not.[10] Statutes passed in 1885 in France had also legalized time bargains in public and other securities and recognized "bargains for the delivery of provisions and agricultural produce" if "their *aim and object* is the actual delivery of the produce," although lack of delivery on such contracts was not penalized.[11] The Federal Code of Switzerland held a similar position, allowing time bargains except for those "which, in the guise of time bargains, are a mask for gambling operations": that is, those with "no intention of buying or selling" and "no delivery of goods."[12]

Legislation in Germany in 1896 was the most radical, prohibiting all futures trading done on established produce exchanges. German merchants in these exchanges rebelled by establishing "voluntary associations . . . outside the law" which operated as informal markets.[13] The British representative in Berlin sent a long note elaborating the "acute stage of things" in Germany, recounting the averse response of German merchants to this regulation and asserting that "time-bargains fulfilled a mission, valuable in itself, of equalizing and leveling differences of demand and supply."[14] The commercial codes of Greece, Russia, Sweden, and Norway, in contrast, made no mention at all of gambling in options and futures.[15] Finally, in a move characteristic of aggressive American capitalism, the United States Congress debated a bill legalizing options and futures contracts, with or without delivery. Introduced in the House of Representatives in December 1895, a bill for "regulating the sale of certain agricultural products, defining 'options' and 'futures' and imposing taxes thereon and upon dealers therein" wasted no time with the moral question of gambling, insisting rather that the state ought to profit from speculative practices.[16]

While the specific definitions of options and futures trading remained tentative, what can be inferred from these erratic strategies was the overarching interest in distinguishing legitimate market practices from gambling methods. In the United States and Britain, this boundary was drawn most clearly along lines of class. Liberal paternalism joined with market interests to protect the general public from get-rich-quick swindles of all sorts. In the late nineteenth and early twentieth century, such concerns were evident in the publication of manuals, moralistic tomes, and guidelines for futures trading.

Treatises like *Gold Bricks of Speculation* (1904), by John Hill, a member of the Chicago Board of Trade, claimed that "the success of the swindler in the guise of brokers, commission merchants, investment agencies, etc. is largely due to a misconception on the part of the public as to what speculation really is."[17] The work sought to distinguish between the gambling of "bucket-shops" (which duped small investors through the manipulation of price quotations), false corporations, pyramid schemes, and the like; and the regulated mechanism of the Chicago Board of Trade, the largest commodities exchange in the world. Surveying the entire landscape of false methods of investment and trade, this volume offered a series of explanatory chapters on legitimate commercial exchanges, their regulation, and the utility of futures trades, particularly those which were settled without delivery, "the strongest weapon in the hands of those opposed to 'futures.'"[18] The author explained that under standardized and uniform conditions, when contracts were executed "in the same manner and are exactly similar as to quantity or unit," and with the "intent . . . to deliver," delivery was often "idle and unnecessary."[19] Here, legitimate futures trades were those conducted on an official, organized, and respectable exchange. The validity of the futures contract was tied to its intent, which rendered the question of actual delivery inconsequential.

In Britain and India, the criticism of illicit futures trades focused more on the fact of nondelivery, particularly in the case of transactions regulated by the indigenous Indian mercantile law. More broadly, beginning in the 1890s in Britain, moralists and merchants alike became concerned with distinguishing legitimate speculation from its counterfeit. In 1902, a Parliamentary Select Committee was appointed "to inquire into the increase of public betting amongst all classes."[20] The public debate inspired by the inquiry sought definitions for new sorts of betting and wagering practices. For example, a volume which appeared a year after *Gold Bricks* entitled *Betting and Gambling: A National Evil*, published with the support of the York Anti-Gambling League, reiterated not only the usual concerns about working-class idleness but considered specifically the democratizing of market activity through the expansion of commercial information, the growth of joint stocks requiring lower minimum investments, and the popular appeal of false contrivances that mimicked commercial enterprise.[21]

Included among its articles on "the Ethics of Gambling," "Gambling Among Women," and "Gambling and Citizenship," a piece by the editor of the *Investor's Review* on "Stock Exchange Gambling" recounted the history of the "spirit of unbridled lust after unearned wealth" spreading throughout the general public.[22] Arguing that limited liability had broadened the horizons for popular investment, the author bemoaned the spread of fraudulent market information that had accompanied the expansion of public commercial information. This, along with the emergence of the £1 share, which had promoted the "excessive capitalization" of "all manner of enterprises," had ensured the swindling of masses of shareholders.[23] Still, the article's broader argument insisted that stock exchange regulation could not offer the most effective antidote to this growing menace. After a discussion on the impossibility of reforming the fundamental human drive for gain, and the productive place of speculation in the history of British trade and finance, the author insisted that the only "palliative" for the problem would be the strict regulation of public commercial information.[24] Reflecting the hesitation of official British policymakers in penalizing market practices, the argument offered a perspective relevant for the Indian context. In Britain, the standardization and regulation of commercial information presented an alternative to criminalizing new speculative activities; in India, the two trends coincided.

The Idea of the Market and the Ethics of Speculation in India

In the subcontinent, the growing public anxiety over gambling as an economic crime reflected, first, India's presence as an exporter of primary products in an increasingly integrated world market and, second, the greater standardization of its domestic economy. The expansion of the railway by the 1880s in particular mapped and regularized a broader web of exchange in primary goods.[25] As abroad, the introduction of the telegraph created an expanded and more efficient circulation of commercial information among both official sources and indigenous merchants. This revolution in internal transport and information also informed a supralocal experience of "the market": a newly imagined abstraction generated through a greater rationalizing of the material world and speed of exchange. Expanded commercialization and monetization of exchange in this period "steadily increased the capacity of bureaucrats, policy-makers, politicians, reformers and experts to capture and manipulate that central cognitive invention of capitalism, 'the economy.'"[26]

In the form of the free market specifically, the economy furthered a model of Nature itself as a system of balance and order, expressed as natural flows of supply and demand. By the early 1900s, this vision of British political economy came increasingly under attack by Indian nationalists, who critiqued free-market operations as the systematic drain of Indian wealth and sought instead state-sponsored national economic development.[27] And by 1905, the Swadeshi movement demanded an end to Britain's exploitative use of Indian resources, joining economic questions with nationalist imperatives. In that same year, the first Indian Industrial Conference, held at Benares alongside the meeting of the Indian National Congress, called for the expansion of commercial and industrial education, and the compilation of information on indigenous methods of trade, finance, and organization.[28] A year earlier, the Bengal Chamber of Commerce, a voice for British trade in Calcutta, put forward a scheme for a program of modern commercial education at Presidency College, and in 1905 the Commerce and Industry Department established the Commercial Intelligence Branch.[29] As the market became the corollary of the emerging Indian civil society, the question of legitimate commercial practices assumed greater prominence in public debates about gambling and market ethics, an index of the modern subject and citizen-to-be.

The question of gambling as a distortion of market practices resonated within a broader debate over Indian economic development. While the characterization of indigenous commercial practices as high risk and unproductive dated back to the eighteenth century, only in this later period did the issue attract public attention and government regulation. Histories of Indian capitalism have highlighted the ways in which caste and kinship-based commerce enabled subtle strategies of risk management. The business enterprise of the family firm managed diverse financial and trading portfolios in astute risk-minimizing arrangements. These were founded on the extensive access to capital and credit afforded by the family firm, a form of organization so protected against risk and so generative of investment that it precluded the necessity of the joint-stock association.[30] Still, historical attention to the techniques of local capitalisms informs, but does not override, questions concerning their legitimacy. In India, the criminalization of indigenous speculative methods reflected earlier trends in civil law on trade and charity: community, as family, kinship, and caste, was rendered incompatible with productive capital, and indeed became an alibi for the dark underbelly of market activity. As the market was institutionalized as a lived supralocal abstraction, it increasingly structured everyday experience, as did new distinctions between respectable and illegitimate trade. The categories of public and private, as before, informed this distinction and the corollary question it raised: was the market a game of skill, or was it sustained by an addiction to chance and risk?

Marwaris and Traditional Methods of Speculation and Hedging

While gambling was identified with major speculative markets and a variety of commercial groups across north India, Marwaris in particular became the focus of controversy, particularly in Calcutta. Like other north Indian commercial groups, Marwaris operated the intermediary trade between domestic producers and consumers and foreign exporters and importers. But they also had a long history in finance and speculation and gained vast fortunes in futures trading in the late nineteenth and early twentieth centuries; by the 1920s, these fortunes were invested in industrial enterprise. Marwari migration from their homeland in Rajasthan reflected the geography of antigambling legislation beginning in the 1880s. Migrating in large numbers to Bombay in the 1880s, and then to Calcutta beginning in the 1890s, they earned windfall profits through speculation, particularly in opium (with which they had been associated since the later part of the eighteenth century) and jute.[31] The first was a commodity whose exports to China were unstable and in decline by the early 1900s.[32] The second—raw jute and its products, such as hessian—was a sector of the world market controlled by India by 1920.[33] Marwaris first migrated to Bombay and the Deccan in central India with the cotton boom in the 1860s; and the bulk of migration to Bombay occurred earlier than Calcutta, in the period from 1860 to 1880.[34] By 1901, the Marwari population of Bombay was 7,000, and grew at a steady pace to 12,000 by 1911. In Calcutta, the Marwari population rose rapidly, from about 2,000 in 1891 to 15,000 in 1911.[35] By 1915, they had become the dominant force in the jute trade, operating as intermediary *banias*, that is, commission agents and financiers to British managing agencies trading in that commodity.[36]

Traditional institutions in Rajasthan, informal speculative markets were also popular among other trading groups with moneylending histories. In Bombay in the 1880s, the most prominent speculators were not Marwaris but rather Gujarati Hindus (of the *Bhatia* commercial caste), Parsis, and Muslims, particularly the Ismailis.[37] Indigenous methods of futures trading among all these communities combined speculative and hedging transactions, though they became increasingly associated with dangerous risk-taking activity. Historians have highlighted the speculative profits and accumulations of Marwaris and other groups but leave vague the various types of transactions that constituted speculation more generally. Their classification was intimately linked to the concern over public gambling, which remains unaddressed in Indian economic history.

Four basic types of *sowda* (a word meaning bargain, negotiation, or common-law contract) were associated with indigenous speculative practices.[38] First was the standard forward trade, the basic futures transaction that promised and settled delivery of a certain amount of a particular commodity on a given day. Futures trading more broadly was encompassed by the term *satta* (speculation) or the settling of multiple forward trades without delivery, either through payment or a reinstitution of the promise for delivery based on an adjusted commission rate.[39] Third were the *teji mundi* transactions, or what were called "trading in differences" by British observers.[40] C. A. Bayly has described the use of *teji mundi chittis* (letters or tickets prescribing ownership) in the early nineteenth-century opium trade. These, he explains, were "the nearest thing . . . in the Indian trade to joint-stock companies whose shares [were] sold in the market" although there was "no question of limited liability."[41] In effect, *tejimundi* transactions operated like the stock-jobbing practices on the London exchange, without the performance of actually buying shares. *Tejimundi chittis* would pass through the hands of merchants who would buy and sell units of commodities among themselves and profit (or lose) on price differences. Finally, *badni* transactions, a form of time-bargaining which was akin to options dealing, were particularly common in the grain market. These would secure the right to buy or sell commodities for a particular period of time at a fixed rate.

These practices and their variants were discovered and classified in police and public-gambling investigations between 1895 and 1920. All, at one time or another, were associated with either wagering on chance or with the games that were fixed and manipulated. This classification reflected the anxiety over economic crimes and legitimate market activity, as stated above, but also over the flourishing of new forms of recreational gambling which were not directly connected to market activity. Some of these new forms of wagering for amusement operated like lotteries, in which bets were taken on numbers; these were, in fact, games based on price quotations transmitted telegraphically. Other recreational gaming mimicked the conventions of business and was conducted in bazaar areas. These new types of gambling for amusement also fueled the interest in distinguishing between respectable and counterfeit trade. Indeed, illegitimate trading practices were first identified through the regulation of recreational gambling.

Bombay, 1887–1890: Defining the Gamble and the Wager

As stated above, the first acts regulating gambling in India addressed public disorder and the gathering of the populace in what were termed "common gaming-houses" located in town centers within a three mile radius of railway stations. This first set of regulations was passed between 1866 and 1868 in the various presidencies and provinces. Bombay Presidency was the first to amend these provisions. Legislation in 1887 extended their purview to areas outside of town centers, and in 1890, the Bombay legislature broadened the definition of gaming itself to include wagering. This development, in turn, set the stage for greater regulation of vernacular practices.

In an 1886 report, the commissioner of police in Bombay argued that gambling had spread outside the city of Bombay to its suburbs to "establishments where raw youths and old men (apparently respectable) daily resort to."[42] The act in operation, Bombay Act III of 1866, the Public Gambling Act, had provided for the search, seizure, arrest, and summary trials of people found in common gaming houses. The common gaming house was a "house, room, or place, in which cards, dice, tables or other instruments of gaming are kept or used for the profit or gain of the person owning, occupying, using or keeping such house, room, or place."[43] As with other statutes in British India, and indeed Britain, the 1866 act focused primarily on the potential for disorder in public gathering places and in streets; it did not penalize gambling or playing games for money in private houses.

The Bombay Prevention of Gambling Act (IV of 1887) amended the 1866 act by making it applicable to the island of Salsette, where gambling had spread, and by giving the governor general the prerogative to extend it to "any local area in the Presidency of Bombay."[44] The basic provisions of the 1866 act remained intact. In addition to providing for the arrest of the owner of the common gaming house, it established fines of up to Rs. 200 or one month's imprisonment for any person found in a common gaming house, who would be "presumed, until the contrary be made to appear, to have been there for the purposes of gaming."[45] In addition to the standard summary jurisdiction of such offenses, the act also allowed for broad rights of search and seizure. Any superintendent of police who had "reason to suspect any . . . place to be used as a common gaming-house" had the authority to empower an officer to enter, search, take all persons into custody, and seize all "instruments of gaming."[46] In a feat of circular reasoning, the statute also established that "when any cards, dice, gaming-table, counters, cloth, board or other instruments of gaming used in playing a game, not being a game of mere skill, are found in any house, room or place . . . it shall be evidence, until the contrary is made to appear, that such house . . . is used as a common gaming-house and that the persons found therein were there . . . for the purposes of gaming, although no play was actually seen by the Magistrate or Police Officer."[47] Suspects could also be taken into custody without evidence that they had been playing for any money; primary evidence consisted of the recovery of "instruments of gaming." Witnesses brought before the magistrate were also to be "freed from all prosecutions" for any involvement in gambling before the time of their testimony.[48]

In 1887, then, evidence of gambling was tied to the discovery of instruments of gaming and to the use of those instruments for a game that could be open to the public in general. Still, the distinction between private amusements and public gaming remained slippery, as the concerns of a letter of appeal sent to the Government of Bombay recounted: "Section 7 states that any room or house in which there are cards and dice is a gaming house and all persons in that house are gamblers. Unless dice or cards are defined all Hindus from the Himalaya . . . to Ceylon will be considered gamblers, because, when marriages take place the father of the bride gives to the bridegroom . . . play things . . . played either with cowries or dice and consequently these articles will be found in all Hindu houses and all the Hindus will be found playing with them during the Diwali Holidays and on other occasions when they have no work."[49] Pointing to the broad interventionary powers of the act, the appeal addressed the potential of regulating traditional forms of recreation. Still, in 1887, officials were less interested in traditional games than in potential for disorder in town centers. Thus, a member of the Bombay Governor's Council explained as he moved the first reading of the bill: "If Marwaris like to go on betting which of two kites will fly the higher, or which of two drops of rain will first fall from the eaves of a house, Government cannot stop them. But I think the Council will agree . . . that we do not want a Monte Carlo within twelve miles of Bombay, and that we ought to have the power to put down organised gambling establishments of this kind, which must exercise a most demoralising influence on the people."[50]

But by 1889, "rain gambling," a practice brought to Bombay by Marwaris, had come under attack. *Barsat ka satta*, literally, rain speculation, was a popular pastime in Rajasthan during the monsoon season. Coincident with the anticipation of rains in an extremely hot and dry desert climate, rain betting took many forms. Bets would be wagered on how much rain would fall in a particular time period, or when the rains would come and for how long. A recreation widespread in Rajasthan, it was largely associated with migrants from Jaipur and Ajmer States, commercial men who introduced it to their clients and colleagues. Most rain gambling occurred informally, among friends. As its popularity heightened, the practice also became an organized pastime, with commercial men running betting stalls that followed standardized procedures: the clouds and sky would be examined three times a day and bets taken accordingly within set time limits. While some such betting operations were given to deception, many operated as small-scale public lotteries. The growing concern over rain gambling focused both on its concerted promotion of risk taking through wagering and on its deceptive potential as an organized recreation run by tight-knit coteries, most often of traders and bazaar merchants. The prohibition of rain gambling thus betrayed concerns over indigenous commercial practice and ethics first in Bombay, and later, as we shall see, in Calcutta.

In July of 1889, the Government of Bombay introduced a bill to amend the Bombay Prevention of Gambling Act of 1887. Its Statement of Objects and Reasons insisted that "the prevalence of a new form of gambling, known as 'Barsat ka Satta,' wagering on the rainfall . . . has caused incalculable harm and has had a very demoralizing effect, particularly on the youths of the City of Bombay . . . [and] has even attracted gamblers from the Mofussil."[51] The bill was introduced in response to a series of events beginning in 1888 in connection with the closing of a large and conspicuous conglomeration of rain gamblers in downtown Bombay. In October, an establishment run by two Gujaratis, Narotamdas Motiram and Hemraj Khimji, was raided by police and declared a common gaming house. According to the police evidence, the enterprise maintained a highly organized system of wagering which depended upon "instruments of gaming," such as the rain gauge:

> Narotamdas . . . rented a large shed near Mowbadevi for the purpose of what is called Rain-Gambling and has paid to the owner a sum of Rs.

6,600 in advance, . . . one year's rent. The shed is divided into about 31 stalls which are sublet to different persons at rents ranging from Rs. 161 to Rs. 130 per mensem. These stalls are used for the purpose of registering bets or wagers for or against a fall of rain within a particular period of time. The stall-keepers register bets and very often register themselves.

Two principal appliances are used for the purposes of the betting . . . One . . . [is] a rain-gauge. It is admittedly used for betting purposes only, and is no sense a scientific instrument. The other . . . is a mere wooden gutter or trough inclined at a certain angle and attached to the roof of the house. Bets are laid whether within a certain time water will flow from the so-called rain-gauge, . . . or whether the flow of rain-water will or will not strike a certain wooden cone in falling from the gutter. . . . The odds depend on the state of weather, and there is a current bazaar rate which is publicly offered. The betting house is frequented by a large number of persons . . . as many as 500 to 700 . . . at a time.

Large sums of money change hands and the stall keepers make a profit by exacting a commission. The betting is chiefly for cash, but accounts are opened with known customers.[52]

However, the chief magistrate of Bombay acquitted Motiram and Khimji, arguing that while the law had prohibited gambling as a form of *gaming*, it had not specifically prohibited *betting or wagering* of any kind. The government then appealed to the Bombay High Court, where the decision of the chief magistrate was sustained.[53] The High Court opinions all asserted that gambling in both Britain and India referred to a variety of activities of "many kinds and degrees . . . and the Legislature has, in fact, drawn a marked distinction between them."[54] Gambling as wagering, they argued, referred broadly to betting on an outcome of pure chance; it did not include risk taking as a participant in a game, sport, or contest (such as a card game, where participation always included potential for manipulation).

In his judgment, the chief magistrate undertook an examination of the many meanings of *gambling* in colloquial and legal usage. While the term applied generally to "forbidden games," it also included legal lotteries, raffles, and wagering on sports such as horse racing, a pastime popular in British clubs throughout India. Gambling was "also used in popular language to denote commercial speculation in transactions dependent wholly or partially on chance."[55] Referring to indigenous *tejimundi* transactions, and trading in differences in stock exchanges, he explained that "what is sometimes termed gambling on the stock exchange is a familiar illustration of the popular use of this term; and transactions commonly known as opium and cotton betting (*aphin-ka-satta, kapus-ka-satta*) are of much the same general character.... The essence of this kind of speculation is that it depends on what is practically pure chance, and those who take part in it can by no skill or efforts of their own exercise any control over the result."[56]

While the case's public prosecutor had deployed the public/private distinction, arguing that the Motiram's establishment was a public betting house and that it posed a threat to the community, the chief magistrate and High Court judges insisted that the main question remained the distinction between gaming and wagering. Indeed, the attorney for the defense had even admitted that the accused ran a public betting house but that betting per se was not illegal. Citing authorities on history of gambling legislation in Britain, the magistrate asserted that in British common law, all games and wagering were "prima facie lawful," and that the history of legislation in Britain made clear that only gaming associated with public disorder had been criminalized: "There can ... be no gaming in the technical sense unless there be a game. The making of a bet cannot ... be called playing at a game. Gaming and betting are essentially different things, and have always been very differently regarded by the Legislature. These considerations will show that wagering at horse-races ... on other popular contrivances for promoting betting, are in India at present perfectly legal, however objectionable they may be deemed on grounds of public morality."[57]

In addition, Justice Jardine of the Bombay High Court argued that a rain gauge could not be construed as an instrument of gaming: the device "registers quantity just as the watch in the hand of the Judge at a horse-race registers time, or as a thermometer is used to register heat or a barometer the pressure of the atmosphere. Its use resembles further the use of these instruments in that it does not introduce any element of chance into the betting."[58] Furthermore, Hindu law mirrored British law before 1845, "when wagers were considered lawful contracts, although particular descriptions of them, such as gaming with dice, cards, &c., were rendered illegal by statute."[59] Similarly, the chief magistrate objected to the flexible interpretation of an "instrument of gaming" required to penalize the defendants: "For all I know to the contrary bets may have been laid whether the accused in the present case will be convicted or discharged by the Chief Presidency Magistrate, but I trust that my present judgment may not be deemed an 'instrument of gaming' merely because some bets may be dependent on it."[60] Another High Court judge argued that a game required a "contest" and "an active participation of certain persons." But neither element was present in rain gambling, in which "the operation of nature . . . is brought within easy observation by the gauge or the gutter to wager on its uncertainty. But there is no contest, no players, and no participation by the betters save as on-lookers."[61]

These decisions incited the Bombay legislature to take action, and in late 1889, a bill to amend the Bombay Prevention of Gambling Act of 1887 was introduced in the Bombay Council. Passed in May 1890, the amending act opened the definition of gaming to "include wagering." It also provided for the first time a definition for instruments of gaming, which referred broadly to "any article used as a subject or means of gaming."[62] This was a radical departure from both British and Indian precedent. Wagering could now be penalized as a public nuisance—one which, according to the advocate general of Bombay, caused people to squander vast sums of their own, as well as those "entrusted to [clerks and employees] by their masters."[63]

The 1890 Bombay measure set the stage for the amendment of gambling legislation in other parts of India. This introduction of wagering into the law on public gambling informed a growing debate over the legitimacy of speculative practices, or market wagers, and the ethics of saving and spending more generally. This debate emerged in Bengal in the late 1890s with a wave of criticism over the spread of rain betting, run largely by Calcutta's Marwari community. Ironically, in the case of *Empress v. Narotamdas Motiram*, the chief magistrate had argued that speculation on commodities and shares was, like rain betting, perfectly legal because it qualified as wagering: that is, as an activity based on chance and so not open to criminal manipulation or fixing. Even before wagering was criminalized in Bombay in 1890, market speculation had been interpreted as an engagement with chance, rather than an exercise of skill.

Thus, before 1890, the definition used by judicial authorities to distinguish illegal forms of gambling from speculation tended to codify it as a risky endeavor. This association between market speculation and the play of chance (as opposed, for example, to hedging, or risk-minimizing activities) re-emerged in the Calcutta public debate over rain betting, which generated a rich discussion on market ethics. Was gambling on the fall of rain homologous with speculative practices? If so, did rain gambling threaten to spread bad habits that were intrinsic to market speculation, habits that promoted the very idea of the market as a dice game, rather than as a rational system? The discussion over rain gambling in Calcutta brought together three issues: the question of gambling and public disorder, the relationship between wagering and market speculation in general, and the relationship between wagering and indigenous speculative practices in particular.

Calcutta, 1896–1897: The Bengal Rain-Gambling Act, Public Debates, and Marwari Protest

The first public report of rain gambling in Bengal appeared in 1894 during a period of accelerated Marwari migration to Calcutta. In the August monsoons of 1894, Sir John Lambert, the commissioner of police, submitted an official note on rain gambling, emphasizing that the activity was concentrated in the Burrabazar area of northern Calcutta. Burrabazar was Calcutta's wholesale and speculative commercial center, dominated and inhabited by Marwaris, who had settled there as early as the 1860s. Since the police had from their very first investigations declared rain gambling an issue of public disorder in north Calcutta, it is important to establish a basic picture of its commercial and spatial geography. Beginning in the 1870s, Marwaris started buying up land in the area, pushing out established wealthy Bengali landlords.[64] Geographically, Burrabazar was a classic South Asian bazaar area, approximately two square kilometers in size, and structured by narrow lanes, alleyways, crowded market spaces, and roads bustling with people transporting goods. Architecturally, houses were most often built around courtyards, with doorways and front rooms leading onto streets. Marwari homes and places of business overlapped. The agents of the firm would conduct their business in their offices or *gaddis* located in front rooms facing streets, where the firms' *munims* or accountants would be found. Shops and showrooms would also be located at the front, and *godowns* were situated either on the other side of the entry way or at a back entrance.[65] In Calcutta and elsewhere, speculation markets were held in places called *baras*. These were closed courtyards or alleyways, which could be entered through guarded doorways that opened onto streets. Inside, the *baras* were lined with small stalls and could be as rowdy as the floor of any officially organized commodities exchange. Marwari agents sat cross-legged on cushions negotiating deals, while *chaprasis* (runners) carried sales information between them. The center of Burrabazar was without doubt the *Aphin Chowrasta*, or the "Opium Crossing": at the intersection of Cotton and Mullick streets, which by the late 1890s had become the center of speculation in cotton and opium particularly but which also included *baras* for all the other major commodities.[66]

The 1894 Police Commissioner's Report recounted the history of rain gambling in Calcutta as an effect of Marwari presence in that city:

> Rain gambling was first introduced by the Marwaris about 20 years ago. They are born gamblers, and are certain to have play and wagering of some kind or another. It has always been confined to one part of the town, viz., to Cotton Street. Up to 1882 or thereabouts, Marwaris who engaged in rain gambling used to assemble on the street.... This led to obstruction of one of the crowded thoroughfares; so the leading Marwari opened out premises in that street, No. 67 [Cotton Street], containing a large courtyard, where the gamblers could assemble.
>
> ... In 1867 there was only one betting house. About 12 years ago, a second house opened, and in 1891 a third house: all these close to one another.
>
> In former years betting was chiefly confined to Marwaris. Gradually others have been attracted, and now crowds of all races collect: Europeans, Arabs, East Indians, West Indians, Native Christians, Jews, Hindus, Muhammadans, Arabs, native females, and even children.[67]

Like the description of the major rain gambling establishment of Bombay, this report also focused on its organized nature, and indeed its mimicking of indigenous commercial practice: "Attached to the gaming house are a certain number of *modees* or *baniahs* [agents] who register bets for the proprietor; and they charge the proprietor a commission of one pice [1/4 of an *anna*, which was 1/16 of a rupee] on each ruppee won, and also a commission of one anna to the ruppee to the successful wagerer."[68] Moreover, the police commissioner recounted, aside from one major opponent, the respectable Marwari merchants of the area remained uninterested in the issue: "Of the respectable residents in Cotton Street, Sheubux Bogla, a rich [Marwari] man, whose house is close to no. 67, Cotton Street, is the chief opponent. Also a few others, but as a rule, I do not find that the respectable native gentlemen of that part of the town care much about it. Still the state of things is such that a scandal may at any time arise."[69]

On July 6, 1895, Surendranath Banerji, the prominent Congress leader, introduced the question of rain gambling in the Bengal Legislative Council. Contrary to the initial police report, he claimed that the practice had become a "serious nuisance to the respectable inhabitants of the neighborhood where it was carried on." But the lieutenant-governor, Sir Charles Elliot, refused to consider such a measure, arguing that it would be "practically impossible to put down betting in private houses." While reformists like Banerji were interested in providing legal mechanisms for penalizing rain betting establishments as common gaming houses, Elliot had insisted that they were *private* spaces that were not obviously open to regulation. On the other hand, the lieutenant-governor also asserted that "if the particular form it [gambling] has taken . . . were stopped, it would break out in some other form, and if driven to secrecy, it might be even more harmful than if practiced openly." Thus, while Elliot supported a laissez-faire response to this "private" pastime, he also explained that rain betting was indeed conducted openly. The difficulty in mapping this recreation within social space reflected the confusion over whether rain betting qualified as innocuous private amusement or infectious public recreation.[70] This would become a crucial point of debate in 1896–1897, as the issue drew wider public attention.

Nine months after Surendranath Banerji raised the question in the Bengal Legislative Council, in April of 1896, the Government of Bengal received a memorial from "about 200 residents of the neighborhood of the gambling houses" complaining about the acute nature of the problem. The memorial, which was promptly passed on to the Home Department in Delhi, was a one-page condemnation of the "vicious practice of rain-gambling." It argued that "many leading native bankers and merchants addicted to it have ruined themselves and become bankrupts, and . . . they have brought also untold misery upon their families by their extravagant expenditure in [this] pursuit."[71] Moreover, the memorial narrated the threat to public morality through the corruption of indigenous women, a theme which would become a leitmotif in antigambling discourse: "Many young women of respectable parentage, given to this habit, have been spoilt, and have had recourse to means of bad livelihood."[72] Finally, the document asserted that rain gambling did not operate as an innocent game determined purely by chance, but rather as a conscious manipulation. Thus they submitted that "the rain gamblers of Calcutta who have formed themselves into a league ... are a dishonest set of people and deceive the players in sundry ways. They have in their employ a man named Shivanunda Tewary, who though formerly by profession a cook, has amassed several lakhs [several hundred thousand] of rupees as their agent." Calling upon the Government of Bengal to take action, the memorialists demanded legislative checks "in the interests of public morality."[73]

After reviewing another report from the commissioner of police, which confirmed the growing popularity of rain gambling, the Bengal government circulated the memorial to five prominent civic associations for opinions over the summer of 1896. All but one responded that legislation was necessary, since rain gambling had spread "to a large class of people who are not Marwaris."[74] Beginning in September, when it became clear that the government was contemplating legislation to suppress rain gambling, virtually all the major Calcutta English-language newspapers published articles and editorials on what seemed to have become Calcutta's favorite pastime.[75] Some native-owned newspapers were interested in exposing the potential for police oppression in such statutes. More broadly, they condemned the hypocrisy of the Bengal government, and indeed the Government of India, which protected wagering on horses and conducted trade (most particularly in opium) that promoted wagering in futures prices. While some journals warned against legislating morality, others insisted only on consistency of policy: if the government was going to outlaw rain gambling, then it ought to address all of its other forms, including those connected with trade.

Commenting on the broad powers of the police, a September 1896 editorial in the nationalist *Amrita Bazar Patrika* argued, for example, that under the current gambling law, "it is only the poor natives who suffer" under police inspection. It agreed that while rain gambling was "a great evil," the "remedy ... may be worse than the disease."[76] Two days later, an article in that paper emphasized that Surendranath Banerji had been forcing his will in the Calcutta Corporation, a municipal organization that had supported anti–rain gambling legislation. According to the report, other prominent Bengali members, such as Bhupendra Nath Bose, had been prevented from "criticis[ing] the administration" on the issue of gambling. Again, rather than accepting the gambling question as an issue of public disorder, the paper redirected the question towards a critique of the government's investment in wagering. In the process, it argued that gambling and wagering in commodities and shares were one and the same, and that moral condemnation, rather than containment of dangerous elements in Burrabazar, ought to be the central focus of public discussion.[77] An article published six months later, just before the rain gambling bill was introduced, argued again that the "chief objection" was "on the score of police oppression" and that "the subordinate police should not be furnished with another engine to interfere with the liberty of the subject."[78] As the paper expressed concern about governmental transgressions of civil liberties, it confirmed that gambling included market-based speculation of all kinds.

Other papers also insisted that the practice of rain gambling remained almost indistinguishable from commercial activities, but did so in order to *legitimate* both and expose the futility of potential regulations. The *Hindu Patriot*, whose editor, Kristodas Pal, was active in the loyalist British Indian Association, also entered the debate in September.[79] An editorial on rain gambling agreed that "the promoters of the legislation are inspired by honorable motives" and that "no one would deny that gambling has been among the besetting sins of the human race since the earliest of times, [as] the pages of the *Mahabharata* . . . bear melancholy evidence." But nevertheless, gambling remained a common amusement, a tolerated evil practiced not only "on the sly in the drawing-room," but on the race track and during the holiday of Diwali, when it would be "elevated to the dignity of a time-honored custom." Arguing that legislation in Bombay had been passed not on moral concerns, but as a response to nonpayment, the *Patriot* insisted that "no nation can be made virtuous by Acts of Parliament. . . . The attempt to stop rain-gambling is . . . positively unintelligible in the absence of any attempt to stop other forms of gambling." Thus they claimed rhetorically, that "if rain-gambling is to be stopped . . . then . . . 'forward' transactions of every kind, whether in Government papers, gold and other shares, or jute or opium or indeed in any other kind of produce . . . ought to be suppressed also."[80]

In early October 1896, the *Statesman* reprinted an article from the *Indian Empire*, in which the correspondent had described his visit to the largest rain-gambling establishment in Burrabazar.[81] This exposé left the question of legislation unaddressed but offered rather a titillating peek into the elusive gambling community. Evoking the patterns of indigenous business, it exposed a curious and closed economic culture:

> I entered by a door, quite wide. . . . I was in a position to have a complete view of the spacious quadrangle where stood about fifty persons. They all looked as if negotiating . . . some business. All around the quadrangle, there are wooden platforms under tin sheds, divided into separate stalls, about twenty in number. . . . I noticed one word was being uttered by everyone,—it was *khayaga*, which literally means "will you eat?" What could this signify? . . . I don't know if the shrewd Marwari would at once detect me for a newcomer. Here a person . . . handed over a four-anna bit to a stall-keeper. The little shining thing was held up in the hand, and the stall-keeper kept on crying out for about two minutes, *puchis me khayaga* (will you eat at twenty-five); *khaya khaya* (I have eaten, I have eaten) was heard from the crowd. The crier stopped vociferating, opened his *khatta* [account] book . . . and made certain entries.[82]

After describing the crowd, consisting of natives as well as Eurasian and European *topiwallas* (hat-wearers, or non-natives), the author went on to explain the complicated anticipations and transactions involved in settling a wager. Sometimes there would be no cash exchange. "You took ten rupees from the Saheb to pay to that Marwari if it does not rain, but you did not take anything from the Marwari to pay the Saheb if it rains," the author asked of one Jalji, a broker. "That Marwari is known to us," Jalji replied. "He is a man of money and has his *guddi* [office] in Burra Bazar."[83] The dialogue considered in some detail Marwaris' potential for unfair advantage in the game, an edge secured by closed credit and represented benignly by the informant as risk management:

> 'Supposing if I [the reporter] were to do as that Marwari has done in this transaction, would I have to deposit fifty rupees with you?'
>
> 'Oh, yes, certainly. Otherwise the transaction would not be complete. But there are some Bengalee Baboos whom we know well and to whom we give credit. The fact is, like every other business, we take cash when we think it is unbusiness [*sic*] like to do otherwise.'
>
> 'Then, betting against rain is pretty much confined to Marwaris and a few others who are well known to you?'
>
> 'Why? Anybody is at liberty to bet against rain, that is, to accept the

HEDGING BETS   165

responsibility of paying if it rains. Known persons only have credit—that's all.'

'Then you mean to say that, if it does not rain today, that Marwari will earn ten rupees without having to deposit anything, whereas any other men, not known to you, would have to deposit fifty rupees with you if he meant to earn that amount of ten rupees[?]'

'Exactly so.' . . .

' . . . You say [the] Marwari can gamble without cash, while all others must deposit cash with you. Is this not an advantage to some extent to your own people?'

'No doubt, it is. But I think known customers are allowed credit in every other business. Is this not so?'

. . . Our conversation . . . had to be given up owing to an interesting event. All of a sudden there was a rush of a large crowd in the quadrangle. All eyes were turned upwards towards the heavens. . . . It was then nine o'clock. There was something like the buzzing of ten thousand bees.

' . . . Sir, some rainy clouds have appeared on the horizon. . . . Those on the terrace, who are called the *Rungbaz* experts, are making signs. The rate has come down. . . . The anti-rain parties are now anxious to make their way out of the difficulty. Look there, that Marwari comes and wants now to be *for* rain! That's the way to lessen his responsibility.'

. . . There was a heavy fall of rain at about ten.[84]

The account narrated classic tropes: the customs of Marwari business flowed easily into gambling conventions, and vice versa. Access to credit reserves, as well as a shared internal knowledge of the rhythms of the game, revealed how community ties might influence outcomes. The journalist's investigation of Marwari recreation, then, shed light on the operation of their slippery commercial habits and rendered the community itself a topic of public discussion. This account, like others, exposed a malaise over community and family as a structure for legitimate trade. In Bombay, the discourse on rain betting had provoked a discussion primarily about the relationship between the gamble and the just trade; in Calcutta, however, this debate was supplemented by a concern over community as the mechanism for business. The focus on the Marwaris and their customs in particular publicly produced an anthropology of the community, which had by the late 1890s dominated virtually all forms of indigenous trade in Calcutta. Indeed, kinship-based economic organization seemed to produce a biological predisposition to the aleatory, and to cheating. Responding to another article in the *Hindu Patriot*, which had asserted that "no foul play was practiced in [rain] gambling,"[85] the *Statesman* explained that it was among the European, Eurasian, and non-Marwari native community, "rather than among the Marwaris, with whom speculation of the kind is second nature, that [rain gambling was] productive of the most mischief, economic and moral."[86]

Another exposé appeared a few days later on October 9 in the generally loyalist and native-owned *Indian Mirror*. "The literature on rain-gambling is steadily growing," this op-ed began. The author recounted his firsthand experience at the "den at Burra Bazar," which he had visited for "five days in succession." Referencing particularly the charitable activities of the owners of the establishment and the Marwari production of status and respectability, the account wove rain gambling into the texture of indigenous mercantile culture: "The gamblers, I soon found, are not the demons that I had expected them to be. Some of them are even pious according to their lights. Old Tewary [the infamous and prosperous ex-cook of the citizens' memorial], almost an octogenarian, daily feeds a large number of *Sadhus* [holy beggars].... Contributions are sent to the Pinjrapole [animal shelter] at Sodepore. The agitation [against rain gambling], I learnt, has been set afoot by a man from Allahabad, who came to open a shop on his own account" and who refused to give a deposit of Rs. 10,000 demanded by the owners of the rain gambling establishments. "Tewary is strictly honorable in meeting the bets lost by the acceptors. The statement that only rich people are paid, and the poor are sent away with the aid of sticks, is utterly false."[87]

Furthermore, the article highlighted the practical difficulties of regulating gambling of all sorts, including stock markets and futures trades. Chance and uncertainty had always captured the imagination and informed a variety of everyday activities and experiences. Thus gambling ought to be condemned through moral education, rather than legislation and police intervention:

> Do not take me for a friend of the gamblers.... Human nature seeks to pry into the future. Hence Astrology and other sciences, true or false I do not care.... I shall not speak of betting on the turf, and the ruin it frequently leads to. I shall not speak of the operations of the stock

market.... I shall speak, however, of the mercantile world. Are there not such things as forward transactions? Jute is bought and sold along before the ground is tilled to receive a single seed.... It is not known who will win, and who will lose by the time of delivery. There is nothing in these transactions that can take them out of the category of gambling.

Is there a merchant that disapproves of such transactions?... The fact is, there is nothing in ethical science that condemns the courting of chance.... But acquisition of wealth should not be easy. There should be labor—hard labor—for acquiring wealth.... Gambling ... creates a desire to incur risk.... Hence loss, and even ruin.[88]

Like many voices in the debate over rain gambling in September and October 1896, this op-ed agreed that there was little distinction between gambling, wagering, and everyday market practices.

Marwaris themselves furthered this assertion in their appeals, which together constituted the first major civic performance of any Marwari community in India. In February of 1897, a petition to the new lieutenant-governor, signed by 1,290 persons, spoke on behalf of "the undersigned Citizens and Residents of Calcutta, Members of the Marwari Community." Dated February 9, this long document addressed the accusations of the earlier memorial, first objecting to the allegation that rain gambling had caused ruin in the "Commercial World." Further, it asserted that tales of the ruin of native women were fabrications that libeled all native communities, who "guard their females jealously." Thirdly, the memorialists denied that rain gambling was practiced as a fixed game: "The rain is independent of human control. So is the overflowing.... There is not one body which habitually bets in favour, and another habitually against rain. *Each person* bets according to his inclination. This is all. In what way is cheating possible?"[89]

After also rebutting that rain gambling caused a public nuisance, the petition then delved into the ethics of trade. Agreeing with popular opinions that held that "every man is a gambler by nature," the memorialists cited the common European pastimes of card playing and horse racing.[90] In addition, "transactions recognised as legitimate by law and society, specially, such as relate to stocks and shares, to opium, and even to commodities of commerce and trade," the petitioners insisted, "fully partake of the nature of gambling, inasmuch as gain and loss in these cases are determined by events of chance." Echoing the opinion of Sir Charles Elliot in 1895, the memorial concluded with the assertion that if rain gambling were made illegal, even more dangerous forms of gambling would emerge in secret.[91]

However, rather than confirming the innocuous nature of the recreation, this argument only nurtured suspicions about the risky, unfair, and imprudent nature of Marwari commercial practices. Thus, the mover of the Bengal Bill for the Suppression of Rain-Gambling warned that "it is possible as they [the Marwaris] anticipate, that the Marwaris will devise some new form of gambling on its suppression. They have ... introduced in Bombay a system of betting on the number of cotton bales sold daily in the London market, not unlike the well-known betting on the prices realised at the Government opium sales in Calcutta [*tejimundi* speculations]."[92] The discourse on rain gambling opened a reproach and regulation of vernacular market conventions. Government critics, for example, emphasized that notions of community and caste obligation challenged, rather than informed, commercial and social respectability. Thus the mover of bill claimed that "the Government has reason to know that the more respectable Marwari residents would be glad to see this gambling suppressed, although they are prevented by caste obligations from openly announcing their view."[93] Official rhetoric confirmed that Marwari caste networks precluded not only legitimate commercial practice, but civic performance.

The February 1897 Marwari memorial, in contrast, offered itself as a public statement of organized citizens. Speaking out against the government validation of a personal feud, the petitioners argued that anti–rain gambling forces had acted on private and dishonorable motives: "The prime-mover in the matter is an individual who has been actuated by malice against Babu Shew Nandan Tewary, the lessee of the house where the bets are principally made." Marwaris drew a distinction between themselves and their petty accusers, failed competitors in the rain gambling trade. Emphasizing that the April 1896 antigambling memorial was "not a genuine expression of honest indignation or right feeling," they attempted to undermine its legitimacy as a civic statement: "Signatures are easily obtained, for envy and jealousy are important factors in human conduct."[94]

The Marwari memorial went unanswered as the Legislative Council prepared to introduce the Bill for the Suppression of Rain-Gambling in March of 1897. Five days before the meeting of the council, a letter from one Babu Premsook Das, who claimed to be a "Member of the Rain-Gambling Managing Committee," attached yet another memorial from the Marwari community, along with a letter and clippings from many of the newspaper articles cited above. The letter again addressed the spuriousness of the earlier petition lambasting rain gambling: "It is no exaggeration to say that that memorial has been signed by a number of nondescripts many of whom have sentiments of private grudge against Babu Sew Nandan Tewary, the lessee of the house in which bets are principally made."[95] The attached Marwari memorial, dated February 15 and signed by 910 persons "of various callings," reiterated the points made in the February 9 petition, including their judgment that the anti–rain gambling forces had "made personal reflections of the most reckless kind against Babu Shew Nandan Tewary."[96] While reasserting that chance informed all sorts of legitimate activities, this document also posited that rain gambling demanded skill, and even scientific knowledge: "Rain-gambling conduces to the promotion of science which no other form of betting does, in that your memorialists have on that account devoted much time to the study of metereology [!], with the result that in many parts of the *country*, if not generally, their reports as to the likelihood of a fall of rain are more highly valued and relied on than the reports of the Metereological Department, and your Memorialists would gladly place their reports at the disposal of Government."[97]

    The Legislative Council remained unpersuaded and introduced the bill on March 20, 1897. Unlike the Bombay Act of 1890, which had inserted wagering of all sorts into the definition of gambling, the Bengal Bill sought specifically to criminalize rain gambling as a form of public gambling, identifying the betting establishments as common gaming houses and rain gauges as instruments of gaming: "All that [the bill] insists upon is that if the Marwaris choose to indulge in gambling, they shall not be permitted to do so in houses where the public is invited."[98] The suppression of rain gambling thus emerged as a measure concerning public disorder, one which intended only to prevent private recreation from becoming a public nuisance. As the president of the Bengal Council argued, "Marwaris [may] remain in their own courtyards and have as many of their European friends as they please . . . and bet away til midnight if they like, provided [they do not run] common-gaming house[s]."[99] The bill, the lawmakers claimed, did "not attempt to regulate people's conduct by any moral considerations whatever. It aims simply and solely at a matter of Police."[100] The Government of Bengal thus resisted the public criticism, articulated in a spate of editorials following the introduction of the bill, that it was seeking to legislate morality with repressive measures.[101]

Rather than manage slippery definitions of gaming and wagering, and so engage in moral debate, the bill deployed the categories of public and private to enforce security. The discourse both for and against rain gambling had characterized it as a recreation of the innately risk-taking Marwari community. Like a peculiar sort of esoteric custom, it would be allowed only as private amusement and was considered dangerous when organized for the public in general. If Marwari kinship-based commercial organization made private what ought ideally to be public contractual exchange, its leisure practices made public what ought to have been private pecadillos.

Moreover, the rain-gambling scandal evinced suspicions of community and caste-based civic performance that claimed public import. Thus, lawmakers ignored the self-construction of Marwaris as a body of "citizens of Calcutta" protesting the government's validation of a personal feud.[102] This civic performance became more elaborate as the bill passed through the council. On March 26, in what the *Indian Daily News* called a "monster protest meeting" at the Dalhousie Institute, and which continued on the next day at the large courtyard of the main rain gambling establishment at No. 68 Cotton Street, a mass of Marwaris settled on six resolutions to be sent to the government.[103] According to a detailed article in the *Statesman*, which printed the texts of the resolutions, "long before the meeting opened, the hall was literally packed from one end to the other, there being scarcely any room for the large number who flocked around every passage." The "most orderly" gathering consisted of a wide variety of respectable commercial men, including "leading merchants, shroffs, bankers, tradesmen and heads of firms."[104] The speeches for the chairman and the movers of the resolutions had been written in English and were read by volunteer English speakers, then translated.[105] The resolutions addressed police oppression, asked for a more impartial inquiry into the practice of rain gambling, declared the anti–rain gambling memorial to be "'reckless, exaggerated and misleading,'" and denied any allegations of bankruptcy or commercial disruption. The fifth resolution was the most daring, proposing that the "Marwari community of Calcutta abstain . . . altogether from having anything to do with Government opium sales [and] *teji mundi* speculations" for at least one day, and then consider the possibility of a longer strike.

Calling the government's bluff succeeded temporarily. The Legislative Council agreed to postpone the discussion of the rain gambling bill until the next week, and the Marwaris continued their opium speculations. The public debate continued, with major English newspapers and native vernacular papers offering their opinions on the bill.[106] On April 3, the Bengal Rain-Gambling Act was hurriedly passed before the coming of the next monsoon.[107] On the 6th, Hukmi Chand Chowdury, the chairman of the Marwari Public Meeting, sent a telegram of protest to the secretary to the Government of India in the Legislative Department. On the 9th, a new memorial from the "Marwari Community of Calcutta, assembled at a Public Meeting, held at no. 68, Cotton Street on the 9th day of April, 1897" was sent to Elgin, the viceroy. The Bengal government swiftly wrote to the viceroy, explaining that "the meeting at which the memorial was adopted *was not a public but a private one*, and . . . it was thus of no importance."[108] Community again had precluded the possibility of civic expression. The viceroy signed the act on May 10, and on the 18th of that month, Chowdhury again sent a Marwari protest telegram, this time all the way to the secretary of state for India in London, but to no avail.

Punjab Province and the City of Delhi, 1898–1900: Opium Gambling and Early Surveys of Indigenous Speculative Practices

The rain gambling agitation in Bengal drew attention to elusive indigenous commercial arrangements in areas of north India in the late 1890s. In Bengal, a wide variety of appeals *opposing* the Rain-Gambling Act—from those offered by nationalists concerned about police repression, to vernacular newspapers condemning the hypocrisy of the government, to the Marwaris themselves—had insisted that gambling and trade were mutually inclusive endeavors. This assertion, ironically, produced a greater interest in customary trading practices and counterfeit contracts.

In December of 1898, Rai Bahadur Madan Gopal, a member of the Punjab Legislative Council, introduced the question of suppressing rain gambling in that province. While there had been no public outcry, and indeed little evidence that this habit had infected that region, a bill was drafted to amend the Punjab Public Gambling Act of 1867 to incorporate rain gambling within its provisions. The governor of Punjab then sent the draft bill to "all Commissioners and Superintendents of Divisions" for comment, asking each specifically to outline the extent of the rain gambling problem.[109]

What emerged was less a confirmation that the scourge of Calcutta had spread westward than a confused survey of speculative practices and games of chance in the small trading entrepôts of Punjab Province and in its major commercial center, Delhi. The inquiry into the extent of rain gambling began a process of enumerating spurious forms of mercantile practice that had remained unregulated by commercial and financial statute. As responses were returned to the governor throughout 1899, it became clear that the more important questions for district commissioners and superintendents concerned the legitimacy of various sorts of *teji mundi* and *badni* transactions, particularly in the opium and grain markets. The inquiry into gambling opened broader questions about unstandardized trading procedures and the need for more stable criteria distinguishing between criminal and legitimate transactions.

Most responses simply stated that they could not find evidence of rain gambling in their districts, but that the bill would be of great benefit for Punjab, suppressing as it did a most "objectionable practice."[110] But areas that included bustling entrepôts offered more elaborate speculations. The deputy commissioner of the Gujarat Division confirmed that rain gambling was virtually unknown in that region but did give an account of his experiences in Rajputana and in the town of Rewari in Gurgaon District, about forty miles southwest of Delhi, a junction in the textile and grain trade between Punjab and the United Provinces:

> I do not remember it [rain gambling] in the present Lahore or Rawalpindi Division. Something of the kind was rampant, however, in the country between Ajmere and Meerut about 1893 ... and was based in the Ajmere sales of opium, I think, as well as those of Calcutta.... In Rewari ... there were then, I was informed, several rather well-to-do traders of the Aggarwal and Dhussar communities (I think) who made this form of speculation their chief business. It was looked upon as a kind of 'Badni,' or time-bargaining, and was hardly reprobated, probably because it required some capital and was so not likely to lead the younger sons or confidential accountants of big firms into mischief.... If however, it has been developed as a regular gambling show by a certain class

(commonly Marwaris), it is not unlikely to produce even more demoralization than the notorious rain-game itself.[111]

While the ill repute of rain gambling Marwaris had already marked them as questionable traders, a wide array of other mercantile groups were also suspect. The superintendent of the Delhi Division, for example, explained that "the Punjabi of all classes is notorious for this gambling spirit, and 'badni' transactors have, I believe, attracted notice ever since the Province was annexed."[112] Similarly, the deputy commissioner of Rawalpindi described Punjabi merchants in that area as uninterested in rain gambling, but involved in "betting on the prices realizable at the large central marts for wheat &c, on any given date."[113] Cross-referenced papers from the United Provinces recounted an appeals court case of nine Aggarwal merchants accused in 1896 of running a common gaming house for opium speculation.[114]

The responses also included detailed police reports about the culture of opium gambling in Delhi, Rewari, and Agra, all longtime market towns.[115] Even before the Bengal anti–rain gambling agitation, local police in the Punjab had tried to contain informal speculative markets under the public disorder provisions of the 1867 Public Gambling Act. These early surveys revealed that by 1898 police investigations had already mined a great deal of raw data on opium speculation. These reports detailed various types of betting on commodity prices but did not attempt to distinguish customary negotiations such as *teji mundi* speculations (or betting on the rise and fall of the market) from games of chance. In 1894, the deputy inspector of police for Rewari, for example, explained that there had been only a few opium speculation shops, but that by late 1898, forty-five had been opened in this town. Their business depended upon the calculation of the average price of a carton of Benares and Patna opium on the Calcutta market, which would be "made known to these shop-keepers by means of telegrams from Calcutta on [the] very [same] day." Then, acting as commission agents, the shopkeepers received deposits ranging from 1 to 10 percent per bet; betting consisted of estimating the average value of opium cartons and their rise and fall of that price according to daily market fluctuations:

> Suppose *A* betted a bargain with *B* at 5 per cent and paid the amount and estimated the average price per packet of opium Rs. 995. If this ... price falls according to the result of the auction [of opium in Calcutta],

A is entitled to get Rs. 100 instead of his five, or if the case is different, *A* loses his Rs. 5 which *B* gains. In this way hundreds of people bet according to their estimation, and thus gain or lose money.

After the agreement is made, the shopkeeper enters the name of the man who bets, the sum and price estimated in his account book (*bahi*), and a copy of it is given to him by the shop-keeper, on a slip of paper (*chitti*). After this the people wait for the arrival of a telegram from Calcutta, which reaches here at about 2pm which decides the bargain.

In the early part of every month the people from different quarters and the neighboring towns come here.... As if in a fair, [they] crowd the main streets of the town from 10am to 4pm, and conveyances and carriages do not find way to pass through.[116]

This account described a type of wagering necessary for *teji mundi* speculation, a practice which operated much like stock jobbing or the buying and selling of shares purely for profit, except that here there were no shares or joint stocks. In this case, there was no evidence that opium had actually been bought and sold: this was market speculation pure and simple, without the aim of any organized investment. Nevertheless, success in the betting required detailed knowledge of the opium market, in which these traders no doubt participated. The practice demanded that merchants exercise their predictive skills and draw on the strength of their information networks to Benares, Patna, and Calcutta. It was perhaps this unabashed performance of privileged access to local information, which was then used to predict and indeed make a game of official and standardized prices, that was most unsettling. Citing the recording of information in *bahis* and *chittis*, the inspector argued that the whole enterprise misused public commercial information under the protection of unregulated indigenous trading practice. Moreover, some of the largest agents in the business "began to pay income tax upon the income realized from [these] bargain[s]." This channel of official legitimation apparently "made them bolder, and they [remained] fully convinced that they [were] doing nothing against the law." Such convictions, he bemoaned, also nurtured the practice in Delhi, Agra, Kanpur, and Jaipur.[117]

The Punjab police reports also provided new evidence of games of chance generated by the swift telegraphic relay of prices, evidence which supported the idea that all speculation on opium incorporated some form of criminal activity. The superintendent of police at Delhi, for example, described a newly popular numbers lottery dependent upon daily quotations of opium prices and extensive indigenous commercial networks:

> The shop-keepers here have paid agents in Calcutta who . . . watch the opium market most carefully and communicate daily by wire to the shopkeepers the state of the market, that is prices at which the different qualities of opium per case are being sold. . . . Ordinarily three to four telegrams are received. Apart from intimating the actual prices of cases the agents in Calcutta also wire advising what in their opinions will be the average price per case. . . . With the help of the above information the shop-keepers here give odds. Bettings are made either on the last two figures; the particular figures must be exact otherwise the shop-keeper wins the bet. . . . All bets are recorded in books with foils and counterfoils. . . . After the sales have been completed, the agents telegraph *in cipher* the average realized per case. The public, as far as I can gather, have to depend *purely on chance*, and invariably lose. . . . The average being telegraphed in cipher and known entirely to the shop-keepers and their agents, gives the business a very doubtful appearance, and it would seem to provide for dishonest practices.[118]

Again, this report warned that indigenous merchants' private culturally coded (and secret) communications would necessarily manipulate legitimate markets and make them fixed games. Legally unregulated customary norms ensured that wagering based on chance, which continued to be legal everywhere but in Bombay, would masquerade as proper trade.

The Punjab inquiry expressed anxieties inspired by the greater standardization of commercial information in India. As price information became more readily available and constitutive of the market as an idea, gambling threatened to misrepresent market principles and produce a "fatal fascination for the native mind."[119] Customary forms of speculation not only distorted trade; they publicized a mistaken understanding of the market itself. Local gambling establishments, requiring very small investments and promising high returns, promoted the market as an untamed and fluctuating force and emphasized its aleatory nature.[120] Thus the Punjab discourse on opium gambling articulated a dialectic of indigenous mercantile deception: opium speculators at once exaggerated the unfettered vagaries of the market and duped their unsuspecting clients by manipulating it. Such were the conclusions of the "respectable" opinions solicited by the Punjab government. These reiterated a standard script recounting the material ruin of countless innocent victims and opium gambling's "very injurious . . . effects on trade and equally pernicious . . . effects on the morals of the public."[121]

But despite these exposés, the Punjab government, with the assent of the Government of India, concluded in 1901 that rain gambling had not affected that province, and evidence on opium gambling had been neither extensive nor conclusive. Referring to the opium speculations, the Home Department explained that the Punjab bill aimed at suppressing "not a form of gambling" but "a form of betting on the average price of monthly opium sales in Calcutta." Well known there and elsewhere, "this particular form of betting . . . could not . . . be effectually stopped, any more than any other form of betting could be."[122] The Government of India thus protected its long-held and viciously protected investment in the opium trade with a nod to the legal distinction between gambling and wagering. Nevertheless, the Punjab inquiries had initiated a more specific discussion of customary commercial norms and their respectability.

The Criteria for Proper Trade: The United Provinces Inquiry into Opium, Grain, and Silver Gambling, 1906–1911

While inconclusive, the Punjab inquiry of 1899–1900 had brought informal speculation and futures markets to the attention of the Government of India and local administrations. Its references to the popularity of opium gambling in Agra had unsettled officials in the United Provinces (UP) who, beginning in 1906, began investigations into the various forms of market-based gambling in their districts. These surveys sought to identify new forms of speculative activity, but also to classify them more specifically as legitimate or illegitimate forms of trade. Legislation suppressing gambling, officials argued, demanded an elaboration of the criteria for ethical market practice. This became particularly important in the UP, as proposed legislation by 1910 echoed Bombay and called for the incorporation of all forms of wagering within the definition of gambling.

The UP surveys elaborated especially the multifarious forms of opium gambling, but also detailed the lesser-known activities of grain, silver, and even indigo gambling prevalent in that province. Many reports reiterated a narrative of moral condemnation, now a template for antigambling discourse, which invoked the ruin of the poor, women, and children and objected to the use of commercial information as a mechanism of deceit. Focusing on opium gamblers' closed networks of information, the district magistrate of Saharanpur, for example, described their maneuvers for ensuring unfair advantage: "It is ... possible for a gambler who has large sums involved to watch the sales by his agents, and if he sees things are likely to be unfavourable to his principal, to endeavor by himself bidding ... for the last few chests sold at the monthly sale." Such tail-end bidding would "raise the average to a price beyond that which [would] be disadvantageous to his principal. It is clear ... that this form of gambling is one which is eminently unfair to the speculator, as it is possible for one gambler ... *with large interests involved or for a combination of such gamblers* so as to arrange matters that the public *must* be fleeced."[123] This criticism, like many others in the UP, presupposed standards of fair and legitimate competition; the above citation might have served as a diatribe against monopolistic trading practices. The magistrate dismissed any analogy between gambling and legitimate speculative trade: "It may be argued that it [opium gambling] is not different from stock exchange transactions or speculating in wheat or in any other commodity ... in my opinion there is a vast difference and ... a stop should be put, *once and for all*, to this most pernicious and far-reaching form of gambling."[124] In effect, he called at once for the prohibition of commercial gambling and for the clarification of acceptable trading procedures. Indeed, more than in any previous inquiry, the gambling investigations in the United Provinces debated the intricacies of speculative practices. Thus, the commissioner of Meerut District claimed that the above conclusion had "greatly ... exaggerated the chances against the wager" and added that such arrangements assumed a "requisite skill and knowledge."[125]

In Agra, a city with an infamous history of opium gambling, reports grappled with establishing criteria for legitimate transactions even as they articulated moral reproach. The deputy collector of that city named "rain-gambling, silver-gambling, grain-gambling, cotton-gambling, &c." as the "cognate forms of opium-gambling," which had "enticed young and old alike in its treacherous charm." Its most deleterious effect was its "impression—a false impression ...—that it [was] a sort of trade, whereas it [had] not the least show of it." "Big firms," which maintained "their separate telephones from the Government telegraph office," promoted "daily gambling [in which] even labourers who get two *annas* a day after their hard day's labour are tempted to invest two or three *pice*. . . ." Thus the public's economic imagination would be weaned on "fond" but ill-conceived "hopes for future gain."[126] Nevertheless, while calling for legislation suppressing such games, this opinion also insisted that "it is desirable to protect legitimate commercial speculations" and thus called for a provisional clause in the draft legislation stating that " 'transactions in which delivery of goods is contemplated may be exempted from the operation of the Gambling Act.' "[127]

Similarly, the High Court Vakil (the public prosecutor) for Agra tried to juggle the demands of the "respectable people of Agra" and the necessities of commerce: "By an amendment in the telegraph guide the Government can prohibit that no telegram relating to the price of opium chests be sent from any station. But this might interfere with legitimate trade and hence it is urged that legislation can be of avail to suppress the gambling."[128] He complained that opium gambling was "conducted in public markets with all the notoriety of a trade business." Grain and silver gambling were also performed this way. Indeed, the very existence of these counterfeit practices demanded that "bonafide transactions in grain and silver should be maintained." Thus, he called for a comprehensive amendment to the UP Public Gambling Act, one which would "include not only opium-gambling, but all forms of speculative gambling, e.g. rain and silver, with a saving clause that bona fide trade transactions, *in which delivery of goods* is contracted . . . on the due date, will not be affected."[129]

Thus opinions in the UP suggested that the principle of contract (and its focus on an a priori intention) could be harnessed to regulate informal and customary speculative procedures. The completion of the contract, as well as its bona fide intention, would be evidenced in the delivery of goods, a standard criterion to distinguish legitimate from criminal practices. According to an opinion from Aligarh, the transactions "under the vernacular names of *badni, satta* and others . . . consist of [an informal] contract for the delivery of commodities on a specified future day, but in nine cases out of ten it is not the intention of the parties . . . to call for or give delivery from or to each other . . . though colorable provisions for the completion of purchase are not infrequently inserted."[130] The absence of a formal, written contract in a customary trade, when combined with a lack of delivery, rendered that agreement's intentions unverifiable and therefore suspect. In this way, the inquiry into the criminal potential of speculation offered a new channel for the imposition of contractual principles into the indigenous mercantile law. "Respectable" informants insisted that while the enforcement of delivery might become "the subject of adverse criticism [among] commercial people; [it] would no doubt be welcomed by the educated classes."[131]

However, since futures trades were often settled without delivery, officials remained hesitant about incorporating such provisions within a draft bill. Near the end of the inquiry in November 1906, the secretary to the UP Legislative Council expressed concern that a law attempting specifically to restrict "wagering on the price of opium, silver, grain, or any other commodity" would include "certain stockjobbing transactions" which were perfectly legal in Britain.[132] Though the UP governor visited Agra in 1908 and spoke vehemently against opium gambling, the question of legislation was put off until April of 1910, when, during a heightened period of speculation in the increasingly unstable world opium market, a member of the UP Legislative Council again moved a resolution for legislation.

The years from 1908 to 1910 saw windfall speculative profits, particularly for Marwaris in Bombay and Calcutta, whose aggressive tactics threatened not only supply and demand predictions for the opium market but treaded on the potential earnings of British managing agencies.[133] Rumors of vast and spuriously amassed fortunes furthered the interest in setting criteria for respectable trade and in publicizing indigenous commercial procedures. In 1910, the UP government appointed a committee to inquire again "into the evils of opium[,] grain[,] and silver-gambling . . . and to consider whether any, and if so what steps can be taken to put a stop to them." The committee was to assist the Legislative Council in framing a law which would prohibit "transactions which [were] contrary to the public good" but which did not extend "to those which [were] bona fide incidents of trade, or legitimate operations of the share or other markets."[134]

On the first of August, the committee heard statements from fifteen witnesses, mostly from Agra and its environs. Some members of the committee also visited the Seth ki Gali (literally, the alley of wealthy merchants), the bustling center of opium speculation in Agra, and "personally inspected the operations of the bookmakers." The witnesses included police inspectors, magistrates, and municipal commissioners from Agra, Mathura, and Muzaffarnagar, many of whom explained that much speculative gambling, including that in silver and grain, remained confined to wealthy merchants; only opium gambling constituted a threat to public order.[135] Indeed, some descriptions of grain and silver gambling read as outlines of basic futures trading procedures: "[One] sort of gambling is to buy grain before it is sown even, at certain rates for a certain date, and the man never or very seldom gives grain at the date, but gives the loss or profit as the case may be at the day's market rate. This sort of gambling was much resorted to by richer grain merchants here in the *mandi* [grain market], but dishonestly crept in [in] different forms . . . [so that] each party tries to lower or raise the market rate by fictitious purchases on that date and in this way tries to defeat the winner."[136]

Such statements exposed a tension between the exchange of material goods and the emergence of the market as a virtual process in which fictitious goods might hold the same value as actual ones. Merchants engaged in speculation had already normalized the latter picture, as a statement to the committee submitted by the secretary of the Agra Trades Association evidenced. It outlined the simple logic of hedging and speculative procedures in the *badni* transaction, a legitimate contract for a time bargain in which parties settled on prices and so bet against market fluctuation.[137] This lengthy statement from a reputable and publicly organized merchant association prompted the committee to send a questionnaire specifically soliciting mercantile opinions. Most responses expressed concerns about legislation to regulate "speculations incidental to commercial life."[138] The Upper India Chamber of Commerce, an organization of British interests based in Kanpur, saw, for example, "no essential distinction between the operations known as *tezi-madda* [*teji mundi*] and what is known as 'option dealing' on the London Stock Exchange, which, although in actuality gambling pure and simple has met with the acceptance, if not approval, of the commercial world."[139]

In early 1911, the UP Legislative Council drafted a bill "to prohibit wagering on the price of opium," the most pernicious form of speculation according to government evidence. An awkward proposal revealing anxieties over the transmission of commercial information, the bill attempted to ferret out legitimate futures trades from their criminal counterparts. A common gaming house would now include a place "in which wagering on the price of opium is carried on for the profit or gain" of the operator "or which is used as an office or place for the receipt or record of such wagers . . . whether the wagers are received by means of the post or in any way whatsoever."[140] But, hesitant to enact these broad provisions, the UP government put the measure aside, invoking the "uncertain state of the opium trade in India."[141] Still, the gambling menace sustained its momentum as a public issue, and in 1917, new legislation was enacted. The United Provinces Public Gambling Amendment Act ultimately remained reticent on the distinctions between legitimate and illegitimate speculation, instead inserting wagering into the definition of gambling, as the Bombay Act of 1890 had done. As in Bombay, this measure allowed broad powers of police discretion to identify and then shut down common betting or wagering houses.[142]

Indeed, in Bombay, it was clear that patterns of police arrests, rather than the law, had drawn the boundaries between legitimate and criminal activity. A 1910 police commissioner's report on the procedure for gambling arrests in that city delineated two distinct categories of speculation: the first referred to practices "difficult to class as illegal," and the second to those that were "plainly illegal." The first category included futures trades that resulted in delivery, though often, the commissioner stated, even these contracts were settled by paying "merely the difference in price." Since this form of speculation was "based on the desire and ability inherent in a large proportion of the mercantile class to anticipate the 'market,'" it remained questionable whether "these wagering contracts or 'time bargains'" fell within the purview of the Bombay Gambling Act. The second sort of "plainly illegal" activity included betting on the numbers of estimated sales of any commodity, or on prices, without any buying or selling.[143]

This was a slippery distinction that threatened to criminalize a wide array of unwritten customary contracts. While a formal written contract might be satisfactory proof of intent to deliver and of the trade itself, an unwritten wager, which resulted in a similar setting of differences in prices, could be more readily construed as "betting pure and simple." This of course did not mean that indigenous merchants refrained from using readily communicated price information simply for numbers lotteries. Still, the exact nature of legitimate speculative practices remained vague and dependent upon the judgment of the police. Indigenous merchants thus sought to protect themselves from criminalization by publicly appropriating the moral reproach of gambling, a discourse in which they had begun to participate by 1910.

In 1910–1911, such reproach emerged in Bombay as a response to the question of government regulation of horse racing, which, though openly accepted as a form of wagering, had been protected by the administration. As earlier in Calcutta, nationalist and reformist opinions sought to expose official hypocrisy. In October of 1911, the Bhatia Mitra Mandal, an organization of Gujarati merchants, sent a letter to the governor of Bombay demanding the suppression of horse racing, which had been "the cause of curse and ruin in [not only in their] own ancient historical community" which was "at present pursuing great and peaceful commercial enterprise" but had "to a great extent shaken the Commercial morality . . . of other mercantile communities at large." The organization argued that "enlightened commercial communities," such as their own and those represented in the influential Bombay Native Piece-Goods association, vehemently opposed the "vices on the Turf." The continued government sanction of horse racing, rather than any indigenous fascination with risk and propensity for deceit, had sustained the addiction among native merchants.[144]

The Bhatia Mandal posited respectability as a central concern of the native commercial community. Referring specifically to *abru* the Gujerati term for reputation, the organization claimed that horse racing had caused not only material devastation, but had shaken the ethical foundations of its community: thus merchants resorted to "extortions, . . . frauds, falsification of accounts, cheating, etc. . . . for the purpose of saving their reputation (Abru)."[145] Here, their reformist critique of gambling attempted to legitimize traditional norms of credit and commercial association. Presented in an invocation of an ancient and timeless culture, *abru*, which was manifest in ties of kinship and codes of honor, was not the source, but the casualty, of the gambling menace. Amongst the "enlightened commercial community," these ties structured an ethics of reputation, and did not channel secret manipulations. Such assertions stood in marked contrast with the 1897 memorials of Marwaris against the rain-gambling bill, in which the Marwari community spoke as economic actors, meteriologists, and "citizens of Calcutta." The Bhatia community demanded that their reputation be aligned with respectability, and that public morality, if not the law, should validate the *culture* of indigenous commerce. In the process, these merchants presented their commercial ethics as a treasured cultural code; it was in this way that their "great and peaceful commercial enterprise" might be recognized as economic prowess and not potential thievery. The protest at once appropriated and resisted the central modernizing protocol of capitalist development: the distinction between community and capital, or more broadly, culture and economy.

Gambling, Commercial Respectability, and the Suppression of Cotton Gambling in Bengal, 1911–1912

As the Bombay Council debated the Race-Course Licensing Act of 1912, which regulated but did not eliminate horse racing in that city, the gambling question returned to center stage in Calcutta over a new wagering scheme that made use of the availability of daily cotton prices from London and New York. Unlike the public debates of 1897 over rain gambling, the condemnation of cotton gambling was both swift and universal. This greater uniformity of opinion reflected the standardizing influence of nationalist and middle-class social reform agendas, as well as the nature of the game, which was tied less obviously than opium or grain gambling to speculative enterprise. The cotton gambling scare also reflected the growing regulation and classification of economic crimes by the Calcutta Police, itself evidence of the expanding reception of "the market" as an idea and everyday experience.

In 1910, the chief inspector of police in Bengal put forward a scheme for a Criminal Intelligence Bureau "for centralizing information regarding crime and criminals." The general index for its "Information on Record" recorded a panoply of criminal types, including dacoits, burglars, and poisoners, but also elaborated two new subsets: the swindler and the money forger. The category of "swindlers" included, among other things, "bogus firms and commission agents," "bogus collectors of charitable subscriptions," "personators of long lost relatives," "cheats who profess . . . to turn baser metals into gold," "defrauders of Banks," "bogus collectors of subscriptions, other than charitable," "telegraphic money-order cheats," "bogus marriage negotiators," "forged *hundi* cheats," that is, those who falsified indigenous bills of exchange, "personators (native and European) who by negotiating bad cheques obtain advances, loans, etc.," and "cheats who obtain goods and money under false pretenses, by representing themselves as the agents of notable personages." The category of money-forgers referred to both "coiners" and "note-forgers." "Coiners" were divided into "local coiners," "foreign coiners," and "Marwari and Rajputana... coiners," while "note-forgers" included those who forged "promissory notes..., currency notes, [and] bank notes."[146] Evoking the illicit underbelly of market activity, such classification revealed a greater concern for control over procedures for trade, commercial association, and credit.

In 1912, this anxiety focused on a new amusement discovered in Calcutta, a numbers lottery operating through the daily fluctuations in raw cotton prices. In March of 1912, the Government of Bengal reported to the Government of India that this new form of wagering had instigated "a serious increase of poverty and crime."[147] From its inception, the public discussion of cotton gambling affirmed the logic of free market exchange and its imagined ethical foundation, the even playing field. The report from the Bengal government described cotton gambling as a game of crafty skill and unfair advantage, one which employed commercial knowledge to dupe and manipulate uninitiated players. Like rain gambling, this new practice was characterized as a fixed game rather than a free and open competition:

> A shop is opened at which tickets are sold showing in one column the serial numbers 1 to 10; in a second column the amount paid by the customer opposite the serial number on which he lays his wager; and in a third column the amount which the owner agrees to pay if the number which the customer has backed is eventually declared to be the winning number. The amounts wagered naturally vary with the means of the customer and the sum offered as a prize varies from twice to over one hundred times the value of the stake. The winning number is theoretically obtained by posting on a board the five times of cotton future and demand sale quotations from America and England which are obtained daily from Reuter's telegraphic quotations. The five quotations are added together and divided by five and the last figure of the sum thus obtained is declared to be the winning number. It is reported, however, that with few occasional exceptions the number on which the fewest wagers have been laid is declared to be the winner; and there is no doubt that the owners of these shops take advantage of the ignorance of the public to announce a figure which will involve the lowest expenditure in prizes. [It is] apparent that pure and simple gambling is in question. It

has no relations whatever to the cotton trades and the cotton quotations appear to have been adopted as a suitable criterion for bets, merely because they were beyond the risk of being influenced....

The system has now spread downwards to a social stratum in which the gamblers are incapable of securing the adoption of the correct figure. From the specimen tickets which have come to the notice of the Government, it appears that the poorest sections of the community are being widely attracted by the excitement of cotton gambling. The stakes laid are frequently as low as one anna and even women and children of the poorest classes are being tempted to speculate on the winning figures. Although . . . individual stakes are often so trifling, it is believed that in the aggregate the sums which change hands daily are enormous.[148]

This picture mirrored previous accounts of informal futures trading: cotton gambling induced a blind devotion to pure chance, incarnate in a new deity called the market, all the while manipulating, deceiving, and ruining its victims. Or rather, the very fixed nature of the game encouraged an ignorant and fatalistic understanding of market forces; the open contest of legitimate trade, in contrast, would have demanded that uncertainties be skillfully managed.[149] But cotton gambling was also different from indigenous speculation because it had "no relations whatsoever to the cotton trades." Its obvious operation as a lottery allowed an almost homogenous public condemnation, one which insisted upon the distinction between proper and illegitimate trade. During the rain gambling controversy of 1897, even "respectable" voices had argued that gambling and commerce were inseparable endeavors. By 1912, public criticism ignored this practical analogy and promoted the separation of gambling and commerce into distinct categories, though debate remained as to the actual practices they represented.

In May of 1912, the Bengal Legislative Council formally took up the issue, but potential legislation was deferred after the Calcutta High Court acquitted two men accused of running cotton-gambling shops. The judges in *Ram Pretap Nemani and Another v. King Emperor* echoed the earlier 1887 decision of the Bombay High Court, holding that cotton gambling was a form of straightforward wagering, rather than gambling (that is, a scheme for cheating), and therefore still legal in Bengal.[150] The prosecutors had offered various exhibits seized by the police as instruments of gaming including boards containing the telegrams of cotton prices, a canvas signboard showing the name of the firm, boards showing odds, a tin ticket revealing the number 9, the day's winning digit, and a box containing Rs. 410. These, the court held, were not evidence of cheating or a fixed game, but of "betting pure and simple."[151] According to a member of the Legislative Council, on the day of the acquittal, several Calcutta papers reported that "25 cotton gambling shops were opened in one street," carrying on "a roaring business."[152]

Police activity soon heightened, and in early July, nine cotton-gambling establishments located in the Bow Bazaar section of Calcutta were raided on complaints of obstruction and public nuisance.[153] That same week, the Bengal government received an unsolicited letter from the Marwari Association of Calcutta. This organization, established in 1898 shortly after the relentless protest of that community against the suppression of rain gambling, demanded the immediate elimination of cotton gambling. Rejecting its earlier laissez-faire position, the community presented a by-now established narrative of moral reproach. The representation recounted that for "some time past, this form of gambling has been rather violent all over Calcutta . . . [and] the city is thickly dotted over with gambling booths run by unscrupulous persons." It bemoaned the ruin of "both the middle and poorer classes," who "find the temptation irresistible and . . . stake their honest earnings, sometimes even the small savings of a lifetime . . . only to lose and lose for ever."[154] Invoking their own commitment to social order and respectability, Marwaris spoke paternally, as commercial sages, elaborating the moral tragedy that accompanied material ruin:

> Driven to desperation, many people resort to unfair and sometimes positively dishonest means to find the where-withal to live and continue the hopeless endeavors to recover their losses. It is a matter of public knowledge that many a family has been disgraced and ruined in this way, the bread-winners having been sent to jail either for embezzlement or for some other criminal offense of a similar nature. If popular stories . . . are to be relied upon, the womenfolk of the lower classes also seem to have been affected to some extent by this vice of betting on cotton figures. The Committee therefore consider it no exaggeration to say that this new form of gambling is a social evil of the gravest magnitude which has brought disgrace upon many families and has reduced count-

less others to the condition of extreme poverty and therefore [must] be put down with a strong hand.... Another submission of the Committee in this connection is that the new law should be elaborate enough to bring within its purview every other possible forms [sic] of mischievous gambling.[155]

Calcutta's public discourse echoed this opprobrium in the few months following the representation, and reached a crescendo in September and October of 1912. The practice was condemned in a number of English-language papers (both native and British), including the *Amrita Bazar Patrika*, the *Indian Mirror*, the *Hindu Patriot*, and the *Telegraph*, and in a wide array of vernacular journals.[156] While cotton gambling was not often specifically associated with Marwaris as rain gambling had been, this history did continue to haunt the community. In early October, the *Amrita Bazaar Patrika* printed an exposé of cotton-gambling saloons and "new devices of robbing public money":

> That these [saloons] do a roaring trade is apparent from the large staff maintained by them.... In [one] booth which is styled a club, there is a rather well-furnished ante-room, where Marwaris, probably the promoters of the business, smoke the hookah of content while their clerks register bets in the outer rooms.... Men of poor intelligence and very small means ... are an easy prey.... It is no uncommon sight to see a group of cotton-figure punters discussing in earnest the science of finding the winning number.... Another excrescence ... is the cotton-figure bank.... These so-called banks offer an astounding rate of interest to investors. They remind one of a fraudulent enterprise revealed sometime back in the States.[157]

In the vernacular press, no less than sixteen articles appeared in various papers appealing for legislation on the issue. The *Basumati*, a Bengali weekly with a circulation of approximately two thousand, called in mid-September for the commissioner of police to "take the evidence of respectable men in camera against cotton-gambling." The *Daily Bharat Mitra*, a local Hindi paper with a circulation of three hundred, explained that the illicit business was carried on openly in the major thoroughfares of Burrabazar, including Cotton and Mullick streets and in the Chitpur Road. It called for the "attention of the Marwari and other associations of Burrabazar towards their duty in the matter," asking the residents of Cotton Street, "which become[s] a virtual pandemonium every night" to "follow the example of the residents of Bow Bazar, who have, by their complaints, been able to [close] the gambling dens of their quarter."[158]

In early November 1912, a question in the British Parliament asked specifically whether legislation had been considered to stop this new practice in Calcutta, pressuring the Government of India to take action.[159] The Home Department then insisted that the cotton numbers game had become a "mania" in Calcutta and considered emergency measures to suppress the practice, since no law could be drafted until the Bengal Legislative Council returned to session in January of 1913. At the suggestion of the viceroy, the Bengal administration then considered establishing an "ordinance . . . promulgated by the Governor General to provide a temporary remedy for the particular evil of cotton-gambling." The power of ordinance had been reserved for "cases of emergency" and had been exercised in Bengal on six occasions previously. Still, officials in Bengal argued that such a measure would extend only to cotton gambling, with no power to suppress other potential forms of wagering. The Calcutta High Court decision had necessitated an amended public gambling law to avoid future resort to such piecemeal interventions.[160] The public outcry quieted as arrests continued in October and November of 1912, and in March of 1913, the Bengal Public Gambling Amendment Bill was passed in council. Bengal Act IV of 1913 reiterated the law in Bombay, establishing that "'gaming includes wagering or betting (except wagering or betting upon a horse-race.)'"[161]

Jute Gambling in Bengal:
From Swindlers to Businessmen

For the Marwari community specifically, cotton gambling had offered an opportunity to alleviate doubts about the legitimacy of their trading practices. For the first time in its history, the Marwari Association, which by 1900 had established a professional arm in the Marwari (later Bharat) Chamber of Commerce, had spoken publicly against gambling in order to promote itself as a bastion of respectability. This new strategy sought to exorcise the ghost of rain gambling, as well as illicit elements within the community itself that had been exposed in recent arrests. Increased Marwari public and civic participation, as evinced in the association and the Chamber of Commerce, in demands for greater representation in the Calcutta Municipal Corporation, and, by the 1920s, in the presence of members of the community in the Bengal Legislative Council itself, informed a growing public discussion about the legitimacy of informal and customary commercial procedures.[162]

In Calcutta, suspicions about informal commercial conventions had heightened as indigenous trade began to compete with, rather than complement, British interests. In the fast-growing trade in raw jute and jute products (such as hessian, or burlap and gunny sacks), Marwari futures markets threatened the rhythms of this vastly profitable export trade.[163] Marwari exchanges or *baras* for futures speculation (that is, for *satta*, also known in Bengal as *fatka*) in jute first opened in Burrabazar in the 1905–1906 crop season. With units of transaction as low as five bales of jute, these markets attracted a wide net of investment. The Calcutta *fatka* market in jute not only marked Marwaris as a force to be reckoned with; it also destabilized the operations of the jute mills, run by British interests. Dependent on raw jute bought on a spot basis, British agencies managing these mills had little experience with forward trading and hedging procedures in this commodity. Speculative quotations from futures markets were telegraphed up-country and began to form the basis of raw jute pricing, which in turn upset millowners' financing and expectations for supply and demand.[164]

By 1911–1912, as the Calcutta public demanded the suppression of the cotton-figure numbers game, British traders initiated a two-decade condemnation of the *fatka bazaar* in jute. In 1912, the British members of the Calcutta Baled Jute Association complained that the *fatka bazaar* had begun to attract everyone from "members of the Bar Library" to "tramway conductors . . . and *bhistis* [watermen]."[165] A year before, the Indian Jute Mills Association (IJMA), the voice of British jute millowners and managing agents, wrote to the Bengal Chamber of Commerce, the premier organization of British traders in eastern India, for support in exposing jute gambling.[166] The IJMA letter obsessed particularly on the propagation of false contracts within informal Marwari *baras* (futures exchanges), emphasizing the distinction between genuine and counterfeit transactions:

> The Committee of the Indian Jute Mills Association address[es] you with reference to the use of what have come to be known as "pink" and

"white" contracts and to [their] ... effect on the legitimate jute market. ... The contracts have been introduced by the Marwari community.... [They] purport to evidence the purchase and sale of jute, and they have the appearance of relating to genuine transactions. ... However, in hardly any of the cases in which these contracts pass does a delivery of jute take place; and provision is made in the concluding paragraph of the contract form for the payment of differences.

... It is understood that to give the transaction the further appearance of genuineness it is usual for the buyer to ask the seller to declare the mark [quality] or marks to be delivered under the contract.

The gambling thus made possible has resulted in the attraction of many Marwaris who have no interest in the genuine jute market besides giving scope to those already interested in it to indulge in absolute speculation. And the effect on the genuine market has ... been great.[167]

Interest in curbing Marwari competition thus fixated on the protection of a "real," material market, and its natural mechanism of supply and demand, through the enforcement of contracts for delivery. But this was a tricky proposition, as speculative and hedging transactions of the most legitimate nature in other commodities were often settled without actual delivery. Aware of this possibility, IJMA presented a further clarification of the law of contract, enclosing a brief presented by their counsel advising on pink and white transactions with Marwari brokers. It explained that "a section of the Marwari community," which had been "deprived of the pleasures of rain gambling" and was unable to gamble in the shares market due to its "moribund condition," had "invented a means of satisfying their craving for the gains of chance in a system of contracts purporting to evidence the purchase and sale of jute, but [the counsel] believe in no single instance has jute ever been delivered under them." They advised IJMA that "these contracts [were] void," that is, unenforceable under the Indian Contracts Act, 1872, "so far as they [were] wagering transactions" but considered whether they were illegal. Their answer underlined the foundation of the principle of contract: "We are of the opinion that ... Pink and White Contracts, entered into by parties with the common understanding and intention that no delivery of jute should be given and taken ... are null and void."[168]

In a second letter to the Bengal Chamber of Commerce, IJMA again emphasized the indigenous propensity for the unstandardized and uncertain by reiterating the homology between rain gambling and Marwari mercantile practice. It recounted that Marwaris "congregate together in the public street as much as they did in the days when they watched the clouds and the water spouts in Burra Bazar, . . . and . . . books of a very similar character to those kept for the purposes of registering bets . . . in connection with rain gambling are now kept as records subsidiary to 'pink' and 'white' contracts."[169] Invoking Marwaris' defense of rain gambling sixteen years before, jute millowners argued that customary account keeping would by its very nature distort written forms of contract. Echoing contemporaneous criticisms of informal speculation markets in the United Provinces, this reproach pinpointed gambling as the very prototype for all forms of indigenous commercial exchange, and chicanery as its mechanism.

But pressured jute millowners did not manage to convince the Bengal Chamber of Commerce, which represented a wide variety of export trades and industries, to take action. While the chamber insisted that its members were "alive to the evils" of such false contracts, it concluded that "there would be considerable difficulty . . . in urging legislation," as it was "not by any means certain that different interests would all be in [its] favour."[170] The chamber resisted the demand for regulation through legislation, which threatened to control British trading interests as well. Meanwhile, the growing presence of police in the Burrabazar area after the Bengal Public Gambling Act of 1913 attested to the continued association of indigenous merchants with illicit activities. In 1913–1914, the Marwari Chamber of Commerce and the Marwari Association sent a series of letters to the Bengal Chamber of Commerce appealing for help in exposing the police harassment of Burrabazar traders. The Marwari organizations had sent letters to the Commissioner of Police complaining of several instances of "molestation by the police" of piece-goods traders, respectable men who, during the loading and unloading of their *godowns*, had been taken to the *thana* (local headquarters) to be questioned and detained on charges of street obstruction.

While wagering did not constitute the central focus of these arrests, they did prompt Marwari concern about the community's public reputation. In a letter to the commissioner of police in September of 1913, the Marwari Association explained that it "fully appreciat[ed] the raids of the police on the rain and cotton gambling dens . . . but the methods adopted . . . in putting down streets obstruction [sic] are open to serious objection on the ground that . . . they inflict unnecessary hardship on the people, are calculated to affect trade injuriously and to render the police extremely unpopular."[171] Consciously promoting the legitimacy of their operations, the association sent letters again in 1914, calling for the protection of Burrabazar from the spread of the *goonda* (hooligan) classes. Marwaris called for the improvement of police arrangements in that area and claimed that because Burrabazar was "the most important trade centre and the most densely built and populated area of the town," it afforded "excellent opportunities for the lawless classes to carry on their nefarious trade."[172]

Here, Marwaris asserted their central role in Calcutta's commercial life. Responding to the production of its illegitimacy, the community had by 1914 begun to embrace civic duty, demanding the enforcement of the distinction between legitimate and illegitimate trade. By the 1920s, prominent Marwari leaders turned directly to the possibility of legislation to protect their informal futures markets. Leaving behind their appeals to the police, the Marwari Association, the Marwari Chamber of Commerce, the new and more reformist and nationalist Marwari Trades Association, and the Bengal National Chamber of Commerce, an organization which included the most influential Marwaris in Calcutta, all backed two bills calling for the regulation of "wagering associations." The first circulated in various drafts in the Bengal Legislative Council between 1924 and 1926. Written by Debi Prosad Khaitan, an industrialist leader in the Marwari community, a founder of the Federation of Indian Chambers of Commerce and Industry, and nonofficial member of the Bengal Council, the bill attempted to address the concerns of "a large number of prominent merchants" in favor of "restrict[ing] gambling."[173]

The bill did not speak for the Marwari community specifically, but rather for the place of indigenous commerce in the interests of trade in general. Khaitan's Statement of Objects and Reasons was the first attempt at legalizing, regulating, and so legitimating indigenous speculative practices in India.[174] It began by explaining that there existed "various Exchanges in the Northern part of Calcutta which have been started on the principle of the Bombay Cotton Exchange and the Liverpool Exchange. These exchanges are controlled and supervised solely by Indians; and in the Vernacular, these are called Baras." Invoking already established markets in commodities futures, Khaitan elaborated on the procedures for buying and selling within indigenous exchanges, and on the need for regulation:

> Baras have been established for Jute, Hessian, Shares, Linseed and Cotton. *Bona Fide* businessmen, hedgers, speculators and gamblers—a mixture of elements—deal at these Baras. No written contracts are made in connection with transactions . . . though every transaction is entered in the books of the buyer and seller and initialled by the opposite party. Each Saturday a rate is fixed on the basis of which differences are paid and received the following Monday and the contract continues at the rate fixed. This payment of differences each week end continues until the delivery date, when in the case of Hessian, Shares and Linseed the parties have a right to offer or demand delivery and they often do so. In the case of Jute and Cotton the differences only are settled on the basis of the rate at the due date.[175]

Khaitan then called for legislation, referencing the difficulties in distinguishing between gambling and trade, proclaiming the honorable concerns of native merchants:

> It is very difficult for one not acquainted with the nature of the Baras to discriminate between a purely speculative and "mixed" Bara. Two Baras in the past were raided by the Police. One, a Cotton Bara quite different from the two classes described above was purely a gambling house, whereas the Sugar Bara was of a mixed character, since deliveries used to be effected in it. Such raids upon a "mixed Bara," while they fail to stop gambling upset business very much. . . . Under the circumstances, suitable legislation is necessary in order that the gambling may be checked while business may not be hampered. Indian businessmen honestly want to stop all sorts of gambling in Burra Bazar but without Government cooperation it is impossible to do so.

The bill assumed the difficult task of providing for comprehensive and standard procedures for informal exchanges, while allowing them the option to remain informal. *Baras* could choose to be registered under the Indian Companies Act and to formulate articles of association, and so constitute themselves as "Exchange Associations," which were to follow rules of written contract with the right to offer and demand delivery of goods "in a manner recognized by [each particular] Trade" and establish minimum quantities for transactions.[176]

The Wagering Associations Bill included provisions for a Central Board of Exchange to coordinate and regulate the activities of exchange associations, and to collect information on them for government use. It was to be constituted by "(a) three persons to be elected by the Bengal Chamber of Commerce; (b) three persons to be elected by the Bengal National Chamber of Commerce of whom at least two shall be Marwaris; (c) representatives of Exchange Associations . . . ; [and] (d) the Secretary to the Local Government in the Department of Commerce, *ex-officio*." However, the bill also allowed for another category of association, the "Wagering Association," which could choose to operate informally: it was defined as "an Exchange Association not complying with [the relevant sections of the act establishing procedures for exchange associations]." The local government had the prerogative, after reviewing reports from the central board and conducting its own inquiries, to declare any exchange association or wagering association a "Proclaimed Wagering Association," to be prosecuted as a common gambling house.

The regulatory power of the bill rested in the standardization of procedures for all futures and speculative markets, indigenous or otherwise. But it left a space open for "private," unregistered customary operation. This, the Bengal government argued, made it difficult for wagering associations to be managed with the same scrutiny as official exchanges, as there would be no standards for judging informal institutions without required by-laws. Members of the Commerce Department, which as a whole was "in favor of trades organizing proper Exchanges and bringing the members of those exchanges under discipline and control," complained that there were no penalties for failure to register under the bill.[177] Indeed, one Commerce Department opinion stated bluntly that "this is an attempt by a Marwari to prevent Marwaris from gambling. I am not very hopeful of its success."[178]

The Wagering Associations Bill was formally introduced in the Bengal Legislative Council in July of 1926, but it was never pursued due to the close of that council's session. In 1927, at the opening of a new council, the Marwari leader P. D. Himatsingka, a nonofficial member, Congress supporter, and lawyer with ties to the reformist Marwari Trades Association, introduced the Futures Markets Bill, modeled on Khaitan's measure.[179] The new bill reiterated its predecessor almost exactly but was received with less skepticism, as it allowed for the local government to exempt from regulation associations which had proven their commitment to *"bona fide* trade or industry."[180] In addition, it specifically exempted "all Associations affiliated to the Bengal Chamber of Commerce," in effect excluding British trade from regulation. Still, Himatsingka attempted again to legitimize informal speculative practices. But he employed a new strategy; he did not refer specifically to indigenous *baras*, but spoke objectively of the necessity for futures markets. Not emphasizing the particularity of indigenous trading practices, as Khaitan had done, but rather implying their de facto similarity with rational and modern procedures, Himatsingka promoted the progressive functions of futures markets in general. His Statement of Objects and Reasons thus began,

> Transaction[s] in commodities for future delivery are an important future of modern business. They enable traders to minimise the risk that they have to undergo in their legitimate business due to constant fluctuations in the price of all commodities, brought about by world factors. Transactions of this nature have been systematised in the commercial world by the establishment of institutions which in America and other European countries are known by the name of Exchanges. . . . The economic utility of Futures Markets or Exchanges was summarized by the London Jute Association in the memorial submitted by them to the Secretary of State for India. They say "The value of the futures system . . . needs no emphasis. [The Liverpool, New York, and New Orleans cotton associations] and the analogous market for Cotton recently established in Bombay [under the Bombay Cotton Contracts Act of 1922] working on scientific principles and under authoritative control, serve to provide a continuous market for the producer and consumer, to steady the market and prevent . . . "scares" . . . to reduce the risks of the *bona fide* trader and therefore, to restrict gambling."[181]

Though he did call for suppressing "baras which are of a purely gambling nature," his statement more generally incorporated indigenous practices within a language of scientific efficiency. Customary practices did not counteract modern principles, he argued, and community organization, he implied, did not skew the workings of capital.

The Futures Markets Bill circulated for opinion and was granted sanction to be introduced in 1927, but it, too, was left unaddressed.[182] From the late 1920s through the 1930s, the Indian Chamber of Commerce, Calcutta, an organization established in 1926 and dominated by Marwari industrialists, continued to write to the Government of

Bengal complaining of police raids on bona fide speculative markets and the unjustified confiscation of account books. In 1928, the chamber wrote to the Bengal Commerce Department complaining that "any Police informer or any other irresponsible person ... can go and lodge information with the Police that gambling is being carried on at the premises of a certain Association, and that fact is itself sufficient to bring about a raid by the Police."[183] In 1929, its annual report asserted that the police had tried to extort funds from the East India Jute Association, an organization of indigenous jute interests affiliated with the chamber, by threatening raids.[184] Its 1930 report reprinted a letter sent to the Political Department relaying the acquittal of prominent merchants from Indian firms who had been accused of running a common gambling house and "subjected to ... excessive humiliation, loss and injury."[185] In 1932, the chamber again recounted the unfair police raids on the premises of the Gunny Trades Association.[186]

Criminal procedure thus continued to remind indigenous trade of its illicit history.[187] The emergence of gambling as a potent public issue reflected a long official discomfort with customary trading practices. The gambling question delineated a battleground where economy might be disjoined from culture, and a rational system of exchange from the irregularities of convention. Critics of gambling had assumed the illicitness of indigenous trade because of its internal ties of kinship, which, they argued, necessarily promoted the "unfair advantage" of the gamble, or the fixed game. As Marwaris realized in 1897, the performance of material prowess would not suffice to validate them as legitimate economic actors. Indeed, stories of their vast speculative accumulations only rendered them more suspect of deception and manipulation.

The public face of indigenous commerce, its reputation and legitimacy as a trading sector, thus demanded that an impeccable moral uprightness be produced outside the contested terrain of commercial ethics. As early as 1912, and certainly by the 1920s, indigenous commercial groups, and Marwaris in particular, embraced social respectability to assert the compatibility of their customary trading arrangements and modern market principles. As chapters 2 and 3 have shown, social respectability was performed increasingly through investment in modern forms of philanthropic endeavor. But more significantly, respectability also involved a greater privatization of the idea of family among merchant groups. By the 1920s, indigenous merchants completed the family firms' incarnation as Hindu Undivided Family, a legal invention of the nineteenth century, in impassioned demands for the protection of this "private" arena of cultural autonomy. The next chapter turns to this defense of the HUF in the face of reformist social legislation, considering commercial groups' embrace of private autonomy to enforce cultural orthodoxy, all in the service of public material progress.

5

Economic Agents, Cultural Subjects

Gender, the Joint Family, and the Making of Capitalist Subjects, 1900–1940

> We need to organize ourselves ... [to assert] the contribution which the business classes are making to the civil and economic development of the country. To assert our rightful place in the public affairs ... we must organize ourselves to a man. ... The gentlemen from the labourite group ... are ... accentuating the cleavage between the Indian capital and labor. ... The idyllic school of economists ... declare that modern methods of large-scale commerce and large-scale industry are foreign to the Indian genius and culture. Against the cumulative opposition from the various sources, the Indian businessmen must make their way. How else are they to achieve success except by perfect organization of their forces and resources?—ANANDJI HARIDAS, Presidential Address, Inaugural Meeting, Indian Chamber of Commerce, Calcutta, 1926

IN 1926, THE INAUGURAL MEETING of the Indian Chamber of Commerce announced the emergence of "native commerce" as a class, as capital personified with a consciousness and a will. As a form of commercial organization, the chamber of commerce marked a shift in the social world of capital in India, encapsulating a half-century of market governance. Unlike the extended family or the caste council, it was a corporate body under law, a civic association and an arrangement of economic men. The first all-India native chamber of commerce, and origin of the Federation of Indian Chambers of Commerce and Industry (FICCI), the Indian Chamber consolidated interests that had reaped massive profits during the First World War.[1] Still, despite these material conquests, the public persona of indigenous capitalism spoke of substantial challenges. The business classes, their leaders insisted, were engaged in the universal battle between capital and labor. As they inserted themselves into this master position and monopolized economic agency as bearers of capital, their difference nevertheless loomed large. Thus they addressed long-held assumptions about their old-fashioned ways, challenging them by speaking for "Indian genius and culture." As these commercial and industrial leaders laid claim to representing the public by managing the market, they also elaborated culturalist discourses: applauding modern market ethics, they became capitalist ethnics.

Interested in this relationship between market ethics and ethnics, between agency and subjectivity, this chapter considers key social reform discourse of the 1920s, especially the publicizing of status-of-women questions, as an archive for the history of market society in India. In the 1920s, indigenous merchant-capitalists began to manage the question of capitalism's difference as a question of culture, speaking both as nativist nationalists *and* as defenders of community orthodoxy. Far from an age-old leftover, the culturalist call to protect the joint family, which expertly deployed the colonial public/private distinction, evinced an active appropriation of capitalist modernity's valorization of market value. Vernacular capitalists staked a place in the colonial global, and did so through the gendered production of the local, especially in the defense of the joint family system.[2]

By the time of the First World War, the standardization of market practice had engendered greater suspicion of kinship-based commercial activity and the operations of the family firm. And by the 1920s, commercial groups directly addressed this malaise via their expanded civic participation in native chambers of commerce, through demands for greater representation on civic bodies such as port trusts and municipal corporations, and in their roles as informants on official policy on tariffs, trade, and currency. As historians have emphasized, the spread of nationalism fortified the ascendancy of vernacular capitalists, who promoted themselves as managers of and experts on the wealth of the emerging nation.[3] But with the historical emergence of modern Indian Economic Man, the masculine subject of rational interest, came figurations of Woman, as site of culture, of community protection, and as collective political subject of rights discourses.[4] This chapter elaborates on capitalism's modes of governing through the social reform discourse of the 1920s. The discourse on women and family in this period acts a lever for opening the relationship of capital and community. By this I mean not only the relationship of capital and nation, but the social life of capital more broadly, in its various incarnations as family, clan, caste, and ethnic/communal identity.

Histories of indigenous capitalism address social-reform discourses only summarily, if at all. This is a surprising gap, given the rich research on the symbolic centrality of marriage and the exchange of women for the circulation of credit, the consolidation of business alliances, and insurance. Commercial arrangements were not simply "prescribed by codes of conduct for kin, by recipes for relatives," but rather reflected the dynamic production of family itself.[5] While histories of indigenous capitalism have emphasized that kinship did not refer to a set of static rules for sex-gender relations, but rather a management of inseparable commercial and social imperatives, they have not considered the emergence of the family as a subject of public contestation or its public representation as a cultural system.[6] Research in gender studies, in contrast, has engaged public discourse on family as a key site for the genealogy of colonial modernity.[7] Feminist scholarship has engaged questions concerning the relationship of law, cultural discourses, and economic formations, particularly through the problem of women's inheritance and property rights. Such studies have examined the law as a site for comparing the institutionalization of cultural orthodoxy (especially in personal law) with the institutionalization of capitalist development and individual private property rights.[8] Highlighting the Marwari story in capitalist subject formation, this chapter brings histories of capitalism into conversation with feminist approaches. Vernacular capitalists' claims to market governance were mediated by the fortification of the joint family and by orthodox formulations of culture as a political script. As such, this chapter explores idioms of gemeinshaft as effects of a politics of gesellschaft.

Social reform holds a prominent place in Marwari caste histories, which were written extensively beginning in the 1930s. They recount internal community battles over the age of consent and widow remarriage as the birth pangs of a modernist consciousness, characterizing social-reform movements as indices of the community's moral progress and exorcism of backward customs.[9] Secondary literature on the emergence of the Indian capitalist class has highlighted distinctions between orthodox and social-reformist Marwaris along material lines, as a class distinction "between *banians*, still very dependent on their British connections, and men . . . who had become business magnates in their own right." Ethnographies, for their part, have portrayed Marwaris as strong examples of community performance in an emergent colonial-national public culture.[10] Unpacking this disciplinary distinction between Marwaris as economic actors and as cultural ones, we pursue debates in social reform as condensing a long history of negotiation over the joint family and its capacities as vehicle for modernizing capitalist agency.

In the late nineteenth century, upwardly mobile urban mercantile groups began to support local and regional social reform movements that sought to modernize customary practices, often by reinterpreting ancient textual authorities. The rise of nationalist ideologies coincided with the emergence of gendered community publics as well as communal violence, conservative movements for cultural preservation, and modernist critiques of anachronistic customs.[11] By the 1920s, Hindu mercantile castes, like other upwardly mobile urban middle-class groups, were actively engaged in debates over the necessity of social reform. The more conservative sectors of indigenous commerce, especially among Gujaratis, Marwaris, Aggarwal *banias*, and Jains, entered these public debates on a large scale after the First World War. By this time, the marriage customs of Hindu joint families, particularly child marriage, had come under rigorous public scrutiny. Liberal nationalist reformists introduced legislation to amend age-old practices that propagated the caste system and its corrupt practices. The public discussion over the status of women contemplated female education, applauded women's domestic contributions, and promoted their protection through reformed marriage customs. These discourses reflected the gendered production of an authentic (and bourgeois) Indian Culture, a process at the heart of nationalism's hegemonic visions.[12] Conservative sectors of the commercial world responded particularly to the government entry into the private and autonomous sphere of native culture centered on the joint family. They embraced the ancient authority of the Hindu Undivided Family and its unmediated role as protector of native women.

Among the most vocal were Marwaris, whose orthodoxy was matched by the reformism of some of the community's most prominent members, including Har Bilas Sarda, the drafter of the controversial Child Marriage Restraint Act of 1929. As recent converts to and lavish supporters of the Indian National Congress, devotees of Gandhi, and as promoters of "Hindu culture," Marwaris were at the center of all-India social reform debates. Indeed, new rifts within the community, with conservatives resisting any legislative interference in social and religious customs, and reformers calling for legislation to raise the age of consent and exhorting its members to implement female education, reflected tensions between capital's modernizing market governance and capitalism as located in historical difference. Battles between Marwari modernizers and orthodoxy attest to the homogenizing and localizing forces of capitalist transformation.

The sections below elaborate on the complicated history of the Hindu Undivided Family as an alibi for the family firm, a major theme of the chapters in part 1, and then on the production of respectability given the history presented in chapter 4. Beginning with the period from 1905 to 1920, the analysis first charts the changing public discussion of the HUF in the context of key shifts in the commercial law of partnership, which sought aggressively to place it under the purview of contract. If earlier native responses to government regulation had spoken in favor of indigenous mercantile law, by the twentieth century, commercial groups increasingly deployed the HUF and its culturalist authority to resist intervention. Turning to Marwari social-reform discourse, the analysis then highlights new public affirmations of the joint family as an economic mechanism, a theme finessed by both modernizing and conservative sectors of the community. The validation of kinship-based capitalism *through* the defense of the HUF is then pursued in important public debates on the age of consent, child marriage, and intercaste civil marriage in the 1920s. As we shall see, influential Marwari contributions to these debates cast the joint family as a source of cultural autonomy (the orthodox view) and as an object of community regulation in the service of public stability (the nationalist and reformist imperative).

From Economic to Cultural Mechanism: Changing Public
Representations of the Joint Family Firm, 1905–1920

As Marwari social-reform debates of the 1920s represented the joint family as an ancient religio-cultural institution, all sides of the debate drew authority from the ancient texts that were used in the early nineteenth-century colonial codification of the HUF's property and inheritance procedures. Conservatives cited primarily the *Dharmashastras* as sources of ancient custom, and the HUF as a time-tested arrangement. Liberals invoked the Vedas, as well as Puranic sources, as the originary texts of a "pure" Hinduism before its decay into an irrational system dominated by *kuriithiyan*, or evil customs.[13] Either way, this promotion of the joint family, and in particular the invocation of the HUF as an operative legal fiction, marked a departure from commercial groups' earlier public representations of the coparcenary unit. As chapter 3 discussed, as early as the mid-1880s, the government had solicited opinions from prominent Marwaris on legislation concerning the devolution of joint rights and liabilities and its potential recoding of family trusts along contractual principles. Rather than protest these proposals by buttressing the HUF as a protected and sanctified religious system, these opinions had argued that contractual relations only ever approximated, but could not assume, the customary operations of indigenous mercantile law. The jointness of the *Mitakshara* system was to be understood as an instrument, but not the end, of the activities of the family firm. Consequently, the opinions of two of the most powerful Marwari traders of the period had insisted on the authority of mercantile convention, rather than that of personal law, as the basis for critiquing legal interventions.[14] Culture had not yet become an alibi for commerce embedded in kinship.

From the 1880s, companies law and income tax provisions had brought the family firm into the public eye and posed it as potential object of regulation. British mercantile concerns, subject to the provisions of the Companies Act as limited liability joint stocks or as partnerships, had demanded that native firms also be regulated as contractual partnerships. Legislators equivocated on this question: they allowed family firms to elude the civil law, insisting rather that their operations fell under the authority of Hindu personal law. This solution had offered only an incomplete escape from regulation, since it delegitimized indigenous commercial practices as directed away from the public. Furthermore, the British compilation of personal law had privileged the authority of ancient texts, an authority that had been previously modulated by the specificities of situation and community arbitration.[15] But if the rules of joint succession were systematized and made open to judicial intervention, the influence of kinship on indigenous mercantile law continued to plague legislators and British traders alike. The impetus towards regulating the family firm's organization and operations under the law of contract accelerated throughout the 1890s and afterwards, particularly with new investigations into gambling and false trading practices.

A longtime complaint of British traders concerned the irregularity and unenforceability of trading arrangements with indigenous firms. The constitution of native firms shifted depending on the birth of sons within joint families and the marriage of daughters into other families. This fluidity allowed the management of debt and the transfer of capital between retail, wholesale, and moneylending concerns. British traders worried that native firms' familial structure helped them evade contractual obligations, particularly in the case of debt. In the 1890s, British mercantile interests approached the Government of India to help rectify this slipperiness by calling for an amendment of the Code of Civil Procedure to more rigorously enforce the contractual disciplines of legal partnership in the guise of enabling "persons carrying on business in co-partnership to sue and admit of their being sued . . . under their trade or professional names." Accordingly, the Judicial Department discussed the "question of Hindu joint families," which "constantly ar[o]se in connection with partnerships, especially in connection with execution proceedings." As one legal advisor to British trade explained to government officials, "Trading in the name of a deceased grandfather, or of an infant child . . . or in that of a deity as being emblematical of good luck, is unknown in England, and where a firm is composed of a number of persons as members of a joint Hindu family, there would be nothing easier than for the insolvent party to state that he was the only member of the firm, the property having been previously disposed of to other members, who would be exempted from responsibility in the event of the insolvent party swearing that he alone constituted the firm."[16]

The Home Department also cited the authority of the advocate general of Bombay, who argued that in India "a very common defense to suits is the denial of partnership." In response, legislation for registration of partnerships was posed as a possible strategy for managing "fluctuating and undefined bodies" engaging in trade and moneylending.[17] These proposals were left unelaborated, and judicial opinions held that measures for regulating family firms as contractual partnerships posed difficulties in practice. But this official discussion did imply that in the mid-1890s, indigenous firms did not categorically evoke the religious sanctity of the Hindu Undivided Family to defend themselves from commercial regulation. A common practice in resisting the intervention of contract and the courts in indigenous mercantile matters was, according to the Bombay advocate general and reports from British interests such as the Calcutta Trades Association and the Bombay Chamber of Commerce, the simple denial that the category of partnership applied to the family firm.[18]

However, the question of establishing the standard registration of all partnerships persisted, and in 1907, a draft bill on this subject was circulated to prominent indigenous chambers of commerce for opinion, including the Bengal National Chamber, the Marwari Chamber, and the Bombay Native Piece-Goods Merchants' Association. By this time, vernacular capitalists had not only become organized in such civic bodies, but the influence of the Swadeshi movement had also helped to publicize native commerce as a foundation for India's economic development. The 1907 bill was the first draft legislation to outline specific provisions for the registration of family firms. It defined a "partner" as "every person who is a member of or sharer in a Partnership as defined by the Indian Contract Act, 1872, and in the case of an undivided Hindu family having a share or interest in such Partnership or carrying on by itself a family business, every member of such family." Further, it required all family firms to register in each place where they conducted business (rather than simply at the home office) and established provisions for a registering officer with powers to demand that any firm or partnership "disclose . . . all the alterations and additions in the constitutions, membership or general nature of the business of the Firm or Partnership," in addition to requiring the standard disclosure of such information.[19]

British trading interests represented in the Bengal Chamber of Commerce, and the Madras, Karachi, Rangoon, Upper India (Kanpur), and Bombay chambers supported the bill wholly or with minor amendments. Native merchants, however, were less enthusiastic. While the Marwari Chamber of Commerce did not express an official opinion on the bill, it is important to remember that one of its most influential functions was the arbitration of disputes with non-Marwari traders. In its first year of operation, for example, the Marwari chamber settled 1,081 of 1,198 disputes between Marwaris and British and other mercantile partnerships.[20] This active engagement in informal arbitration kept the intervention of the courts at bay and protected the kinship-based operations of Marwari traders.

The Bombay Native Piece-Goods Merchants' Association was less reticent, and it sent a lengthy response to the Home Department in March of 1908. A body established in 1882 and dominated by Gujarati merchants, the association had sent one hundred members to the founding of the Indian Merchants' Chamber, a broader organization of Bombay-based trading interests including Gujaratis and a smaller number of prominent Parsis and Muslims. Taking a didactic tone, the opinion emphasized the weakness of the proposed legislation rather than any threat posed by it to the joint family, here represented as perfectly legitimate form of commercial organization:

> The Committee is of opinion that ... such legislation ... which has been under the consideration of Government and [the] mercantile community of India for the last fifty years without any effect, will be met with a general disapproval.
>
> ... A very considerable part of the native mercantile community of India is composed of firms carried on by joint Hindu families from generations to generations [*sic*] which are called family firms, the members of which are not only males but also females, both adults as well as minors. Every member of the family upon his birth becomes a coparcener not only in the family property but also in the family concern. Each of the individuals composing a joint Hindu family has an interest in such property and business ... which varies according to his or her own status; for instance, males ordinarily take specific shares, and in the case of females, daughters are entitled to maintenance and marriage expenses until their marriages, and widow of the deceased members are entitled to maintenance and provision for a suitable residence, and in some cases mothers are entitled to share equally with their son and step-son.
>
> In a family business owned by a large Hindu joint family, there must be deaths and births occurring within short intervals. According to the ordinary law in force as to partnerships, upon the death of a member of

the partnership firm, the same stands dissolved. Upon the birth of a child in a joint Hindu family, he becomes interested in the family business. The death in such a case would mean the dissolution of the firm, and the birth would bring about a reconstitution of the firm.... If the legislation as to the registration of partnerships were to be enacted, [a] considerable amount of trouble, annoyance and inconvenience would entail upon such family firms to register the constant and successive changes in... membership.... The work of the registration department would not only be cumbersome, it would be converted into a regular machinery for noting the births and deaths of a part of the population [i.e., women and children] which is outside the scope and object of the proposed legislation.[21]

The bill elicited a discussion of the joint family and Hindu law, but one that emphasized the legitimacy of the firm as family instead of the sanctity of the HUF. Linking the proposed extension of the purview of contract with governmental procedures for enumerating and surveying bodies, the association presented the joint family as a commercial mechanism with a responsibility to females and children, one which followed the ordered prescriptions of personal law. While the Bombay merchants resisted a culturalist argument, the joint family did appear as a codified and efficient system of material organization, posed in contrast with the confused reasoning of the draft bill. The association thus invoked two different logics: that of the joint family, a codified rather than customary arrangement in which commercial organization and kinship were mutually inclusive, and that of the rule of law, in which commerce (as public endeavor) and family (expressed as authority over women and children) were mutually exclusive. Officials struggled to align these but ultimately put the bill aside.

The commercial joint family again emerged as a problem for all-India fiscal legislation a decade later in proposals for an excess-profits tax on individuals, companies, firms, and Hindu Undivided Families with incomes exceeding 50,000 rupees. The First World War had brought increased profits for industrialists and traders, particularly in cotton, jute, coal, and cement, which the Government of India sought to skim for the war effort. The Super-Tax Act, passed in March of 1917, however, was not enacted as a temporary war measure, but rather as a permanent addition to India's fiscal machine. Directed specifically at trading profits, the measure addressed British interests with primary offices in India, as well as indigenous traders and industrialists operating as family firms: "The families who are affected are the joint-families engaged in commerce, and they approximate much more closely than the ordinary families to the status of the firm."[22] Still, despite the specific target of legislation, the family firm was read via the more universal category of the HUF. In Legislative Council debates preceding the act, British officials reiterated that the Hindu Undivided Family was in fact analogous to the contractual partnership or firm, and indeed to the joint-stock company. Like the Income Tax Act of 1886, the proposed legislation sought to tax families as wholes, rather than the shares of individual members, thereby maximizing the number of family firms open to excess-profits tax. But in 1886 debates, officials had argued for assessment of the HUF as a whole due to its *excessive jointness*, a principle which rendered it radically distinct from the modern joint stock. In contrast, the 1917 measure addressed the HUF as a commercial mechanism and a form of corporate economic life. According to one member of the council, the analogy with companies and firms was straightforward, since in either case,

> you find that there is always a residue left in the hands of these semi-corporations, i.e., a company does not divide the whole of its profits, but keeps a considerable sum back and puts it to reserve. In the same way partners do not spend all the income they have made; they leave a considerable portion with the firm; and in the same way, a Hindu family ... does not spend the whole of its income ... but leaves some in the family purse which goes on accumulating.... Therefore ... it is clear that you cannot let off from taxation the residue which is kept by each of these semi-corporations.[23]

The Indian members of the Legislative Council disagreed. They criticized procedures that would tax the Hindu family at the source but that would allow partnerships and joint stocks to deduct the amounts paid out to individual members or shareholders.[24] However, unlike native arguments in 1886 that had called for the assessment of individual members of the HUF rather than the family as a whole, these opinions asserted that super-tax law "would be penalising the Hindu religion, would be placing a disability on those following the Hindu law, and would encourage the division of Hindu families."[25] Madan Mohan Malaviya, the Congress conservative and spokesperson for Hindu orthodoxy, argued that "owing to the particular constitution of the joint Hindu family, members of such families would be exposed to a serious disadvantage." Reading the family firm primarily as the HUF, Malaviya argued that it would be difficult to determine which shares of the profits were allotted to individual members (and therefore not eligible to super-tax) and which constituted its corporate "residue." In order to obtain the benefits of deductions allowed to companies and partnerships, he insisted that "members of a joint Hindu family . . . must expose themselves to the danger of the breaking-up of the joint family"; otherwise, they would have to "submit to a higher taxation."[26] As Bhupendra Nath Basu, the prominent reformer from Bengal, explained, the government threatened either to penalize financially or to disrupt a time-honored institution exactly because of its cultural difference:

> The Hindu joint-family . . . cannot be easily split up. They have continued probably for centuries and for generations, and until some disruptive force comes in, it is not likely that the joint family does break up, especially in business families. And, therefore, the position will be that they will not be able to divide the income finally as has been proposed by this Bill. . . . I hope the tenacity of Hindu family life will continue in spite of adverse legislation, but is it fair to that family . . . that they should be in this way penalised, persecuted because they chose to follow ancient custom, because they do not choose to see the great advantages . . . religious or otherwise, accruing from division.[27]

The act as passed did make provisions for the deduction of expenses "actually expended" for the maintenance of any member of the joint family, a compromise reluctantly accepted by the Indian members-in-council.[28] The Super-Tax Act of 1917 had sought to regulate the joint commercial family as a trading mechanism: that is, to align its operations with models of contractual organization. In the process, native opinions publicized the indigenous trading firm as the HUF, a timeless instrument of culture, to be protected for its own sake. In so doing, they asserted that the act threw a wedge between trading families' cultural obligations and economically rational calculations. This argument at once presupposed the embeddedness of kinship and commerce and promoted them as separate and competing imperatives. Native opinions began with the assumption that the trading families to be affected by the legislation were both pious and very amenable to capitalist reasoning. Indeed, the threat of the HUF's division stemmed from the possibility that material calculations might ultimately trump the authority of ancient tradition. If the Indian members claimed that the law had been the catalyst for this tension, their insistence on the ominous threat of division reinforced the imperatives of culture and economy as distinct and exclusive logics. In this mitosis, kinship was reimagined as the source of culture, as a source of stability as well as stasis, and as a set of codes at odds with both the dangers and promises of capitalist development.

Such defenses of the Hindu Undivided Family were counterpoints to commercial groups' more aggressive postwar strategies for civic representation. Divesting themselves of the marks of kinship, merchants demanded access to public bodies as indigenous commercial and financial experts. In 1926, for example, the Royal Commission on Currency and Finance convened to consider a gold standard for India and to recalibrate the rupee's rate of exchange. They brought in witnesses from the Marwari Chamber of Commerce, Bombay; the Gujarati-dominated Indian Merchants' Chamber and Ahmedabad Millowner's Association; the Marwari Trades Association, Calcutta; and D. P. Khaitan from the Indian Chamber of Commerce, Calcutta, the Marwari-dominated organization that had recently broken off from the Bengal National Chamber of Commerce.[29] Only five years earlier, in 1921, the Marwari Association of Calcutta had sent a memorial to the viceroy asking for greater representation in civic administration and policymaking committees.[30] The community unabashedly presented itself as the voice of native commerce. This, they claimed, was a voice that had been systematically excluded from decision-making procedures affecting indigenous business concerns:

> Indian merchants in Bengal have always . . . depended on the Government for the recognition of their claims and adoption of . . . means to . . . facilitate their trade and remove their grievances. Their quietness . . . has been misunderstood and on the civic and administrative bodies . . . only persons who do not come into contact with Indian merchants, or study their needs and wishes [are included]. . . . If the constitution of any public body, e.g., Port Commissioners, Calcutta Improvement Trust, Railway Local Committees, and Commissions &c . . . be scrutinised, it will be found that . . . the Marwari community, though occupying such an important position in trade and commerce, [has] been rigorously excluded. The result has been that the real views and wishes of the

Indian Mercantile Community on this side of India have remained unexpressed and the Indian merchants are greatly dissatisfied.[31]

This new civic strategy coincided with the expansion of local representative bodies after the First World War, the setting aside of seats on municipal bodies for "Indian Commerce," and the domination of Marwaris in virtually all sectors of Calcutta's trade. But as Marwaris emphasized their status as influential economic actors in the 1920s, they also turned more consciously towards the preservation and reform of the community's social customs. The intensification of social-reform debates within the community coincided with their attempts to secure a commercial and industrial hegemony, and more broadly, a civic presence. For the first time, Marwaris presented the family separately from the commercial mechanism of the firm, as a source of self-regulation, performed particularly through the control of women in kinship exchange. This regulation of women in marriage informed the emergence of Marwari males as legitimate actors in political economy. As Marwaris' political representation and participation in sovereignty expanded—as they re-presented themselves as legitimate colonial and national subjects, claiming to be proxies for vernacular practitioners of capitalism—they elaborated new disciplines for caste, clan, and family.[32]

Public Association and Social-Reform Discourse within the Marwari Community

The interwar period saw the consolidation of Marwari community organizing that had begun at the end of the nineteenth century. Formal associations were organized on a castewide basis, and also along the subcaste ties of the two largely endogamous kinship groups that comprised the community: Agarwals (also spelled Aggarwal and Agrawal), whose ancestral homes were located primarily on the northeastern border of Rajasthan and in Ajmer, Jaipur, and Bikaner states; and Maheshwaris from Jaipur and the northern Shekhawati region of Rajasthan. These groups began to reconstitute their local *panchayats*, or caste councils, into civic associations in the first two decades of the twentieth century.[33] Both established associations for all-India representation around the time of the war. Maheshwaris and Agarwals in the Central Provinces founded the Maheshwari Mahasabha in 1912 and the Marwari Agarwal Mahasabha in 1918. (*Mahasabha* refers to a large assembly or congress of smaller associations.) Both civic organizations broadly supported social reform, though to varying degrees depending on the issue. Reflecting the geography of Marwari migration in the three decades before the First World War, local delegates from around India convened in yearly meetings of these bodies. Calcutta also remained a focal point of civic association and a microcosm of the varieties of reformist and conservative opinions expressed throughout the subcontinent. The Marwari Association of Calcutta had been founded in 1898, a year after the rain-gambling controversy, and remained a pillar of orthodox Agarwal opinion through the 1920s. In 1903, Maheshwaris and Agarwals organized a Calcutta Vaishya (the broad term for all trading castes) Sabha, or association, that advocated for social-service issues in Burrabazar. In 1913, reformist Calcutta Marwaris of both subcastes founded the Marwari Relief Society for volunteerism in public health efforts. In 1922, orthodox leaders in Calcutta founded the Didu Maheshwari Panchayat, which had split off from that city's progressive Maheshwari Sabha. In 1935, the All-India Marwari Federation, created from the merger of the two community Mahasabhas, held its first session in Calcutta.[34]

These burgeoning community organizations brought with them the proliferation of Hindi journals discussing caste-based social customs and religious traditions. Though often circulated locally, they published information on the community throughout India. One of the first, the *Marwari*, was published out of Fatepur, in the Shekawati region, from 1907 to 1908. In Calcutta, the *Maheshwari* circulated in Burrabazar from 1909 to 1911, and from 1918 to 1931, the *Marwari Hitkarak* (Marwari welfare-advocate) drew a broad Maheshwari and Agarwal audience.[35] Among the early publications that have been preserved and catalogued are the reformist *Marwari Sudhar* (Marwari reform/uplift), published in Arrah (Bihar) and circulated in Calcutta, and the *Marwari Agarwal*, the journal of the Marwari Agarwal Mahasabha, published in Indore and circulated to its members throughout India.

These reformist journals reiterated the necessities for female education, the elimination of backward customs, and the responsibility of *dan* or social welfare. One such piece, entitled "Marwari Samaj me Kuriithiyan [Condemnable practices in Marwari society]," elaborated the customs threatening the community's decline: "bal vivahe aur ayogya vivahe [child marriage and marriages in which partners are not suited to each other]; "vriddh vivahe aur kanyavikray [the marriage of old men and the sale of young girls]"; "phajulkarchi [extravagance and useless expenditure]," especially on marriage and religious rituals; "ashliltha [obscenities]" such as whistling at women; and "maadak dravya sevan [the consumption of intoxicating substances]" such as *pan* (betel leaf laced with chewing tobacco), cigarettes, and liquor. Written by a Marwari community leader based in Rajasthan, the article asserted that this decay originated in lack of education among both men and women.[36] Reflecting the community's historical association with illegitimate trading practices, articles also drew attention to the popularity of gambling within the community and its addictive potential. One even argued that "phatka bi jua ka ek ang athhva prakar hi he [speculation is itself a component or type of gambling]."[37] Reformist literature continually tied the reform of such bad habits and customs with an ethics of community self-regulation structured by respect for and protection of women; women's status constituted a focal point for progressive programs. As one piece on Marwari "Sthri-Samaj [female society]" asserted, "sthri jati ke sudhar ke sath hi hamari unnathi ki hal ho jayegi [the difficulties of our development will be resolved only with the uplift of women]."[38]

In their gendered discourse of community identity, Marwari reformers echoed the social-reform narratives of other literate, nationalist, upwardly mobile middle-class groups. Like them, Marwaris also emphasized the need for community development in the service of national progress. But more specifically, as Marwaris asserted their expertise in the management of the wealth of the nation, they advocated social progress as a reconstitution of the community's economic ethics, as a discipline on private expenditure and excess. As the industrialist Jamnalal Bajaj, a supporter of Gandhi, a Congress funder, and the president of the Marwari Agarwal Mahasabha, explained at that organization's annual meeting in 1926, Marwaris "should not only accumulate wealth" but also "spend it for the benefit of the country."[39] Urging his community not to deal in foreign cloth and advocating resistance against the drain of wealth to Britain, Bajaj's presidential address condemned "extravagance on wedding," the customs of child marriage and purdah,[40] and the "craze for ornaments."[41] The economic ethics of the community, Bajaj argued, were mirrored in its social practices, and as he urged the direction of wealth to public efforts, he demanded greater asceticism within marriage arrangements, the transfer of dowry and gifts, and household consumption. A restructured economy of marriage exchange, grounded in the education of women and the elimination of child betrothals, would purify the community in two ways: first, by revitalizing in it a Hindu asceticism, and second, by promoting the community's prudence as distributors and managers of wealth.[42] In this way, Bajaj asked that Marwari moral economy be recoded as an economic morality in which marriage customs would reflect the community's place in political economy.

However, if reformers inscribed social customs within an ethics of thrift and productivity—that is, virtues central to capitalist market exchange—they did not demand the reconstitution of Hindu marriage as a civil contract. The reformist platform consciously carved out the private household as a microcosm of Marwari civic ethics, but it never abandoned the idea of the joint and extended family as the foundation of social life. Progressive literature often spoke of the virtues of Western business methods and philanthropic efforts and consciously produced parallels between the worldviews of Marwari businessmen and Western capitalists. As one article proudly propounded about Americans and Marwaris: "Dono hisab-kithab me bare pukke hothe hein. Dono kubhi hazar-lakh se niche bathein nein karthe [Both are very accurate in accounts and bookkeeping. Neither ever discusses affairs worth less than a thousand lakhs (100,000,000)]."[43] Nevertheless, Western marriage customs were criticized for their unstable status as civil contracts. An article from the *Marwari Agarwal* of 1921, entitled "Vivahe Bandan" (Marriage ties), complained that while marriage "ek dharmic bandan mana gya he [has been respected as a religious bond]," in America, marriage "ek prakar ka sowda ho gya he [has become a sort of bargain or contract]."[44] *Sowda* was a term used by merchants to refer to the immediate, negotiated reciprocity of commercial exchange, here presented as distinct from the gift of woman in marriage. Divorce was characterized as a curious custom propagated by women's capriciousness: "As long as the wife remains happy, everything is fine. But when there is even the hint of a squabble [*zara sa khatpat*] the wife will go running to the courthouse with an application to dissolve the bond."[45] Contractual marriage posed the threat of divorce, social instability, and female ruin, particularly for women married at a young age.[46] The courthouse and the law could offer them only superficial protection; in contrast, Marwari reformists advocated the control and protection of women and girls as a community duty.

For reformers, then, the joint family resisted the operations of contract, while at the same time promoting national productivity and progress. While the HUF was not itself a market mechanism, it could, they asserted, sustain an indigenous ethics coincident with the imperatives of modernity. Here, Marwari social-reform discourse revealed the long history of suspicion with that strange creature of the bazaar: the family firm. Buttressing the firm, the Hindu joint family emerged as a model of social and material management, and so quietly legitimated indigenous modes of commercial practice. The social-reform agenda thus publicized joint kinship as the foundation for culture and for capitalist development.

Seeking to legitimize the joint family, Marwari progressives accommodated and supported nationalist legislative interventions in Hindu marriage customs. In the 1920s, a series of such proposals placed the reformist production of community at odds with Marwari orthodoxy. Orthodox opinions publicized the joint family differently: not as the source of an ethics of national progress, but as a mechanism of private cultural autonomy, and as the basis of an alternative Hindu public. Emphasizing the cultural specificity of the HUF, conservatives defended the joint family system as an ancient code that regulated social and material affairs. The social reform legislation of the 1920s thus revealed the codification of kinship both as a symbol of a particular Indian modernity and as the bastion of Indian tradition.

Marwari Responses to the Age-of-Consent Question, 1922–1924

In late 1921, Rai Bahadur Bakshi Sohan Lal, a nonofficial member of the Legislative Assembly from Punjab, introduced a bill to amend the Indian Penal Code to raise the age of consent for girls from twelve to fourteen years of age. The measure sought to "reduce the death rate amongst married girls of immature age and amongst infants" and was "expected to improve the physical constitution, longevity and mental strength of the progeny." Linking the health of the nation with the regulation and protection of women's reproductive capacities, the bill reflected an established biopolitics of social reform, and the long history of the "politics of colonial masculinity" that accompanied it.[47] The protection of girl children produced an elaborate medical discussion on women's bodies and puberty. Among Marwaris, as with other communities, the discourse on the physical health of the community also expressed concerns over masculinity and the decay of the male body.[48] The bill addressed threats produced by the practice of child marriage, a custom understood to be propagated especially among "families of high classes," of which wealthy Marwaris were considered a part.[49]

In 1891, the age of consent had been raised from ten to twelve, although the law remained largely unenforced.[50] The 1922 bill again raised the age at which intercourse would be considered rape, and therefore a criminal offense, punishable by transportation or ten years' imprisonment. Sohan Lal was quite sure that as in 1891, a "storm of controversy" would surround the bill, "in view of the custom of child marriage," but insisted that the age of consent should regulate acts within and outside the marital relation.[51] It was presented as a purely medical measure, a scientific concern which overrode any customary authority: "In England . . . [and] . . . in other civilized countries of Europe and America the age of consent for the purposes of the offence of rape is not below sixteen years; and therefore the age of consent of the girl, so far as the offence of rape is concerned, requires to be raised to sixteen years; but having regard to the custom of early marriage still prevailing amongst high classes of Hindus and Muhammadans, only a medical step is recommended for the present, and fourteen years is fixed as the age before which sexual intercourse even by the husband with [his wife's consent] . . . must be legally prohibited and be made an offence within the definition of rape in the Indian Penal Code."[52]

Fearing that the measure would be perceived as an undue interference in the "rites and usages" of Hindus and Muslims, officials surveyed the presidencies and provinces for potential opposition by orthodox sections of the public. In September of 1922, a judicial branch summary of the local government opinions emphasized the difficulties the measure would pose for conservatives throughout India; reports from Bengal, Punjab, Bihar and Orissa, and the Central Provinces were particularly cautious. Home Department opinions cited the authority of prominent orthodox men such as Rai Bahadur Hariram Goenka, a Calcutta Marwari industrialist and honorary magistrate, who reasoned that the "very rare number of cases" of spousal rape accusations was "an indication that very rarely indeed do immediate, as apart from ultimate, evils follow" from early marriage of girls.

Goenka's letter, solicited by the Government of Bengal, spoke not for the Marwari community, but for orthodox Hindus in general. Concerned particularly with the potential for criminalizing boys and men married to girls below the age of fourteen, he warned that the measure would disturb indigenous cultural norms, and indeed undermine the protections offered to women by the Hindu family. "Punishing the husband" on a charge of rape, he insisted, "would mean condemning the wife also to lifelong misery," as men would not return to their wives after imprisonment, and young girls would "practically have to lead the [lives] of widow[s]." Indeed, "such enforced widowhood" was "likely to lead to results far worse than those that are apprehended from a young man and a girl, just under 14 years of age, living as man and wife."[53] Women's social protection and cultural stability thus trumped the supposedly universal imperatives of medicine and public health: "The object which the mover of the Bill seems to have in view is to protect the health of the girl-wife and her children. In other words, the Bill is an attack on the custom of early marriage prevalent in the Hindu society. Many things can be said both for and against this custom, but I have no mind to enter into any controversy. If Hindu custom needs reform, the reform ought to come from within and not from without. Interference with social customs, based on religious laws ... is highly undesirable. As regards the Hindu society . . . there are several forces at work to bring about a change in the custom [of child marriage] and I do not see any necessity of legislating for the purpose."[54]

Responding to the unqualified authority of medical science invoked by the framer of the bill, Goenka retaliated with the authority of "custom," a set of practices "based on religious laws," which only an undefined mass called "Hindu society" ought to regulate. The Hindu family was the domain of an ancient religio-cultural code, one with its own logic of progress, to be preserved from intervention. The orthodox stance left no room for a discussion of that infamous subset of the HUF, the family as commercial firm, or for marriage as a material imperative. Debates over commercial and fiscal reform had previously posed the Hindu Undivided Family as an obstacle to commercial and fiscal progress. The orthodox stance on social reform reinforced this view by insisting that the Hindu family eluded a material logic. Or rather, it argued that the material organization of the family was wholly determined by its cultural imperatives, so that its primary material function would be that of social welfare, or the protection of women.

This culturalist argument stood in contrast with the visions of the future drafter of the Child Marriage Restraint Act of 1929, Har Bilas Sarda, who at the time held the post of the officiating district judge of Ajmer.[55] Sarda's elaborate response argued that while the abolition of child marriage ought to have "the sympathy of every right-minded person," the use of criminal law to eliminate it was an "overzealous" and intemperate response to the problem. "The proposer of the . . . legislation," he argued, "completely ignored the great and unmistakeable influence which nature and heredity," referring to India's physical climate, which had been commonly accepted as the source of a lower age of puberty, "combined with traditional notions of domestic and marital affairs and social environment . . . exercise over the mind and the physical constitution of boys and girls."[56] Medical science had to be considered in the context of "social environment," a structure that had not simply to be defended for itself, but to be recognized as a cultural system "which control[ed] and regulat[ed] the lives and happiness of millions of human beings."[57] Any successful reform would have to grapple with culture as a potent system of meaning, rather than override it through the deployment of criminal law.

The 1922 bill to amend the age of consent was defeated on its second reading, but the measure was revived in 1923 by Sir Hari Singh Gour, a zealous reformer and nonofficial member of the Legislative Assembly, who instigated a new a tug-of-war over the issue.[58] Reproducing the earlier proposal, Gour's original bill (introduced in February 1924) raised the age of consent within and outside marital relations from twelve to fourteen years. Following its review, the Select Committee amended the measure to accommodate conservative opinion, raising the age of consent only to thirteen within marriage, and to fourteen without. In discussion, Gour again amended the proposal and raised the age to fourteen within marriage and sixteen for all other circumstances. Ultimately, in 1925, the government proposed its own official bill, passed in September 1925 (Act XXIX of 1925), which again recalibrated the ages to thirteen within and fourteen outside of marriage.[59] Opinions were solicited on the original proposal of February 1924 in the spring and summer of that year. Local government officials again reiterated their concerns over offending the orthodox public and consulted associations representing that sector.

Goenka again returned an opinion, and reiterated that "social reforms must proceed from within and ... society is fast moving in that direction." His criticism, however, concentrated on the regulation of native girls' marriage age; he offered "no objection to the age of consent being raised to 14 years or even higher as against strangers."[60] The religious and cultural authority of Hindu customs could thus sanctify sexual relations otherwise constituted as rape. This assertion further ossified Hindu kinship as a protected code for the exchange of women and girls, and the regulation of their reproductive roles: "both [the] Shastras and equally secred [sic] customs enjoin consummation of marriage after menstruation."[61]

The Marwari Association of Calcutta echoed this opinion almost exactly. Speaking for the "orthodox Hindu community" (as in economic affairs they claimed representation of "Indian commerce"), the association affirmed that "the consummation of marriage on the attainment by the wife of the age of puberty is regarded as religious duty."[62] The criminalizing of men married to girls under the age of thirteen would thus "not only mean disgrace and trouble in many ways to the families of the husband and wife but will also spell utter ruin to the wife for life." Reform, the Calcutta Marwaris reiterated, had to begin from within "Hindu society," though they lauded the raising of the age of consent to fourteen "outside the marital connection" as "a step in the right direction."[63] Marwari orthodoxy thus sought to legitimize the joint family as a symbolic order, one which determined the material arrangements of the household, and most particularly the welfare and protection of women and girls. Again, the association refrained from specifying the legislation's particular implications for the joint family firm: marriage became a question of culture, and kinship only a code for the family's sex-gender relations.

During the debates over Gour's age-of-consent bill, two measures promoted by Marwari reformists concerning the marriage age for boys were also circulated for discussion. The first, the Bengal Child Marriage Prevention Bill, was drafted by Debi Prosad Khaitan in 1924; the second, a bill to prevent the marriage of young Hindu boys, was proposed by Rang Lal Jajodia, a nonofficial member of the central Legislative Assembly. A member of a prominent Marwari industrialist family who became a lawyer and politician, Khaitan was active in the early 1920s in the Marwari Association and later was affiliated with the more progressive and nationalist Marwari Trades Association.[64] Though his bill sought to prevent "Hindu child marriage in Bengal," the measure prohibited only the marriage of boys under the age of eighteen. It provided for one month's imprisonment and a fine of up to one thousand rupees for any male guardian over eighteen who contracted such a marriage.[65] Khaitan's Statement of Objects and Reasons echoed and cited the authority of Marwari reformist discourse:

> The causes of public health and education have greatly suffered by the unfortunate practice of child-marriage. . . . The *Shastras* prescribe that *Brahmacharya* [celibate studenthood, the classical Hindu conception of the stage of life preceding marriage] should be practiced at the age of 20 years and more. This injunction was closely observed by Hindus for several centuries, when they were recognised to be on a high level in every way. Their downfall synchronised with the adoption of evil customs, of which child-marriage is one.
>
> As the first stage [of reform] I propose that the minimum age for the marriage of boys may be fixed at 18. Some . . . feel that the age had better been fixed at 16 to start with. The All-India Marwari Agarwal Mahasabha fixed the minimum age at 16. The general feeling seems to be in favor of 18.[66]

In this pre-lapsarian, progressive version of Hindu cultural decline and revival, ancient texts served not to sanctify child marriage, but to villify it. Khaitan's statement invoked the pure and indeed modernist mandates of the classical Hindu scriptures, which sustained no contradiction between material well-being and ethical conduct. Indeed, referring specifically to *Brahmacharya*, Khaitan's explanation referenced a classical model for Hindu marriage and the joint family as a moral and material project. British officials in the Bengal government sympathized with the aims of the bill, though many remained concerned about orthodox backlash. Ultimately, these concerns, along with further deliberations for all-India legislation, prevented the introduction of Khaitan's provincial bill.

In December of 1924, after Khaitan's proposal had failed, Rang Lal Jajodia, a Calcutta Marwari and a moderate reformist, took up the cause of Hindu boys in the central legislature. His draft was identical to Khaitan's except that it reduced the minimum age of marriage for boys to sixteen. Jajodia attempted to introduce the bill through the assembly sessions of 1925 and early 1926, but it ultimately lapsed. Echoing Khaitan's statement, in his defense of the measure he explained that "neither the *Ramyana* or the *Mahabharata* nor the tenets of Yajnyabalk [Yajnavalka] ... which ... Hindus unanimously hold in the highest veneration and the rules of which [they] consider scrupulously binding ... prescribe early marriage." Moreover, the health of the nation, measured by "prevailing economic distress, the abnormal rate of Infant Mortality and increasing number of girl widows," required "the serious attention of all thoughtful men." Raising the minimum age of marriage for boys, he argued, "will have a simultaneous effect on the marriageable age of girls as well."[67] Reasoning thus, both Khaitan and Jajodia attempted to accommodate vocal and obstinate orthodox opinion. Both measures left the age of consent for girls at the legal minimum, and so preserved the symbolic and material crux of marriage custom: the gifting of girls, which was the glue binding joint families and family firms. These proposals did not directly tamper with orthodoxy's investment in the marriage of girls at puberty. What rendered them "progressive" was their reconceptualization of the joint family as an institution in service of modernization, both scientific and economic.

Again, Marwari reformers sought to legitimize the HUF as a foundation for national welfare, an institution in which indigenous cultural conventions did not contradict universal material imperatives. This reformist legislation thus demanded that Hindus eschew "evil customs" and so promote, rather than undermine, economic well-being within the joint family and for the public in general. In these proposals, the regulation of boys would ensure their responsible management of female social productivity, since raising the age of consent for males would result in marriages to healthy, properly mature young women, lower infant mortality, and, in the case of the husband's death, fewer child widows. Reformists thus asserted that the ethical management of the joint family would be wholly consistent with material development, as their selective citation of classical Hindu texts evidenced. The orthodox position, in contrast, legitimated the age-old customs of the joint family as culture pure and simple: an autonomous arena of Hindu ethics separate from public material concerns. At the center of these competing discourses was the HUF, a private system for the regulation of females, sanctioned by ancient authority, which for reformers contributed to public welfare, and for the orthodox constituted the foundation of an alternative Hindu public.

Marwari Resistance to Marriage as a Civil Contract:
The Special Marriage Act of 1923

Through the 1920s, Marwaris, in their public incarnations as commercial experts, advocated for capitalist industrial development, all the while proceeding in business as family firms. The public defense of the joint family on the part of both progressives and conservatives informed this adherence to indigenous methods of commercial organization. While Marwari social reformers in particular promoted the joint family as the origin of a productive ethics for capitalist development, they spoke less of the family firm in their advocacy of Indian commerce and industry. Reports of the Indian Chamber of Commerce, for example, did not publicize the family firm per se, but rather highlighted the specificities of indigenous business organization in their protests of regulatory legislation, particularly those to do with income tax and companies law. Such complaints often focused on the interventional powers of the income-tax officer in "private business affairs" and its effects on the Hindu Undivided Family.[68] In addition, kinship ties continued to structure modern forms of contractual organization. Marwari industrialists protected the kinship-based control of their newly organized public limited liability companies through the mechanism of the managing agency, a family firm which would hold the majority of shares in the concern.[69] In 1926, for example, Marwaris lobbied for the strict control of managing agencies over the directorships of joint stocks when members of the managing firm owned more than three-quarters of the shares in the company.[70] By the 1920s, Marwari commercial and industrial interests protected kinship-based organization not by promoting the validity of an indigenous mercantile law and the model of the family firm, but rather by rallying for the joint family as an absolute limit not to be transgressed by the law. Social reform and cultural protectionism, both of which sought persistently to legitimize the Hindu joint family, were central to Marwari strategies for commercial and industrial dominance. At a time when indigenous firms had become subject to greater contractual regulation in business matters, the codified legal creature called the HUF, now a valuable cultural and symbolic currency, shielded the jointness and fluidity of kinship-based commerce. Marwari responses to the idea of civil marriage in particular reveal this management of the growing monopoly of the law of contract over market relations.

The issue of establishing provisions for marriage as a civil contract emerged between 1921 and 1923, when Hari Singh Gour proposed an amendment to the Special Marriage Act of 1872. Inspired by Henry Maine's proposals for the removal of "caste disabilities," the first Special Marriage Act had provided for civil marriage in India among persons who professed no religion: that is, for those who claimed to be neither Muslims, Hindus, Christians, Jains, Parsis, nor Sikhs. In addition to serving reformist groups outside traditional religious folds, such as Brahmos, the measure offered an option for those who wished to marry across religious communities, with the condition that they abandon any religious affiliation. Gour presented his amendment in response to trends in case law proceeding the 1872 act, and in particular a Privy Council decision which held that not only did Hinduism resist simple renunciation, but that in addition, Buddhists, Jains, and Sikhs *counted* as Hindus for the purposes of succession and marriage.[71] Accommodating these juridical trends, the first version of the Special Marriage Amendment Bill provided for a form of civil marriage for those who *professed* to be Hindus, Jains, Sikhs, Buddists, Muslims, Christians, and Parsis. After discussion in the Select Committee, the bill excluded Muslims, Christians, and Parsis, who, under the provisions preserved from the 1872 act, could enter secular marriages by renouncing their faiths. However, for Hindus, Jains, Sikhs, and Buddhists who had been rendered legally incapable of renouncing their religions, the Special Marriage Amendment Bill offered civil marriage as an option for those "professing" these faiths.[72] The measure thus posited civil marriage as a legitimate relation among "Hindus" and enabled intercaste marriages among its various castes and "sects" (understood as Sikhs, Jains, and Buddhists).

Again, orthodox opinions from around India reacted to the measure as an attack on the sacrament of Hindu marriage and the sacred institution of the joint family. In mid-1921, during the first circulation of the bill, Debi Prosad Khaitan, the Calcutta reformist, wrote to the Government of Bengal as honorary secretary of the Marwari Association of Calcutta. Uncharacteristically, in this opinion the association did not openly identify itself with the "orthodox Hindu community." Rather, it spoke for Calcutta Marwaris as a whole, as representatives of "Hindu society." They reacted strongly to what they saw was a central contradiction in the measure: while the bill provided for civil marriage, it codified this relation as a form of Hindu marriage. Contractual principles thus threatened to override customary procedures and so undo the jointness central to Hindu social relations:

> Marriage in Hindu society is a purely religious question and, as laid down in the Shastras, is . . . among the most sacred of all sacraments. My Association can never agree to its being reduced to a civil contract and the purity of the Hindu society being torn up by the roots. . . .
>
> [A] marriage outside the . . . sphere [of religion] or in a different form can in no sense be said to be Hindu marriage at all. . . . Although according to the Shastras the inter-marrying people and their descendants will not have any right to the joint Hindu family home or to the worship of the family idol, there will be nothing to prevent them from claiming such a right under a law of the nature proposed. It will mean absolute defilement of the Hindu family home and idol and subvert the entire Hindu social organization. My Committee are not sure that marriages between different castes, being only civil contracts, will not be dissoluble although under the proposed law they will be called Hindu marriage.[73]

Even as some Marwaris began to promote the reform of marriage customs, they, along with the orthodox, sought to validate the joint family as a foundation of social and material organization. Marriage practices might be rethought, but the coparcenary property relations they cemented, which structured the operations of the family firm, were to be off-limits for government intervention. Unlike protests from many other noncommercial sectors of the Hindu community, this Marwari response elaborated on the standard "cry of 'Religion in Danger.'"[74] Its emphasis on inheritance procedures and the management of family trusts reflected particularly the embeddedness of kinship in extensively negotiable economies of material and symbolic exchange. The opinion did echo many others that expressed outrage at the bill's sanctioning of intercaste marriage. At the same time, the Marwari Association argued that the measure would "perpetuat[e] the evils of the caste system" by creating new subcastes under the guise of civil matrimony. Here, Marwaris again highlighted problems for inheritance, as a proliferation of subcastes would only give "rise to internecine quarrels, dissensions and complications," so dividing "Hindu society" and indeed weakening "the sentiment in favor of nationalism."[75] This decisive protest of civil marriage reflected Marwaris' earlier resistance to contractual models of commercial exchange. Marriage as a contract opened another channel for the entry of civil law into customary practice, and so the operations of the family firm. But while Marwaris emphasized the proposed legislation's impact on the material arrangements of inheritance and succession, they now defended them *as a cultural code*, as a recipe for social relations. Moreover, the emphasis on inheritance represented extended ties of marriage and lineage as the joint household, evincing a deployment of the legal category of the HUF, which coded broad networks of mercantile consanguinity and affinity as joint family coresidence.

The final act remained a purely permissive measure, but it did clarify the consequences for succession in the case of civil marriage: "The marriages under this act of any member of an undivided family who professes the Hindu, Buddhist, Sikh or Jaina religion shall be deemed to effect his severance from such a family."[76] Significantly, the entry into civil marriage immediately negated the right to "enter into any religious office or service, or to the management of any religious or charitable trust."[77] Hindu personal law would have no authority over such contracts, and their laws of succession and inheritance would follow the civil law provisions of the Indian Succession Act of 1865.[78] Thus attempting to distinguish personal law from civil procedure, the bill enforced the civil contract as at once wholly outside Hindu inheritance, and yet as the basis of an intracaste marriage for all castes "professing the Hindu faith."

Marwaris continued to protest, claiming that the introduction of contractual marriage as an option among Hindus would undermine Hindu inheritance. The Marwari Association's response to a proposed 1927 amendment to the Special Marriage Act, for example, plainly reiterated the dangers of civil marriage. The amendment, which was never passed, provided for civil marriage among persons who professed to be Muslims, Christians, or Parsis. With these changes, civil marriage would become a mechanism not only for intercaste, but also intercommunity marriage. Speaking for their community as well as for an abstract Hindu public, the Marwari Association asserted that "for a Hindu a non-religious and non-denominational marriage is inconceivable and there is no escape from the marriage ritual for him if he chooses to marry and remain a Hindu."[79] Indeed, such a measure would "seriously affect the existing Hindu laws of succession, inheritance, etc., and [would] thus practically destroy Hindu society."[80] The disruption would bring material chaos and moral anarchy: "A law of this nature will permit a man or woman to run after and marry every other man or woman who he or she may take a fancy to and to separate and begin life afresh according to each other's fancy.... What society will then be like can better be imagined than described."[81]

The Child Marriage Restraint Act of 1929: The Logic of Reform and Orthodoxy

If Marwaris agreed that the joint family resisted contractual relations, battles among them emerged with the question of legislating the age of child marriage. By the close of the 1920s, the age-of-consent question had become an attack on child marriage in particular. Har Bilas Sarda, a proponent of Hari Singh Gour's reformist interventions and an ultra-modernist, reintroduced the question in 1926 as a member of the central Legislative Assembly. The debates over the Sarda Bill, as it was called colloquially, incited the active participation of Marwaris throughout India. Their positions reflected the thematics of reform and protectionism building throughout the 1920s, and again highlighted the joint family as the site for the production of claims to public sovereignty and private cultural autonomy.[82]

Sarda gave notice to introduce his bill regulating the age of marriage in December of 1926. In February 1927, the bill was introduced in the Legislative Assembly, and set the marriage age at twelve for girls and fifteen for boys.[83] Government reports were gathered throughout July 1927, and then the bill circulated for public opinion. In March of 1928, the meeting of the Select Committee amended the bill by raising the age of marriage to fourteen for girls and eighteen for boys, and then again solicited public opinion. In late 1927, a list of thirty-nine associations and public bodies sent unsolicited petitions directly to the Government of India. Among the eight memorials received in its favor was one from the Young Marwari Sabha, Karachi. Among the thirty-one organizations that sent testimonials against it were the Marwari Chamber of Commerce, Calcutta; a public meeting of Sanatanist Hindus of Calcutta; the Burrabazar Hindus of Calcutta; the Sanatanists of Kanpur; the Marwaris of Hinghanghat (Central Provinces, near Nagpur); the Marwari Agarwal Sabha, Bombay; and the Hindu Sabha of Arrah, in Bihar; all these represented Marwaris either exclusively or in large part.[84]

In addition to outlining fines and imprisonment for those contracting child marriages, the first draft accommodated orthodox groups by providing that a girl of eleven could be married by obtaining a license of marriage from local magistrates. Opinions solicited for this draft included the Calcutta Marwari Association and the more liberal Marwari Chamber of Commerce, Bombay. The Calcutta association criticized the provision allowing for the marriage of eleven-year-old girls, arguing that the very need for the magistrate's permission would "introduce a system of marriage by license, an element of the civil marriage, in[to] the Hindu society and [also] the curse of litigation of a ruinous nature."[85] More broadly, it reasserted the unmitigated authority of the Shastras, asserting that child marriage was a purely religio-cultural question as distinct from the concerns of economy: "It is conveniently forgotten that the constitution of the Hindu society is many centuries old, and that, had that constitution been so fundamentally defective as it is now depicted to be, the Hindu community would have been wiped away from the face of the earth long ago. The present deplorable condition of the society is due chiefly to economic causes, and it is futile to expect any improvement simply by raising the marriageable age of girls and boys."[86]

The Marwari Chamber of Commerce, Bombay, on the other hand, "whole-heartedly agree[d]" with the "spirit" of the bill and attempted a compromise among the varied positions within the community. Recognizing that "the present is a most opportune moment for stamping out the social custom of child marriages which is widespread evil eating into the vitals of the Hindu Society," it cited the authority of the Agarwal Mahasabha and the Maheshwari Sabha, which, combined, "cover[ed] practically almost the whole population of the Vaishyas [commercial castes] of Northern India."[87] It reported that both organizations recommended twelve as the marriage age for girls, and for boys, sixteen and eighteen, respectively. To accommodate orthodox conventions, the chamber also lauded the provisions for the marriage of girls at the younger age of eleven.[88]

The Bombay Marwari chamber cautiously furthered the platform of reformist Marwaris who dominated powerful industrial concerns, all the while attempting to accommodate the conservative and primarily commercial sectors of the community. Responding to the amended bill in a second letter of June 1928, the organization explained that while the majority of its membership was against the bill, its board supported it.[89] Reflecting opinions on Khaitan's and Jajodia's bills from 1924 and 1925, many Marwari reformists supported the higher marriage ages for boys with little opposition but concentrated on fixing the age for girls at twelve. In 1928, responding to the amendment to the bill raising the ages to fourteen for girls and eighteen for boys, the Marwadi (Marwari) Agrawal Sabha of Bombay "wholeheartedly" supported the bill but indicated that twelve would be preferable to fourteen in the case of girls.[90] The Marwari Sammelan, another progressive Bombay cultural organization, again agreed with eighteen for boys, but recommended twelve for girls.[91] Only the Rajputana Provincial Ladies Conference, which, Sarda explained, was "composed in a proponderating degree of Marwari women," demanded "emphatically" the "immediate passing" of the bill with no amendments.[92]

Still, many Marwari men from smaller towns in India echoed Calcutta Marwari orthodoxy and, protesting any tampering with marriage ages, rejected the bill outright. A 1928 government listing of 157 petitions sent against the bill included the Marwari inhabitants of three different towns in Madras Presidency; the Jain inhabitants of forty different towns throughout north, central, and eastern India; the Agarwal Mahajan of Fatepur (Rajasthan); "the Marwari Inhabitants of Palasbari"; and the Sanathan Dharma Sabha, Bhiwani, in the Shekhawati region. In 1928, the Calcutta Marwari Association wrote yet again on the amended bill, but this time it appropriated the language of economic welfare to further their position against any tampering with the age of marriage, arguing that "in a country like India where there is no Poor Law Funds [sic], unemployment relief, National Health insurance, etc., for which the British Government spends millions every year," the marriage of girls and boys at young ages provided a safeguard against poverty.[93] Promoting the joint family as a social welfare mechanism, such arguments affirmed the growing influence of claims to national welfare in social reform discourses, even as these arguments contested the intervention of the state.

Reformist aims finally triumphed, and the Child Marriage Restraint Act was passed in 1929, establishing the minimum ages for marriage at fourteen and eighteen for females and males, respectively.[94] Public health, the reproductive future of the nation, the physical strength of its body, and the very moral fiber of the nationalist cause were at stake. As Sarda summarized in a Legislative Assembly debate in early 1929, "we must no longer refuse to remedy the wrong inflicted on the helpless ... women of India. If you refuse to [do so], people might well ask, what right have you to demand that justice should be done to you by a foreign power ruling over the country."[95] The ethical power of national sovereignty rested on the protection of its women, as subjects first of the nation, and only secondarily of their communities. In this sense, the Child Marriage Restraint Act, the culmination of a decade of social reform proposals, undermined the predominant interests of Marwaris both orthodox and reformist: the promotion of the joint family as the locus of women's protection and control, and so the promotion of community as the primary arena of patriarchal authority.[96] As Mrinalini Sinha has argued, the Sarda Act codified for the first time a universal liberal subject, the female subject of rights, thus challenging the communitarian "colonial conception of the relationship between state and society."[97]

The broad Marwari participation in the Sarda debates—as protest and as qualified support—confirmed the central feature of the social-reform debates within the community: public legitimation of the joint family and resistance to the extended purview the civil law of contract. If conservatives sought the Hindu Undivided Family's autonomy from public regulation, social reformists attempted to align its patriarchy with the aims of national progress. In the process, the domain of family was promoted as a private space, distinct from the civic public, and either wholly disjoined from it (the orthodox view) or continuous with it (the reformist). By the 1920s, Marwaris had appropriated the colonial categories of public and private first introduced in late nineteenth-century legislation to regulate market activity and charitable gifting. Since at least the 1880s, this increasingly influential commercial group experienced the tensions between the public/private distinction and their market practices, embedded in patriarchal kinship ties. In both the cultural protectionist and social-reform discourse of the Marwaris, the contractual relations of the public, those of civic and market exchange, were kept wholly distinct from the kinship-based relations of private marriage exchange, as evinced by the particularly vociferous reaction of the community to the very notion of civil marriage.

Marwari community identity and self-representations disjoined kinship from commerce, though they continued to reproduce each other in the mercantile world. But this deployment of public and private, this disjuncture between commerce and kinship, or capital and community, also supported Marwari strategies for commercial and industrial dominance. Marwari families promoted themselves as firms with the commercial expertise to manage the wealth of the nation, while firms, organized in chambers of commerce, protected their kinship-based organization and promoted the ancient sanctity of the HUF. Marwaris, like other emergent communities of the industrial bourgeoisie, thus participated in public sovereignty as economic experts and promoted their autonomy in the realm of the cultural. The precolonial mercantile bargain with sovereignty was thus reconstituted and affirmed: participation in sovereignty was indeed here coincident with mercantile autonomy, though the bargain now demanded a divided subjectivity, one which reflected the divorce of economy, as a public project, from culture, a private one. In the making of the colonial subject as capitalist, those who, like Marwaris, claimed to be legitimate agents of Capital became, at the same time, subjects of Culture.

Conclusion

Colonial Modernity and the Social Worlds of Capital

> Mr. Mittal, India's wealthiest expatriot, belongs to an ethnic group called Marwari that traditionally believes it's critical for companies to maintain family ownership. But that kind of involvement is becoming increasingly difficult in one of the world's hottest economies. . . . "We have to put behind our family interest for the interest of the industry and the shareholders at large," he says.—ERIC BELLMAN AND PAUL GLADER, "Breaking the Marwari Rules," *Wall Street Journal*, July 10, 2006

AS INDIA SHARES IN GLOBAL capitalism's future, the Indian capitalist populates the world financial press: Indian Economic Man draws a renewed attention at the turn of the twenty-first century. In recent years, the *Wall Street Journal* has intently followed the maneuvers of the steel magnate Laxmi Mittal. A 2006 article entitled "Breaking the Marwari Rules," complete with vivid color wedding photos of Mittal's garlanded son and daughter-in-law, offered a condensed ethnography of Marwari life, briefing its readers on the community's history and its strict codes of kinship in business practice. It emphasized that Mittal Steel's takeover of its chief rival, a Belgian company, had been secured by relinquishing long-held principles of family ownership; could it be that, unlike his ancestor at the turn of the twentieth century with whom we began this study, Indian Economic Man had finally distinguished capital from community, economy from culture? Certainly, the visuals that accompanied the text, displaying Rajasthani marriage rituals intact and preserved in full glitter, assured readers that culture flourished in its proper place—in the festive Hindu extended family—and as distinct from the steely mergers and acquisitions of the business world.

A Speculation on the Market and Colonial Subject

The capitalist of today has had a long history of subject formation. Detailing folds of hegemony, this book has addressed the making of vernacular capitalists as modern subjects. In the 1870s, indigenous market ethics operated relatively autonomously, governed by caste-based councils, and more broadly, conventions that allowed for an extensive negotiability between the symbolic values of kinship, lineage, and community, and the material values of credit, trade, and investment. By the 1920s, the value systems of the indigenous mercantile law, and the authority of community and corporate social forms grounded in kinship, came to be validated and reproduced through claims of cultural protection. Investigating the capitalist as a prism for modern forms of governing, this book has considered the genealogy of the colonial subject through a new lens. In 1912, the delegates at the Indian Industrial Conference had bemoaned the state of Indian Economic Man, who held "no economic ambition . . . [only] longing for *Nirvana*."[1] Such modernizing conjurings conveyed anxieties concerning the colonial subject as *economic* subject and especially as entrepreneurial capitalist actor.

The "most abstract and accessible account of the so-called colonial subject," as Spivak has argued, "would be that class . . . of indigenous functionary-intelligentsia who . . . acted as buffers between the foreign rulers and native ruled."[2] A native informant and hegemonic agent, the colonial subject is ubiquitously evoked through Macaulay's famous pronunciation in his "Minute on Education," which called for a political class "Indian in blood and colour but English in taste, in opinions, in morals and intellect."[3] It is important to note, however, that Macaulay also envisioned the colonial subject as economic actor, posing the East India Company government as an agent of moral and material progress: "It would be . . . far better for us that the people of India were well governed and independent of us, than ill governed and subject to us; that they were ruled by their own kings, but wearing our broadcloth and working with our cutlery; than that they were performing their salaams to English collectors and English magistrates, but were too ignorant to value, or too poor to buy, English manufactures. To trade with civilised men is infinitely more profitable than to govern savages."[4]

One might say that for Macaulay, the telos, that is the end and the fulfillment of empire, was the making of economic, and not political subjects. Civilized subjects were to be economic agents, so perfectly governed by market values that they could be politically sovereign (under "their own kings"). Indeed the very interests and choices of civilized colonial subjects—their ethico-political agency—would act out, through the valuing of English manufactures, the script of supply and demand for the benefit of England.[5] Macaulay's vision of a society of economic subjects, whose political agency would be trumped by their economic instrumentality, could launch a genealogy of market society in India today. This book has pushed such a project by investigating colonial liberalism and its "arrangement of economic men," to borrow Foucault's conceptualization.[6] Macaulay's prophetic words also evoke Marx's famous description of the capitalist, a "bearer" whose "subjective purpose" emerges only instrumentally, as an acting out of the metahistorical agency of capital.[7] Most thoroughly in Marx, but also in Foucault, the figure of Economic Man—as naturalized individual, practitioner of capitalism, and object of governance—opens to a critique of the autonomous, intending subject. In this critical spirit, the previous chapters have pursued the legal installation of Economic Man, mapping the enforcement of market ethics grounded in contract and its focus on unmediated, a priori intentionality. The chapters have also pursued vernacular capitalists in this spirit, reading them not as *Homo economici* but rather as subjects of market governance, thus problematizing their claims to economic agency alongside the making of new cultural subjectivities.

In his lectures on liberal and neoliberal governmentality, Foucault charts the figure of the self-interested economic subject (*le sujet d'intérêt*) of political economy as supplement to the political theory of sovereignty and the subject of law and right (*le sujet de droit*).[8] Taking a colonial route, we have charted the making of an economic subject of interest *as* a subject of law and of sovereignty. Law is a key site for examining the colonial abstraction of exchange relations in the late nineteenth century. Institutionalizing the lineaments of market society, and arranging capital's social power in a public/private wording, colonial law carved out a space for the free circulation of capital unbound by culture. The ideal subject of civil law governing the market was an individual with rational consciousness and a will effected through contract, who valorized market value. At the same time, as research in economic and social history demonstrates, other value systems—*jati*, *gotre*, ancestry, marriage—sustained the exchange and production relations of the colonial economy. These codings, and their corresponding notions of social and corporate life, which are sometimes given the name "status," did not disappear with the emergence of new disciplines of contract. This book has thus followed the making of a legitimate bearer of capital in India by working in between the study of vernacular market cultures, on the one hand, and the colonial production of economy/culture on the other.

Law, Translation, and Non-Negotiable Sovereignty

In 1887, judicial authorities in Assam were perplexed by the case of one Nasiram Lachiram, a Marwari retailer who died near Shillong, intestate and without heirs. A rare case of an indigenous merchant devoid of the markings of family and community, its central question focused on whether the deceased's property, that is, his share of the firm to which he belonged, should escheat (revert) to the Crown, or to the "State from which the merchant comes."[9] Lachiram was a migrant trader from Bikaner in Rajasthan, the princely state identified as his domicile. Juridical precedent seemed to indicate that the property should return to the Bikaner state treasury. As the British judge of the Assam Valley districts noted, "[it] is well known [that] few of our Marwari merchants are permanently domiciled in Assam.... Marwari merchants ... residing in Assam for purposes of trade do not acquire a new domicile [and] therefore succession to the moveable property of the deceased is regulated by the law of Bikaner."[10] The Bikaner court judge also asserted that "according to the laws of the [Bikaner] state, the whole property of the heirless must be made over to the [Bikaner] State Treasury.... Lachiram [is a] resident of the Bikaner territory.

[He] had [his] house and traffic here.... Therefore... the amount of money [the deceased's share of his commercial enterprise] is to be paid to the Bikaner State."[11]

The case ultimately went to the advocate general. While many precedents had been offered to him in favor of the transfer of funds to Lachiram's domicile, his response was brief and unelaborated: "I am of opinion that the property of a Marwari merchant trading in Assam who dies without heirs escheats to the Crown and not to the State to which he belonged."[12] Despite his "traffic" in Rajasthan, Lachiram's presence as a trader in Assam here erased the territorial and political claims of the Raja of Bikaner. This decision rendered the merchant a subject of British India on the basis of his participation in commerce, a domain solely under the authority of the Crown. Ruling exclusively over this domain, colonial sovereignty stood above indigenous political and social geographies. This performance of authority marked a significant change from earlier patterns of political negotiation, where "material exchange at various sites... occupied disparate, overlapping and plural domains of power."[13]

The previous chapters have sought to historicize the disembedding of the market from social geographies of trade and credit, as well as to demonstrate the impossibility of such disembedding. The focus on the (mis)translations of civil and criminal law abstracting "the market" has highlighted the distinction between law as a logic, and law as *nomos* or the conventions of localized practice. Through its own fictions, colonial law enabled and managed new, virtual forms of capital, among them corporate persons, trusts, and speculation in imagined goods. Investigating law as site for the staging of capital as modernity, this analysis has charted a universal value system in the making. It has charted the ways in which indigenous practices were made commensurate with a new value system structured by contract and the idea of "general public utility." At the same time, it has been attentive to the traces of incommensurability in that value system, to the ways in which indigenous practices elided translations such as "coparcenary partnership," "Hindu Undivided Family," "trust in mortmain," and "public/private."

Stages of Capital, Scenes of Community

Histories of Indian capitalism have contested master narratives of modernization that exorcise community or gemeinschaft corporate life from models of capitalist practice. They have done so by addressing the diverse workings of market cultures on the ground, thus focusing on the continuities between community and capital. The preceding chapters have supplemented this research by asking a different question: in what ways did colonial governance enforce a distinction between the kinship-based forms of corporate life that structured indigenous market practice, and the social world of capitalist modernity? Shifting the focus from continuities between community and capital, culture and economy, this book has investigated the production of the oppositions themselves in colonial context, and the ways in which they were challenged *and* institutionalized, especially by vernacular practitioners of capitalism.

As colonial sovereignty hedged bets across economic progress and cultural preservation, indigenous capitalists hedged political investment in the public stage of economy and in private, protected sites of culture. Following both processes, this study has highlighted these various stagings of community—both public and private—that constituted capitalist modernity in India. It has elaborated the stages of capital, both temporal and spatial, implemented by market governance, investigating them particularly as scenes of community. The colonial installation of a gesellschaft, with its many new contractually based forms of corporate association, I have argued, produced new codings of mercantile corporate life as gemeinschaft. The trajectory of Indian Economic Man from capitalist de facto to capitalist de jure saw vernacular market actors enable new social formations of capital—the company, the public/private trust, the chamber of commerce, indeed the nation itself—even as they affirmed the patriarchal authority of the joint family, religious orthodoxy, and the currency of culture. Enacting public/private as economy/culture, vernacular capitalists rendered the ethico-political currencies of their market practices negotiable with modernity, in service of the non-negotiable authority of capital and modern sovereignty. As gambles and as risk management, these hegemonic strategies open new histories of subject formation and modes of subjection in liberal regimes of market governance.

Notes

Introduction

1. Marcus Walker's *Wall Street Journal* article "India Touts its Democracy in Bid to Lure Investors Away from China" quotes B. G. Srinivas, senior vice president and head of the Europe, Middle East, and Africa division for Infosys Technologies, the Indian software-outsourcing company, who comments, "'In economic terms, India has already paid the sunk fixed costs of democracy.' . . . As a result, 'India has civil infrastructure such as a more effective legal system to protect contracts.'"

2. An editorial by Caspar Weinberger (2006), the chairman of *Forbes* magazine and former U.S defense secretary under Ronald Reagan, is representative of the explicit referencing of India's colonial history in current assessments of India's capitalist future: "Because of its years under British rule, [India] has a long tradition of familiarity with English and of upholding the rule of law. . . . It has joined China in becoming a magnet for economic growth" (Weinberger, "India: On Every Business Agenda"). Similarly, British historian Paul Johnson writes, "India has this precious tradition [of freedom of thought and expression], as well as the rule of law, both of which are legacies (I am proud to say) of British rule. The rule of law is essential to long-term investment on the largest possible scale" (Johnson, "Current Events," 37).

3. New-agey philosophies of corporate governance, espoused by CEOs both Eastern and Western, employ the *Gita* to learn "self-mastery" for leadership and attracting fortune (Engardio and MacGregor, "Karma Capitalism"). The Indian management guru C. K. Prahalad has pronounced the Mahatma himself as an ideal manager, a "master strategist" and motivator. The economist Arindham Chaudhuri has asserted that Gandhi was "'the perfect case of adopting styles to suit the culture,'" breaking ground

in a "'follower-centric'" leadership style that took account of existing conditions before setting forth policy (cited Ganapathi, "India Inc. Discovers Mahatma Gandhi").

4. Indian Industrial Conference, "Summary of Proposals," *Report of the Indian Industrial Conference*, 1912, lix–lx. The figuration of Indian Economic Man is preceded here by an account of Western Economic Man and his transfiguration from profit-oriented taskmaster to benevolent civilizer: "The conception of an 'economic man' in western economics has been very limited. He was at one time depicted as a man bent on making profits, . . . as a man stern and determined, with hardly any heart and feelings. Ideas have now changed and the modern 'economic man' of the West is depicted with a kindly face indicating benevolent intentions. Now let us picture an Oriental and especially an Indian 'economic' man: . . . His ragged dress . . . his wife and children . . . cares of dissolution of partnership . . . division of parental property . . . and lastly no economic ambition . . . [only] longing for *Nirvana*."

5. Rai Bahadur Lala Baij Nath, "Indian System of Banking and Other Business," *Indian Industrial Conference Report*, 1908, 144–45.

6. These processes are elaborated in Stokes, *The English Utilitarians and India*.

7. The classic study is Washbrook, "Law, State and Agrarian Society in India."

8. The term "development regime" is borrowed from Ludden, "India's Development Regime," which poses "the economy" as the "central cognitive invention of capitalism" (258).

9. In his classic text of historical and economic sociology, *The Great Transformation*, Karl Polanyi charts a period beginning in the late eighteenth century when what he calls "the self-regulating market," or "the economy" emerged as distinct and "disembedded" from society and customary norms. Polanyi argues that in industrializing England, the state intervened to produce the self-regulating market, destroying older forms of exchange marked by "reciprocity" and "redistribution" and transforming society into a nexus of impersonal relations. The attention to the market as effect of governance resonates for the colonial context and in contemporary development discourses. For a reading of Polanyi in the context of development, see Rankin, *The Cultural Politics of Markets*, 23–32. But the idea of "the economy," as Polanyi uses it, must be historicized, as is the project in Timothy Mitchell's *Rule of Experts* and indeed here. Here, I also rethink Polanyi's temporizing of the distinction between premodern/"embedded" and modern/"disembedded" market society. Recent work in Indian economic and social history rightly challenges Polanyi's

temporizing. See especially Subrahmanyam, "Introduction," 5–11. Studies in European history are also engaged in unpacking the embedded/disembedded distinction. For a summary, see Natalie Zemon Davis, "Conclusion." Still, I find the term "disembedding" a useful shorthand for processes by which sovereignty produces the market as its object.

10. Chakrabarty's attention to the translation of lifeworlds into labor and history in *Provincializing Europe* informs the project here. I address the translation of the lifeworlds and the hegemonies of vernacular merchant-capitalists into new languages and hegemonies of capitalist modernity and historical agency.

11. The distinction was famously elaborated by Ferdinand Tönnies, who distinguished gemeinschaft, "community," grounded in status, tied to birth, kinship, and the rights and duties derived therefrom, and gesellschaft, "society," based on the bilateral and impersonal arrangements of contract. See Tönnies, *Community and Civil Society* [*Gemeinschaft und Gesellschaft*], first published in 1887. Writing about three decades before Tönnies, Henry Sumner Maine coded this distinction as status versus contract in his analysis of Roman law, *Ancient Law*, first published in 1860. Maine then applied the distinction to his study of village communities in India in *Village Communities in East and West*, the product of a six-year stint as legal member of the Viceroy's Council in India. The gemeinschaft/gesellschaft distinction has been popularized variously in classic texts of sociology and economic anthropology. Marx's analysis of historical modes of production has, of course, finessed the distinction, as has the work of Max Weber, particularly his analysis of law and market ethics in *Economy and Society*. Polanyi's *Great Transformation* has nostalgically echoed Maine's vision of village community, even as he critiques the market as model for social relations. For a summary of these perspectives, see Polanyi, "Aristotle Discovers the Economy."

12. These moves are detailed in the two sections that follow, "The Historiography of Vernacular Capitalism in India" and "Market Governance in Colonial/Postcolonial Studies."

13. The most quoted line from this famous speech is a figuration of the native informant: "We must at present do our best to form a class who may be interpreters between us and the millions whom we govern; a class of persons, Indian in blood and colour, but English in taste, in opinions, in morals, and in intellect." Macaulay, "Minute of 2 February 1835 on Indian Education," 729. I follow Spivak's theorization of the colonial subject as hegemonic actor, and as ancestor of the postcolonial native informant. See Spivak, *A Critique of Postcolonial Reason*, esp. 359–64. Because the colonial subject's articulation of otherness legitimizes the authority of colonial

discourse by reversal, Spivak calls for "a persistent attempt to displace the reversal, to show the complicity between native hegemony and the axiomatics of imperialism" (37), a call that informs the project here.

14. For the definitive postcolonial theorizing of the subject, and the relation between subjectivity, agency, and instrumentality, see Spivak, *A Critique of Postcolonial Reason*. Summaries of Spivak on the subject can be found in Birla, "History and the Critique of Postcolonial Reason" and Birla, "Postcolonial Studies."

15. The concept of complicity as being "folded in" draws from the thematic of the fold (*le pli*) pursued in a range of poststructuralist philosophy. See especially Derrida, "The Double Session"; also Deleuze, *The Fold*.

16. Partha Chatterjee has called this the "framework of universal history." See Chatterjee, *The Nation and Its Fragments*, 33.

17. South Asian history has been at the forefront of the study of world capitalism. In particular, it has offered critiques of world-systems theory and its core-periphery model and overdetermined methodology. The foundational text of world-systems theory is Wallerstein, *The Modern World System*; for a brief summary of work in this field, see his *World-Systems Analysis*. For a representative discussion of the concept and practice of histories of world capitalism, see Bose, ed., *South Asia and World Capitalism*. Ludden, "The World Economy and Village India, 1600–1900"; and Washbrook, "South Asia, The World System and World Capitalism," both in that volume, discuss South Asia as a region, rather than merely periphery, so posing the project of studying world capitalism as an interaction among situated histories. Bose, *A Hundred Horizons*, pursues globalization via the study of regions, highlighting the material and cultural flows of the Indian Ocean, which he emphasizes is "best characterized as an 'interregional arena' rather than as a 'system'" (6). Here, Bose elaborates the research of K. N. Chaudhuri, whose richly textured narratives of the period before 1750 engage the historicity of lived space/time. See Chaudhuri, *Asia Before Europe* and *Trade and Civilization in the Indian Ocean*.

18. Guha, in *History at the Limit of World History*, addresses the concept of a world history of capital as template for all historical transition. Approaches from postcolonial and subaltern studies have variously addressed the staging of a universal history of capital and the problem of difference. See especially Chakrabarty's *Provincializing Europe* and *Rethinking Working-Class History*; Partha Chatterjee's *The Nation and Its Fragments* and *Politics of the Governed*; and Spivak, *Critique of Postcolonial Reason*, especially 67–111 on Marx's "Asiatic Mode of Production."

19. See Foucault, *Sécurité, territoire, population* and *Naissance de la biopolitique*. For summaries of these lectures, see Lemke's "Birth of Bio-

Politics" and "Foucault, Governmentality, and Critique"; see also Gordon, "Governmental Rationality." For a theorizing of the uses and limits of Foucault in colonial contexts, see Stoler, *Carnal Knowledge*, especially chap. 6 on the "circuitous colonial route" (144) to Foucault, as well as her *Race and the Education of Desire*.

20. Foucault, lecture at the Collège de France, Apr. 4, 1979, translated by and cited in Gordon, "Governmental Rationality," 23. The full text of this lecture can be found in Foucault, *Naissance de la biopolitique*. The original French reads: "La société civile, c'est l'ensemble concret à l'interieur duquel il faut, pour pouvoir les gérer convenablement, replacer ces points idéaux que constituent les hommes économique. Donc, *homo economicus* et société civile font du même ensemble, c'est l'ensemble de la technologie du gouvernamentalité libérale" (300).

21. Marx, *Capital*, 1:254.

22. The "Hindu rate of growth" was a phrase popularized in the 1970s by the Indian economist Raj Krishna, evoking India's slow growth rate. For an overview of the economy/culture formulation, see Adams, "Culture and Economic Development in South Asia." One notorious example of the ur-formulation is Lal, *The Hindu Equilbrium*. A functionalist outline of the relation of culture and economic development as "causal, correlative or relatively autonomous" is found in Thompson, "Culture and Economic Development." An example of the current dialogue on traditional cultures and modern corporate governance in the management world is Silos, *Management and the Tao*. With the decline of structural adjustment policies, development discourses now seek to acknowledge and manage culture in service of economic development, especially in gender projects. In the 1990s, the World Bank launched a gender and development theme, as well as one dedicated to culture as a resource for sustainable development; both are good examples. Amartya Sen's *Development as Freedom* engages the problem of culture and economic development, especially in his discussions of gender and human rights. For critical approaches to discourses of culture and indigeneity in development talk see Spivak, *Critique of Postcolonial Reason*, and Gupta, *Postcolonial Developments*. A study of the production of the neoliberal female subject in Nepal, Rankin's *The Cultural Politics of Markets* presents a lucid overview of the culture/economy binary in development and planning discourse.

23. Foucault's term "the conduct of conduct" is discussed later in this chapter in the section "Economy as a Problem of Law: Contract and the Conduct of Bazaar Conduct."

24. Rajat Ray, "Asian Capital in the Age of European Domination." Responding specifically to Clifford Geertz's notion of the bazaar as an arena of "peddling and petty credit transactions," Ray distinguishes the

bazaar from both the "subsistence economy of the millions of peasants, artisans and pedlars, operating on metallic currency rather than paper credit," as well as the "Western business and financial sector, lubricated by bank paper and financed at the bank rate" (552). See also Rajat Ray, "The Bazaar." For a social history of the bazaar as site of material exchange across the long durée from the late eighteenth to the early twentieth centuries, see Yang, *Bazaar India*. Mapping the bazaar empirically and as counterpoint to the colonial construction of the Indian village, Yang explores local marketplaces to deconstruct the idea of "the bazaar," a centerpiece of the "imaginative geography of Orientalism" (9). For a contemporary reading of the bazaar and vernacular capitalism through the visual culture of markets, see Kajri Jain, *Gods in the Bazaar*.

25. Studies of the social and economic history of class formation, agrarian production, and the expansion of trade and markets all take account of kinship-based capitalism for the ancient, early modern, and modern periods. More specific to the discussion at hand are histories of mercantile groups for the period after 1750. The foundational work on the merchant family as economic agent and on merchant groups as "intermediary capitalists" is C. A. Bayly, *Rulers, Townsmen and Bazaars*. Other representative examples include Douglas Haynes's study of Gujerati merchants, *Rhetoric and Ritual in Colonial India*, and Rudner's work on the Nadukottai Chettiars, *Caste and Capitalism in Colonial India*, both of which address the late colonial period, and mercantile groups' status production through gifting and marriage. Kinship and credit in the Sindhi mercantile diaspora are addressed in Markovitz, *The Global World of Indian Merchants, 1750–1947*; on Marwari entrepreneurship, see Timberg, *The Marwaris*. Subrahmanyam and Bayly, "Portfolio Capitalists and the Political Economy of Early Modern India," details the diversity of enterprises conducted by kinship-based capitalism.

26. In a reading of Polanyi, for example, Subrahmanyam summarizes that "it is now often argued that even in capitalist society, the economy remains embedded within society. No 'laws of motion' determine the working of the economy... but instead, power, politics and social relations impinge on the economic in manifold ways." See "Introduction," in Subrahmanyam, ed., *Money and the Market in India*, 7. The attention to these themes in nineteenth- and twentieth-century European history reflects established trends in South Asian history. In an essay on contemporary revisions of Polanyi in European history, Natalie Zemon Davis highlights recent scholarship that challenges the distinction between premodern/embedded and modern/disembedded practices. See Zemon Davis, "Conclusion." Summarizing essays in this volume, Zemon Davis emphasizes that "modern market relations continued to be 'embedded' with other

institutions and practices. . . . Commercial operations on both a local and international scale are informed by legal contract and calculations of rational interest, on the one hand, and by 'liens de clientele,' on the other" (288–89).

27. See, for example, the articles in Ray, ed., *Entrepreneurship and Industry in India, 1800–1947*. The functional role of economic rationality also emerges in social histories such as Bayly, *Rulers, Townsmen and Bazaars*; Timberg, *The Marwaris*; Markovitz, *Global World of Indian Merchants*; and in many other less-textured analyses, such as Taknet, *Industrial Entrepreneurship of Shekhawati Marwaris*.

28. Partha Chatterjee has argued that the call to an "Indian" history of capitalism veils colonial power in the name of an "authentic" native agency. See Chatterjee, *The Nation and Its Fragments*, 26–34.

29. Partha Chatterjee elaborates the complications of a "peculiar history of Indian capitalism" in a critique of Washbrook's "Progress and Problems." Ibid., 30–34.

30. Natalie Zemon Davis, "Religion and Capitalism Once Again?" Zemon Davis here revisits Clifford Geertz to read the memoir of Gluckel of Hamlen, the Jewish merchant woman celebrated by Werner Sombart in *Die Juden und das Wirtshaftslieben* [*The Jews and Modern Capitalism*] (1911). Exposing the functional role of rationality in Sombart's descriptions of Jewish merchant culture, and in the tradition of work following Weber's *The Protestant Ethic and the Spirit of Capitalism*, such as that of R. H. Tawney, Zemon Davis calls for engagement rather with Geertzian "webs of meaning" and "conceptual structures," reading Geertz against the grain of his own work on tradition versus modernization in Indonesia. For a recent example of such work in the case of East and Southeast Asian capitalisms, see Brook and Luong, eds., *Culture and Economy*. For South Asia, examples of this kind of anthropologically informed approach can be found in studies such as Haynes, *Rhetoric and Ritual*; Rudner, *Caste and Capitalism*; and Yang, *Bazaar India*.

31. The supplementary relationship of social history, which seeks to capture the details of the everyday, and history as critical practice attentive to the limits of that impetus to capture, is addressed in Birla, "History and the Critique of Postcolonial Reason."

32. See especially Marshall, *Bengal: The British Bridgehead*; Bayly, *Indian Society and the Making of the British Empire*; and Subramanian, "Capital and Crowd in a Declining Asian Port City."

33. *Company Raj* refers to the period of East India Company rule, officially dated from 1772, when the first governor general (Warren Hastings) took office, to 1858, when the Government of India Act transferred the governing authority of the Company directly to the British Crown.

The East India Company had arrived in the subcontinent as a trading concern in the seventeenth century. In 1757, deploying its mercenary army in Calcutta, it conspired with influential indigenous merchants to depose the ruler of Bengal, and in 1765 assumed control of that state's treasury and land revenue. The conquest of Bengal launched almost a century of territorial expansion in which conquest produced access to new land revenue, which financed Company trade, which in turn financed more conquest. The role of indigenous merchants in this expansion, and in the trade and revenue systems of the seventeenth, eighteenth, and early nineteenth centuries, has been addressed in a range of studies. See the essays in Subramanyam, ed., *Merchants, Markets and the State in Early Modern India, 1770–1870*; Asiya Siddiqi, ed., *Trade and Finance in Colonial India*; and Bayly, *Rulers, Townsmen and Bazaars*. Subrahmanyam, *The Political Economy of Commerce*, is a key study of trade and politics between 1500 and 1650. On the role of indigenous credit in the economy of late eighteenth-century Western India, see Subramanian, *Indigenous Capital and Imperial Expansion*. On trade in southern India from 1600 to 1750, see Mukund, *The Trading World of the Tamil Merchant*.

34. See Kumkum Chatterjee, *Merchants, Politics and Society in Early Modern India*; and Sudipta Sen, *Empire of Free Trade*, 11–18 and passim. Attentive to merchants' negotiations with sovereign authorities, K. N. Chaudhuri's analyses remain models for the social history of merchants in the precolonial and early colonial periods. See Chaudhuri, *Asia before Europe*, and *The Trading World of Asia and the English East India Company, 1660–1760*.

35. See especially Markovitz, *Indian Business and Nationalist Politics, 1931–39*; and Tripathi, ed., *Business and Politics in India*. A careful biography of a key figure of the period is Kudaisya, *The Life and Times of G. D. Birla*.

36. As in Yang, *Bazaar India*, especially chap. 5, "Traders, Merchants and Markets, 1765–1947," which presents a thick description, in the spirit of K. N. Chaudhuri; Bagchi, *The Presidency Banks and the Indian Economy 1876–1914* and *Capital and Labour Redefined*; Bose, ed., *Credit, Markets, and the Agrarian Economy of Colonial India*; Bose, *Peasant Labor and Colonial Capital*; and Ludden, *An Agrarian History of South Asia*.

37. Individual studies are too numerous to list here. For an overview of colonial studies as an intellectual formation see Dirks, *Scandal of Empire*, and also Dirks, ed., *Colonialism and Culture*. Representative studies, as well as syntheses of research in the field of colonial knowledge/power, include Said, *Orientalism*; Guha, *A Rule of Property for Bengal*; Cohn, *Colonialism and Its Forms of Knowledge*, and *An Anthropologist among the Historians and Other Essays*; Spivak, *Critique of Postcolonial Reason*; Cha-

krabarty, *Provincializing Europe*; Partha Chatterjee, *Nationalist Thought and the Colonial World* and *The Nation and Its Fragments*; Stoler, *Carnal Knowledge and Imperial Power*; Mamdani, *Citizen and Subject*; Prakash, ed., *After Colonialism*; Metcalf, *Ideologies of the Raj*; and Breckenridge and Van der Veer, eds., *Orientalism and the Postcolonial Predicament*. Strong examples of research on gender and colonial knowledge in India include Mani, *Contentious Traditions*; and Sinha, *Colonial Masculinity*. The now-long history of subaltern studies encompasses a broad range of questions on the politics of hegemony, historical agency, representation, and difference. The volumes are to be found in Guha et al., eds., *Subaltern Studies*, vols. 1–present. Overviews of the contributions and debates in subaltern studies are available in Chakrabarty, "A Small History of Subaltern Studies"; Spivak, "Subaltern Studies: Deconstructing Historiography"; Prakash, "Writing Post-Orientalist Histories in the Third World"; Chaturvedi, ed., *Mapping Subaltern Studies and the Postcolonial*; and Ludden, ed., *Reading Subaltern Studies*. My reading of subalternity as political inside/outside and as historical methodology can be found in Birla, "History and the Critique of Postcolonial Reason."

38. In postcolonial cultural studies, key texts on subjectivity and the politics of representation include Spivak, "Can the Subaltern Speak?"; and the essays in Bhabha, *The Location of Culture*. On gender history and the collective subject "woman," see Sinha, *Spectres of Mother India*.

39. See Cohn, "Law and the Colonial State." Important products of this process included the *Code of Gentoo Laws, or Ordinances of the Pundits*, compiled for Warren Hastings by N. B. Halhead and published in 1776; Charles Hamilton's *Hedaya: A Commentary on Muslim Laws*, published in 1791; and H. T. Colebrooke's translations of the *Dharmashastra Smriti* of Yajnavalka, Vijnesvara, and Jimutavahana, or the compilation of laws on Hindu succession and inheritance under the *Mitakshara* and *Dhayabaga* systems, first published in 1810. See also P. V. Kane, *The History of Dharmasastra*.

40. This interest is clear in the mid-nineteenth-century jurisprudence of Henry Maine. See his *Ancient Law*. Beginning in the 1870s, British legal thinkers began publishing legal digests of Hindu personal law and its application to customary practice. Important examples are Mayne, *Treatise on Hindu Law and Usage*, first published in 1878; and Trevelyan, *Hindu Law as Administered in British India*.

41. This process has been highlighted by a variety of work in South Asian legal studies. J. D. M. Derrett has outlined the standardization of personal laws in a variety of studies on inheritance procedure, charitable endowments, and the modern Hindu code. These works will be cited as appropriate in the following chapters, but an overview can be found in

Derrett, *Religion, Law and the State in India*. The tensions between the rule of law and customary modes of arbitration, both Hindu and Muslim, are also addressed in Cohn, *Colonialism and Its Forms of Knowledge*, and earlier in his "From Indian Status to British Contract." These questions are also addressed in Metcalf, *Ideologies of the Raj*. The production of the Muslim personal law is surveyed in J. N. D. Anderson, "Islamic Law and Its Administration in India" and "The Nature and Sources of Islamic Law." See also Michael R. Anderson, "Islamic Law and the Colonial Encounter in British India"; and Tahir Mahmood, *Muslim Personal Law*. The standardization of British criminal law also depended upon the privatizing of Muslim and Hindu laws; see Fisch, *Cheap Lives and Dear Limbs*; and Singha, *A Despotism of Law*.

42. Nair, *Women and the Law in Colonial India*, provides a discussion of the standardization of elite monogamous marriage and the restriction of women's reproductive and labor choices, especially among peasant and tribal groups. On the problem of slavery as domestic practice and legal form, see Indrani Chatterjee, *Gender, Slavery and Law in Colonial India*. The gendered and classed colonial construction of community itself is addressed in Singha, "Colonial Law and Infrastructural Power." Chandra, *Enslaved Daughters*, and Mukhopadhyay, "Between Community and State," examine the adoption of the gender ideologies of the Brahminical tradition for the regulation of women's sexuality. On law and the production of tradition, see Mani, *Contentious Traditions*. For a discussion of the gendered effects of the codification of personal law in postcolonial India, see Parashar, *Women and Family Law Reform in India*. The history of colonial law has informed analyses of contemporary feminism and law in India; see Menon, *Recovering Subversion*; Menon, "Rights, Bodies and the Law"; and Ratna Kapur and Brenda Cossman, "On Women, Equality and the Constitution." Sunder Rajan, *The Scandal of the State*, contextualizes gender and postcolonial citizenship via the colonial legal regulation of women's bodies and the production of woman as site of difference.

43. Much of this work has focused on temple control in south India. See Appadurai, *Worship and Conflict under Colonial Rule*; Breckenridge, "From Protector to Litigant"; Dirks, *The Hollow Crown* and "From Little King to Landlord"; and Muldiar, *State and Religious Endowments in Madras*.

44. On the reconstitution of family in the colonial period, see Indrani Chatterjee, ed., *Unfamiliar Relations*; Uberoi, ed., *Family, Kinship and Marriage in India*; and Chakrabarty, "The Family, Fraternity, and Salaried Labor," in *Provincializing Europe*, 214–36. The literature on domesticity as integral part of nationalist discourse is vast, with a concentration of work on Bengal. See, for example, Chakrabarty, "The Difference-Deferral of Colonial Modernity"; Partha Chatterjee, "The Nationalist Resolution of

the Women's Question" and chaps. 6 and 7 of *Nation and Its Fragments*; Sarkar, *Hindu Wife, Hindu Nation*; Majumdar, "Marriage, Modernity and Sources of the Self"; and Ray, *Engendering India*.

45. Cornish, *The Hindu Joint Family*, 18. While produced in cases concerning native Christians, by the 1870s, this precedent was also applied to Muslim communities. An 1878 Calcutta High Court decision established that Muslims would be "'governed by the Hindu law of coparcenary if . . . they have lived in a state of joint family as Hindus do both as regards food and caste.'" *Rup Chand Chowdhry v. Latu Chowdhry*, 3 Indian Law Reports Calcutta 97, also cited in Cornish, *The Hindu Joint Family*, 20. This precedent was gradually overturned in favor of Muslim laws of succession in all cases in Bengal, Assam, and the United Provinces. In 1900, an Allahabad High Court decision held that Muslim law was to be applied strictly and decisively over customs of inheritance that had previously been understood as overriding Muslim law; *Jammya v. Diwan*, 23 Indian Law Reports Allahabad 20, also cited in Cornish, *The Hindu Joint Family*, 21. But the customs of Muslim families and commercial groups continued to be adjudicated through Hindu law in other areas. In Bombay, a series of cases from the 1860s through to 1905 relating to the mercantile Khojas and Bohras of the Ismaili community (considered converts from Hinduism) affirmed the authority of Hindu succession, particularly for joint family businesses. See Cornish, *The Hindu Joint Family*, 22–23.

46. See Bayly, *Rulers, Townsmen and Bazaars*, 374–93.

47. Rudner's study of the "banker's trust" of the Nattukottai Chettiars offers the most detailed elaboration of this point. See especially Rudner, "Banker's Trust and the Culture of Banking among the Nattukottai Chettiars of Colonial South India"; see also Rudner, *Caste and Capitalism*, 89–103. The circulation of indigenous negotiable instruments, or *hundis*, has provided social and economic historians with extensive evidence of the efficiency and geographical expanse of "family" credit.

48. I am here borrowing Spivak's conceptualization of consanguinity and coresidence from her reading of the communal mode of power in "Subaltern Studies," 359.

49. These processes are presented in Dirks, *Castes of Mind*.

50. This argument will be primarily concerned with the *Mitakshara* HUF, though it will also address Anglo-Indian jurisprudence on *Dhayabhaga* families that affected both systems of joint property, particularly in chapter 2. The *Dhayabhaga* system asserted the absolute discretion of the father, restricted only by moral considerations, in the management of ancestral property. The sons acquired interest in the ancestral property only on the father's renunciation, caste-exclusion, or death. At that time, they succeeded to the patrilinial ancestral property and the property of the father

for undivided shares of fixed proportion. For a discussion of the intricacies of management, partition, and alienation in both systems, see Derrett, "The History of the Juridical Framework of the Joint Hindu Family."

51. I refer to the model put forth in Subramanyam and Bayly, "Portfolio Capitalists."

52. The most comprehensive example of an economic and social history of Marwari merchants is Timberg, *The Marwaris*. See also his "A North Indian Firm as Seen Through Its Business Records, 1860–1914." Many other studies of Marwaris exist as part of the economic histories of agricultural production, finance, and trade in this period, as well as in the political economy of nationalism; these will be referenced as relevant in the chapters. For ethnographic studies, see Hardgrove, *Community as Public Culture*; and Babb, *Alchemies of Violence*. Hardgrove's attention to Marwari public cultural performance adds to Timberg's economic history, but Hardgrove is not concerned with questions of capital formation and the vast body of social/economic history into which Timberg writes. These two stories are not, of course, distinct. The production of the public was intimately tied to new discourses on the economy.

53. The 1911 Census of India counted 15,000 Marwaris in Calcutta and another 12,000 in Bombay, out of an approximate total population of 525,000 Marwari immigrants throughout India. Timberg, *The Marwaris*, 88–89 and 114.

54. A detailed description of these patterns of immigration can be found in ibid., chap. 3 and appendix A.

55. For a summary of these caste histories, and the social mythology of Marwaris, see Babb, *Alchemies of Violence*, especially chap. 4 and 5.

56. See, for example, Bose, *Peasant Labor and Colonial Capital*; Chakrabarty, *Rethinking Working-Class History*; Ludden, *Peasant History in South India*; Prakash, ed., *The World of the Rural Laborer in Colonial India* and *Bonded Histories: Genealogies of Labor Servitude in Colonial India*; and Omkar Goswami, *Industry, Trade and Peasant Society*.

57. See especially Mitchell, *Rule of Experts*; on India, see Ludden, "India's Development Regime"; Prakash, *Another Reason*; Sudipta Sen, *Empire of Free Trade*; Manu Goswami, *Producing India*; and Kalpagam, "Colonial Governmentality and 'the Economy.'" Prakash highlights native elites' appropriation of the categories of Indian difference upon which universalizing narratives of colonial science and technology were premised, a concern that resonates here. Other important studies of the economy that have informed the growing literature include Buck-Morss, "Envisioning Capital"; and Tribe, *Land, Labour and Economic Discourse*.

58. Mitchell, *Rule of Experts*, 7.

59. Mitchell's argument relies on a somewhat semantic assertion that

"the economy" does not emerge until Keynesian economic science and that thinkers like Polanyi, Dumont, and Foucault use the term *the economy* anachronistically, confusing economy as a practice (as in political economy) with the economy as an abstract object. Chronologically, this can be contested with evidence of the German historical school; see Manu Goswami, *Producing India*, 335. More broadly, while the economy as an abstract matrix of economic science was certainly not yet formed in the nineteenth century, political economy as a practice of governing always presupposed and produced an object and social space of governance, a site of production and exchange to be abstracted later by economic science. Marx's critique of political economy, as a particular casting of the social, informs the project here. A summary of eighteenth-century political economy as a casting of public and social space informing mercantilism and empire in India can be found in Sen, *Empire of Free Trade*, chap. 4.

60. Mitchell, *Rule of Experts*, 85.

61. On symbolic capital, see Bourdieu, *Outline of a Theory of Practice*.

62. For Mitchell, "the economy" is a "set of practices for producing ... [the] bifurcation" of the world into "material and cultural" domains; both a "method of staging the world as though it were divided in this way into two, and a means of overlooking this staging, and taking the division for granted." Mitchell, *Rule of Experts*, 82–83.

63. In the case of India, the economic visions of nationalist intelligentsia such as R. C. Dutt and Dadabhai Naroji have been prominent subjects of analysis in the study of the economy. This nationalist discourse contributed to the coding of vernacular capitalism as a cultural formation. The asymmetrical relationship between "native" capitalists and nationalists precedes the postcolonial asymmetry of the capitalist class and the nation-state. See Birla, "Capitalists Subjects in Transition." For a study of the tensions between the postcolonial capitalist class and the state, see Chibber, *Locked in Place*.

64. Foucault, "Governmentality," 102. One among many examples of political economy as a method of analysis of the already-constituted categories of state and economy is Tomlinson, *The Political Economy of the Raj*. Social-history approaches such as Bayly, *Rulers, Townsmen and Bazaars*, offer evidence for the constitution of the state and the economy as distinct domains, though they do pursue the epistemological and governmental questions that concern recent work historicizing the economy as an object of governance.

65. Foucault, *Sécurité, territoire, population* and *Naissance de la biopolitique*. Scott, "Colonial Governmentality"; and Meuret, "A Political Genealogy of Political Economy." Foucault's essay entitled "Governmentality" is a translation, by Pasquale Pasquino, of the Feb. 1, 1978, lecture at

the Collège de France. For Foucault's mapping of the relationship between the self-interested subject, the "subject of interest" or "*le sujet d'intérêt*" of political economy, and the subject of law/rights, "*le sujet de droit*" of the political theory of sovereignty, see especially *Naissance de la biopolitique*, lecture, Mar. 28, 1979, 281–86. For Foucault, the will and desire of the self-interested economic subject is the foundation of the technology of liberal governmentality, where agency and choice are affirmed even as governable subjects are produced as calculable.

66. Foucault, "Two Lectures."

67. Foucault, *Naissance de la biopolitique*, especially lecture, Apr. 4, 1979.

68. This point is rightly emphasized in Timothy Mitchell's critique of Foucault. Still, Foucault's research on government draws attention to political economy as a practice that presupposes and produces its object; see also note 59 above.

69. Sudipta Sen, *Empire of Free Trade*, 16–17. Ranajit Guha's now classic *Rule of Property for Bengal* elaborates the varieties of political economy, particularly physiocratic, at play in the 1793 Permanent Settlement of Bengal.

70. Sudipta Sen, *Empire of Free Trade*, 119, 88, and passim.

71. Free-trade rhetoric was used to privilege the activities of Company merchants. As Sudipta Sen explains, citing from the Proceedings of the Governor General in Council in the Department of the Ceded Provinces, March 17, 1803, "the new 'freedom' of trade proclaimed by the colonial economic order . . . promised to strive 'in its fullest extent' to afford every 'facility and convenience to the merchant in the dispatch and disposal of his goods.'" *Empire of Free Trade*, 119. Free-trade rhetoric enabled monopoly; indeed, the Charter Act of 1813 did not affect the Company's monopolies in two key commodities: indigo and opium. For a discussion of the Company's methods of extraction, and discourses veiling them, in the late eighteenth century, see Dirks, *Scandal of Empire*, chap. 4.

72. The East India Company state deployed notions of public and private rights that were later abstracted into the legal categories of public/private. Under the Company, the terms *public* and *private* were directed specifically at defining physical boundaries of local marketplaces—bazaar, *hat* (a periodic or temporary village market), and *ganj* (a small, fixed-time market) alike—and distinguishing them from the private property of zamindars (landlords). As Sudipta Sen has shown, the "permanent settlement of marketplaces" in Bengal in the 1790s defined markets as "legal site[s] for sales and contracts of all things vendible" and as public spaces, not subject to the private duties of zamindars, on whose lands these marketplaces existed. *Empire of Free Trade*, 138–39. This locating of

public space as distinct from private in marketplaces is elaborated in chapter 4, in the controversy over indigenous speculation markets.

73. Recent studies on India that have drawn attention to processes that imagined and concretized the economy as a template for the nation make reference to law, but the study of law as governmental technology remains unelaborated. See, for example, Ludden, "India's Development Regime"; Manu Goswami, *Producing India*; Kalpagam, "Colonial Governmentality and 'the Economy' "; and Prakash, *Another Reason*.

74. See Aristotle, *The Politics*, bk. 1, chaps. i–xiii, for the foundational definition of *oikonomia* as the distribution and management of the household: that is, of the realm of necessity. *Oikonomia* includes acquiring goods, and Aristotle distinguishes between its just and natural forms of acquisition directed at self-sufficiency, conducted via exchange without excess or remainder, and unnatural exchange for surplus and profit, which has no limits. Smith's notions of "natural price" versus "market price" rewrite this Aristotelian distinction; *Wealth of Nations*, bk. 1, chap. 7. The authority and relevance of these categories until the twentieth century is evinced in essays like Polanyi, "Aristotle Discovers the Economy." Foucault has analyzed Rousseau's entry in the *Encyclopédie* on political economy as a key example of eighteenth-century political philosophy's attention to economy as household management. See Jean-Jacques Rousseau, "Discourse on Political Economy"; and Foucault, "Governmentality," 92.

75. Foucault, "Governmentality," 95.

76. See Foucault, *Sécurité, territoire, population*, lecture, Apr. 5, 1978, 360–61: "Il va falloir manipuler, il va falloir susciter, il va falloir faciliter, il va falloir laisser faire, il va falloir autrement dit, gérer et non plus réglementer." See also Gordon, "Governmental Rationality," 17–20.

77. See Singha, *A "Despotism of Law"*; and Hussain, *The Jurisprudence of Emergency*. Hussain addresses Foucault's narrow notion of law, which is distinguished from the apparatus of security. The distinction betrays Foucault's lack of engagement with colonialisms, in which law itself is an apparatus of security. See Hussain, *Jurisprudence of Emergency*, 14–16. I approach colonial law for capitalist development as a mechanism for the security and the predictability of markets; see especially chapter 4 on gambling and criminal law. Legal scholars outside of colonial studies who use the governmentality framework have critiqued Foucault's notion of law as "pre-modern harbinger of absolutism" (Hunt and Wickham, *Foucault and Law*, 59). These authors argue that Foucault uses the term "right" and "rights" interchangeably, therefore confusing the king's right as imperative command with modern notions of civil and human rights: "This slippage from right to rights . . . leads Foucault . . . to disparage the transformative capacity of rights within modern political systems" (45).

Such assessments miss the point of Foucault's critique of liberal government, which is to locate the mechanics of power *even in* "transformative" discourses of liberal freedom. Foucault's analysis contemplates the full register of the force of law, a move especially useful for colonial studies, where discourses of rights—legal, political, cultural—emerged *through*, and not just in opposition to, sovereign right.

78. For an important deployment of the concept of the conduct of conduct in the colonial production of modern subjects by means of "new habits of social discipline," see Scott, "Colonial Governmentality," 47, and 40–52, passim.

79. Translation mine. See Foucault, *Sécurité, territoire, population*, 196–97, for the definition of conduct: "Ce mot 'conduite' se réfère a deux choses. La conduite, c'est bien l'activité qui consiste à conduire, la conduction si vous voulez, mais c'est également la manière dont on se conduit, la manière dont on se laisse conduire, la manière dont on est conduit et dont, finalement, on se trouve se comporter sous l'effet d'une conduite qui serait acte de conduite ou de conduction." In "The Subject and Power," Foucault emphasizes that "to govern, in this sense, is to structure the possible field of action of others" (221).

80. Under Company rule, political economy directed at landed wealth had produced revenue settlements that sought to buttress landlords (*zamindars*) and yeoman-peasants (*ryots*). The legal history of the period from c. 1870–1930, an era of the accelerated global expansion of finance capital, evinces a new interest in a new kind of economic subject, classical political economy's self-interested, contracting, risk-managing agent. For a discussion of discourses of risk and the modern subject, see O'Malley, "Uncertain Subjects."

81. The writings of the prominent late nineteenth-century common law jurists involved in standardizing modern contract law (from Britain and the United States, including jurists working on colonial law, such as Sir Frederick Pollock) are collected in the Association of American Law Schools, ed., *Selected Readings on the Law of Contracts*. For a genealogy of contract-law theory from a governmentality perspective, see O'Malley, "Uncertain Subjects." See also Gordley, *The Philosophical Origins of Modern Contract Doctrine*; Peter Benson, "Introduction"; and Hamburger, "The Development of the Nineteenth-Century Consensus Theory of Contract."

82. Weber, *Economy and Society*, 1:312.

83. To do so, the historical method here begins at the empirical limit, approaching the world of the bazaar as "culture alive": that is, a "vanishing present" of living practice that requires attention to the dynamic translation of lifeworlds. On the concept of "culture alive," see Spivak, "Cultural Talks in the Hot Peace," 329. The question of culture as a name for differ-

ence is further theorized in "Translation as Culture." For my account of writing history from the limit, see Birla, "History and the Critique of Postcolonial Reason." In this analysis, culture operates as a name for historical difference, an intervention inspired by Chakrabarty, "Two Histories of Capital" and "Translating Life-Worlds," both in *Provincializing Europe*; and Chakrabarty, "Marx after Marxism." The attention to the naturalizing of culture as difference also draws from critical political theory and recent work on culture in globalization, especially Spivak and Appadurai. Appadurai works through distinctions between culture as a "virtually open-ended archive of differences," "the subset of those differences that constitutes the diacritics of group identity," and "culturalism" (*Modernity at Large*, 11–16). The literature on globalization and the relationship between capitalism and culture is growing rapidly. For an overview of the anthropology of globalization as a framework for the study of advertising, the commodity form, and cultural difference in contemporary globalizing India, see Mazzarella, *Shoveling Smoke*. Representative works from cultural studies include Lowe and Lloyd, *The Politics of Culture in the Shadow of Capital*; and Yúdice, *The Expediency of Culture*. For important critiques of culture discourses in liberal pluralism, see Balibar, "Is There a Neo-Racism?"; and David Scott, "Culture in Political Theory."

84. See Maine, *Ancient Law*; Weber, *Economy and Society*, especially vol. 1; and Maitland, *State, Trust and Corporation*.

85. Marx, "On the Jewish Question." In a reading of Hegel, Chatterjee emphasizes that in the *Philosophy of Right*, the idea of the corporate is itself indeterminate, marking an "interface between family and civil society [where] no objective line separates the private from the public." Partha Chatterjee, *The Nation and Its Fragments*, 233.

86. Marx unfortunately naturalizes the figure of this acquisitive individual in a culturalist frame, as a Jew, a move that would be undermined by his own critique. The critical strength of Marx's reading of the liberal social contract stems from its exposure as dissimulation of "universal human emancipation," an idea grounded in Marx's concept of species-being, a notion of the social that does not presuppose the individual as a priori subject. Marx's theorizing of the social entails the possibility of imagining community outside the gemeinschaft/gesellschaft distinction. See Marx, *Economic and Philosophical Manuscripts of 1844*, esp. 322–58. If in "On the Jewish Question" Marx critiques the false abstraction of the liberal social contract, in "Excerpts from James Mill's *Elements of Political Economy*" he emphasizes that political economy abstracts exchange as a model for social relations: "Economics established the estranged form of social commerce as the essential . . . form appropriate to the vocation of man" (266).

87. This process is explored especially in chapter 3. The notion of "layered sovereignty" and its colonial recasting is elaborated in Jalal, *Self and Sovereignty*.

88. For important summaries of feminist political theory, see Benhabib and Cornell, eds., *Feminism as Critique*; Pateman, *The Sexual Contract*; Butler and Scott, eds., *Feminists Theorize the Political*; and Joan Scott, *Gender and the Politics of History*.

89. Habermas's *Structural Transformation of the Public Sphere* codes the public as a space for rational-critical discussion and a ground for the agency of civil society. Published a year after Polanyi's *Great Transformation*, Arendt's *Human Condition* charted the disembedding of the market phenomenologically, seeing in modernity the invasion of the *oikos* into *polis*—the private world of base necessity (the *oikos* as defined by Aristotle) into the realm of ethical public life: that is, citizenship. This collapse of the public/private order inaugurated the "rise of the social," a public space divested of human agency and directed at the technical management of the economy. Though Arendt's analysis reproduces an ahistorical and masculinist *oikos/polis* distinction, her broad critical gesture, to expose the production of the public *as* market, and the human agent as its instrument, speaks to our concerns. For a feminist critique of Arendt, see Benhabib, "Models of Public Space." Arendt's argument opens research on the techno-bureaucratic nexus of the economy, as well as biopolitics, as in Foucault and more recently, Agamben. See Foucault, *Society Must Be Defended*; and Agamben, *Homo Sacer*.

90. Habermas, *Structural Transformation of the Public Sphere*. Important texts that follow Habermas's notion of the public as space of collective agency include Freitag, *Collective Action and Community*; Freitag, ed., *Culture and Power in Benaras*; and Haynes, *Rhetoric and Ritual*. On voluntary associations and civic space, see Watt, *Serving the Nation*; on Hindi as idiom for a vernacular public sphere, see Orsini, *The Hindi Public Sphere 1920–1940*.

91. See especially David Scott, "Colonial Governmentality." For a feminist critique of Habermas, see Fraser, "Rethinking the Public Sphere" and "What's Critical about Critical Theory?" On the inadequacy of the Habermasian model for India, see Kalpagam, "Colonial Governmentality and the Public Sphere in India." More broadly, postcolonial approaches in anthropology have challenged Habermas's nation-state framework, using more robust notions of public and urban life as sociability. See Appadurai, *Modernity at Large*; and Breckenridge, ed., *Consuming Modernity*, which theorize public culture and contemporary diasporic public spheres in the context of contemporary globalization.

92. I draw here from Spivak's theorizing of the distinction between re-

presentation as portrait, and representation as proxy in Marx; see *Critique of Postcolonial Reason*, especially chap. 3. On the role of this distinction in history writing, see Birla, "History and the Critique of Postcolonial Reason" and "Postcolonial Studies."

93. Critical attention to the historical recounting of indigenous political agency is, of course, a foundational gesture of subaltern studies.

94. Partha Chatterjee, *Nation and Its Fragments*. The state/market and state/civil society binaries are further challenged in the concept of "political society." See Partha Chatterjee, *Politics of the Governed*, 38–40 and passim.

95. Partha Chatterjee, *Nation and Its Fragments*, 234.
96. Ibid., 238.
97. Ibid., 10.
98. Ibid., 236.
99. Marx called this "fictitious capital"; *Capital*. vol. 3, chap. 25.

1. The Proper Swindle

1. Poovey, *The Financial System in Nineteenth-Century Britain*, 2.

2. This chapter, its citations, and its archival sources (and their deployment/phrasing in this argument) are elaborated from my own earlier original research, first presented in Birla, "Hedging Bets," chap. 1.

3. Poovey, *The Financial System*, 2. For a discussion of the "homogenization of financial space" in this period, see Manu Goswami, *Producing India*.

4. On the law merchant and its incorporation into English common law, see Remfrey, *The Sale of Goods in British India* and *Commercial Law in British India*.

5. Poovey, *The Financial System*, 2.
6. Harris, *Industrializing English Law*, 2.

7. Maitland, *State, Trust and Corporation*, 119. Maitland's foundational essays in the political and legal theory of community, states, trusts, and corporations were first published between 1900 and 1904. On the "Bubble Act" (6 Geo. I c.18 [1720]), its role in the reconstruction of the national debt, and the proliferation of unincorporated joint-stocks, see Harris, *Industrializing English Law*, 60–78.

8. Poovey's introduction to *The Financial System* presents a lucid survey of the world of Victorian finance and especially the history of the national debt and stock exchange. For studies summarizing key aspects of financial and commercial law in nineteenth-century Britain, see Harris, *Industrializing English Law*; Lester, *Victorian Insolvency*; Likhovski, "A Map of So-

ciety"; Stebbings, *The Private Trustee in Victorian England*; and Mitchie, *The London Stock Exchange*. The relationship between law and economic developments in industrializing Britain is surveyed in David Sugarman and G. R. Rubin, "Towards a New History of Law and Material Society in England: 1750–1914."

9. See Government of India, *Indian Evidence Act (Act I of 1872)* and *Indian Contract Act (Act IX of 1872)*. The contract act elaborated types of contracts (contingent, void agreements); detailed definitions of subsidiary notions of agreement, consent, coercion, fraud; and outlined the conditions for their performance, including the appointment and authority of agents.

10. Here I revise Foucault's assertion that with Smith's announcement of the totality of the economic process, political economy becomes a "science laterale," a mode of knowledge for sovereignty, but no longer an art of governing. It is exactly colonial sovereignty that presumes the ability to govern totally in this way. See Foucault, *Naissance de la Biopolitique*, especially lecture, Apr. 4, 1979, and Gordon, "Governmental Rationality," especially 14–22.

11. Meyer, Burns, Cotton, and Risley, "Commerce and Trade," 264.

12. Home Charges were levies made on Indian subjects to cover a range expenses and enable the transfer of wealth from India to Britain; they were presented to Indian subjects as charges for being governed. Indian nationalists famously attacked the Home Charges as channels for what they called the "drain of wealth" from India to Britain. The charges covered the cost of running the secretary of state's India Office in London, the costs of wars in the South Asian region and abroad, the purchase of military stores, pensions for British military and civilian officials, and a guaranteed 6 percent interest on British investment in Indian railways.

13. Meyer, Burns, Cotton, and Risley, "Commerce and Trade," 263–66. On the inland customs hedge, see Moxham, *The Great Hedge of India*.

14. Meyer, Burns, Cotton, and Risley, "Commerce and Trade," 267.

15. Bayly, " 'Colonial Rule and the 'Informational Order,' " 284. On the use of law to enforce a new public circulation of information after 1830, see also Fisher, "The East India Company's 'Suppression of the Native Dak.' " For an overview of the geography of knowledges on the economy in the late nineteenth and early twentieth centuries, see Manu Goswami, *Producing India*.

16. Washbrook, "Law, State and Agrarian Society in Colonial India," 677.

17. See Rudner, "Banker's Trust and the Culture of Banking," especially 420–26, and Rudner, *Caste and Capitalism*.

18. Bagchi, "The Transition from Indian to British Indian Systems of

Money and Banking." Bagchi emphasizes that the "organized"/European-style and "unorganized"/Indian-style sides of the money market/banking sector existed under a "mutually recognized division of spheres of activity" after about 1860 (518). For an elaboration, see Bagchi, *The Evolution of the State Bank of India*, vol. 2. See also Ray, "Asian Capital in the Age of European Domination."

19. Jerry D. Leonard, "Foucault and (the Ideology of) Genealogical Legal Theory." Citing Foucault, Leonard argues that legal systems are "'mode[s] of political and economic management which exploit . . . the difference' between legitimacy and illegitimacies" (139).

20. The distinction is informed especially by Max Weber's reading of law and economy. See his *Economy and Society*, vol. 1, esp. 311–12.

21. In this book, see also the sections of the introduction entitled "Historicizing Economy as Object and Practice of Government" and "Economy as a Problem of Law: Contract and the Conduct of Bazaar Conduct." The Hindi term for the practice of economy, *arthavyavastha*, is derived from Sanskrit and embodies the root *artha*, both "meaning" and "wealth."

22. The household as social imaginary for governance supplements feminist analyses addressing the discourses and pyschogeographies of "home" in the nineteenth-century imperial formation; see Grewal, *Home and Harem*; and Burton, *Dwelling in the Archive*.

23. For a discussion of the 1844 and 1856 acts and statistics, see Harris, *Industrializing English Law*, 284–89.

24. NAI, Legislative Department, May 1882, part A, nos. 9–117, K.W. 3, proc. no. 23, Abstract of the Proceedings of the Legislative Council of the Governor-General of India, Aug. 3, 1881.

25. There were forty-seven mills in operation in Bombay by 1875, and seventy-nine by 1883. Tomlinson, *The Economy of Modern India*, 109.

26. NAI, Legislative Department, May 1882, part A, nos. 9–117, K.W. 3, proc. no. 10.

27. Ibid.

28. Ibid.

29. This point is elaborated in chapter 4 of the present volume.

30. NAI, Legislative Department, May 1882, part A, nos. 9–117, K.W. 3, proc. no. 91, from Kristodas Pal, Secty of the British Indian Association, Calcutta, to the Government of Bengal, Judicial, Political and Appointment Departments.

31. The opinions responded to the joint stock as a British-run and British-modeled organization. As the officiating judge of Calcutta's Court of Small Causes explained, "It is desirable that the laws relating to such a subject as mercantile companies should be as nearly as possible the same in India as in England." NAI, Legislative Department, May 1882, part A,

nos. 9–117, K.W. 3, proc. no. 81, from R.S.T. MacEwan to the Secty of the Government of Bengal, Nov. 5, 1881.

32. NAI, Legislative Department, May 1882, part A, nos. 9–117, K.W. 3, proc. no. 78, memorial from Munshi Sada Sukh Lal, late Government Translator, North-Western Provinces and Oudh, to the Secty to the Legislative Council of India, Jan. 31, 1882.

33. NAI, Legislative Department, May 1882, part A, nos. 9–117, K.W. 3, proc. no. 78, emphasis added. He went on to suggest specific provisions that should be implemented in the new act, including a section to prevent directors from repurchasing the property of their bankrupt joint stocks at public sale. This provision was not included in the final act, and "investment banking" in joint stocks through the managing-agency system was popularized in Bombay and Calcutta by the second decade of the twentieth century.

34. NAI, Legislative Department, May 1882, part A, nos. 9–117, K.W. 3, proc. no. 88, from Babu Bullaram Mullick, Officiating Judge of the Court of Small Causes, Sealdah, to The Undersecretary of the Government of Bengal, Nov. 17, 1881.

35. NAI, Legislative Department, May 1882, part A, nos. 9–117, K.W. 3, proc. no. 86, from Babu Protap Chandra Ghosh, registrar, Joint-Stock Companies, Calcutta, to Undersecretary to the Government of Bengal, Nov. 14, 1881.

36. NAI, Legislative Department, May 1882, part A, nos. 9–117, K.W. 3, proc. no. 86.

37. Ibid.

38. NAI, Legislative Department, May 1882, part A, nos. 9–117, K.W. 3, proc. no. 91.

39. Thus, the liquidator of a company ought not appoint his partner as a legal advisor, as "it would be highly objectionable to allow a family arrangement of this kind." NAI, Legislative Department, May 1882, part A, nos. 9–117, K.W. 3, proc. no. 86.

40. This was so much the case that in order to buttress limited liability, the act introduced *un*limited liability for directors of companies for up to one year after the declaration of bankruptcy. This was tempered by the rule that former directors were not personally liable for any debts incurred after they ceased to occupy that position. NAI, Legislative Department, May 1882, part A, nos. 9–117, K.W. 3, proc. no. 25, Statement of Objects and Reasons.

41. Ibid.

42. NAI, Legislative Department, May 1882, part A, nos. 9–117, K.W. 3, proc. nos. 28–30 recount the long history of the Calcutta Trades Association, a group organized to assist in the settling of debts among British traders in Calcutta. In the mid-1870s, it began a campaign to become recog-

nized as a public association and legal entity so that it could sue on behalf of creditors it represented. The result was section 26 of the act, which allowed for the incorporation of not-for-profit public associations. See chapter 2 for elaboration on this new legal category of nonprofit public and civic association.

43. On the *Mitakshara* joint family, see the introduction of the present volume. For an outline of the principles of *Mitakshara* inheritance, see Derrett, "The History of the Juridical Framework of the Joint Hindu Family," 17–47.

44. R. S. T. Ewan explained that "the Bill refers mainly to English public companies and to associations modeled on the form of English joint-stock companies." NAI, Legislative Department, May 1882, part A, nos. 9–117, K.W. 3, proc. no. 81.

45. NAI, Legislative Department, May 1882, part A, nos. 9–117, K.W. 3, proc. no. 45, letter from W. C. Capper, Judicial Commissioner, Oudh, to Secty to the Government of the North-Western Provinces and Oudh, Nov. 10, 1881.

46. As one scholar described it, the law interpreted Hindu firms as family businesses rather than business families. Richard Fox, *From Zamindar to Ballot Box*, 143.

47. NAI, Legislative Department, May 1882, part A, nos. 9–117, K.W. 3, proc. no. 82, from Babu Sreenath Roy, Judge of the Small Case Court, Howrah, to the Secty to the Government of Bengal, Judicial, Political and Appointment Departments, Nov. 11, 1881.

48. *Samalbai v. Someshwar* (1880), as cited in Desai, *The Law of Partnership in India and Pakistan*, 65.

49. The law of partnerships in India was finally articulated in statute in the Indian Partnership Act (1935), which emphasized the contractual nature of a partnership composed of individuals for business, as distinct from the family business conducted by members of a Hindu joint family for the benefit of the family (an asset of the HUF). See ibid., 26. The British Partnership Act of 1890 defined partnership as "the relation that subsists between persons carrying on a business in common with a view to profit." For an elaboration, see Pollock, *Digest of the Law of Partnership*.

50. NAI, Legislative Department, May 1882, part A, nos. 9–117, K.W. 3, proc. no. 90, from H. W. I. Wood, Secty, Bengal Chamber of Commerce, to Secty to the Government of Bengal, Judicial, Political and Appointment Departments, Dec. 10, 1881.

51. Foucault, "Governmentality," 99.

52. See the section on the Hindu Undivided Family in the introduction of the present volume. It is important to note again that though Hindu family firms were the focus of public discussion, non-Hindu family firms were also subject to the privatizing category of the HUF, which had been applied variously to non-Hindus since the 1860s. See introduction, note 45.

53. In 1874, Rs. 1 = 22d; in 1894 the rate had fallen to Rs.1 = 13d. Rothermund, *An Economic History of India*, 43.

54. Customs revenue decreased in this period from Rs. 25 million to Rs. 16 million; land revenue increased only slightly, from Rs. 200 million to Rs. 250 million; but Home Charges increased to due to the fall in exchange from £13.5 million (Rs. 147 million) to £15.8 million (Rs. 270 million). Ibid., 43–44.

55. The pressures of the fiscal burden were buttressed by increased military expenditures, which in turn were prompted by government support of British commercial concerns in Upper Burma, which was annexed in 1886.

56. NAI, Legislative Department, February 1886, part A, nos. 113–63.

57. Act XXXII of 1860. See Pal, *The Law of Income Tax in British India*, 5–82.

58. Ibid., 81.

59. See ibid. and M. P. Agrawal, *The Taxation of Charity in India*, 13.

60. These required every person in a profession or trade whose profits were Rs. 500 and up to take out a certificate for his work and pay a sum specified based on annual income. Again, there was a general notice of the act and then demand for voluntary returns. See Pal, *Law of Income Tax*, 83–114.

61. Ibid., 96 (for text of 1870 act); 134 (for text of 1871 act); 152 (for text of 1872 act).

62. NAI, Legislative Department, February 1886, part A, nos. 113–63, appendix A26.

63. The question of the tax-exempt status of religious organizations was also affected by the invention of the public charitable organization, which is discussed in chapter 2 of the present volume.

64. NAI, Legislative Department, February 1886, part A, nos. 113–63, proc. no. 114.

65. NAI, Legislative Department, February 1886, part A, nos. 113–63, appendix A11, Abstract of the Proceedings of the Legislative Council of the Governor General of India, Opinion of T. C. Hope, Jan. 11, 1886.

66. NAI, Legislative Department, February 1886, part A, nos. 113–63, notes of the Legislative Department. The Criminal Jurisdiction Bill, or "Ilbert Bill," of 1883 was the first piece of legislation to call for the removal of restrictions against native judges presiding over cases involving Europeans; the bill passed with the condition that in such cases the juries were to be at least half European.

67. For example, NAI, Legislative Department, February 1886, part A, nos. 113–63, appendix A11, remarks of Viswanath Narayan Mandlik, Jan. 11, 1886, in the Legislative Council of India. He strongly supported the

assessment of the wealthier classes but argued that "direct taxation, like income-tax, ... is obnoxious to the people."

68. NAI, Legislative Department, February 1886, part A, nos. 113–63, proc. no. 114, speech of Auckland Colvin.

69. For a legal analysis of taxation and its relationship to political subjecthood and citizenship in the British and British colonial contexts, see Likhovski, "A Map of Society."

70. The definition of partnership was unstable at this time. The 1880 judicial precedent had established the Hindu family firm as customary: that is, produced through the operation of law. Partnership is commonly understood as an association that is a result of contract, but that definition was not written into statute in India until 1935. In the 1880s, partnership might have been interpreted as a contractual association, but also as an association created by the operation of law. See Desai, *The Law of Partnership in India and Pakistan.*

71. NAI, Legislative Department, February 1886, part A, nos. 113–63, proc. no. 146, letter from Babu Trailokya Nath Mitra, Secty of the Indian Union, to Secty to the Government of India, Legislative Dept., Jan. 19, 1886. He proposed that "it be distinctly provided that the incomes of the individual members of the firm or family will be assessed and not their joint income, for the reason that exempting small income is applicable as much to persons who live jointly or carry on a joint business as to those who live or carry on business separately."

72. Ibid.

73. NAI, Legislative Department, February 1886, part A, nos. 113–63, proc. no. 154, letter from the President of the British Indian Association, Calcutta, to the Secty to Government of India, Legislative Dept., Jan. 26, 1886.

74. NAI, Legislative Department, February 1886, part A, nos. 113–63, appendix A11, speech of G. H. P. Evans, in Legislative Council of the Governor General of India, Jan. 11, 1886.

75. NAI, Legislative Department, February 1886, part A, nos. 113–63, proc. no. 154, letter from the President of the British Indian Association to the Secty to the Government of India, Legislative Department, Jan. 26, 1886.

76. NAI, Legislative Department, February 1886, part A, nos. 113–63, proc. no. 114, emphasis added.

77. Smith, *The Wealth of Nations*, bk. 1, chaps. 7–8. For a recent summary of Smith's notion of surplus, see Vaggi, "The Classical Concept of Profit Revisited."

78. This thematic of economy as impossible model of governance is elaborated by Foucault in his 1977–79 Collège de France lectures. The

lecture of Mar. 28, 1979, in *Naissance de la Biopolitique* addresses the totalizing project of liberal political economy via the invisibility of Adam Smith's "invisible hand," a theme that ties to his analysis of laissez-faire, the conduct of conduct, and the *"conduite"* of the self-governing liberal subject. See the introduction of the present volume, in the section "Historicizing the Economy as an Object and Practice of Government." See also Gordon, "Governmental Rationality," 14–21.

79. The managing agency system was a distinguishing feature of the late colonial economy. A managing agency was a private partnership firm that consisted of British businessmen who managed a wide range of joint-stock companies and provided them with commercial and financial services. Managing agencies had senior partners in Britain and junior representatives in India, and were key instruments in the foreign control of the Indian economy. At the end of the nineteenth century, there were about sixty such agencies, mostly based in Calcutta. For a history of the managing agency system and the racial politics of British businessmen, see Misra, *Business, Race, and Politics in India*.

80. On the "unorganized" banking sector, see Bagchi, "Transition from Indian to British Indian Systems."

81. In the early nineteenth century, Hindu law had a limited purview over the affairs of trade; the "traditions of the merchants" held authority over the personal law in cases dealing with trade. See Bayly, *Rulers, Townsmen and Bazaars*, 421. While the classical Sanskrit texts referred to the duties of the Vaishya merchants and to the ethics of profit and usury, they remained reticent on the procedures for exchange and credit. A canonical sourcebook on negotiable instruments explains that "neither of the law books of Hindus [or] Muhammadans contain any reference to negotiable instruments as such." Bashyam and Adiga, *The Negotiable Instruments Act, 1881*.

82. A *darshani hundi*, for example, might have only three days, or over a week, to be cashed or re-endorsed, depending on the ties between creditor and recipient. See Birla, "Hedging Bets," chap. 1; and Bashyam and Adiga, *The Negotiable Instruments Act*, for elaborations. On *hundis* in the context of the homogenization of financial space, see Manu Goswami, *Producing India*, chap. 2.

83. A Select Committee, consisting of a few members of the Legislative Council, would be convened when a legislative matter required further consideration.

84. NAI, Legislative Department, Jan. 1882, part A, nos. 1–211, proc. no. 206, speech of Whitley Stokes in the Legislative Council of India, Dec. 7, 1886.

85. NAI, Legislative Department, Jan. 1882, part A, nos. 1–211, proc. no. 96.

86. Ibid.

87. NAI, Legislative Department, Jan. 1882, part A, nos. 1–211, appendix I, letter from J. F. McConnell, Manager, Agra Savings Bank, to Secty, Board of Revenue, North-Western Provinces, Dec. 13, 1867.

88. NAI, Legislative Department, Jan. 1882, part A, nos. 1–211, proc. no. 97, Second Report of the Select Committee, 1878.

89. NAI, Legislative Department, Jan. 1882, part A, nos. 1–211, proc. no. 124, translation of pamphlet by Lala Nanak Chand.

90. NAI, Legislative Department, Jan. 1882, part A, nos. 1–211, proc. no. 206, and Bashyam and Adiga, *The Negotiable Instruments Act*, 10.

91. Report of the Select Committee on the Negotiable Instruments Act, published in the *Gazette of India*, 1879, vol. 75, cited in Bashyam and Adiga, *The Negotiable Instruments Act*, 17–18.

92. *Juggomohun Ghose v. Manichund*, 7 Moore's Indian Appeals 263. Discussed in Bashyam and Adiga, *The Negotiable Instruments Act*, 18.

93. See Cohn, "Law and the Colonial State," in *Colonialism and Its Forms of Knowledge*.

94. *Edelstein v. Shuler and Co.* (1902), 2 King's Bench 144, cited in Bashyam and Adiga, *The Negotiable Instruments Act*, 19.

2. Capitalism's Idolatry

1. Maitland, *State, Trust and Corporation*, 69.

2. Ibid., 69.

3. Ibid., 76.

4. Ibid. Maitland here refers to the great monopoly corporate conglomerates of the United States, later dismantled under antitrust legislation.

5. A principle inherited from Roman law in which the sovereign power might select categories of aggregate or collective bodies to hold property in perpetuity, mortmain had a long history in English jurisprudence. By the late eighteenth century, it referred to the inalienable and perpetual condition of property held in corporation for religious or charitable purposes. For an early history of mortmain, see Raban, *Mortmain Legislation and the English Church*. For a primary source history, see Tyssen, *The Law of Charitable Bequests*, and *New Law of Charitable Bequests, being an account of the Mortmain and Charitable Uses Act, 1891*. Figurative usage of *mortmain* is "based on the notion that the 'dead hand' refers to the posthumous control exercised by the testator over the uses to which the property is to be applied." Simpson and Weiner, eds., *Oxford English Dictionary*, 2nd ed., s.v. "mortmain."

6. The 1601 statute was the Statute of Charitable Uses, 43 Elizabeth c. 4.

For specific cases and acts relating to the law of mortmain to 1929, see Tudor, *Tudor on Charities*, 8–12. *Tudor on Charities* is the fifth edition of the comprehensive overview of the law of charitable trusts written by Owen Davies Tudor, a barrister of the Middle Temple. Specific changes in the law of charities across the late nineteenth century can be found by cross-consulting the first four editions, published in 1854, 1862, 1889, and 1906. See Tudor, *The Charitable Trusts Act, 1853*; and Tudor, *The Law of Charitable Trusts*, 2nd, 3rd, and 4th editions.

7. Georgian Mortmain Act (9 Geo. 2 c. 36) cited in Tudor, *Tudor on Charities*, 2.

8. For a brief history of superstitious trusts and a list of cases in nineteenth-century England directed specifically against "Popish superstitions," as well as equivocal decisions from Ireland, see Tyssen, *The Law of Charitable Bequests*, 336–58. On nineteenth-century critiques of "Popery" and Hinduism in the contested space of British national identity, see Birla, "Converting the Unconverted."

9. Tudor, *Tudor on Charities*, 12, emphasis added.

10. For a history of the private trust as social and legal form, see Stebbings, *The Private Trustee in Victorian England*.

11. Ibid., 4–11.

12. Ibid., 14–15.

13. The Trustee Act of 1888, the Trust Investment Act of 1889, and the Trustee Act of 1893. For a discussion of these measures and the circumstances leading to them, see ibid., 15–19.

14. The Public Trustee Act 1906 (6 Edw. VII c. 55). See Stebbings, 59–62. See also Polden, "The Public Trustee in England, 1906–1986."

15. The concept of symbolic capital, the porous boundaries between it and material capital, and its central place in the study of the "economy of practices" are elaborated especially in Bourdieu, "Structures, Habitus, Power: Basis for a Theory of Symbolic Power," in *Outline of a Theory of Practice*, 159–97.

16. See Rudner, *Caste and Capitalism in Colonial India*; and Bayly, *Saints, Goddesses, Kings*.

17. See Appadurai, *Worship and Conflict under Colonial Rule*; Breckenridge, "From Protector to Litigant"; Dirks, *The Hollow Crown*; and Muldiar, *State and Religious Endowments in Madras*.

18. Haynes, "From Tribute to Philanthropy," 341. This argument is placed in a broader social and political context in chapter 7 of his *Rhetoric and Ritual in Colonial India*, esp. 121–29.

19. Rudner, *Caste and Capitalism in Colonial India*, 193 and 147. For an earlier period, see his "Religious Gifting and Inland Commerce in Seventeenth-Century South India."

20. See, for example, Mansfield, "Religious and Charitable Endowments and a Uniform Civil Code"; and Jain, *Outlines of Indian Legal History*.

21. Gregory Kozlowski, *Muslim Endowments and Society in British India*, 194.

22. On "anomalous Muslims," see Cornish, *The Hindu Joint Family*, esp. 22–23, and the introduction to the present volume, section entitled "The Hindu Undivided Family." Kozlowski, *Muslim Endowments and Society in British India* discusses the Mussulman *Waqf* Validating Act of 1913 as reflecting the dominant perception of Muslim endowments, particularly family *waqfs*, which were considered central for the maintenance of the declining Muslim landed aristocracy.

23. The legal use of Vedic texts is outlined in a canonical contemporary text of jurisprudence, Saraswati, *The Hindu Law of Endowments*, 18–28.

24. Ibid., 27.

25. Derrett, *A Critique of Modern Hindu Law*, 377.

26. Ibid., 377.

27. Laidlaw, *Riches and Renunciation*, 291–96.

28. Ibid., 296. For a summary of the context-specific framework of Hindu and Muslim jurisprudence, see Cohn, *Colonialism and Its Forms of Knowledge*, 57–75.

29. On the concept of layered sovereignty, see Jalal, *Self and Sovereignty*.

30. Kumkum Chatterjee, *Merchants, Politics and Society in Early Modern India*, 85.

31. Ibid., 84.

32. Derrett, *Critique of Modern Hindu Law*, 380.

33. Societies Registration Act, 1860, sections 1 and 20, reprinted in Anand, *The Societies Registration Act*, 44 and 140.

34. Aggarwal, *The Law of Religious and Charitable Endowments*, 86.

35. NAI, Legislative Department, May 1882, part A, nos. 9–107, K.W. 3, proc. nos. 28–36. Section 26 of the Indian Companies Act provided a framework for the not-for-profit limited liability corporation as distinct from the public charitable organization.

36. NAI, Legislative Department, Feb. 1886, part A, nos. 113–63, appendix A27. For an extended discussion, see Birla, "Hedging Bets," chap. 2.

37. NAI, Legislative Department, Feb. 1886, part A, nos. 113–63, appendix A25, Report of the Select Committee of the Legislative Council of India, emphasis added. By "colorable" legislators generally meant counterfeit or illegitimate gifts serving self-interest. In the British context, as stated earlier, these included "deathbed" gifts that interfered with inheritance, and gifts that served "Popish idolatries," such as gifts to maintain priests who would pray for dead persons. In India, "colorable gifts to idols"

was a broad and slippery category, including gifts for what were deemed superstitious purposes, gifts to invented deities, and gifts that could be tapped into in times of need or for other purposes.

38. As John Mansfield has argued, endowments under personal law are different from trusts "under which a distinction is drawn between legal and equitable title," even though endowment and trusts share "ideas concerning fiduciary obligation." Mansfield, "Religious and Charitable Endowments and a Uniform Civil Code," 75. The predominance of the legal notion of trust as mirroring Hindu practice is perhaps best illustrated by M. K. Gandhi's promotion of trusteeship, which emerged in the second decade of the twentieth century as the ideal role for Indian business in its relation to the nation: the controllers and managers of the nation's property for the benefit of the nation itself. See Gandhi, *My Theory of Trusteeship*.

39. Mukherjea, *The Hindu Law of Religious and Charitable Trust*, 7, and Aggarwal, *The Law of Religious and Charitable Endowments*, 82.

40. Mukherjea, *The Hindu Law of Religious and Charitable Trust*, 7.

41. Aggarwal, *The Law of Religious and Charitable Endowments*, 82; Mukherjea, *Hindu Law of Religious and Charitable Trust*, 7.

42. Mukherjea, *The Hindu Law of Religious and Charitable Trust*, 34.

43. Mukherjea discusses the "legal ideas underlying various types of Hindu religious and charitable institutions" and provides an overview of these sources. He concludes by emphasizing that Hindu law offered only "scanty" rules for the regulation of endowments. Ibid., 33–51, quote on 49. Vedic and Shastric authorities were reticent on the primacy (and specificity) of intention. Though even the classical *Smriti* sources selectively codified in the Hindu law, including Manu, Narada, and Yajynavalka, were silent on the notion of a trust, the idea itself emerged by the 1920s as a standard paradigm for the property relations of indigenous endowments.

44. See note 14.

45. Aggarwal, *The Law of Religious and Charitable Endowments*, 90.

46. Srinivasan, *Tax Treatment of Private Trusts*, 4.

47. Mukherjea, *The Hindu Law of Religious and Charitable Trust*, 48.

48. The idea of the gift as an exchange, and part of an economy, has been addressed by a long tradition of social and economic theorists, each offering a staging/temporizing of exchange relations. The anthropology of exchange has argued that the gift cannot be separated from the notion of a calculated reciprocity. Mauss's *The Gift* is the seminal text in this effort. He informs Polanyi's notion of "embedded" or primitive economies in *The Great Transformation*, a temporizing challenged here. Bourdieu's *Outline of a Theory of Practice* critiques Mauss by narrowing the gap between the "primitive" economy of the gift and modern capitalist exchange. The gift

economy, he argues, is as rational and calculating as its modern descendant; it therefore rests upon a misrecognition, a willful ignorance of its own calculatedness. Thus, Bourdieu's theory of symbolic capital asserts the embeddedness of the "primitive" misrecognition of calculated gift exchange within the practices of modern capitalism. Derrida's *Given Time: 1. Counterfeit Money* goes farther by conceptualizing the gift as (im)possible. Here, circulation, exchange, and reciprocity are not simply understood as being *instituted* by the gift as in the Maussian tradition, but rather, as constituting its condition of possibility. The gift requires receipt, and yet in very the moment of its reception it is undone. Like narration, which provides the possibility for the event, or "the present," exchange enables the gift, the "present" to be both possible and impossible. The temporal coding of primitive/modern in Mauss is here rethought through the problem of the gift as vanishing present. This theoretical genealogy resonates in our argument: We chart how British Indian case law enforced the distinction between the gift and market exchange. In one temporal schemata, the indigenous gift, as idolatry and excess, was to be radically outside modern market exchange, and in another, "modern" charity remained outside modern market exchange as its inside, its logical exception.

49. 13 Moore's Indian Appeals 270. The case is also discussed in Saraswati, *The Hindu Law of Endowments*, 145–46. I have reproduced the (albeit bastardized) Anglo-Indian spellings of the cases to be cited, since they have been memorialized as such in legal digests and literature.

50. Derrett, "The Reform of Hindu Religious Endowments," 319.

51. Ibid., 318; see also Derrett, *Introduction to Modern Hindu Law*, 493–98, on the status of the deity as property owner in modern Hindu law. Despite his rich empirical observations, Derrett reproduces orientalist discourses when he uses the term *idol* to refer to the deity. An idol is the object of idolatry, broadly understood as the irrational worship of an object or thing. Referring to the deity as an idol thus mistranslates both the experience of worship and the agency of the worshipper, who animates the deity through ritual practice. Colonial discourses, legal and governmental, consistently use the term *idol*, and it is only reproduced here when it appears in direct citations from sources.

52. Derrett, "The Reform of Hindu Religious Endowments," 320.

53. Thapar, *A History of India*, 1:162.

54. Derrett, "The Reform of Hindu Religious Endowments," 320.

55. *Prosonna Kumari Debya and another v. Golab Chand Babu*, 2 Law Reports, Indian Appeals 145. Also discussed in Saraswati, *The Hindu Law of Endowments*, 147–48.

56. Saraswati, *The Hindu Law of Endowments*, 149; Mukherjea, *The Hindu Law of Religious and Charitable Trust*, 160, 258.

57. Judgment, *Prosonna Kumari Debya v. Golab Chand Babu*, emphasis added. The implication of the judgment on trustee responsibility is discussed in Saraswati, *The Hindu Law of Endowments*, 149.

58. Saraswati, *The Hindu Law of Endowments*, 148. See also Mukherjea, *The Hindu Law of Religious and Charitable Trust*, 278–79 and 296, for later judgments that follow this precedent and establish the right of the *shebait* to alienate income and parts of the corpus of the endowment, while the deity's propriety right still remains inalienable.

59. The limits on the powers of alienation develop in a chain of cases beginning with *Maharani Shibessouree v. Mothooranath Acharjo*, 13 Moore's Indian Appeals 270. These developments are summarized by Mukherjea, *The Hindu Law of Religious and Charitable Trust*: "No sale or mortgage of debuttar property would be binding on the deity unless it is supported by legal necessity or benefit to the idol" (278). The burden of proof of "legal necessity," or pressure upon the estate to sell a part of its corpus, rested on the *shebait*, and in the case of a *matha*, on its manager (381). Later cases supporting this 1869 decision are *Seena Peena Reena v. Choklingam*, 31 Law Reports, Indian Appeals 83 (1904); *Abhiram Goswami v. Syama Charan*, 36 Law Reports, Indian Appeals 148 (1909); and *Palanippa v. Devasikamony*, 44 Law Reports, Indian Appeals 147 (1916).

60. *Manohar Ganesh Tambekar v. Lakhmiram Govindram*, 12 Indian Law Reports Bombay 247 (1887). The legal implications of the case are discussed in Saraswati, *The Hindu Law of Endowments*, 117–26.

61. Saraswati, *The Hindu Law of Endowments*, 118.

62. Mukherjea, *The Hindu Law of Religious and Charitable Trust*, 160. For an elaboration of this foundational argument, see Bagchi, *Juristic Personality of the Hindu Deities*.

63. The judges argued simply that though it was customary for the *sevaks* to divide up the offerings and donations to the deities at their discretion, this did not imply ownership of any kind. *Manohar Ganesh Tambekar v. Lakhmiram Govindram*, 12 Indian Law Reports Bombay 247. This section of the judgment is also discussed in Saraswati, *The Hindu Law of Endowments*, 125–26.

64. Saraswati, *The Hindu Law of Endowments*, 124.

65. Like the Hindu Undivided Family, and indeed the modern company, the deity as legal person was understood both as a sort of corporate entity and also an individual owner.

66. "Legal necessity," of course, itself reinforced the power of the courts over indigenous gifting.

67. The role of the *sevak* was to conduct the distribution and management of the deity's household, or its *oikonomia*. That power of distribution and management was to be distinct from the *sevak*'s personal profit.

68. Derrett, "The Reform of Hindu Religious Endowments," 319.

69. Parry, "The Moral Perils of Exchange," 78–79.

70. Ibid.

71. For description of *Diwali puja*, see Bayly, *Rulers, Townsmen and Bazaars*, 377; Parry "The Moral Perils of Exchange," 81–82; and Laidlaw, *Riches and Renunciation*, 364–87.

72. On mercantile asceticism, see Bayly, *Rulers, Townsmen and Bazaars*, 384–85; Laidlaw, *Riches and Renunciation*, 359–63; and Haynes, "From Tribute to Philanthropy," 343–44.

73. Derrett, "The Reform of Hindu Religious Endowments," 322.

74. For an interesting example from the 1930s, see Rudner, *Caste and Capitalism*, 151–57.

75. Mr. Gopal Bagri, an income tax accountant and prominent member of the Marwari community of Nagpur, was of great assistance in compiling this information. With the help of a *munim*, or family accountant, I examined the *dharmada* accounts of retail shops connected with the Nagpur-based firm of Bansilal Abirchand, a Marwari firm from Bikaner, in the private collection of Mr. and Mrs. Krishna Daga. This firm financed the East India Company in the late eighteenth century. In the 1880s, its patriarch, Kastur Chand Daga, had been bestowed with the title "Seth." In the early twentieth century, the firm continued to dominate large-scale banking and the grain trade in central India. By the second decade of this century, it had, like many large Marwari firms, established cotton-ginning and spinning concerns in and around Nagpur. I examined the cash (*rokad*) and account (*bahi*) books and charity or religious accounts (*dharmada khatas*) from local retail concerns of Bansilal Abirchand from the early twentieth century. These included the daily ledger from the retail cloth shop of Ramchandar Ramchandardas of Hinganghat for 1907–8; the Branch Office cash book of the Berar Manufacturing Company Ltd. of Jabbalpur for 1907; and the yearly accounts for the cotton-spinning mills of Bansilal Abirchand in Hinganghat for 1921. For more detail, see Birla, "Hedging Bets," chap. 2.

76. *Dharmada Khata*, 1907, of the cloth shop of Bansilal Abirchand, at Hinganghat, near Nagpur.

77. That is, the dominance of dead accumulated labor over living labor power: "By the purchase of labour-power, the capitalist incorporates labour, as a living agent of fermentation, into the lifeless constituents of the product, which also belong to him." Marx, *Capital*, 1:292.

78. This rule was established in 1833. Mukherjea, *The Hindu Law of Religious and Charitable Trust*, 134.

79. The *Mitakshara* had a range of schools that covered differences of practice in southern, western, northern, and central-east India. In the

Punjab, British colonial authorities actively buttressed customary law, which mediated the application of the *Mitakshara*.

80. Derrett, "The History of the Juridical Framework of the Joint Hindu Family," 28–30.

81. *Mitakshara* I, iii, 27, in Colebrooke, *The Law of Inheritance According to The Mitacshara*, 18–19.

82. Under the *Mitakshara*, formal partition of ancestral property was allowed only under specific morally defined circumstances. On partition and survivorship, see Derrett, "Juridical Framework of the Joint Hindu Family," 31. For a contemporary discussion of the rules and precedent for partition, see Mitra, *The Law of Joint Property and Partition in British India*.

83. Derrett, *Introduction to Modern Hindu Law*, 252–53, emphasis in original.

84. The Tagore Law Lectures of 1887 elaborate these developments. See Henderson, *The Law of Testamentary Devise as Administered in India*.

85. *Jagat Mohini Dossee v. Sokheemony Dossee*, 14 Moore's Indian Appeals 289, emphasis added.

86. Saraswati, *The Hindu Law of Endowments*, 137.

87. As Mukherjea explains in reference to this case, "Once the intention to dedicate is established the subsequent acts and conduct of the trustees, even if they amount to breaches of trust, would not invalidate the endowment." Mukherjea, *The Hindu Law of Religious and Charitable Trust*, 168–69.

88. *G. M. Tagore v. U. M. Tagore*, 9 Bengal Law Reports 377. This measure is discussed in Trevelyan, *Hindu Law as Administered in British India*, 505–8.

89. *Bhupati Nath v. Ram Lal*, 37 Indian Law Reports Calcutta 128. The decision came from a full bench of the Calcutta High Court; see M. P. Agrawal, *The Taxation of Charity in India*, 316.

90. Mukherjea, *The Hindu Law of Religious and Charitable Trust*, 138.

91. Occurring in the Deccan (the plains of western India) in 1875, the riots saw peasants attack moneylenders who ran the exploitative system of debt bondage in the region.

92. See Islam, "The Punjab Land Alienation Act and the Professional Moneylenders."

93. Rules limiting debt liability to within one lifetime were introduced in the 1830s. The introduction of individual legal responsibility attempted to restrict the perpetuity of debts in the HUF, which previously had been passed on along with ancestral property. See Bayly, *Rulers, Townsmen and Bazaars*, 392.

94. Agrawal, *The Taxation of Charity in India*, 534–36.

95. Srinivasan, *Tax Treatment of Private Trusts*, 30.

96. Derrett, *Critique of Modern Hindu Law*, 379.

97. NAI, Legislative Department, February 1886, part A, nos. 113–63, text of the Indian Income Tax Act.

98. See NAI, Legislative Department, March 1917, part A, nos. 94–106, on the Super-Tax Act of 1917 and its particular interest in extracting profits from indigenous industry, especially from Marwaris in Calcutta.

99. Pal, *The Law of Income Tax in British India*, 297.

100. Ibid., 298.

101. According to Agrawal, "It appeared from the language of section 41 of the IT Act, 1922 [the section on liability of trusts], that the taxation of . . . artificial juridical persons was not outside the contemplation of the Act." *The Taxation of Charity in India*, 539.

102. Commissioner of income tax, *Madras v. The Therava Patshala*, by manager, Armachalaur Chetty, 51 Madras Law Journal 123, cited in Jain, *Annotated Digest of Income-Tax Cases, 1886–1942*, 137.

103. Commissioner of income tax, *Bihar and Orissa v. Himayam Raza*, 1936 All India Reporter, Patna 532, in Jain, *Annotated Digest of Income-Tax Cases*, 140, emphasis added.

104. Pal, *The Law of Income Tax in British India*, 408.

105. NAI, Home Department, Judicial Branch, November 1888, part A, nos. 202–54, Bill to Provide for the Vesting and Administration of Property Held in Trust for Charitable Purposes.

106. NAI, Home Department, Judicial Branch, part A, July 1914, nos. 265–87, Administration of Religious and Charitable Endowments in India, appendix II, "Act No. VI of 1890, An Act to Provide for the Vesting and Administration of Property Held in Trust for Charitable Purposes."

107. NAI, Home Department, Judicial Branch, November 1888, part A, nos. 202–54, proc. no. 224, letter from of G. E. Knox, Acting Legal Remembrancer to the Government, NW Provinces and Oudh, to The Secty to the Government of the NW Provinces and Oudh, July 28, 1886.

108. NAI, Home Department, Judicial Branch, November 1888, part A, nos. 202–54, proc. no. 224.

109. The 1887 ruling in *Manohar Ganesh Tambekar v. Lakhmiram Govindram*, the Dakor Temple case, discussed above, had stated that Hindu trusts in the name of deities *could* qualify as public charitable institutions, but only for the purposes of section 539 of the Civil Procedure Code. Section 539 of the 1882 Civil Procedure Code, entitled "Of suits relating to public charities," provided procedures for the interference of the court "in case of any alleged breach of any express or constructive trusts." That is, Hindu religious trusts might be construed as public charitable trusts when competing parties to trusteeship needed to settle their

claims. Thus Hindu religious trusts might be construed as public institutions in order to enable court intervention and regulation of their affairs. However, normatively speaking, in 1890, Hindu religious trusts, large or small, were not considered public charitable trusts and so were rendered private by default. See *Manohar Ganesh Tambekar v. Lakhmiram Govindram*, 12 Indian Law Reports Bombay 247. For the 1882 Civil Procedure Code, see also Sarkar, *The Civil Procedure Code*.

3. For General Public Utility

1. Gandhi elaborates the concept through a series of interviews and articles in the 1920s and 1930s. For an overview, see M. K. Gandhi, *My Theory of Trusteeship*.

2. Maitland, *State, Trust and Corporation*, 127.

3. "Non-negotiable" is used here specifically for its evocation of absolute value—the absolute value of colonial sovereignty, and indeed of the modern sovereignty of the "people" in the nation form, as opposed to *absolutism*. Critical studies of liberalism and empire have investigated the absolute nature of the modern domain of the political. See, for example, Mehta, *Liberalism and Empire*; and Chakrabarty, "In the Name of Politics."

4. Drawing on Spivak's use of the term, I use *worlding* here broadly to indicate the forceful making of a world, and more particularly, one that according to Spivak "generates the force to make the 'native' see himself as 'other.'" Spivak, *Critique of Postcolonial Reason*, 212; see also chap. 3 of that work. For Spivak, worlding operates through mechanics of othering, and, as elaborated in more recent work, also marks the possibilities of alterity. In *Death of a Discipline*, for example, she poses "the planet"—a name for an alterity that we inhabit—as a replacement for "the globe," which has been mapped, and made recognizable by the violent making commensurate of Capital (70–73).

5. The reforms of 1909, also known as the Morley-Minto reforms, increased the number of nonofficial Indian members in the central (Imperial Legislative) council and the provincial councils, and strengthened links between them and municipal and district boards. It also established the notorious system of separate electorates, in which the eligible Indian voting body was divided into distinct communities. The Montague-Chelmford reforms of 1919 elaborated the separate electorate system, expanding indigenous political representation in the central and provincial councils by giving them elected (rather than nominated) majorities.

6. Dept. of Commerce and Industry, Commercial Intelligence Branch,

Nov. 1917, part A nos. 1–7, "Compilation of a Handbook of Commercial Information for India."

7. NAI, Department of Commerce and Industry, Commercial Intelligence Branch, June 1917, part A, no. 5.

8. For a discussion of new forms of philanthropy in this period via a study of Gujerati trading groups, see Haynes, *Rhetoric and Ritual*, 121–29.

9. Sarkar, *The Civil Procedure Code*.

10. *Manohar Ganesh Tambekar v. Lakhmiram Govindram*, 12 Indian Law Reports Bombay 247.

11. As we shall see, by the 1930s there were four categories of trust, reflecting the double world of contractual and customary gifting: the public charitable trust, the public religious trust (a subset of the public charitable category), the private religious trust (not charitable in the legal sense, taxable, and encompassing indigenous gifting practices not legitimated by the courts as publicly beneficial), and the secular private trust (a taxable contractual economic arrangement for purposes of inheritance or not-for-profit activity).

12. The literature on such debates is well developed and focuses largely on the influential Hindu temples of the south. See the section "Historiography of Sovereignty, Endowments, and Mercantile Gifting" in chapter 2 of the present volume.

13. A recent study of Marwari charitable activity in Bikaner state in Rajputana alone evinces the growth of traditional gifting in the period from approximately 1880 to 1940. According to this estimate, in this half-century, Marwari groups operating in Bikaner founded a variety of institutions in that state and in their ancestral Rajasthani villages: twenty-three Sanskrit *pathshalas*, or centers of religious education; twenty Anglo-vernacular schools; eighteen middle schools and high schools; thirty-four public libraries; thirty-seven Ayurvedic hospitals; eighteen "aleopathic" or modern hospitals; seventy-two wells, cisterns, and stepwells; and twenty-one *dharmshalas*, or rest houses. See Sharma, *Marwari Vyapari*, 144–64, section entitled "Shiska, Sarvjainik Swasthay Evm Samaj Kalyan ke Vikas Vyapari Varg ka Yogdan" [The contribution of the business classes to the development of education, public health and social welfare]. This chapter has lists of donors and the names of their endowments in each of the categories cited. Bikaner was the princely state home for many Marwaris, which may explain the dense landscape of traditional gifting here. Still, areas of Marwari immigration throughout India evince influential local institutions through which status and authority were produced. By 1911 there were approximately 525,000 Marwaris spread throughout India, and another 743,000 in the states of Rajputana. See Timberg, *The Marwaris*, 107 and 114. Timberg's Rajputana numbers use a broad definition of

"Marwari *bania*" and include the Khandelwal, Oswal (Jain), Saraogi (Jain) kinship groups, as well as the Marwari Agarwals and Maheshwaris. His all-India numbers are estimated on the basis of population samples of Oswals, Agarwals, and Maheshwaris only.

14. This precedent was set in *Commissioner of Income Tax Bihar and Orissa v. Himayam Raza*, 1936 All India Reporter, Patna Series, 532. Cited in Jain, *Annotated Digest of Income Tax Cases 1886–1942*, 140.

15. Caste histories, while self-serving, provide evidence of the variety of forms of mercantile gifting. The prominent Marwari histories include Kedia, *Bharat me Marwari Samaj*, esp. chap. 6. On the variety of social welfare and reformist associations which emerged within the community particularly in the nationalist period, including the Marwari Relief Society, Calcutta, see Barua, *Me Apni Marwari Jati ko Pyar Karta Hun*, which outlines the range of traditional Hindu and nationalist endeavors in the context of family histories; Modi, *Desh ka Itihas me Marwari Jati ka Sthan*; and Bhandari, Gupta, and Soni, *Agarwal Jati ka Itihas*. See also Taknet, *Industrial Entrepreneurship of Shekhawati Marwaris*; and Sharma, *Marwari Vyapari*.

16. I was granted access to the original trust deed of this institution, Sri Poddareshwar Ram Mandir Trust Deed (in Hindi), in the possession of Sri Ramkrishan Poddar. Information also drawn from interview with Sri Ramkrishan Poddar, Nagpur, India, April 19, 1995.

17. See also the section "The Invisible Hand Plays Dead" in chapter 2 of the present volume; and Derrett, "The History of the Juridical Framework of the Joint Hindu Family"; also Derrett, *Introduction to Modern Hindu Law*, 365–90.

18. This question was also significant for Government of India's obligations in the case of the growing number of trusts holding government securities. If family members could reclaim parts of an endowment, the Government of India might become endlessly liable. Trusts established by local rajas had invested in government securities as early as the late eighteenth century. See the story of Maharaja Amrit Rao of Poona, NAI, Home Department, Judicial Branch, June 1889, part A, proc. no. 82, elaborated in Birla, "Hedging Bets," chap. 3. The notes to the Indian Securities Act, 1885, refer to the "king of Oudh's investments for his relatives" and his trust properties. See NAI, Legislative Department, October 1885, part A, nos. 230–70, notes section, letter from R. E. Hamilton, Asst. Secty to the Government of India, Department of Finance and Commerce, to the Comptroller General, Dec. 29, 1883. Mercantile firms were also great investors in government securities, and their growing trust properties offered new channels for such investment.

19. See Government of India, *Indian Contract Act (Act IX of 1872)*.

20. NAI, Legislative Department, Oct. 1885, part A, nos. 230–70, Indian Securities Act Papers, note by C. P. Ilbert, Finance Member of the Legislative Council of India.

21. NAI, Legislative Department, Oct. 1885, part A, nos. 230–70, Indian Securities Act Papers, appendix A42, "A Bill to amend the law relating to Government Securities."

22. NAI, Home Department, Judicial Branch, Nov. 1888, nos. 202–254, proc. no. 230, Letter from the Commissioner, Jabbalpur Division, to Registrar, Judicial Commissioner's Court, Central Provinces, July 6, 1886.

23. NAI, Home Department, Judicial Branch, Nov. 1888, nos. 202–254.

24. For Central Provinces opinions, see ibid.

25. On Raja Gokul Dass, see McEldowney, *Colonial Administration and Social Developments in Middle India*, chap. 8.

26. NAI, Home Department, Judicial Branch, Nov. 1888, nos. 202–254, proc. no. 230, Opinion of Seth Gokul Dass Rai Bahadur.

27. NAI, Home Department, Judicial Branch, Nov. 1888, nos. 202–254, proc. no. 232, letter from the Officiating Commissioner, Nagpur Division, to the Registrar, Judicial Commissioner's Court, Central Provinces, July 6, 1886; and proc. no. 234, letter from Seth Kastur Chand Daga to Officiating Commissioner, Nagpur Division, June 30, 1886.

28. Legislation aligning customary commercial organization with contractual partnership did not come into being until the Indian Partnership Act of 1932.

29. See text of the Charitable Endowments Act, Act VI of 1890, Section 3(2), Appendix II in NAI, Home Department, Judicial Branch, part A, July 1914, nos. 265–87.

30. See Bayly, *Rulers, Townsmen and Bazaars*, 414.

31. NAI, Department of Finance and Commerce, Separate Revenue Branch, part A, nos. 203–6, proc. no. 204.

32. NAI, Department of Finance and Commerce, Separate Revenue Branch, part A, nos. 203–6, proc. no. 205.

33. NAI, Department of Finance and Commerce, Separate Revenue Branch, part A, nos. 203–6, notes.

34. NAI, Home Department, Public Branch, Sept. 1895, part A, nos. 248–55. See also Anand, *The Societies Registration Act (Act no. XXI of 1860)*.

35. NAI, Home Department, Public Branch, Sept. 1895, part A, nos. 248–55, proc. no. 249, letter from the Secty, Sind (Hindu) Mutual Family Relief Fund to the Secty to the Government of India, Revenue Department.

36. NAI, Home Department, Public Branch, Sept. 1895, part A, nos. 248–55, proc. nos. 251–52, Case Summary of the Solicitor to the Government of India, Aug. 9, 1895.

37. NAI, Home Department, Public Branch, Sept. 1895, part A, nos. 248–55, proc. no. 249.

38. NAI, Home Department, Public Branch, Sept. 1895, part A, nos. 248–55, proc. nos. 251–52.

39. Indian Companies Act Papers, NAI, Legislative Department, May 1882, part A, nos. 9–107, K.W. 3, appendix F. Procs. nos. 28–36 of this file cover the history of section 26, which was written into the act in response to the memorials of the Calcutta Trades Association, a British-run society that facilitated credit disputes among British and Indian merchants.

40. NAI, Home Department, Public Branch, May 1897, part A, nos. 175–89.

41. Ibid., proc. no. 176, emphasis in original. The Punjab Mutual Hindu Family Relief Fund fought for registration under section 26 of the Companies Act; see ibid., proc. nos. 180–84.

42. *Commissioner of Income Tax Bihar and Orissa v. Himayam Raza*, 1936 All India Reporter, Patna Series, 532. Cited in Jain, *Annotated Digest of Income-Tax Cases, 1886–1942*, 140. After 1947, this attitude eroded and as the courts began to validate indigenous notions of charity.

43. *Delrus Banoo Begum v. Nawab Syed Asghur Ally Khan*, 15 Bengal Law Reports 167, cited in Agrawal, *The Taxation of Charity in India*, 475.

44. *Ranchordas Vandravandas v. Parvatibai*, 26 Law Reports, Indian Appeals 71. This precedent is also reiterated in a canonical sourcebook on Hindu law, Mulla, *Principles of Hindu Law*, section 405, which explains that a "gift or bequest to dharam is void for vagueness and uncertainty; so also is a bequest for good work."

45. *Purmanundass v. Venayek Rao*, 9 Law Reports, Indian Appeals 86 (1882); *Morarji Cullianji v. Nenbai Indian*, 23 Indian Law Reports Bombay 351 (1893). These are also cited as precedents in the tax-exempt status of *dharmshalas* in Agrawal, *The Taxation of Charity in India*, 188.

46. Judgment, *Jugalkishore v. Lakshmandas Raghunathdas*, 23 Indian Law Reports Bombay 659 (1899).

47. Ibid.

48. *Gordhan Das v. Chunilal*, 30 Indian Law Reports Allahabad 111 (1907).

49. Ibid.

50. NAI, Legislative Department, Legislative Branch, Jan. 1867, part A, nos. 17–19, proc. no. 18, letter from C. A. Dodd, Personal Assistant to the Inspector-General of Police, North-Western Provinces, to R. Simon, Secty to the Government of the North-Western Provinces, Sept. 10, 1866. The

inspector-general of police in the Punjab also reiterated that he attached "the greatest importance" to this measure "as the history of thuggee proves that poisoners often select such places to operate on travelers." See NAI, Legislative Department, Legislative Branch, Mar. 1867, part A, nos. 30–31.

51. NAI, Legislative Department, Legislative Branch, Jan. 1867, part A, nos. 17–19, proc. no. 18, draft of *Sarais* Bill.

52. Ibid.

53. NAI, Home Department, Judicial Branch, part A, June 1912, nos. 200–203, proc. no. 200, petition of Suraj Mal and Bajrang Lal to the District Magistrate and Collector, Gorakpur, Sept. 10, 1910.

54. Ibid. This proceeding (no. 200) also contains "The humble petition of Suraj Mal and Bajrang Lal, sons of Lalji Mal, caste Aggarwala [Marwari], residents of Bazar Bharouli, Tappa Deoria, Paragana Salempur Majhouli, District Gorakpur" to John Prescott Hewett, Lieutenant-Governor, the United Provinces of Agra and Oudh, from which this citation originates. This document is hereafter referred to as Petition to John Hewett, Feb. 1912.

55. Petition to John Hewett, Feb. 1912. Also NAI, Home Department, Public Branch, November 1910, part A, nos. 17–26.

56. NAI, Home Department, Judicial Branch, part A, June 1912, nos. 200–203, proc. no. 200, letter from J. W. Hose, Chief Secty to the Government of the United Provinces, to the Secty to the Government of India, Home Department, Apr. 3, 1912.

57. Petition to John Hewett, Feb. 1912, emphasis in original.

58. Ibid., emphasis in original.

59. Ibid.

60. NAI, Home Department, Judicial Branch, part A, June 1912, nos. 200–203, proc. no. 200, Questions and Answers in the United Provinces Legislative Council, Mar. 13, 1912.

61. NAI, Home Department, Judicial Branch, part A, June 1912, nos. 200–203, proc. no. 202, opinion of the Advocate General on the question of whether a *dharmshala* comes under the *Sarais* Act. In October of 1912, the Marwari Association of Calcutta sent a memorial to the Home Department protesting this decision: NAI, Home Department, Judicial Branch, October 1912, part B, no. 50.

62. NAI, Home Department, Judicial Branch, Part A, 1923, file no. 660, Legislative Department pamphlet on "Attitude of Government on the Subject of Social Legislation" by C. W. Gywnne.

63. NAI, Home Department, Judicial Branch, part A, July 1914, nos. 265–87, appendix II, diagram of proposed bills, their application, nature and appointment of controlling body, and terms of audit. This file includes

documents pertaining to the history of charitable endowments legislation in the late nineteenth century, and is cited below in the context of the Religious Endowments Conference of 1914.

64. Ibid.

65. NAI, Home Department, Judicial Branch, Part A, 1923, file no. 660, Legislative Department pamphlet on "Attitude of Government on the Subject of Social Legislation" by C. W. Gywnne.

66. NAI, Home Department, Judicial Branch, part A, July 1914, nos. 265–87, Miscellaneous Papers: The Hon'ble Dr. Rashbehary Ghose's speech on the twentieth March 1908 in introducing the Public Charities Accounts Bill, emphasis added.

67. NAI, Home Department, Judicial Branch, part A, July 1914, nos. 265–87, letter to the Local Governments from H. Wheeler, Secty to the Government of India, Home Department, Feb. 11, 1914.

68. NAI, Home Department, Judicial Branch, Feb. 1916, part A, nos. 121–22, Sir Ibrahim Rahimtoola's Charities Registration Bill.

69. NAI, Home Department, Judicial Branch, part A, July 1914, nos. 265–87, Miscellaneous Papers, Speech by the Hon'ble Mr. Ibrahim Rahimtoola in introducing the Bill for the Registration of Charities.

70. NAI, Home Department, Judicial Branch, part A, July 1914, nos. 265–87, extract from a letter to Government of Madras from Mr. Sheshagiri Iyer and Govindharaghava Iyer.

71. NAI, Home Department, Judicial Branch, Dec. 1915, part A, nos. 30–31.

72. NAI, Home Department, Judicial Branch, part A, July 1914, nos. 265–87, letter from H. Wheeler, Secty to the Government of India, to Sir T. W. Holderness, Undersecretary of State for India, May 6, 1914, states that "we particularly asked local Governments to see that the orthodox element was represented . . . , but I am afraid that they rather failed to make nominations accordingly. The representatives sent up were all practically of the modern educated class; it is not implied that they were any the worse on that account, but it is important to remember that this was so, and there have been some mutterings in the press about it."

73. Rudner, *Caste and Capitalism in Colonial India*, 191.

74. NAI, Home Department, Judicial Branch, part A, July 1914, nos. 265–87, appendix III, Memorandum of Sri Ramaswamy Chetty.

75. NAI, Home Department, Judicial Branch, part A, July 1914, nos. 265–87, Historical Summary (Unofficial) from the Madras Point of View.

76. *Peesapati v. Kanduri* (1915), Madras Weekly Notes 842, cited in Agrawal, *Taxation of Charity in India*, 475.

77. NAI, Home Department, Judicial Branch, part A, July 1914, nos. 265–87, notes of the Home Department.

78. Ibid.

79. NAI, Home Department, Judicial Branch, Mar. 1915, part A, nos. 325–28.

80. NAI, Home Department, Judicial Branch, Sept. 1919, part A, nos. 92–93, A Bill to Provide more effectual control over the administration of Charitable and Religious Trusts.

81. It is important to note also that "Religious and Charitable Endowments" became a provincial transferred subject under the Montagu-Chelmsford reforms of 1919. Dyarchy meant that provincial Indian executives were in charge of trust administration, which was nevertheless to be decided in the courts. See NAI, Home Department, Judicial Branch, part A, file no. 415, 1924.

82. See the section "The Deity is Liable" in chapter 2 of the present volume.

83. NAI, Home Department, Judicial Branch, part A, file no. 430, 1924, notes of the Home Department and text of Hindu Religious and Charitable Trusts Bill.

84. Ibid.

85. Ibid.

86. On the commensurability of Muslim and Hindu as critique of minority/majority formulation, see Jalal, *The Sole Spokesman*.

87. Government of India, *Legislative Assembly Debates*, Feb. 28, 1924, The Hindu Religious and Charitable Trusts Bill, 1060.

88. Government of India, *Legislative Assembly Debates*, Sept. 16, 1924, Dr. Hari Singh Gour's motion to refer the Hindu Religious and Charitable Trusts Bill to a Select Committee, 3504–21.

89. Ibid., 3518.

90. Speech of Madan Mohan Malaviya, Government of India, *Legislative Assembly Debates*, Feb. 19, 1926, 1544.

91. NAI, Home Department, Judicial Branch, part A, file no. 415, 1924, letter from Honorary Secty, Bar Association, Delhi, to the District Judge, Delhi, May 26, 1924.

92. Home Department, Judicial Branch, file no. 123, 1924. The jurisprudence on perpetuities is discussed in the section "The Invisible Hand Plays Dead: Mortmain, the HUF, and the Question of Perpetuities" in chapter 2 of the present volume.

93. Speech of K. Rama Aiyar on the Chettiar community in Government of India, *Legislative Assembly Debates*, Feb. 28, 1924, 1059.

94. NAI, Home Department, Judicial Branch, part A, file no. 415, 1924, letter from the Honorary Secty, Marwari Association, Calcutta, to the Assistant to the Secty to the Government of Bengal, Department of Education, July 23, 1924.

95. NAI, Home Department, Judicial Branch, part A, file no. 415, 1924, letter from the Marwari Association, Calcutta.

96. Babu Ramkumar Khemka, "American aur Marwari" [The American and the Marwari] compares the commercial and industrial ethos of the two cultures.

4. Hedging Bets

1. This chapter elaborates original research presented in Birla, "Hedging Bets," chap. 4.

2. NAI, Home Department, Judicial Branch, Oct. 1889, part A, nos. 170–78, proc. no. 173, opinion of the Chief Magistrate of Bombay in *Empress v. Narotamdas Motiram* (1888). See also House of Commons, *Report of the Select Committee on Gaming, May 1844*.

3. *Spot price* refers to the market price of a commodity available for immediate sale and delivery.

4. Futures markets theorists have debated whether hedging practices are only concerned with risk reduction, as first argued by Keynes in *The General Theory of Employment, Interest and Money* in 1936, or whether they also anticipate profit and therefore operate as speculative ventures, a theory first propounded by Holbrook Working in 1954 (see *Selected Writings of Holbrook Working*). A general compromise between these two views has been adopted: hedging is understood as both a risk-minimizing endeavor as well as an anticipation of profitable changes in the relationship between spot and futures prices. For a summary of the debate, see Meyer, "Futures Markets as Hedging Markets and the Relative Effects of Speculation on Hedging Effectiveness," 1–20.

5. House of Commons, *Reports from Select Committees and Other Papers on Gambling and Lotteries*.

6. Ibid., 235–62.

7. The British inquiry of 1895 found that in Belgium and Germany legislation had been contemplated to regulate futures exchanges in grain, but it was unimplemented. In the United States, legislation on the sale of agricultural products sought to define and legitimize options and futures contracts rather than penalize them. Ibid., 229–34.

8. Letter from William A.C. Barrington to the Marquess of Salisbury, Sept. 16, 1897, Ibid., 237–38.

9. Letter from Horace Rumbold to the Marquess of Salisbury, Apr. 10, 1897, Ibid., 238.

10. Letter from Sir F. Plunkett to the Marquess of Salisbury, Apr. 13, 1897, Ibid., 240.

11. Letter from Edmund Monson to the Marquess of Salisbury, Aug. 27, 1897, Ibid., 241–43.

12. Letter from F. St. John to the Marquess of Salisbury, Aug. 18, 1897, Ibid., 253.

13. Letter from Frank Lascelles to the Marquess of Salisbury, May 19, 1897, Ibid., 244.

14. Letter from Frank Lascelles, May 19, 1897, Ibid., 245–46.

15. Letters from Egerston, Corbett, and Pakenham to the Marquess of Salisbury, Apr. 13, Aug. 30, and May 8, 1897, respectively, Ibid., 249–51.

16. Text of House of Representatives bill no. 1993, Fifty-forth Congress, in letter from Julian Pauncefote to Marquess of Salisbury, May 7, 1897, Ibid., 254–61.

17. Hill, *Gold Bricks of Speculation*, xv. The book is dedicated to "the Legitimate Brokers who are Members of the Great Exchanges of the Country and to their patrons, the Trading Public, in the hope that it may serve to divorce forever in the public mind Legitimate Speculation from Gambling and Swindling."

18. Ibid., 375.

19. Ibid., 377–78. He further explains, "When a purchase and sale . . . for future delivery is made on the Chicago Board of Trade, it *must* be made with the intention on the part of the purchaser to receive and on the part of the seller to deliver the commodity, although subsequent events may render delivery unnecessary and settlement before the maturity of the contract desirable, without jeopardizing the legality of the contract" (378–79).

20. Rowntree, ed., *Betting and Gambling*, 191.

21. Ibid.

22. A. J. Wilson, "Stock Exchange Gambling," 46.

23. Ibid., 51.

24. Ibid., 47–50, 56–65.

25. These new transportation networks, combined with a depreciating silver currency, produced rises in prices of agricultural commodities and decreases in their price fluctuations after harvests. The reduction of price fluctuations depended, in particular, upon the *prediction* of the potential flows of commodities rather than on their actual movement; standardized freight rates assisted in such predictions, as they facilitated the identification and calculation of local price deviations. See Rothermund, *An Economic History of India*, 34–35.

26. Ludden, "India's Development Regime," 258. On new nexuses of communication and emergence of the economy in India, see also Prakash, *Another Reason*; Manu Goswami, *Producing India*; and Bayly, "Colonial Rule and the 'Informational Order' in South Asia."

27. Ludden, "India's Development Regime," 262.

28. Baij Nath, "Some Factors in the Industrial Development of India," 107, 117. The author makes an argument for the recognition of caste-based divisions of profession in India and calls for a model of development that elaborates on the strengths of this indigenous model of economic organization.

29. Bengal Chamber of Commerce, *Report of the Committee of the Bengal Chamber of Commerce*, 1905, 2:618–25. On the history of the Commercial Intelligence Branch, see Cotton, *Handbook of Commercial Information for India*, 13–14.

30. Bayly, *Rulers, Townsmen and Bazaars*, 420.

31. See Timberg, *The Marwaris*, 161. In the 1860s, several Marwari firms moved from the Malwa region of west central India, the center of opium production, to Bombay to take part in opium futures trading. By the 1850s, Marwari firms in western India had become key organizers of opium shipments from Calcutta to China. See Timberg, "Hiatus and Incubator," 257.

32. This instability offered great potential for speculative ventures. In the period from 1909 to 1913, the British policy of restricting opium exports to China and the Chinese Revolution offered particularly fertile opportunities. Timberg cites the profits of Sir Sarupchand Hukumchand, the head of a major Marwari firm in Calcutta. In 1909, as the Indian market weakened because of export restrictions, Hukumchand bought Rs. 20–25 lakhs (2–2.5 million rupees) of opium on bills of credit. The price increased tenfold, and Hukumchand made approximately 20 million rupees. Sarupchand Hukumchand, Hardutai Chamaria, and J. K. Birla were the key figures in what Timberg calls the "syndicate" of opium speculators in this period. See Timberg, *The Marwaris*, 161–63.

33. Between 1880 and 1889, raw jute brought in an average of 56 million rupees a year in export trade; between 1900 and 1909, this amount had risen to 123 million. Jute was also responsible for Calcutta surpassing Bombay as the origin of British India's exports in the period from 1885 to 1911. See Rothermund, *An Economic History of India*, 40–41. For an in-depth analysis of the jute market in Calcutta, see Omkar, Goswami, *Industry, Trade and Peasant Society*.

34. Timberg, "Hiatus and Incubator," 255–56.

35. Timberg, *The Marwaris*, 89.

36. The futures market in jute (known as the *fatka* market or the *satta* market in jute) was established in the 1905–6 crop season and had become infamously popular by 1912. For a discussion of the *fatka* market in jute, see Omkar Goswami, *Industry, Trade and Peasant Society*, 85–86. As he elaborates, the profits gained enabled Marwaris to finance managing

agencies during the inflationary years of the 1920s, when many British firms found themselves undercapitalized. Marwari moneylenders offered loans at interest rates that were one or two points below the market rate on company debentures. Ibid., 107–9.

37. Timberg, *The Marwaris*, 164.

38. Discussions with Sri Radhakrishna Birla of Pilani, an industrialist in the wool, cotton, and jute markets, whose father had been a speculator in Bombay from approximately 1910 to 1920, were invaluable in sorting out these definitions. His generosity and patience are remembered here.

39. A concise description of the choices available to buyers and sellers in *satta* transactions can be found in "Satta: Vypar Ya Jua?" [Speculation: Business or gambling?], chapter 2 of Radhakrishna Birla, *Bhuli Bathein Yad Karun*, 21–22. If the buyer of the commodity is not ready to take delivery on the given date, the *sowda*, or bargain/negotiation, may be reinstituted with a higher commission to the seller, and vice versa.

40. *Teji mundi* bargains were also called *teji-madda* in north India. *Teji* means fast or quick, and *mundi* or *madda* refers to a slump or a slowing of activity. The term *teji mundi* referred not only to the pace of exchanges in a given market, but also to price fluctuations: the market was said to be *tej* when it was rising and *mundi* when it was falling.

41. Bayly, *Rulers, Townsmen and Bazaars*, 419.

42. NAI, Home Department, Judicial Branch, Sept. 1886, part A, nos. 300–3, proc. no. 301.

43. NAI, Home Department, Judicial Branch, Jan. 1888, part B, nos. 43–46, text of the Public Gaming Amendment Bill.

44. NAI, Home Department, Judicial Branch, Jan. 1888, part B, nos. 43–46, final text of 1887 Bombay Prevention of Gambling Bill, section 1.

45. Ibid., section 5, section 4 of Bombay Act III of 1866.

46. Ibid., section 6, section 5 of Bombay Act III of 1866.

47. Ibid., section 7, section 6 of Bombay Act III of 1866.

48. Ibid., sections 9 and 10, sections 8 and 9 of Bombay Act III of 1866. The final section of the act, section 12, reiterated the right of a police officer to apprehend without warrant any persons found gambling or engaged in bird or animal fighting in public streets and thoroughfares.

49. NAI, Home Department, Judicial Branch, Jan. 1888, part B, nos. 43–46, letter from Vinayak Sitaram Vasungulkar to the Secty to the Government of Bombay, Legislative Department, Mar. 12, 1887.

50. NAI, Home Department, Judicial Branch, Jan. 1888, part B, nos. 43–46, speech of Sir M. Melvill, proceedings of the Council of the Governor of Bombay, July 16, 1887.

51. NAI, Home Department, Judicial Branch, Oct. 1889, part A, nos. 170–78, proc. no. 172.

52. NAI, Home Department, Judicial Branch, Oct. 1889, part A, nos. 170–78, proc. no. 173, judgment of the chief magistrate of Bombay.

53. *Empress v. Narotamdas Motiram and another*, 13 Indian Law Reports Bombay 681.

54. NAI, Home Department, Judicial Branch, Oct. 1889, part A, nos. 170–78, proc. no. 173.

55. Ibid. In its organization, both financial and spatial, Motiram's and Khimji's establishment mirrored the arrangements of speculation markets in particular. See the description of Burrabazar in Calcutta in the section of the present chapter entitled "Calcutta 1896–1897: The Bengal Rain-Gambling Act, Public Debates and Marwari Protest."

56. NAI, Home Department, Judicial Branch, Oct. 1889, part A, nos. 170–78, proc. no. 173.

57. Ibid.

58. Ibid., judgment of Justice Jardine in criminal appeal no. 15 of 1889, made by the Government of Bombay in re *Narotamdas Motiram and another*.

59. Ibid.

60. Ibid.

61. Ibid., judgment of Justice Scott in criminal appeal no. 15 of 1889 made by the Government of Bombay in re *Narotamdas Motiram and another*.

62. NAI, Home Department, Judicial Branch, May 1890, part B, nos. 240–41, appendix N, A Bill to Amend the Prevention of Gambling Act.

63. NAI, Home Department, Judicial Branch, May 1890, part B, nos. 240–41, appendix K, extract from the proceedings of the Council of the Governor of Bombay, Jan. 8, 1890.

64. By 1910, the Calcutta Improvement Trust had instituted a "clearing up" program in which cleared slum lands were sold to Marwaris for the building of shops and mansions. A large number of poor Muslims lost their homes to make way for this gentrification, a situation that informed communal tensions between Marwaris and Muslims in Burrabazar. See Das, *Communal Riots in Bengal, 1905–1947*, 61–62.

65. In interior or upper-story rooms, extended family and kin would share rooms, cooking, and dining spaces.

66. This and related information on the Burrabazar geography of *satta* is informed by a survey of Burrabazar conducted in March 1996. The author was guided by Sri B. L. Sarda, a Marwari whose family home from the late nineteenth century still stands in Burrabazar. In particular, the author visited the *tisi bara* (cotton cloth *bara*) at No. 149 Cotton Street, and the *chandi bara* (silver) at No. 68 Cotton Street. As elaborated later in this chapter, No. 68 Cotton Street housed a large courtyard where the

Marwaris of Calcutta met in protest of the Bengal Rain-Gambling Bill in April of 1897.

67. NAI, Home Department, Judicial Branch, Mar. 1897, part A, nos. 31–42, proc. no. 31, letter from C. W. Bolton, Chief Secty to the Government of Bengal, to the Secty to the Government of India, Jan. 12, 1897.

68. Ibid.

69. Ibid.

70. Ibid.

71. NAI, Home Department, Judicial Branch, Mar. 1897, part A, nos. 31–42, proc. no. 34, "The humble memorial of the undersigned citizens and residents of Calcutta and its suburbs" to Alexander Mackenzie, Lieutenant-Governor of Bengal.

72. Ibid. Thus the memorialists criticized the publicizing of what should have remained private amusement, i.e., rain gambling, through a critique of the "publicizing" of women: respectable women became publicly exchanged in prostitution, the antithesis of the private exchange of women in marriage.

73. Ibid.

74. NAI, Home Department, Judicial Branch, Mar. 1897, part A, nos. 31–42, proc. no. 31. Opinions were solicited from a variety of reformist associations, including Surendranath Banerji's Indian Association, a seat of the Calcutta professional classes; the Central National Muhammadan Association; the Muhammadan Literary Society; and the loyalist and zamindar-based British Indian Association.

75. The rain-gambling controversy is addressed briefly as an example of community identity-formation in Hardgrove, *Community as Public Culture*. Here, I build on my own original research first presented in Birla, "Hedging Bets," detailing the controversy as event of market governance and its culturalist effects.

76. *Amrita Bazar Patrika*, Sept. 15, 1896.

77. *Amrita Bazar Patrika*, Sept. 17, 1896.

78. *Amrita Bazaar Patrika*, Mar. 18, 1897.

79. The British Indian Association represented a Bengali landholding elite, whose forays into commercial enterprise beginning in the 1880s were quickly outpaced by the activities of Marwaris.

80. *Hindu Patriot*, Sept 22, 1896. Furthermore, the editorial reacted strongly to the memorialists' statement concerning the "spoiling" of women engaged in rain gambling; this, they claimed, was a "monstrous assertion" denigrating the "reputation of Native women." The next day, *Capital*, a weekly journal representing British trading interests, published an article entitled "Grandmotherly Legislation," also condemning the regulation of public morals.

81. Both the *Statesman* and the *Indian Empire* were British-owned newspapers.

82. "Rain-gambling in Calcutta, A Visit to the Gamblers," *Statesman*, Oct. 2, 1896. The article is cited in Hardgrove, *Community as Public Culture*, and used as ethnographic evidence. Here, we read the account against the grain.

83. Ibid.

84. Ibid. "*Rungbaz* experts" is a particularly telling oxymoron. It identifies rain gambling as an activity somewhere between artifice and science; *rungbaz* refers to person who is a player, a performer, and one who indulges in amusements.

85. *Hindu Patriot*, Oct. 3, 1896. Defending their stance against skeptics, its editors argued that the cistern which measured the fall of rain was not an "instrument of gaming," as there had yet been no reports of tampering and that payments to winners were faithfully disbursed: "Indeed, to any but the most superficial observer, it must be apparent that the strength and popularity of rain-gambling lies in the popular belief that everything is above board."

86. *Statesman*, Oct. 6, 1896. The *Patriot* claimed that if there had been any reports of foul play in Burrabazar, this was due to the work of "professional *goondas* [hooligans]" and not the Marwari community. By 1914, the Marwaris were themselves writing to the Government of Bengal to protect them from the spread of goondaism in Burrabazar. See letters from Marwari Association and Marwari Chamber of Commerce to Government of Bengal, in Bengal Chamber of Commerce, *Report of the Bengal Chamber of Commerce*, 1913, 2:585–92, and 1914, 2:716–25. In 1926, the Goondas Act did come to regulate this sort of organized crime, but it specifically located the origins of the problem in up-country *darwans* (private guards protecting places of business and carrying commercial information) brought into Calcutta by Marwaris. See West Bengal State Archives, Bengal Legislative Department, May 1923, part A, nos. 1–59, the Goondas Act.

87. "Rain-Gambling in Calcutta," *Indian Mirror*, Oct. 9, 1896.

88. Ibid.

89. NAI, Legislative Department, Legislative Branch, May 1897, part A, nos. 26–54, proc. no. 45, "The humble Memorial of the Undersigned Citizens and Residents of Calcutta, Members of the Marwari community," emphasis in the original.

90. Indeed it asserted that "the Marwari community could tell . . . of the numerous cases in which their coffers have supplied the wherewithal for cards and gambling debts—debts of honor—to be paid." Ibid.

91. Ibid.

92. IOR, Public and Judicial Department Records (L/P&J/6 449), Extract from the Proceedings of the Meeting of the Council of the Lieutenant-Governor of Bengal for the Purpose of Making Laws and Regulations (Bengal Legislative Council), Mar. 20, 1897.

93. Ibid. Surendranath Banerji offered a personal account of the problem to the council: "Only the other day I was having a conversation with one of the foremost men of the Marwari community. He said there was a respectable lady living in Bara Bazar who had taken to rain-gambling; she went through the whole of her money, and then went astray."

94. NAI, Legislative Department, Legislative Branch, May 1897, part A, nos. 26–54, proc. no. 45.

95. NAI, Legislative Department, Legislative Branch, May 1897, part A, nos. 26–54, proc. no. 42, letter from Babu Premsook Das, Member of the Rain-Gambling Managing Committee, to the Chief Secty of the Government of Bengal, Mar. 15, 1897.

96. NAI, Legislative Department, Legislative Branch, May 1897, part A, nos. 26–54, proc. no. 43, memorial from the Marwari community to Alexander Mackenzie, February 15, 1897. Proc. no. 40 of this file identifies the date of this document.

97. Ibid.

98. IOR, Public and Judicial Department Records (L/P&J/6 449), Extract from the Proceedings of the Bengal Legislative Council, Mar. 20, 1897.

99. IOR, Public and Judicial Department Records (L/P&J/6 449), Statement of the President of the Council, Extract from the Proceedings of the Bengal Legislative Council, Apr. 3, 1897.

100. Ibid.

101. An article in the *Amrita Bazar Patrika* of Mar. 24, 1897, had reiterated that the Government was "manufactur[ing] law" to support police oppression. The next day, another article entitled "Morality by Legislation" asked rhetorically, "Why does not the British nation stop the use of intoxicating liquors by an Act of Parliament?" Proc. no. 49 of NAI, Legislative Department, Legislative Branch, May 1897, part A, nos. 26–54, includes a similar series of letters published in the *Indian Daily News*, the *Statesman*, and the *Englishman* during March 20–23, 1897. The *Indian Daily News* of March 20 printed a letter signed "Marwari" which stated that "the new Rain-Gambling Act I regard as an unwarrantable interference with the liberty of the subject. Why should A or Z be at liberty to gamble in Government Paper with impunity (for it *is* gambling after all), while I am to be restrained by a special legislative enactment from placing any money on the behavior of the clouds?" Another letter in that same issue signed "Abandoned Cows, Hacks and Poor Doggies" offered infor-

mation about the charitable expenditures from rain-gambling profits for animal infirmaries assisting students of the Bengal Veterinary School. The same argument was reiterated in a letter to the *Statesman* on March 23, signed "Humanitarian," which also explained, like the Marwari memorial of February 15, that "the game ... teaches one in time to become a weather prophet." The *Englishman* of March 22, 1897, also criticized the bill, stating that there was no need for special enactment against rain gambling if it really was simply a matter of public disorder to be managed by police.

102. This was indeed a momentous event in the history of the Marwari community, who began to organize in civic associations in this period. While the community had organized *panchayats* (caste councils) in the early nineteenth century, the first community organization on modern civic lines, with a memorandum of association, was the Marwari Association of Calcutta, convened in 1898, shortly after the rain gambling bill had been passed. See Timberg, *The Marwaris*, 70–71.

103. "The Rain-Gambling Bill, Monster Protest Meeting," *Indian Daily News*, Mar. 26, 1897, cited in NAI, Legislative Department, Legislative Branch, May 1897, part A, nos. 26–54, proc. no. 49.

104. "Rain-Gambling in Calcutta, A Marwari Meeting," *Statesman*, Mar. 26, 1897. The *Indian Daily News*, cited in NAI, Legislative Department, Legislative Branch, May 1897, part A, nos. 26–54, proc. no. 49, also reported that "nothwithstanding the greatness of the crowd, the meeting was a very orderly and ... in every sense a representative one[;] some of the biggest bankers and merchants belonging to the community were present."

105. The chairman, Hukmi Chand Chowdury, opened with a statement on the serious circumstances that prompted the gathering. "Marwari Meeting," *Statesman*, Mar. 26, 1897.

106. Among the vernacular papers, five articles on rain gambling appeared in the period between March 13 and April 3, 1897. These were in the *Mihir-O-Sudhakar*, a Bengali weekly of about 1,250 subscribers; the *Bharat Mitra*, a Hindi weekly of about 3,000 reported subscribers; the *Sulabh Dainik*, a Bengali daily with a circulation of 3,000; the *Hitavadi*, a Bengali weekly of about 4,000 subscribers; and the *Sahachar*, a Bengali weekly of about 500 subscribers. All except for the *Bharat Mitra* opposed the act. The *Bharat Mitra* criticized the act's hypocrisy given British addictions to horse racing. See Government of India, *Report on the Native Newspapers of Bengal* for the weeks ending March 20, April 3, and April 10, 1897.

107. The *Statesman* published an article on that day explaining that the fall in the rupee price of opium that week had not been due to the Marwaris, as had been rumored by the *Indian Daily News* on April 2. The *Pioneer* of April 3 criticized the new measure, arguing that the "distinction

... between gaming and betting is entirely capricious and arbitrary" and in this connection made reference to Germany's 1896 ban on forward trading as a moral, not material, measure: "When the German Emperor, recently in excess of his passion for shaping the manners and morals of the empire after the young Hohenzollern pattern, endeavoured to put a stop to forward trading in grain, the corn exchanges were promptly deserted."

108. NAI, Legislative Department, Legislative Branch, May 1897, part A, nos. 26–54, notes, letter from the Bengal Government, Apr. 16, 1897, emphasis added.

109. NAI, Home Department, Judicial Branch, Feb. 1901, part A, nos. 1–2, p. 5 of file, letter from the Chief Secty to Government, Punjab to All Commissioners and Superintendents of Divisions in the Punjab, Dec. 20, 1898.

110. Opinions from Peshawar, Derajat, Jullundur, Hoshiapur, Ludhiana, Ferozepur, Lahore, Rawalpindi, Jhelum, Sialkot, and Simla all supported the measure in principle in this way. None of these commented on other forms of potentially dangerous gambling. NAI, Home Department, Judicial Branch, Feb. 1901, part A, nos. 1–2, pp. 11–20. Citation from H. A. Anderson, commissioner and superintendent, Derajat Division, Jan. 21, 1899, p. 13.

111. NAI, Home Department, Judicial Branch, Feb. 1901, part A, nos. 1–2, pp. 21–22, opinion of J. Drummond, deputy commissioner, Gujarat, Jan. 27, 1899.

112. NAI, Home Department, Judicial Branch, Feb. 1901, part A, nos. 1–2, p. 23, opinion of H. C. Fanshawe, commissioner and superintendent, Delhi Division, Mar. 30, 1899.

113. NAI, Home Department, Judicial Branch, Feb. 1901, part A, nos. 1–2, p. 22, opinion of H. P. P. Leigh, deputy commissioner, Rawalpindi, Mar. 11, 1899.

114. NAI, Home Department, Judicial Branch, Feb. 1901, part A, nos. 1–2, p. 27, judgment of *Queen Empress v. Radha Kishan and others*, Agra, June 18, 1898.

115. Opium speculation accelerated in the years between 1895 and 1898, when the revaluation of the rupee reduced already declining shipments of opium to China. Shipments fell to almost half the total average of the previous decade. See Timberg, *The Marwaris*, 51. On the government inquiries on opium that led to speculation in this period, see Richards, "Opium and the British Indian Empire."

116. NAI, Home Department, Judicial Branch, Feb. 1901, part A, nos. 1–2, pp. 25–26, letter from Hatim Mirza, Deputy Inspector of Police, Rewari, to District Inspector of Police, Gurgaon, Nov. 23, 1898.

117. Ibid. In 1896, the "account books and certain sums of money" of

two shops in Rewari were confiscated by the police as "instruments of gaming" under the Public Gambling Act, but the accused were released, as the district magistrate argued that opium gambling did not come under the rules of the Public Gambling Act. This ruling echoed the opinion of the Bombay Chief Magistrate in *Empress v. Narotamdas Motiram* in 1888 (see section in this chapter entitled "Bombay, 1887–1890: Defining the Gamble and the Wager," for a discussion of this case). Similarly, in 1898, the appeals court in Agra acquitted nine men accused of opium gambling in that city, arguing that the law did not cover such a practice. See pp. 26–30 of file for an account of these cases.

118. NAI, Home Department, Judicial Branch, Feb. 1901, part A, nos. 1–2, pp. 31–32, opinion of P. W. Perkins, City Superintendent of Police, Jan. 9, 1899, emphasis in original. The opinion included a list of forty-one persons "holding opium lottery offices in the city of Delhi," mostly concentrated in the area of Egerton Road.

119. NAI, Home Department, Judicial Branch, Feb. 1901, part A, nos. 1–2, p. 25, opinion of R. Humphreys, Deputy Commissioner, Gurgaon District, Dec. 5, 1898.

120. Marwari rain gamblers in Bengal had also expressed such a worldview, insisting that the market mirrored the uncertainty of nature itself.

121. NAI, Home Department, Judicial Branch, Feb. 1901, part A, nos. 1–2, p. 42, opinion of Harhadhian Singh, Honorary Magistrate, Delhi.

122. NAI, Home Department, Judicial Branch, Feb. 1901, part A, nos. 1–2, p. 57, letter from Chief Secty to the Government of India to Judicial and General Secty to the Government of the Punjab, Feb. 1, 1901.

123. NAI, Home Department, Judicial Branch, June 1911, part A, no. 42, p. 31, opinion of G. Bower, District Magistrate of Saharanpur, Mar. 30, 1906, emphasis in original.

124. NAI, Home Department, Judicial Branch, June 1911, part A, no. 42, opinion of G. Bower.

125. NAI, Home Department, Judicial Branch, June 1911, part A, no. 42, letter of H. C. Conybeare, Commissioner, Meerut Division, Apr. 9, 1906.

126. NAI, Home Department, Judicial Branch, June 1911, part A, no. 42, letter of Munshi Lutf Husain, Deputy Collector of Agra, n.d. The letter included a list of eighteen persons who had been financially ruined by opium gambling. Similarly, a note from the magistrate of Matthura included a list of twenty-eight persons ruined in that city. This list enumerated the name and parentage, caste, residence, and dates of participation in the practice. Nineteen of them were listed as "Bania," and also included were "Muhammad," a Darzi, who "sold all his property"; Mutoo, a Kayasth; and Sada Nand, a Khatri. Most had begun gambling sometime between 1899 and 1901. See letter of H. C. Ferard, Magistrate of Muttra, July 28, 1906.

127. NAI, Home Department, Judicial Branch, June 1911, part A, no. 42, letter of Munshi Lutf Husain, Deputy Collector of Agra, n.d.

128. NAI, Home Department, Judicial Branch, June 1911, part A, no. 42, note of Munshi Narain Prasad, High Court Vakil, Agra, July 30, 1906.

129. Ibid.

130. NAI, Home Department, Judicial Branch, June 1911, part A, no. 42, note of Nawab Muhammad Yusuf Ali, Khan Bahadur, Rais of Mendu, Aligarh district, Sept. 27, 1906.

131. Ibid.

132. NAI, Home Department, Judicial Branch, June 1911, part A, no. 42, letter from R. Greeven, Secty, Legislative Council, United Provinces, to Secty to the Government, United Provinces, Nov. 23, 1906.

133. See Timberg, *The Marwaris*, 162–65.

134. NAI, Home Department, Judicial Branch, June 1911, part A, no. 42, p. 8, extract from the Proceedings of the UP Legislative Council, Apr. 18, 1910. The Committee of Inquiry consisted of five members of this council.

135. NAI, Home Department, Judicial Branch, June 1911, part A, no. 42, pp. 45–50, statements relating to opium, grain, and silver gambling in Agra and other places in the United Provinces.

136. NAI, Home Department, Judicial Branch, June 1911, part A, no. 42, p. 45, letter from M. Shyam Lal, Honorary Magistrate, Muzaffarnagar.

137. NAI, Home Department, Judicial Branch, June 1911, part A, no. 42, pp. 11, 51–52, opinion of Lala Koka Mal, Secty of the Agra Trades Association.

138. NAI, Home Department, Judicial Branch, June 1911, part A, no. 42, pp. 53–60, opinions in response to Government of UP letter of August 29, 1910, asking "how far proposals [of the Legislative Councils' Committee] are likely to meet with the approval of the mercantile community of these provinces." It is worth noting that the Marwari Trades Association and the Hindustani Trades Association of Kanpur were both solicited for opinions, but neither responded to the inquiry.

139. NAI, Home Department, Judicial Branch, June 1911, part A, no. 42, p. 56, letter of the Upper India Chamber of Commerce, Oct. 17, 1910.

140. NAI, Home Department, Judicial Branch, June 1911, part A, no. 42, p. 61, draft bill to prohibit wagering on the price of opium.

141. NAI, Home Department, Judicial Branch, November 1911, part A, no. 120, letter from the Lieutenant-Governor, Nov. 13, 1911.

142. See Malik, *A. P. Mathur's Commentaries on Gambling Acts in India*, 79–82.

143. NAI, Home Department, Judicial Branch, June 1911, part A, no. 42, p. 57, letter from the Commissioner of Police, Bombay, to the Judicial Department, Bombay, Nov. 9, 1910.

144. IOR, Public and Judicial Department Records (L/P&J/6 1108), the Bombay Race-Course Licensing Act of 1912, letter of the Bhatia Mitra Mandal, 1911.

145. IOR, Public and Judicial Department Records (L/P&J/6 1108), letter of the Bhatia Mitra Mandal.

146. IOR, Bengal Police Proceedings (P/8929), General Index to the Information on Record of the Criminal Intelligence Bureau, 1912.

147. NAI, Home Department, Police Branch, July 1913, part A, nos. 17–28, proc. no. 25, statement of H. Wheeler, Secty to the Government of India, Home Department.

148. IOR, Bengal Police Proceedings (P/8929), November 1912, part A, nos. 12–21, proc. no. 13, From Chief Secty to the Government of Bengal, to Secty to the Government of India, Mar. 8, 1912.

149. As a popularized experience of the market, this fixed game spread addictive and idolatrous habits, rather than training the rational market actor.

150. The 1887 Bombay High Court case was *Empress v. Narotamdas Motiram and another*. It is important to remember here that unlike Bombay, where "wagering" had been incorporated into the definition of gambling by the act of 1890, the Bengal Rain-Gambling Act had addressed only that practice, resisting any broader amendment of the Public Gambling Act of 1867.

151. *Ram Pretap Nemani v. Emperor*, 13 Criminal Law Journal Reports 603. See also IOR, Bengal Police Proceedings (P/8929), November 1912, part A, nos. 12–21, proc. no. 17. The decision was delivered on June 18, 1912.

152. NAI, Home Department, Judicial Branch, February 1913, part A, nos. 1–7, note by Syed Ali Imam, in appendix to notes.

153. Bow Bazaar was known for its business in prostitution. On the 20th, one Khub Chand Marwari, who owned a raided establishment on Bow Bazaar Street, plead guilty, was fined Rs. 100, and was warned by the presidency magistrate that another conviction would lead to directly to imprisonment; the others were convicted and fined a few days later. IOR, Bengal Police Proceedings (P/8929), November 1912, part A, nos. 12–21, proc. no. 19, letter from Commissioner of Police, Calcutta, to the Chief Secty to the Government of Bengal, July 20, 1912; and proc. no. 21, letter from Chief Secty to the Government of Bengal, to the Secty to the Government of India, Home Department.

154. IOR, Bengal Police Proceedings (P/8929), November 1912, part A, nos. 12–21, proc. no. 20, Letter from Ramdas Chokany, Honorary Secty, Marwari Association, Calcutta, to the Secty to the Government of India, July 2, 1912.

155. Ibid., letter from the Marwari Association.

156. See *Indian Mirror*, Sept. 5, 1912; *Hindu Patriot*, Sept. 30, 1912; *Telegraph*, Oct. 5, 1912; *The Bengalee*, Oct. 19, 1912. For more on the cotton-gambling debate, see Government of India, *Report on the Native-Owned English Newspapers in Bengal* for weeks ending Sept. 14, Oct. 5, Oct. 12, and Oct. 19, 1912. The *Telegraph* lamented that the "abominable trade" of cotton-gambling was "worse than the plague, cholera or smallpox." The *Bengalee* characterized the problem as a different sort of disease, a sexual disorder rather than a virus: "Gambling is a wretched thing, a form of unhealthy excitement which . . . has a disastrous effect upon the character." The *Hindu Patriot* also condemned this "plague" but argued, echoing Bombay merchants, that its origin lay in the infectious government sanction of horse-racing.

157. "Cotton Figure Gambling, New Devices of Robbing Public Money," *Amrita Bazar Patrika*, Oct. 9, 1912.

158. *Basumati*, Sept. 14, 1912; and *Dhainik Bharat Mitra*, Sept. 8, 1912. Other vernacular papers which joined the condemnation were the *Hindi Bangavasi*, circulation 1,500; the *Hitavadi*, a Bengali weekly with a 20,000-person circulation; the *Nayak*, a Bengali weekly, circulation of 1,500–3,000; the *Samaj*, a Bengali weekly with a circulation of approximately 500–800; *Sri Vishu-Priya-o-Anand Bazar Patrika*, a Bengali weekly, circulation 2,500; and the *Star of India*, an Urdu weekly with a circulation of approximately 650. In addition to calling for legislation, some vernacular papers offered creative possibilities for managing the problem. See Government of India, *Report on the Native Newspapers of Bengal*, especially for the weeks ending Sept. 14, Sept. 28, Oct. 5, Oct. 19, Nov. 9, and Nov. 16, 1912.

159. NAI, Home Department, Judicial Branch, Feb. 1913, part A, nos. 1–7, notes summarizing telegram from the Secty of State, Nov. 9, 1913.

160. NAI, Home Department, Police Branch, July 1913, part A, nos. 17–28, notes of H. Wheeler, Secty to the Government of India, Home Department, Nov. 21, 1912; also proc. no. 25, summary by Wheeler and viceroy's draft ordinance.

161. Ibid., proc. no. 25, the Bengal Public Gambling Amendment Bill, as introduced Mar. 17, 1913.

162. By 1923, the Marwari Association flexed their civic muscle by arguing that "a substantial portion of Marwari properties in Calcutta . . . is about one-eighth of the whole" and asked for four seats to be earmarked for the community in the municipal corporation. See papers on the Calcutta Municipal Act, 1923, NAI, Legislative Department, General Branch, July 1923, part A, nos. 23–24.

163. On the Calcutta *fatka* market in jute, see Omkar Goswami, *Industry, Trade and Peasant Society*, 54–63. India captured the world market in burlap by the end of the First World War, which not only vastly increased the demand for sandbags but also wiped out Russia's previously emergent trade in hessian.

164. Omkar Goswami, *Industry, Trade and Peasant Society*, 85–86. Even as "Europeans remained confused about hedge deals for a long time to come," Goswami recounts, "fatka became a permanent feature of the jute trade" (86).

165. Omkar Goswami, *Industry, Trade and Peasant Society*, 85.

166. All jute mills at this time were British owned. Marwaris began to sit on boards of British managing agencies in this industry beginning in the 1920s by gaining stakes in them through financing. The first Indian-owned jute mills were opened by G. D. Birla and Sarupchand Hukumchand in 1922.

167. Letter from the Indian Jute Mills Association to the Bengal Chamber of Commerce, Oct. 25, 1911, in Bengal Chamber of Commerce, *Report of the Bengal Chamber of Commerce, 1911*, 2:167–68.

168. Letter from IJMA to the Bengal Chamber of Commerce, Oct. 25, 1911, ibid., 2:168–70.

169. Letter from IJMA to the Bengal Chamber of Commerce, Nov. 3, 1911, ibid., 2:172.

170. Letter from Bengal Chamber of Commerce to IJMA, Nov. 10, 1911, ibid., 2:174.

171. Letter from the Marwari Association, to the Commissioner of Police, Calcutta, Sept. 11, 1913, ibid., 2:592. Pages 585–93 reprint all the letters in this correspondence.

172. Letter from the Marwari Association, to the Chief Secty to the Government of Bengal, Oct. 7, 1914, ibid., 2:722. Pages 716–25 reprint all the letters in this correspondence.

173. NAI, Home Department, Judicial Branch, file no. 650 of 1926 (650/26), p. 26, letter from Debi Prosad Khaitan, Member of the Bengal Legislative Council, to Secty to the Legislative Dept., Government of Bengal, Aug. 25, 1925.

174. The Bombay Cotton Contracts Act, passed in 1922, and the Bombay Securities Contracts Control Act of 1925 had been instituted to regulate dealings for future delivery in the cotton and securities markets. These measures originated not from indigenous traders, but in government inquiries presided over by British officials and the president of the London Stock Exchange.

175. NAI, Home Department, Judicial Branch, file no. 650 of 1926 (650/26), p. 24, Statement of Objects and Reasons of 1925 draft bill.

176. The minimum quantities established by the bill were set high to protect against gambling with the small investments of the uninitiated public. The quantities were as follows: hessian, 50,000 yards; gunny bags, 20,000 bags; linseed, 30 tons; jute, 250 bales; shares in joint-stock companies, 100 shares when the paid-up amount did not exceed Rs. 10 per share, 25 shares when the paid-up amount was between Rs. 10 and 100 per share, and 10 shares when the paid-up amount exceeded Rs. 100 per share; sugar, 25 tons; and wheat, 25 tons. NAI, Home Department, Judicial Branch, file no. 650 of 1926 (650/26), p. 24, Text of the Wagering Associations Bill, 1926.

177. NAI, Home Department, Judicial Branch, file no. 650 of 1926 (650/26), pp. 3–4, notes of the Commerce Department.

178. NAI, Home Department, Judicial Branch, file no. 650 of 1926 (650/26), p. 4, note of D. C. Chadwick, Oct. 21, 1925.

179. The Marwari Trades Association was an organization of Congress-supporting nationalists who also embraced social reform, such as widow remarriage within the community.

180. NAI, Home Department, Judicial Branch, part A, file no. 1137 of 1927 (1137/27), text of the Futures Markets Bill, 1927.

181. Ibid., Statement of Objects and Reasons for the Futures Markets Bill, 1927.

182. Yet another "Suppression of Wagering Baras Bill" was introduced in 1930 by another nonofficial Member, K. C. Roy Choudhuri, a pro-labor gesture that sought to penalize jute speculators who bet "at the expense of tens of thousands of ignorant mill operatives." It, too, was unaddressed by the Bengal Legislative Council. NAI, Home Department, Judicial Branch, file no. 261 of 1930 (261/30), the Calcutta Suppression of Wagering Baras Bill.

183. Indian Chamber of Commerce, *Annual Report of the Indian Chamber of Commerce, Calcutta*, 1928, 477.

184. Indian Chamber of Commerce, *Annual Report of the Indian Chamber of Commerce, Calcutta*, 1929, 88.

185. Indian Chamber of Commerce, *Annual Report of the Indian Chamber of Commerce, Calcutta*, 1930, 489–91. This report also included a section on "Account Books Taken Away by Police from Indian Mercantile Houses," on 481–87.

186. Indian Chamber of Commerce, *Annual Report of the Indian Chamber of Commerce, Calcutta*, 1932, 52–55.

187. This brought continued claims of social and commercial respectability. In 1938, another Marwari industrialist and legislator in Calcutta, H. P. Poddar, introduced an ultimately aborted bill on public gambling, again condemning and seeking to prohibit popular gambling practices. NAI, Home Department, Police Branch, file no. 24/13/38 (1938).

5. Economic Agents, Cultural Subjects

1. FICCI was established in 1927, and by 1930 had become the premier national organization representing indigenous trade. Its platforms, particularly on the protection of the home cotton textile industry, and the lowering of the exchange rate, were the foundation of the Gandhian Congress' economic policy in the 1920s.

2. The economic value-coding of the colonial global enforced the cultural value-coding of the local. For more on the coding of value, see Spivak's reading of Marx and Foucault through the lever of "value" in *A Critique of Postcolonial Reason*, 104, and her "Scattered Speculations on the Question of Value."

3. See Markovitz, *Indian Business and Nationalist Politics*.

4. For a textured discussion of woman as collective and universal subject of liberal-rights discourses, and so as a counterpoint to the communitarian scripts of colonial society, see Sinha, *Spectres of Mother India*. Examples of the range of work in the history of women's rights in India also include Tanika Sarkar, "Enfranchised Selves"; Majumdar, "'Self-Sacrifice' versus 'Self-Interest'"; and Menon, *Recovering Subversion*.

5. Rudner, *Caste and Capitalism in Colonial India*, 159.

6. For example, Haynes, *Rhetoric and Ritual in Colonial India*; Bayly, *Rulers, Townsmen and Bazaars*; Rudner, *Caste and Capitalism in Colonial India*; Timberg, *The Marwaris*; and Yang, *Bazaar India*. Political, cultural, and social histories of the late nineteenth and early twentieth centuries do, of course, address gender and reformism among the middle class broadly, but they do not detail the positions of mercantile castes.

7. See, for example, Indrani Chatterjee, ed., *Unfamiliar Relations*; and Uberoi, ed., *Family, Kinship and Marriage in India*.

8. Mytheli Srinivas's study of law, women's property rights, and discourses of "conjugality and capital" is a strong example. See Srinivas, "Conjugality and Capital," which focuses on Madras Presidency, where the nationalist period saw an emerging alliance of modernizing capitalist and professional interests, as against landed agrarian elites. Debates over female property ownership reflected "competing visions of family and economy that sought to reconcile conjugality with capital on the one hand and with agnatic kin groups and noncapitalist relations on the other" (957). In this case, the classic battle between capitalism and feudalism was played out in the tensions between a modernizing middle class, both mercantile and professional, promoting capitalist development and male/female individual private property rights, as opposed to the joint-family claims of the landed and feudal classes. The picture is more complicated in the caste-based world of the emergent capitalist class/industrial bourgeoisie,

where agnatic kinship structured capitalist practice. As we argue here, vernacular practitioners of capitalism followed the universalizing bourgeois scripts of capital and challenged them. For broader work on women's rights and questions of property and inheritance, see Basu, "The Personal and the Political"; Kapur, *Feminist Terrains in Legal Domains*; Nair, *Women and the Law in Colonial India*; and Parashar, *Women and Family Law Reform in India*.

9. See, for example, Bhandari, Soni, and Gupta, *Agarwal Jati ka Itihas*, a comprehensive history elaborating an origin mythology of the Agarwal lineage of Marwaris from Maharaja Agre Sen. This text discusses their role in business, religion, nationalism, literature and education, and social uplift. A similar narrative for the Maheshwari lineage of Marwaris is Bhandari, *Maheshwari Jati ka Itihas*. See also Modi, *Desh ka Itihas me Marwari Jati ka Sthan*; and Kedia, *Bharat me Marwari Samaj*. Kedia in particular discusses the reformist criticism of elaborate consumption practices, such as overspending on marriages; see 178–79 and 298–314. For a recent example of this genre, see Jhunjhunuwala, *Marwaris: Business, Culture and Tradition*.

10. See Markovitz, *Indian Business and Nationalist Politics*, 39 and 37–40. Timberg argues that Marwari "entry into industry was both an expression and a cause of the nationalist and reformist impulses of the community." Timberg, *The Marwaris*, 68 and 69–76. For a discussion of early twentieth-century Marwari social-reform associations and institutions in Calcutta as public culture, see Hardgrove, *Community as Public Culture*; for an overview of these associations, see Kudaisya, *The Life and Times of G. D. Birla*, chap. 2. The arguments in this chapter build on my original research of social reform in this period as presented in Birla, "Hedging Bets," especially chap. 5.

11. For an overview of public discourses on and by women in the community-reform and nationalist movements, see Forbes, *Women in Modern India*.

12. The literature on gender and the nation is extensive. On the gendering of nationalism as part of an "imperial social formation," see Sinha, *Colonial Masculinity*, and *Spectres of Mother India*. Key and debated texts in the historiography on nationalism and the women's question include Partha Chatterjee, "The Nation and Its Women" in *Nation and Its Fragments*; and Chakrabarty, *Provincializing Europe*, chap. 5, and "The Difference-Deferral of (A) Colonial Modernity." On the appropriation of the subaltern woman as national symbol, see Spivak, "How to Teach a Culturally Different Book," and "Subaltern Studies: Deconstructing Historiography." Spivak's critique has informed recent studies such as Ray, *En-Gendering India*; and Roy, *Indian Traffic*. The historical literature on the

gendered discourse of community, caste, and culturalist nationalisms is also substantial. See, for example, Sarkar, *Hindu Wife, Hindu Nation*; Singha, "Colonial Law and Infrastructural Power"; Anupama Rao, ed., *Gender and Caste*; and Hasan, ed., *Forging Identities*.

13. The reformist narrative was a familiar one in the nationalist period. It was codified in Nehru's historical tale of India's decline and re-emergence into selfhood, *The Discovery of India*, first published in 1946. See pp. 127–28 for an example of this narrative.

14. See the section "The Trust, the Joint Contract, and the Joint Family Firm" in chap. 3 of the present volume.

15. On the colonial transformation of jurisprudence see Cohn, *Colonialism and Its Forms of Knowledge*; see also Derrett, *Religion, Law and the State in India*; and Mani, *Contentious Traditions*.

16. NAI, Home Department, Judicial Branch, July 1895, Part A, nos. 179–201, proc. no. 190, opinion of E. Leggett, Esquire, to Government of India, Home Department, Sept. 5, 1894.

17. NAI, Home Department, Judicial Branch, July 1895, Part A, nos. 179–201, notes of the Judicial Department, pp. 2–4.

18. Ibid., pp. 1–4, 6.

19. "Draft of An Act for the Registration of Partnerships," reprinted in Bengal Chamber of Commerce, *Report of the Bengal Chamber of Commerce*, 1907, 42–43.

20. Bharat Chamber of Commerce, *Bharat Chamber of Commerce Golden Jubilee Souvenir*, 6. The Marwari Chamber was established in 1900 and changed its name to the Bharat Chamber in 1905.

21. Letter from the Bombay Native Piece-Goods Merchants' Association to the Secty to the Government of India, Home Department, Mar. 17, 1908, reprinted in Bengal Chamber of Commerce, *Report of the Bengal Chamber of Commerce*, 1908, 123–25.

22. NAI, Finance Department, Separate Revenue Branch, Apr. 1917, part A, nos. 66–74, speech by Sir William Meyer in the Legislative Council of India, Mar. 7, 1917. For the discussion of the 1886 Income Tax Act debates, see chap. 1 of the present volume.

23. NAI, Finance Department, Separate Revenue Branch, Apr. 1917, part A, nos. 66–74, speech by G. R. Lowndes in the Legislative Council of India, Mar. 7, 1917.

24. NAI, Finance Department, Separate Revenue Branch, Mar. 1917, part A, nos. 94–106, proc. no. 105, Act VIII of 1917.

25. NAI, Finance Department, Separate Revenue Branch, Apr. 1917, part A, nos. 66–74, speech by Rao Bahadur B. N. Sharma in the Legislative Council of India, Mar. 7, 1917.

26. NAI, Finance Department, Separate Revenue Branch, Apr. 1917,

part A, nos. 66–74, speech by Madan Mohan Malaviya in the Legislative Council of India, Mar. 7, 1917.

27. NAI, Finance Department, Separate Revenue Branch, Apr. 1917, part A, nos. 66–74, speech by Bhupendra Nath Basu in the Legislative Council of India, Mar. 7, 1917.

28. NAI, Finance Department, Separate Revenue Branch, Mar. 1917, part A, nos. 94–106, Act VII of 1917.

29. Government of India, *Royal Commission on Indian Currency and Finance*, vol. 4, *Minutes of Evidence Taken in India*. Indian interests argued for setting the rupee exchange rate in silver at 1s. 4d., as opposed to the artificially high 1s. 6d. that prevailed.

30. The memorial may have been incited by the convening of the All-Indian Income Tax Committee in 1921, which was charged with establishing a plan for consolidation of legislation on taxation of earning and excess profits. Indigenous merchants were not called to participate in the committee.

31. NAI, Home Department, Public Branch, file no. 166 of 1921, part B, letter from the Marwari Association, Calcutta, to the Private Secty to the Viceroy, July 28, 1921.

32. On re-presentation versus representation as proxy, see Spivak, *A Critique of Postcolonial Reason*, 255–65.

33. Taknet, *Industrial Entrepreneurship of Shekawati Marwaris*, 156.

34. Timberg, *The Marwaris*, 67–72.

35. Barua, *Maheshwari Mahasabha Amrit Vallri*, 12. This celebration and construction of Marwari heritage outlines the lineages and ancestral homes that constituted the Marwari caste. The publication of family and lineage histories began as early as the 1890s. According to Barua, one of the first such histories was an elaboration of the Maheshwari lineage published in 1893, the same year as Harishchandra's *Aggarwalon ki Utpatti*, which recounts the *Kshatriya* origins of the Agarwals, both Marwari Agarwals and the Agarwal *banias* of north India, whose ancestral villages were located in present-day Harayana and Uttar Pradesh. In 1898, two more grand accounts of the Maheshwari and Agarwal lineages were published: *Maheshwari Kul Chandrika* and *Agarwal Vansh Komudi*, both by Sukanand Malu.

36. Newatia, "Marwari Samaj me Kuriithiyan."

37. Newardanlal Thulsan, "Jua," 173. Telling of the Marwari management of public discourse on the community's gambling propensities, this article surveyed gambling practices and their moral dangers.

38. Bheya, "Marwari Jati ka Sthri-Samaj," 274.

39. "Aggarwal Marwari Sammelan, Sethji's Address: 'Spend for the Country's Benefit,'" *Forward*, Mar. 17, 1926. This address was delivered

at the eighth meeting of the Marwari Agarwal Mahasabha, convened at Delhi.

40. In the Marwari case, purdah referred generally to the seclusion in the home.

41. "Aggarwal Marwari Sammelan, Sethji's Address: 'Spend for the Country's Benefit,'" *Forward*, Mar. 17, 1926.

42. As K. D. Newatia, the president of the Marwari Agarwal conference, warned in its 1927 meeting, the community had displayed "want of discrimination" in its main virtues, those of "love of religion and peace, commercial skill and munificence." This statement was a calculated response to Marwari involvement in communal violence in Calcutta in the spring of 1926. "All India Agarwal Mahasabha Ninth Session in Calcutta," *Forward*, Apr. 3, 1927.

43. Khemka, "American aur Marwari," 8.

44. "Vivahe Bandan," *Marwari Agarwal* 1, no. 2 (1921): 65.

45. Ibid.

46. Ibid.

47. See Sinha, *Colonial Masculinity*, 171–72.

48. See, for example, the section entitled "Marwari Samaj ki Sharirik Sthhithi" [The physical state of the Marwari community] in the *Marwari Agarwal* 1, no. 2 (1921): 17–23 and 3, no. 2 (1923): 113–15. This section reappeared every few issues.

49. NAI, Home Department, Judicial Branch, file no. 672 of 1922, part A, Bill to Further Amend the Indian Penal Code, Statement of Objects and Reasons.

50. For a discussion of the literature on the 1891 age-of-consent controversy, see Sinha, *Colonial Masculinity*, chap. 4. On the relationship between the discourse on violence to women and emergent public discourse on women's rights, see Sarkar, "A Prehistory of Rights"; see also Bannerjee, *Inventing Subjects*.

51. NAI, Home Department, Judicial Branch, file no. 672 of 1922, part A, notes section, summary note by H. Tonkinson, Dec. 20, 1921.

52. NAI, Home Department, Judicial Branch, file no. 672 of 1922, part A, statement of Objects and Reasons.

53. NAI, Home Department, Judicial Branch, file no. 672 of 1922, part A, letter from Rai Bahadur Hariram Goenka, to the Assistant Secty to the Government of Bengal, Judicial Department, June 26, 1922.

54. NAI, Home Department, Judicial Branch, file no. 672 of 1922, part A, letter of Hariram Goenka.

55. Sarda was from a prominent Marwari family, though he did not speak as a Marwari in his public role as nationalist, legislator, and reformist.

56. NAI, Home Department, Judicial Branch, file no. 672 of 1922, part A, opinion of Har Bilas Sarda, Officiating Additional District Judge, Ajmer, June 17, 1922.

57. NAI, Home Department, Judicial Branch, file no. 672 of 1922, part A, opinion of Har Bilas Sarda.

58. See the section on "The Cultural Orthodoxy of Economic Subjects" in chap. 3 of this volume for an account of Gour's other proposals in the 1920s for the standardization of charitable and religious trusts administration.

59. NAI, Home Department, Judicial Branch, file no. 416 of 1924, part A, nos. 1–38, notes section, summary note by T. Sloan, June 15, 1925, and note by H. Tonkinson, Sept. 3, 1925.

60. NAI, Home Department, Judicial Branch, file no. 416 of 1924, part A, nos. 1–38, letter of Rai Bahadur Hariram Goenka, to the Assistant Secty to the Government of Bengal, Judicial Department, June 13, 1924.

61. Ibid.

62. NAI, Home Department, Judicial Branch, file no. 416 of 1924, part A, nos. 1–38, letter of the Marwari Association, Calcutta, to the Assistant to the Secty to the Government of Bengal, Judicial Department, June 26, 1924.

63. Ibid.

64. In 1928, he drafted a bill to regulate "wagering baras" in order to legitimize Marwari speculative concerns in Burrabazar; see the section on "Jute Gambling in Bengal" in chap. 4 of the present volume.

65. NAI, Home Department, Judicial Branch, file no. 782 of 1924, part B, text of the Bengal Hindu Child-Marriage Prevention Bill, 1924, by Debi Prosad Khaitan.

66. Ibid., statement of Objects and Reasons.

67. NAI, Home Department, Judicial Branch, file no. 1030 of 1924, notes section, letter from Rang Lal Jajodia to Sir Alexander Muddiman, Aug. 5, 1925.

68. See discussion of proposed amendments to the Indian Income Tax Act, Indian Chamber of Commerce, *Annual Report of the Indian Chamber of Commerce*, 1927, 21–22.

69. For a discussion of the Marwari adaptation to the managing agency and joint-stock system, see Omkar Goswami, "Then Came the Marwaris," 225–49; see also his "Sahibs, Babus and Banias."

70. See discussion of the proposed amendment to the Indian Companies Act, 1913, Indian Chamber of Commerce, *Annual Report of the Indian Chamber of Commerce*, 1926, 15–16.

71. NAI, Home Department, Assembly and Council Branch, Dec. 1923, part A, nos. 55–67, extract from Legislative Assembly debates, speech of Sir Hari Singh Gour introducing the Special Marriage Bill, Mar. 22, 1923.

See also Select Committee Report on the final bill, Mar. 14, 1923, in notes section of file. The question of contractual civil marriage emerged first in 1911, when Bhupendra Nath Basu introduced a Special Marriage Amendment bill in the Legislative Council of India, which failed. See IOR, Public and Judicial Department Records (L/P&J/6 1075), The Special Marriage Amendment Bill, 1911. On the problem of professing faith in colonial India, see Viswanathan, *Outside the Fold*.

72. For a discussion of the 1872 Special Marriage Act and the templates it set for later civil marriage acts, postindependence court marriage, and discourses of "love marriage," see Mody, "Love and Law."

73. NAI, Home Department, Assembly and Council Branch, Dec. 1923, part A, nos. 55–67, letter from Debi Prosad Khaitan, Honorary Secty, Marwari Association, Calcutta, to the Assistant Secty to the Government of Bengal, Education Department, June 9, 1921. This statement echoed the association's concerns over Basu's defeated Special Marriage Amendment Bill of 1911. See IOR, Public and Judicial Department Records (L/P&J/6 1075), letter from Ramdeo Chokany, Honorary Secretary, Marwari Association, Calcutta, to Secretary to the GOI, Legislative Department, Nov. 4, 1911.

74. NAI, Home Department, Assembly and Council Branch, Dec. 1923, part A, nos. 55–67, letter from S. G. Hart, Officiating Commissioner of Burdwan Division, to the Secty to the Government of Bengal, Education Department, June 16, 1921.

75. NAI, Home Department, Assembly and Council Branch, Dec. 1923, part A, nos. 55–67, letter from Debi Prosad Khaitan.

76. NAI, Home Department, Assembly and Council Branch, Dec. 1923, part A, nos. 55–67, Act XXX of 1923, An Act to further amend the Special Marriage Act, 1872, section 4, no. 22.

77. Ibid., section 4, no. 23

78. Ibid., section 4, no. 24.

79. NAI, Home Department, Judicial Branch, file no. 294 of 1927, part A, nos. 1–20, letter from the Marwari Association, Calcutta to the Secty to the Government of Bengal, Education Department, June 5, 1928.

80. Ibid.

81. Ibid.

82. Mrinalini Sinha has located the Sarda Act as transformative event in the emergence of the universal female subject of rights "independently of the mediation of the collective identities of communities" (9). See Sinha, *Spectres of Mother India*, esp. chap. 4; also see Sinha, "The Lineage of the 'Indian' Modern" and her "Refashioning Mother India."

83. While the ACT XXIX of 1925 had set the age of consent within marriage to thirteen, it remained unenforced.

84. NAI, Home Department, Judicial Branch, file no. 1024 of 1926, p. 63, list of associations and public bodies whose opinions have been sent direct to the Government of India.

85. NAI, Home Department, Judicial Branch, file no. 1024 of 1926, pp. 160–61, letter from the Marwari Association, Calcutta, to the Secty to the Government of Bengal, Judicial Department, Nov. 29, 1927.

86. NAI, Home Department, Judicial Branch, file no. 1024 of 1926, pp. 161–62, letter from the Marwari Association, Calcutta, to the Secty to the Government of India, Legislative Department, Sept. 29, 1927.

87. NAI, Home Department, Judicial Branch, file no. 1024 of 1926, pp. 238–29, letter from the Marwari Chamber of Commerce, Bombay, Dec. 1, 1927.

88. Ibid., p. 238.

89. NAI, Home Department, Judicial Branch, file no. 1024 of 1926, pp. 306–7, letter from the Marwari Chamber of Commerce, Bombay, June 11, 1928.

90. NAI, Home Department, Judicial Branch, file no. 1024 of 1926, p. 296, letter from the Marwadi Agrawal Sabha, Bombay, to the Secty to the Government of Bombay, June 9, 1928.

91. NAI, Home Department, Judicial Branch, file no. 1024 of 1926, pp. 297–98, letter from the Marwari Sammelan, Bombay, to the Secty to the Government of Bombay, Legislative Department, June 9, 1928.

92. *Legislative Assembly Debates*, Jan. 29, 1929, 191. The conference met on Nov. 19, 1928.

93. NAI, Home Department, Judicial Branch, file no. 1024 of 1926, p. 266, letter from the Marwari Association, Calcutta, to the Secty to the Government of Bengal, Judicial Department, June 1, 1928.

94. It provided different categories of fines and imprisonment for those contracting child marriages. NAI, Home Department, Judicial Branch, file no. 868, 1930, text of Act XIX of 1929, the Child Marriage Restraint Act.

95. *Legislative Assembly Debates*, Jan. 29, 1929, 197.

96. Only a few, though powerful, Marwaris supported the bill without qualification, including members of Federation of Indian Chambers of Commerce and Industry and those affiliated with the nationalist Marwari Trades Association of Calcutta.

97. Sinha, *Spectres of Mother India*, 9.

Conclusion

1. Indian Industrial Conference, "Summary of Proposals," *Report of the Indian Industrial Conference*, 1912.

2. Spivak, *Critique of Postcolonial Reason*, 359.

3. Macaulay, "Minute of 2 February 1835 on Indian Education," 729.

4. Macaulay, "Speech in Parliament on the Government of India Bill, 10 July 1833."

5. This argument is elaborated in the context of the postcolonial industrial bourgeoisie in Birla, "Capitalist Subjects in Transition."

6. Foucault, *Naissance de la Biopolitique*, lecture, Apr. 4, 1979, 300–301; and Gordon "Governmental Rationality," 23.

7. Marx, *Capital*, 1:254. Marx's definition of the capitalist presents "the fundamental critique of the intending subject that sustains Marx's thought." See Spivak, *A Critique of Postcolonial Reason*, 77.

8. Foucault, *Naissance de la Biopolitique*, lecture, Mar. 28, 1979, 281–86.

9. NAI, Home Department, Judicial Branch, Sept. 1887, part B, nos. 337–38.

10. Ibid., letter from H. L. Johnson, Judge of the Assam Valley Districts, to the Secty to the Chief Commissioner of Assam, Aug. 25, 1887.

11. Ibid., letter from Kazi Mohammad Haundulla, Sujangarh, to Deputy Commissioner, Goalpura, June 19, 1887.

12. NAI, Home Department, Judicial Branch, Nov. 1887, part B, nos. 262–64.

13. Sudipta Sen, *Empire of Free Trade*, 38.

References

Archives

India Office Library and Records, London (IOR)
    Public and Judicial Department Records
    Bengal Police Proceedings

National Archives of India, New Delhi (NAI)
    Proceedings of the Home Department:
    Assembly and Council Branch
    Judicial Branch
    Police Branch
    Political Branch
    Public Branch

    Proceedings of Finance and Commerce Department (after 1905, the Finance Department):
    Separate Revenue Branch

    Proceedings of the Commerce and Industry Department:
    Commercial Exhibitions Branch
    Commercial Intelligence Branch

    Proceedings of the Legislative Department:
    General Branch
    Legislative Branch

West Bengal State Archives, Writers Buildings, Calcutta (WBSA)
    Proceedings of the Government of Bengal:
    Legislative Department
    Judicial Department, Judicial Branch

Private Collections
 Account books of the firm of Bansilal Abirchand, in the possession of Krishna and Renu Daga
 Trust deed and minutes of the meetings of trustees, Sri Poddareshwar Ram Mandir and Dharmshala, Nagpur, in the possession of Ramkrishan Poddar, Nagpur

Published Primary Sources

Government Publications
 Bengal Legislative Council Proceedings. Calcutta, selected years.
 Cotton, C. W. E. *Handbook of Commercial Information for India.* 2nd ed. Calcutta: Government of India Central Publications Branch, 1924.
 Government of India. *The Indian Companies Act, 1913 (VII of 1913, as modified up to January 1937).* New Delhi: Government of India Press, 1936.
 Government of India. *Indian Contract Act (Act IX of 1872).* New Delhi: Government of India, 1938.
 Government of India. *Indian Evidence Act (Act I of 1872).* New Delhi: Government of India, 1935.
 Government of India. *Legislative Assembly Debates.* New Delhi, selected years.
 Government of India. *Report of the Census of India 1911.* Vol. 6, parts 1 and 2 (City of Calcutta). Calcutta, 1913.
 Government of India. *Report of the Central Banking Enquiry Committee.* Vol. 1, *Majority/Minority Reports.* Vol. 2, *Written Evidence.* Vol. 3, *Oral Evidence.* Calcutta, 1931.
 Government of India. *Report of the Royal Commission on Currency and Finance.* Vol. 1, *Report.* Vol. 2, *Appendices and Oral Evidence.* Vol. 4, *Minutes of Evidence Taken in India.* New Delhi, 1927.
 Government of Bengal. *Reports on the Native-Owned English Newspapers of Bengal.* Calcutta: Bengali Secretariat Press, selected years.
 Government of Bengal. *Reports on the Native Newspapers of Bengal.* Calcutta: Bengali Secretariat Press, selected years.
 House of Commons. *Report of the Select Committee on Gaming, May 1844.* Irish University Press Series of British Parliamentary Papers: Social Problems, Gambling, vol. 1, and appendices I, II, III. Shannon: Irish University Press, 1968.
 House of Commons. *Reports from Select Committees and Other Papers on Gambling and Lotteries.* Irish University Press Series of

British Parliamentary Papers: Social Problems, Gambling, vol. 2. Shannon: Irish University Press, 1971.

Indian Industrial Conference. *Report of the . . . Indian Industrial Conference*. Amraoti: Indian Industrial Conference, 1905–1917.

Meyer, W. S., Sir Richard Burns, J. S. Cotton, and Sir H. H. Risley. "Commerce and Trade." In *The Imperial Gazetteer of India*, 3:255–313. Oxford: Clarendon, 1908.

Newspapers and Periodicals

Amrita Bazar Patrika (Calcutta)
Capital, A Weekly Journal of Commerce (Calcutta)
Forward (Calcutta)
Hindu Patriot (Calcutta)
Indian Mirror (Calcutta)
Marwari Agarwal (Indore, Hindi)
Marwari Sudhar (Bihar, Hindi)
Modern Review (Calcutta)
Pioneer (Allahabad)
Statesman (Calcutta)

Case Law Reports

Allahabad High Court. *Indian Law Reports*. Allahabad Series. Allahabad, selected years. (Cited as Indian Law Reports Allahabad)

All India Reporter. Nagpur: D. V. Chitaley for the *All India Reporter*, selected years. (Cited as All India Reporter)

Bombay High Court. *Indian Law Reports*, Bombay Series. Bombay, selected years. (Cited as Indian Law Reports Bombay)

Calcutta High Court. *Indian Law Reports*, Calcutta Series. Calcutta, selected years. (Cited as Indian Law Reports Calcutta)

Criminal Law Journal of India. Lahore, selected years. (Cited as Criminal Law Journal)

Incorporated Council of Law Reporting for England and Wales. *Law Reports, King's Bench Division*. London: Incorporated Council of Law Reporting for England and Wales, 1902. (Cited as King's Bench)

Incorporated Council of Law Reporting for England and Wales, Great Britain Privy Council. *Law Reports, Indian Appeals: Being Cases in the Privy Council on Appeal from the East Indies*. London, selected years. (Cited as Law Reports, Indian Appeals)

Madras High Court. *Madras Law Journal*. Madras, selected years. (Cited as Madras Law Journal)

Madras High Court. *Madras Weekly Notes*. Madras, selected years. (Cited as Madras Weekly Notes)

Moore, Edmund F. *Reports of cases heard and determined by the Judicial committee and the lords of His Majesty's most honourable Privy council, on appeal from the Supreme and Sudder Dewaney courts in the East Indies*. London: J. and H. Clark, 1838–73. (Cited as Moore's Indian Appeals)

Other Published Primary Sources

Acharya, Bijay Kishor. *Codification in British India*. The Tagore Law Lectures, 1912. Calcutta: S. K. Banerji and Sons, 1914.

Bagchi, S. C. *Juristic Personality of the Hindu Deities*. Calcutta, 1933.

Baij Nath, Lala Rai Bahadur. "Some Factors in the Industrial Development of India." In Indian Industrial Conference, *Report of the First Indian Industrial Conference 1905*, 107–18. Amraoti: Indian Industrial Conference, 1905.

Bashyam K., and K. Y. Adiga. *The Negotiable Instruments Act, 1881*. 4th ed. Calcutta: Butterworth & Co., 1927.

Bengal Chamber of Commerce. *Annual Reports of the Bengal Chamber of Commerce*. Calcutta, 1900–1920.

Bheya, Kanhaiyalal. "Marwari Jati ka Sthri-Samaj." *Marwari Sudhar* 2, no. 9 (1923): 269–74.

Bhandari, S. R. *Maheshwari Jati ka Itihas*. Bhanpura: Maheswari History Office, 1940.

Bhandari, S. R., K. L. Gupta, and B. L. Soni. *Agarwal Jati ka Itihas*. Indore: Agarwal History Office, 1937.

Bharat Chamber of Commerce. *Bharat Chamber of Commerce Golden Jubilee Souvenir*. Calcutta: 1954.

Cornish, H. D. *The Hindu Joint Family*. Part 1 of *Handbooks of Hindu Law*. Cambridge: Cambridge University Press, 1915.

———. *Partition and Maintenance*. Part 2 of *Handbooks of Hindu Law*. Cambridge: Cambridge University Press, 1915.

Carter, H. G., and F. M. Crawshaw. *See* Tudor, Owen Davies.

Colebrooke, H. T. *The Law of Inheritance According to The Mitacshara*. Calcutta: Thacker Spink, 1869.

Federation of Indian Chambers of Commerce and Industry. *Silver Jubilee Souvenir, 1927–1951*. New Delhi: Federation of Indian Chambers of Commerce and Industry, 1952.

Halhead, N. B. *Code of Gentoo Laws, or Ordinances of the Pundits*. London, 1776.

Hamilton, Charles. *Hedaya: A Commentary on Muslim Laws*. A translation of the work by Ali Ibn Ali Bakr. London: printed by T. Bensley, 1791.

Harishchandra. *Aggarwalon ki Utpatti*. Bombay: 1893.

Henderson, Gilbert Stuart. *The Law of Testamentary Devise as Administered in India: or The Law Relating to Wills in India*. Calcutta: Thacker Spink, 1889.

Hill, John. *Gold Bricks of Speculation: A Study of Speculation and Its Counterfeits, and an Exposé of the Methods of Bucketshop and "Get-Rich-Quick" Swindles*. Chicago: London Book Concern, 1904.

Indian Chamber of Commerce. *Annual Reports of the Indian Chamber of Commerce*. Calcutta: 1926–40.

Jain, B. R. *Annotated Digest of Company Cases, 1913–1939*. Delhi, 1940.

———. *Annotated Digest of Income-Tax Cases, 1886–1942*. Delhi, 1942.

———. *Supplement to the Half-Century Digest of Income Tax Cases*. Delhi, 1937.

Jones, William. *Institutes of Hindu Law or the Ordinances of Menu*. Edited by Standish Grove Grady. 3rd ed. London, 1869.

Kedia, Bhimsen. *Bharat me Marwari Samaj*. Calcutta: National India Publications, 1947.

Khemka, Babu Ramkumar. "American aur Marwari." *Marwari Sudhar* 1, no. 3 (1921): 6–12.

Macaulay, Thomas Babington. *Macaulay: Prose and Poetry*. Edited by G. M. Young. Cambridge, MA: Harvard University Press, 1975.

———. "Minute of 2 February 1835 on Indian Education." In *Macaulay Prose and Poetry*, 724–29.

———. "Speech in Parliament on the Government of India Bill, 10 July 1833." In *Macaulay, Prose and Poetry*, 716–18.

Maine, Henry Sumner. *Ancient Law*. 1860. London: Oxford University Press, 1931.

———. *Village Communities in the East and West*. 2nd ed. London: J. Murray, 1887.

Maitland, F. W. *State, Trust and Corporation*. Edited by David Runciman and Magnus Ryan. Cambridge: Cambridge University Press, 2003.

Malu, Sukanand. *Agarwal Vansh Komudi*. Farrukabad, 1898.

———. *Maheshwari Kul Chandrika*. Farrukabad, 1898.

Marwari Chamber of Commerce. *Annual Reports of the Marwari Chamber of Commerce*. Calcutta, 1930–46.

Mayne, John Dawson. *Treatise on Hindu Law and Usage*. 10th ed. 1878. Madras: Higginbotham, 1938.

Mitra, Ram Charan. *The Law of Joint Property and Partition in British India*. The Tagore Law Lectures, 1895–96. 2nd ed. Calcutta: R. Cambray and Sons, 1913.

Modi, Balchand. *Desh ka Itihas me Marwari Jati ka Sthan*. Calcutta: Raghunathaprasada Simhaniya, 1939.

Mukherjea, Bijan Kumar. *The Hindu Law of Religious and Charitable Trust*. Calcutta: Eastern Law House, 1952.

Mulla, Dinshaw Fardunji. *Principles of Hindu Law*. 3rd ed. Bombay: N. M. Tripathi, 1919.

Newatia, Rameshwar Prasad. "Marwari Samaj me Kuriithiyan." *Marwari Sudhar* 2, no. 6 (1923): 162–65.

Pal, R. B. *The Law of Income Tax in British India*, vol. 2. Calcutta: Eastern Law House, 1940.

Pollock, Sir Frederick. *Digest of the Law of Partnership*. 3rd ed. London: Stevens and Sons, 1884.

Remfry, C. O. *Commercial Law in British India*. The Tagore Law Lectures, 1910. Calcutta: Butterworth, 1912.

———. *The Sale of Goods in British India*. Tagore Law Lectures, 1910. Calcutta: Butterworth, 1912.

Rowntree, B. Seebohm. *Betting and Gambling: A National Evil*. London: MacMillan, 1905.

Saraswati, Prannath. *The Hindu Law of Endowments*. The Tagore Law Lectures, 1892. Calcutta: Thacker Spink, 1897.

Sarkar, Mohim Chandra. *The Civil Procedure Code (Act XIV of 1882) as amended up to March 1894*. Calcutta: Law Publishing Press, 1895.

Thulsan, Newardanlal. "Jua," *Marwari Sudhar* 1, no. 8 (1921): 173–74.

Trevelyan, Ernest J. *Hindu Law as Administered in British India*. Calcutta: Thacker Spink, 1912.

Tudor, Owen Davies. *The Charitable Trusts Act, 1853*. London, 1854.

———. *The Law of Charitable Trusts*. 2nd ed. London: Buttersworth, 1862.

———. *The Law of Charitable Trusts*, edited by L. S. Bristowe and W. I. Cook. 3rd ed. London: Reeves and Turner, 1889.

———. *The Law of Charitable Trusts*, edited by L. S. Bristowe, C. A. Hunt, and H. G. Burdett. 4th ed. London: Sweet and Maxwell, 1906.

———. *Tudor on Charities: A Practical Treatise on the Law Relating to Gifts and Trusts for Charitable Purposes*, edited by H. G. Carter and F. M. Crawshaw. 5th ed. [of *The Law of Charitable Trusts*]. London: Sweet and Maxwell, 1929.

Tyssen, Amherst D. *The Law of Charitable Bequests*. 2nd ed. London: Sweet and Maxwell, 1921.

———. *New Law of Charitable Bequests, being an account of the Mortmain and Charitable Uses Act, 1891*. London: W. Clowes, 1891.

———. *The Law of Charitable Bequests, With an account of the Mortmain and Charitable Uses Act, 1888*. London: William Clowes and Sons, 1888.

Wilson, A. J. "Stock Exchange Gambling." In *Betting and Gambling: A National Evil*, edited by B. Seebohm Rowntree, 45–68. London: Macmillan, 1905.

Secondary Sources

Adams, John. "Culture and Economic Development in South Asia." *Annals of the American Association of Political and Social Science* 573 (2001): 152–75.

Agamben, Giorgio. *Homo Sacer: Sovereign Power and Bare Life*. Translated by Daniel Heller-Roazen. Stanford: Stanford University Press, 1998.

Agrawal, M. P. *The Taxation of Charity in India*. Calcutta: Eastern Law House, 1981.

Aggarwal, S. N. *The Law of Religious and Charitable Endowments*. Chandigarh: Kurana Law Agency, 1977.

Anand, R. L. *The Societies Registration Act (Act no. XXI of 1860)*. Allahabad: Law Publishers, 1966.

Anderson, Benedict. *Imagined Communities*. London: Verso, 1991.

Anderson, J. N. D. "Islamic Law and Its Administration in India." In *Contributions to Indian Law and Sociology*, 105–36. Proceedings of the South Asia Seminar, University of Pennsylvania, 1966. Philadelphia: University of Pennsylvania, 1967.

———. "The Nature and Sources of Islamic Law." In *Contributions to Indian Law and Sociology*, 73–104. Proceedings of the South Asia Seminar, University of Pennsylvania, 1967. Philadelphia: University of Pennsylvania, 1967.

Anderson, Michael R. "Islamic Law and the Colonial Encounter in British India." In *Institutions and Ideologies*, edited by David Arnold and Peter Robb, 165–85. London: Curzon, 1993.

Appadurai, Arjun. *Modernity at Large: Cultural Dimensions of Globalization*. Minneapolis: University of Minnesota Press, 1996.

———. *Worship and Conflict under Colonial Rule: A South Indian Case*. Cambridge: Cambridge University Press, 1981.

Arendt, Hannah. *The Human Condition*. Chicago: University of Chicago Press, 1958.

Aristotle. *The Politics*. Translated by T. A. Sinclair. Edited by Trevor Saunders. New York: Penguin, 1981.

Association of American Law Schools, ed. *Selected Readings on the Law of Contracts*. New York: Macmillan Company, 1931.

Babb, Lawrence A. *Alchemies of Violence: Myths of Identity and the Life of Trade in Western India*. New Delhi: Sage Publications, 2004.

Bagchi, Amiya Kumar. *Capital and Labour Redefined: India and the Third World.* London: Anthem Press, 2002.

———. *The Evolution of the State Bank of India.* Vol. 2, *The Era of the Presidency Banks, 1876–1920.* New Delhi: The State Bank of India, 1997.

———. *The Presidency Banks and the Indian Economy 1876–1914.* Calcutta: Oxford University Press, 1989.

———. "The Transition from Indian to British Indian Systems of Money and Banking." *Modern Asian Studies* 19, no. 3 (1985): 501–19.

Balibar, Etienne. "Is There a Neo-Racism?" In *Race, Nation, Class: Ambiguous Identities,* edited by Etienne Balibar and Immanuel Wallerstein, 17–28. London: Verso, 1991.

Bannerjee, Himani. *Inventing Subjects: Studies in Hegemony, Patriarchy and Colonialism.* New Delhi: Tulika Books, 2001.

Barua, Rishi Jamini Kaushik. *Maheshwari Mahasabha Amrit Vallri.* Calcutta, 1985.

———. *Me Apni Marwari Jati ko Pyar Karta Hun.* Calcutta, 1967.

Basu, Srimati. "The Personal and the Political: Indian Women and Inheritance Law." In Larson, *Religion and Personal Law in Secular India,* 163–83.

Bayly, C. A. "Colonial Rule and the 'Informational Order' in South Asia." In *The Transmission of Knowledge in South Asia,* edited by Nigel Crook, 280–315. Delhi: Oxford University Press, 1996.

———. *Indian Society and the Making of the British Empire.* Cambridge: Cambridge University Press, 1988.

———. *Rulers, Townsmen and Bazaars: North Indian Society in the Age of British Expansion, 1770–1870.* Cambridge: Cambridge University Press, 1983.

Bayly, Susan. *Saints, Goddesses, Kings: Muslims and Christians in South Indian Society, 1700–1900.* Cambridge: Cambridge University Press, 1989.

Bellman, Eric, and Paul Glader. "Breaking the Marwari Rules." *Wall Street Journal,* July 10, 2006, B1.

Benhabib, Seyla, and Drucilla Cornell, eds. *Feminism as Critique.* London: Basil Blackwell, 1987.

Bennett, Tony. "Culture and Governmentality." In *Foucault, Cultural Studies and Governmentality,* edited by Jack Z. Bratich, Jeremy Packer, and Cameron McCarthy, 47–66. New York: State University of New York Press, 2003.

Benson, Peter. "Introduction." In *The Theory of Contract Law: New Essays,* edited by Peter Benson, 1–18. Cambridge: Cambridge University Press, 2001.

Bhabha, Homi K. *The Location of Culture.* London: Routledge, 1994.

Bharat Chamber of Commerce. *Bharat Chamber of Commerce Golden Jubilee Souvenir.* Calcutta, 1954.

Birla, Radhakrishna. *Bhuli Bathein Yad Karun*. Amritsar, 1968.

Birla, Ritu. "Capitalists Subjects in Transition." In *From the Colonial to the Postcolonial: South Asia in Transition*, edited by Dipesh Chakrabarty, Rochona Majumdar, and Andrew Sartori, 241–60. Delhi: Oxford University Press, 2007.

———. "Converting the Unconverted: The Wesleyan Methodist Missionary Society in Ireland and India." *Journal of the American Irish Historical Association* 3, no. 8 (Summer 1990): 70–94.

———. "Hedging Bets: The Politics of Commercial Ethics in Late Colonial India." PhD diss., Columbia University, 1999.

———. "History and the Critique of Postcolonial Reason: Limits, Secret, Value." *Interventions: International Journal of Postcolonial Studies* 4, no. 2: 175–85.

———. "Postcolonial Studies: Now That's History." In *Can the Subaltern Speak?: Reflections on the History of an Idea*, edited by Rosalind Morris. New York: Columbia University Press, 2009 (forthcoming).

Bose, Sugata, ed. *Credit, Markets, and the Agrarian Economy of Colonial India*. Delhi: Oxford University Press, 1994.

———. *A Hundred Horizons: The Indian Ocean in the Age of Global Empire*. Cambridge, MA: Harvard University Press, 2006.

———. *Peasant Labor and Colonial Capital: Rural Bengal since 1770*. Cambridge: Cambridge University Press, 1993.

———, ed. *South Asia and World Capitalism*. Oxford: Oxford University Press, 1990.

Bourdieu, Pierre. *Outline of a Theory of Practice*. Cambridge: Cambridge University Press, 1979.

Breckenridge, Carol, ed. *Consuming Modernity: Public Culture in a South Asian World*. Minneapolis: University of Minnesota Press, 1995.

———. "From Protector to Litigant: Changing Relations between Hindu Temples and the Raja of Ramnad." *Indian Economic and Social History Review* 14, no. 1 (1977): 75–106.

Breckenridge, Carol, and Peter Van der Veer, eds. *Orientalism and the Postcolonial Predicament*. Philadelphia: University of Pennsylvania Press, 1993.

Brook, Timothy, and Luong Hy V., eds. *Culture and Economy: The Shaping of Capitalism in Eastern Asia*. Ann Arbor: University of Michigan, 1997.

Buck-Morss, Susan. "Envisioning Capital: Political Economy on Display." *Critical Inquiry* 21, no. 2 (1995): 434–67.

Burchell, Graham, Colin Gordon, and Peter Miller, eds. *The Foucault Effect: Studies in Governmentality*. Chicago: University of Chicago Press, 1991.

Burton, Antoinette. *Dwelling in the Archive: Women Writing House, Home, and History in Late Colonial India.* New York: Oxford University Press, 2003.
Butler, Judith, and Joan W. Scott, eds. *Feminists Theorize the Political.* New York: Routledge, 1992.
Chandra, Sudhir. *Enslaved Daughters: Colonialism, Law and Women's Rights.* Delhi: Oxford University Press, 1998.
Chakrabarty, Dipesh. *Habitations of Modernity: Essays in the Wake of Subaltern Studies.* Chicago: University of Chicago Press, 2002.
———. "In the Name of Politics: Sovereignty, Democracy and Multitude in India." *Economic and Political Weekly,* July 23, 2005.
———. "Marx after Marxism: History, Subalternity and Difference." In *Marxism Beyond Marxism,* edited by Saree Makdisi, Cesare Casarino, and Rebecca E. Karl, 55–70. New York: Routledge, 1996.
———. *Provincializing Europe: Postcolonial Thought and Historical Difference.* Princeton: Princeton University Press, 2000.
———. *Rethinking Working-Class History: Bengal 1890–1940.* Princeton: Princeton University Press, 1989.
———. "A Small History of Subaltern Studies." In *Habitations of Modernity,* 3–19.
Chatterjee, Indrani, ed. *Unfamiliar Relations: Family and History in South Asia.* New Brunswick, NJ: Rutgers University Press, 2004.
———. *Gender, Slavery and Law in Colonial India.* New Delhi: Oxford University Press, 1999.
Chatterjee, Kumkum. *Merchants, Politics and Society in Early Modern India.* Leiden: E. J. Brill, 1996.
Chatterjee, Partha. *The Nation and Its Fragments.* Princeton: Princeton University Press, 1993.
———. "The Nationalist Resolution of the Women's Question." In *Recasting Women: Essays in Indian Colonial History,* edited by Kum Kum Sangari and Sudesh Vaid, 231–53. New Delhi: Kali for Women, 1989.
———. *Politics of the Governed.* New York: Columbia University Press, 2004.
Chaturvedi, Vinayak, ed. *Mapping Subaltern Studies and the Postcolonial.* London: Verso, 2000.
Chaudhuri, K. N. *Asia before Europe: Economy and Civilization of the Indian Ocean from the Rise of Islam to 1750.* Cambridge: Cambridge University Press, 1990.
———. *Trade and Civilization in the Indian Ocean: An Economic History from the Rise of Islam to 1750.* Cambridge: Cambridge University Press, 1985.
———. *The Trading World of Asia and the English East India Company, 1660–1760.* Cambridge: Cambridge University Press, 1978.

Chibber, Vivek. *Locked in Place: State Building and Late Industrialization in India.* Princeton: Princeton University Press, 2003.

Cohn, Bernard. "From Indian Status to British Contract." In *An Anthropologist among Historians and Other Essays,* 463–82. Delhi: Oxford University Press, 1990.

———. "Law and the Colonial State." In *Colonialism and Its Forms of Knowledge,* 57–75. Princeton: Princeton University Press, 1996.

———. "Representing Authority in Victorian India." In *The Invention of Tradition,* edited by E. J. Hobsbawm and Terence Ranger, 165–209. Cambridge: Cambridge University Press, 1985.

Das, Suranjan. *Communal Riots in Bengal, 1905–1947.* Delhi: Oxford University Press, 1993.

Deleuze, Gilles. *The Fold: Leibniz and the Baroque.* Translated by Tom Conley. Minneapolis: University of Minnesota Press, 1993.

Derrett, J. D. M. *A Critique of Modern Hindu Law.* Bombay: N. M. Tripathi, 1970.

———. "The History of the Juridical Framework of the Joint Hindu Family." *Contributions to Indian Sociology* 6 (1962): 17–47.

———. *Introduction to Modern Hindu Law.* Bombay: Oxford University Press, 1963.

———. "The Reform of Hindu Religious Endowments." In *South Asian Politics and Religion,* edited by Donald Eugene Smith, 311–36. Princeton: Princeton University Press, 1966.

———. *Religion, Law and the State in India.* New York: Free Press, 1968.

Derrida, Jacques. "The Double Session." In *Dissemination.* Translated by Barbara Johnson. Chicago: University of Chicago Press, 1981.

———. *Given Time: 1. Counterfeit Money.* Translated by Peggy Kamuf. Chicago: University of Chicago Press, 1992.

Desai, S. T. *The Law of Partnership in India and Pakistan.* 3rd ed. Delhi, 1964.

Dirks, Nicholas. *Castes of Mind: Colonialism and the Making of Modern India.* Princeton: Princeton University Press, 2001.

———, ed. *Colonialism and Culture.* Ann Arbor: University of Michigan Press, 1992.

———. "From Little King to Landlord: Colonial Discourse and Colonial Rule." In Dirks, ed., *Colonialism and Culture,* 175–208.

———. *The Hollow Crown: An Ethnohistory of an Indian Little Kingdom.* Cambridge: Cambridge University Press, 1987.

———. *Scandal of Empire: India and the Creation of Imperial Britain.* Cambridge, MA: Belknap Press of Harvard University Press, 2006.

Engardio, Pete, and Jena MacGregor. "Karma Capitalism." *Businessweek,* Oct. 30, 2006.

Ewing, Sally. "Formal Justice and the Spirit of Capitalism: Max Weber's Sociology of Law." *Law and Society Review* 21, no. 3 (1978): 487–512.

Fisch, Jorg. *Cheap Lives and Dear Limbs: The British Transformation of the Legal Criminal Law 1776–1817*. Wiesbaden: Franz Steiner, 1983.

Fisher, Michael. "The East India Company's Suppression of the Native Dak." *Indian Economic and Social History Review* 31, no. 3 (1994): 311–48.

Forbes, Geraldine. *Women in Modern India*. Cambridge: Cambridge University Press, 1996.

Foucault, Michel. "Governmentality." In Burchell, Gordon, and Miller, *The Foucault Effect*, 87–104.

———. *Naissance de la Biopolitique: Cours au College de France 1978–1979*. Paris: Seuil, 2004.

———. *Power/Knowledge*. Edited by Colin Gordon. New York: Pantheon, 1980.

———. *Sécurité, Territoire, Population: Cours au College de France, 1977–1978*. Paris: Seuil, 2004.

———. *Society Must Be Defended: Lectures at the College de France, 1975–76*. Translated by David Macey. New York: Picador, 2003.

———. "The Subject and Power." In *Michel Foucault: Beyond Structuralism and Hermeneutics*, edited by Hubert Dreyfus and Paul Rabinow, 208–28. 2nd ed. Chicago: University of Chicago Press, 1983.

Fox, Richard. *From Zamindar to Ballot Box: Community Change in a North Indian Town*. Ithaca: Cornell University Press, 1969.

Fraser, Nancy. "Rethinking the Public Sphere: A Contribution to the Critique of Actually Existing Democracy." In *Habermas and the Public Sphere*, edited by Craig Calhoun, 109–42. Cambridge, MA: MIT Press, 1992.

———. "What's Critical about Critical Theory? The Case of Habermas and Gender." In Benhabib and Cornell, *Feminism as Critique*, 31–56.

Freitag, Sandria. *Collective Action and Community: Public Arenas and the Emergence of Communalism in India*. Berkeley: University of California Press, 1989.

———, ed. *Culture and Power in Benaras: Community, Performance and Environment, 1800–1980*. Berkeley: University of California Press, 1989.

Gandhi, Mohandas K. *My Theory of Trusteeship*. Edited by Anand T. Hingorani. New Delhi: Gandhi Peace Foundation, 1970.

Ganapathi, Priya. "India Inc. Discovers Mahatma Gandhi." *India Abroad/Rediff.com*, Apr. 11, 2003.

Gordley, James. *The Philosophical Origins of Modern Contract Doctrine*. Oxford: Clarendon Press, 1991.

Gordon, Colin. "Governmental Rationality: An Introduction." In Burchell, Gordon, and Miller, *The Foucault Effect*, 1–51.

Goswami, Manu. *Producing India: From Colonial Economy to National Space*. Chicago: University of Chicago Press, 2004.

Goswami, Omkar. *Industry, Trade and Peasant Society: The Jute Economy of Eastern India, 1900–1947*. Delhi: Oxford University Press, 1991.

———. "Sahibs, Babus and Banias: Changes in Industrial Control in Eastern India, 1918–1950." *Journal of Asian Studies* 48, 2 (May 1989): 289–309.

———. "Then Came the Marwaris: Some Aspects of the Changes in the Pattern of Industrial Control in Eastern India." *Indian Economic and Social History Review* 22, no. 3 (1985): 225–49.

Grewal, Inderpal. *Home and Harem: Nation, Gender, Empire and the Cultures of Travel*. Durham: Duke University Press, 1996.

Guha, Ranajit. *History at the Limit of World History*. New York: Columbia University Press, 2002.

———. *A Rule of Property for Bengal: An Essay on the Idea of the Permanent Settlement*. Durham: Duke University Press, 1996.

Guha, Ranajit, et al., eds. *Subaltern Studies*. Delhi: Oxford University Press, 1982–.

Gupta, Akhil. *Postcolonial Developments: Agriculture In the Making of Modern India*. Durham: Duke University Press, 1998.

Habermas, Jürgen. *Structural Transformation of the Public Sphere*. Cambridge, MA: MIT Press, 1991.

Hamburger, Philip. "The Development of the Nineteenth Century Consensus Theory of Contract." *Law and History Review* 7, no. 2: 241–329.

Hardgrove, Anne. *Community as Public Culture: The Marwaris of Calcutta, 1887–1997*. Gutenburg E-books. New York: Columbia University Press, 2002.

Harris, Ron. *Industrializing English Law: Entrepreneurship and Business Organization, 1720–1844*. Cambridge: Cambridge University Press, 2000.

Hasan, Zoya, ed. *Forging Identities: Gender, Communities and the State*. New Delhi: Kali for Women, 1994.

Haynes, Douglas. "From Tribute to Philanthropy: The Politics of Gift Giving in a Western Indian City." *Journal of Asian Studies* 46, no. 2 (May 1987): 339–60.

———. *Rhetoric and Ritual in Colonial India: The Shaping of a Public Culture in Surat City*. Berkeley: University of California Press, 1991.

Hunt, Alan, and Gary Wickham. *Foucault and Law: Towards a Sociology of Governance*. London: Pluto Press, 1994.

Hussain, Nasser. *The Jurisprudence of Emergency: Colonialism and the Rule of Law*. Ann Arbor: University of Michigan Press, 2003.

Islam, M. Mufakharul. "The Punjab Land Alienation Act and the Professional Moneylenders." *Modern Asian Studies* 29, no. 2 (1995): 271–91.

Jain, Kajri. *Gods in the Bazaar: The Economies of Indian Calendar Art*. Durham: Duke University Press, 2007.

Jain, M. P. *Outlines of Indian Legal History*. 4th ed. Bombay: N. M. Tripathi, 1981.

Jalal, Ayesha. *Self and Sovereignty: Individual and Community in South Asian Islam*. London: Routledge, 2000.

———. *The Sole Spokesman: Jinnah, the Muslim League and the Demand for Pakistan*. Cambridge: Cambridge University Press, 1985.

Jhunjhunuwala, Vishnu Dayal. *Marwaris: Business, Culture and Tradition*. New Delhi: Kalpaz, 2002.

Johnson, Paul. "Current Events." *Forbes*, Sept. 5, 2005.

Kalpagam, U. "Colonial Governmentality and 'the Economy.'" *Economy and Society* 29, no. 3 (2002): 418–38.

———. "Colonial Governmentality and the Public Sphere in India." *Journal of Historical Sociology* 15, no. 1 (2002): 36–58.

Kane, P. V. *The History of Dharmasastra*. 5 vols. Poona: Bhandarker Oriental Research Institute, 1968–74.

Kapur, Ratna. *Feminist Terrains in Legal Domains: Interdisciplinary Essays on Women and Law in India*. New Delhi: Kali for Women, 1996.

Kapur, Ratna, and Brenda Cossman. "On Women, Equality and the Constitution: Through the Looking Glass of Feminism." In Menon, *Gender and Politics in India*, 197–263.

Keynes, John Maynard. *The General Theory of Employment, Interest and Money*. London: Macmillan, 1936.

Kozlowski, Gregory. *Muslim Endowments in British India*. Cambridge: Cambridge University Press, 1985.

Kudaisya, Medha. *The Life and Times of G. D. Birla*. Delhi: Oxford University Press, 2003.

Laidlaw, James. *Riches and Renunciation: Religion, Economy and Society among the Jains*. Oxford: Clarendon Press, 1995.

Lal, Deepak. *The Hindu Equilibrium: Cultural Stability and Economic Stagnation in India, c. 1500–1980*. New York: Oxford, 1988.

Larson, Gerald James, ed. *Religion and Personal Law in Secular India: A Call to Judgment*. Bloomington: Indiana University Press, 2001.

Lemke, Thomas. "The Birth of Bio-Politics: Michel Foucault's Lecture at the College de France on Neoliberal Governmentality." *Economy and Society* 30, no. 2 (2001): 190–207.

———. "Foucault, Governmentality, and Critique." Paper presented at the

Rethinking Marxism Conference. University of Amherst. Sept. 21–24, 2000.

Leonard, Jerry D. "Foucault and (the Ideology of) Genealogical Legal Theory." In *Legal Studies as Cultural Studies*, edited by Jerry Leonard, 133–51. Albany: State University of New York Press, 1995.

Lester, V. Markham. *Victorian Insolvency: Bankruptcy, Imprisonment for Debt, and Company Winding-up in Nineteenth Century England*. Oxford: Clarendon Press, 1995.

Likhovski, Assaf. "A Map of Society: Defining Income in British, British Colonial and American Tax Legislation." *British Tax Review* 1 (2005): 158–79.

Lowe, Lisa, and David Lloyd, eds. *The Politics of Culture in the Shadow of Capital*. Durham: Duke University Press, 1997.

Ludden, David, ed. *An Agrarian History of South Asia*. Cambridge: Cambridge University Press, 1999.

———. "India's Development Regime." In Dirks, ed., *Colonialism and Culture*, 247–87.

———. *Peasant History in South India*. Princeton: Princeton University Press, 1985.

———. *Reading Subaltern Studies: Critical History, Contested Meaning and the Globalization of South Asia*. London: Anthem, 2002.

———. "The World Economy and Village India, 1600–1900." In Bose, ed., *South Asia and World Capitalism*, 159–77.

Mahmood, Tahir. *Muslim Personal Law: The Role of the State in the Indian Subcontinent*. New Delhi: Vikas, 1983.

Majumdar, Rochona. "Marriage, Modernity and Sources of the Self: Bengali Women, c. 1870–1956." PhD diss., University of Chicago, 2003.

———. " 'Self-Sacrifice' versus 'Self-Interest': A Non-Historicist Reading of the History of Women's Rights in India." *Comparative Studies of South Asia, Africa and the Middle East* 22, nos. 1–2 (May 2002): 20–35.

Malik, K. K., ed. *A. P. Mathur's Commentaries on Gambling Acts in India*. Delhi: Eastern Book Company, 1973.

Mamdani, Mahmood. *Citizen and Subject: Contemporary Africa and the Legacy of Late Colonialism*. Princeton: Princeton University Press, 1996.

Mani, Lata. *Contentious Traditions: The Debate on Sati in Colonial India*. Berkeley: University of California Press, 1998.

Mansfield, John H. "Religious and Charitable Endowments and a Uniform Civil Code." In Larson, *Religion and Personal Law in Secular India*, 69–103.

Markovitz, Claude. *The Global World of Indian Merchants, 1750–1947: The Traders of Sind from Bukhara to Panama*. Cambridge: Cambridge University Press, 2000.

——. *Indian Business and Nationalist Politics, 1931–39*. Cambridge: Cambridge University Press, 1985.

Marshall, P. J. *Bengal: The British Bridgehead. Eastern India 1740–1828*. Cambridge: Cambridge University Press, 1988.

Marx, Karl. *Capital: A Critique of Political Economy*, vols. 1–3. Translated by Ben Fowkes and David Fernbach. New York: Penguin, 1990–92.

——. *Early Writings*. Translated by Rodney Livingstone and Gregor Benton. London: Penguin 1992.

——. *Economic and Philosophical Manuscripts of 1844*. In *Early Writings*, 279–400.

——. "Excerpts from James Mill's *Elements of Political Economy*." In *Early Writings*, 260–78.

——. "On the Jewish Question." In *The Marx-Engels Reader*, edited by Robert Tucker, 26–52. New York: Norton, 1978.

Mauss, Marcel. *The Gift*. New York: Norton, 1990.

Mazzarella, William. *Shoveling Smoke: Advertising and Globalization in Contemporary India*. Durham: Duke University Press, 2003.

Moxham, Roy. *The Great Hedge of India*. New York: Carroll and Graf, 2001.

McEldowney, Philip. "Colonial Administration and Social Developments in Middle India: The Central Provinces, 1906–1921." PhD diss., University of Virginia, 1980.

Mehta, Uday Singh. *Liberalism and Empire: A Study in Nineteenth-Century British Liberal Thought*. Chicago: University of Chicago Press, 1999.

Menon, Nivedita, ed. *Gender and Politics in India*. New Delhi: Oxford University Press, 1999.

——. *Recovering Subversion: Feminist Politics beyond the Law*. Urbana: University of Illinois Press, 2004.

——. "Rights, Bodies and the Law: Rethinking Feminist Politics of Justice." In Menon, *Gender and Politics in India*, 262–95.

Metcalf, Thomas R. *Ideologies of the Raj*. Cambridge: Cambridge University Press, 1995.

Meuret, Dennis. "A Political Genealogy of Political Economy." Translated by Graham Burchell. *Economy and Society* 17, no. 2 (1998): 225–49.

Meyer, Thomas O. "Futures Markets as Hedging Markets and the Relative Effects of Speculation on Hedging Effectiveness." Columbia University Business School Center for the Study of Futures Markets: Working Paper Series CDFM no. 210, September 1990.

Misra, Maria. *Business, Race, and Politics in British India, 1850–1960.* New York: Clarendon Press, 1999.

Mitchell, Timothy. *Rule of Experts: Egypt, Techno-Politics, Modernity.* Berkeley: University of California Press, 2002.

Mitchie, Ranald C. *The London Stock Exchange: A History.* Oxford: Oxford University Press, 1999.

Mody, Perveez. "Love and Law: Love-Marriage in Delhi." *Modern Asian Studies* 36, no. 1 (2002): 223–56.

Mukhopadhyay, Maitrayee. "Between Community and State: The Question of Women's Rights and Personal Laws." In Hasan, *Forging Identities*, 108–29.

Mukund, Kanakalatha. *The Trading World of the Tamil Merchant: Evolution of Merchant Capitalism in the Coromandel.* Hyderabad: Orient Longman, 1999.

Muldiar, C. Y. *State and Religious Endowments in Madras.* Madras: University of Madras, 1976.

Nair, Janaki. *Women and the Law in Colonial India.* New Delhi: Kali for Women, 1996.

Nehru, Jawaharlal. *The Discovery of India.* Edited by Robert I. Crane. 1946. New York: Anchor Doubleday, 1960.

O'Malley, Pat. "Uncertain Subjects: Risk, Liberalism and Contract." *Economy and Society* 29, no. 4 (2000): 460–84.

Orsini, Francesa. *The Hindi Public Sphere: Language and Literature in the Age of Nationalism.* New York: Oxford University Press, 2002.

Parashar, Archana. *Women and Family Law Reform in India.* New Delhi: Sage Publications, 1992.

Parry, Jonathan. "The Moral Perils of Exchange." In *Money and the Morality of Exchange*, edited by Jonathan Parry and Maurice Bloch, 64–93. Cambridge: Cambridge University Press, 1989.

Pasquino, Pasquale. "Theatrum Politicum: The Genealogy of Capital-Police and the State of Prosperity." In Burchell, Gordon, and Miller, *The Foucault Effect*, 105–18.

Pateman, Carole. *The Sexual Contract.* Stanford: Stanford University Press, 1988.

Pels, Peter. "The Anthropology of Colonialism: Culture, History and the Emergence of Western Governmentality." *Annual Review of Anthropology* 26 (1997): 163–83.

Polanyi, Karl. "Aristotle Discovers the Economy." In *Trade and Market in the Early Empires*, edited by Karl Polanyi, Conrad Arensberg, and Harry Pearson, 64–94. Glencoe, IL: The Free Press, 1957.

———. *The Great Transformation.* Boston: Beacon Press, 1957.

Polden, P. "The Public Trustee in England, 1906–1986: The Failure of an Experiment?" *Journal of Legal History* 10, no. 2: 228–55.

Poovey, Mary, ed. *The Financial System in Nineteenth Century Britain.* New York: Oxford University Press, 2003.

Prakash, Gyan, ed. *After Colonialism: Imperial Histories and Postcolonial Displacements.* Princeton: Princeton University Press, 1995.

——. *Another Reason: Science and the Imagination of Modern India.* Princeton: Princeton University Press, 1999.

——, ed. *The World of the Rural Labourer in Colonial India.* Delhi: Oxford University Press, 1992.

——. "Writing Post-Orientalist Histories in the Third World: Perspectives from Indian Historiography." *Comparative Studies in Society and History* 32, no. 2 (Apr. 1990): 383–48.

——. *Bonded Histories: Genealogies of Labor Servitude in Colonial India.* Cambridge: Cambridge University Press, 1990.

Raban, Sandra. *Mortmain Legislation and the English Church.* Cambridge: Cambridge University Press, 1982.

Rankin, Katherine. *The Cultural Politics of Markets: Economic Liberalization and Social Change in Nepal.* London: Pluto; Toronto: University of Toronto Press, 2004.

Rao, Anupama, ed. *Gender and Caste.* New Delhi: Kali for Women, 2003.

Ray, Rajat. "Asian Capital in the Age of European Domination: The Rise of the Bazaar, 1880–1914." *Modern Asian Studies* 29, no. 3 (1995): 449–554.

——. "The Bazaar: Changing Structural Characteristics of the Indigenous Indian Economy before and after the Great Depression." *Indian Economic and Social History Review* 25 (1988): 263–318.

——, ed. *Entrepreneurship and Industry in India, 1800–1947.* Oxford: Oxford University Press, 1992.

Ray, Sangeeta. *En-Gendering India: Woman and Nation in Colonial and Postcolonial Narratives.* Durham: Duke University Press, 2002.

Richards, John F. "Opium and the British Indian Empire: The Royal Commission of 1895." *Modern Asian Studies* 36, no. 2 (May 2002): 375–420.

Rousseau, Jean-Jacques. "Discourse on Political Economy." In Jean-Jacques Rousseau, *The Basic Political Writings.* Translated by Donald A. Cress. Indianapolis: Hackett, 1987.

Rothermund, Dietmar. *An Economic History of India.* London: Routledge, 1993.

Roy, Parama. *Indian Traffic: Identities in Question in Colonial and Postcolonial India.* Berkeley: University of California Press, 1998.

Rudner, David. "Banker's Trust and the Culture of Banking among the Nattukottai Chettiars of Colonial South India." *Modern Asian Studies* 23, no. 3 (1989): 417–58.

———. *Caste and Capitalism in Colonial India: The Nattukottai Chettiars.* Berkeley: University of California Press, 1994.

———. "Religious Gifting and Inland Commerce in Seventeenth-Century South India." *Journal of Asian Studies* 42, no. 2 (May 1987): 361–79.

Rubin, Gayle. "The Traffic in Women: Notes on the 'Political Economy' of Sex." In *Toward an Anthropology of Women*, edited by Rayna R. Reiter, 157–210. New York: Monthly Review Press, 1975.

Said, Edward. *Orientalism*. New York: Vintage, 1978.

Sarkar, Tanika. "Enfranchised Selves: Women, Culture and Rights in Nineteenth Century Bengal." *Gender and History* 13, no. 3 (Nov. 2001): 546–65.

———. *Hindu Wife, Hindu Nation: Community, Religion and Cultural Nationalism*. New Delhi: Permanent Black, 2001.

———. "A Prehistory of Rights: The Age of Consent Debate in Colonial Bengal." *Feminist Studies* 26, no. 3 (2000): 601–22.

Scott, David. "Culture in Political Theory." *Political Theory* 31, no. 1 (Feb. 2003): 91–115.

———. "Colonial Governmentality." In *Refashioning Futures: Criticism after Postcoloniality*, 23–52. Princeton: Princeton University Press, 1999.

Scott, Joan Wallach. *Gender and the Politics of History*. New York: Columbia University Press, 1988.

Sen, Amartya. *Development as Freedom*. New York: Anchor, 1999.

Sen, Sudipta. *Empire of Free Trade*. Philadelphia: University of Pennsylvania Press, 1998.

Sharma, Girishankar. *Marwari Vyapari*. Bikaner: Krishnajansewa, 1988.

Siddiqi, Asiya, ed. *Trade and Finance in Colonial India*. Delhi: Oxford University Press, 1995.

Silos, Leonardo R. *Management and the Tao: Organization as Community*. Makati City: Asian Institute of Management, 1998.

Simpson, J. A., and E. S. C. Weiner. *Oxford English Dictionary*. 2nd ed. Oxford: Clarendon Press, 1991.

Singha, Radhika. "Colonial Law and Infrastructural Power: Reconstructing Community, Locating the Female Subject." *Studies in History* 19, no. 1 (2003): 87–126.

———. *A "Despotism of Law": British Criminal Justice and Public Authority in North India, 1772–1837*. Delhi: Oxford University Press, 1998.

Sinha, Mrinalini. *Colonial Masculinity: The 'Manly Englishman' and the 'Effeminate Bengali' in the Nineteenth Century*. Manchester: Manchester University Press, 1995.

———. "The Lineage of the 'Indian' Modern: Rhetoric, Agency and the Sarda Act in Late Colonial India." In *Gender, Sexuality, and Colonial*

Modernities, edited by Antoinette Burton, 207–21. New York: Routledge, 1999.

———. "Refashioning Mother India: Feminism and Nationalism in Late Colonial India." *Feminist Studies* 26, no. 3 (2000): 623–44.

———. *Spectres of Mother India: The Global Restructuring of an Empire*. Durham: Duke University Press, 2006.

Smith, Adam. *An Inquiry into the Nature and Causes of the Wealth of Nations*. Edited by Edwin Canaan. Chicago: University of Chicago Press, 1976.

Sombart, Werner. *Die Juden und das Wirtshaftslieben*. Leipzig: Duncker and Humblot, 1911.

Spivak, Gayatri Chakravorty. "Can the Subaltern Speak?" In *Marxism and the Interpretation of Culture*, edited by Carey Nelson and Lawrence Grossberg, 271–313. Urbana: University of Illinois Press, 1988.

———. *A Critique of Postcolonial Reason: A History of the Vanishing Present*. Cambridge, MA: Harvard University Press, 1999.

———. "Cultural Talks in the Hot Peace: Revisiting the Global Village." In *Cosmopolitics: Thinking and Feeling Beyond the Nation*, edited by Pheng Cheah and Bruce Robbins, 329–48. Minneapolis: University of Minnesota, 1998.

———. "How to Teach a Culturally Different Book." In *Colonial Discourse, Post-Colonial Theory*, edited by Frances Burke, Peter Hulme, and Margaret Iverson, 126–51. New York: St. Martin's Press, 1996.

———. "Scattered Speculations on the Question of Value." In *In Other Worlds: Essays in Cultural Politics*, 154–75. New York: Methuen, 1987.

———. "Subaltern Studies: Deconstructing Historiography." In *Subaltern Studies* IV, edited by Ranajit Guha, 330–63. Delhi: Oxford University Press, 1985.

———. "Translation as Culture." *Parallax* XIV (Jan.–Mar. 2000): 13–24.

Srinivas, Mytheli. "Conjugality and Capital: Gender, Families and Property under Colonial Law in India." *Journal of Asian Studies* 63, no. 4 (Nov. 2004): 937–60.

Srinivasan, K. *Tax Treatment of Private Trusts*. New Delhi: National Institute of Public Finance and Policy, 1983.

Stebbings, Chantal. *The Private Trustee in Victorian England*. Cambridge: Cambridge University Press, 2002.

Stokes, Eric. *The English Utilitarians and India*. Oxford: Clarendon Press, 1959.

Stoler, Ann Laura. *Carnal Knowledge and Imperial Power: Race and the Intimate in Colonial Rule*. Berkeley: University of California Press, 2002.

———. *Race and the Education of Desire: Foucault's History of Sexuality and the Colonial Order of Things*. Durham: Duke University Press, 1995.

Subramanian, Lakshmi. "Capital and Crowd in a Declining Asian Port City: The Anglo-Bania Order and the Surat Riots of 1795." *Modern Asian Studies* 19, no. 2 (1985): 205–37.

———. *Indigenous Capital and Imperial Expansion: Bombay, Surat, and the West Coast*. Delhi: Oxford University Press, 1996.

Subrahmanyam, Sanjay, ed. *Merchants, Markets and the State in Early Modern India, 1770–1870*. Delhi: Oxford University Press, 1990.

———. "Introduction." In *Money and the Market in India, 1100–1700*, ed. Sanjay Subrahmanyam, 1–56. Delhi: Oxford University Press, 1994.

———. *The Political Economy of Commerce: Southern India, 1500–1650*. Cambridge: Cambridge University Press, 1990.

Subrahmanyam, Sanjay, and C. A. Bayly. "Portfolio Capitalists and Political Economy in Early Modern India." In Subrahmanyam, *Merchants, Markets and the State in Early Modern India, 1770–1870*, 242–65.

Sugarman, David, and G. R. Rubin. "Towards a New History of Law and Material Society in England: 1750–1914." In *Law, Economy and Society, 1750–1914: Essays in the History of English Law*, edited by David Sugarman and G. R. Rubin, 1–123. Abingdon: Professional Books, 1984.

Sunder Rajan, Rajeshwari. *The Scandal of the State: Women, Law and Citizenship in Postcolonial India*. Durham: Duke University Press, 2003.

Taknet, D. K. *Industrial Entrepreneurship of Shekhawati Marwaris*. Jaipur: South Asia Books, 1986.

Thapar, Romila. *A History of India*. Vol. 1. New York: Penguin, 1966.

Thompson, Herb. "Culture and Economic Development: Modernization to Globalization." *Theory and Science*, 2001. http://theoryandscience.icaap.org/content/vo1002.002/thompson.html. Accessed Sept. 28, 2005.

Timberg, Thomas. "Hiatus and Incubator: Indigenous Trade and Traders, 1837–1857." In Siddiqi, *Trade and Finance in Colonial India*, 250–64.

———. *The Marwaris: From Traders to Industrialists*. New Delhi: Vikas, 1978.

———. "A North Indian Firm as Seen through Its Business Records, 1860–1914: Tarachand Ghansyamdas, A 'Great' Marwari Firm." *Indian Economic and Social History Review* 8, no. 3 (1971): 264–83.

Tönnies, Ferdinand. *Community and Civil Society*. Translated by José Harris and Margaret Hollis. 1887. Cambridge: Cambridge University Press, 2001.

Tomlinson, B. R. *The Political Economy of the Raj*. London: Macmillan, 1979.

Tribe, Keith. *Land, Labour and Economic Discourse*. London: Routledge and Kegan Paul, 1978.

Tripathi, Dwijendra, ed. *Business and Politics in India: A Historical Perspective.* New Delhi: Manohar, 1991.

Uberoi, Patricia, ed. *Family, Kinship and Marriage in India.* Delhi: Oxford University Press, 1993.

Vaggi, Gianni. "The Classical Concept of Profit Revisited." In *Perspectives in the History of Economic Thought.* Vol. 3, *Classicals, Marxians and Neo-Classicals,* edited by Donald E. Moggridge, 1–9. Brookfield, VT: Edward Elgar, 1990.

Viswanathan, Gauri. *Outside the Fold: Conversion, Modernity and Belief.* New York: Columbia University Press, 1998.

Walker, Marcus. "India Touts its Democracy in Bid to Lure Investors Away from China." *Wall Street Journal,* Jan. 30, 2006.

Wallerstein, Immanuel. *The Modern World System.* 3 vols. New York: Academic Press, 1974, 1980, 1989.

——. *World-Systems Analysis: An Introduction.* Durham: Duke University Press, 2004.

Washbrook, David. "Law, State and Agrarian Society in Colonial India." *Modern Asian Studies* 15, no. 3 (1981): 646–721.

——. "Progress and Problems: South Asian Economic and Social History, c. 1720–1860." *Modern Asian Studies* 22, no. 1 (1988): 57–96.

——. "South Asia, the World System and World Capitalism." In Bose, ed., *South Asia and World Capitalism,* 40–84.

Watt, Carey A. *Serving the Nation: Cultures of Service, Association and Citizenship.* New Delhi: Oxford University Press, 2005.

Weber, Max. *Economy and Society: An Outline of Interpretive Sociology.* Edited by Guenther Roth and Claus Wittich. 2 vols. New York: Bedminister Press, 1968.

——. *The Protestant Ethic and the Spirit of Capitalism.* New York: Routledge, 2001.

Weinberger, Caspar. "India: On Every Business Agenda." *Forbes,* Feb. 13, 2006: 37.

Working, Holbrook. *Selected Writings of Holbrook Working,* compiled by Anne E. Peck. Chicago: Chicago Board of Trade, 1977.

Yang, Anand. *Bazaar India: Markets, Society and the Colonial State in Gangetic Bihar.* Berkeley: University of California Press, 1998.

Yúdice, George. *The Expediency of Culture: The Uses of Culture in the Global Era.* Durham: Duke University Press, 2003.

Zemon Davis, Natalie. "Conclusion." In *Autour de Polanyi: Vocabularies, théories et modalités des échanges,* edited by Phillipe Clancier, Francis Joahnès, and Pierre Rouillard, 283–90. Paris: De Boccard, 2005.

——. "Religion and Capitalism Once Again? Jewish Merchant Culture in the Seventeenth Century." *Representations* 59 (1997): 56–84.

Index

Afghan Wars, 53
Agarwals, 18–19, 202, 212–13, 299n9
Agarwal Vansh Komudi (Malu), 301n35
age of consent, 202–3, 216–22, 227–31, 304n82, 305n94, 305n96
Aggarwalon ki Utpatti (Harishchandra), 301n35
Ahmedabad Millowner's Association, 211
All-India Marwari Federation, 213, 221
Amendment Act VII of 1939, 98–99
American Civil War, 40–41
Ancient Law (Maine), 241n11, 247n40
anomalous Muslims. *See* Ismailis
anthropology of globalization, 254n83
Appadurai, Arjun, 254n83
Arendt, Hannah, 256n89
"Aristotle Discovers the Economy" (Polanyi), 241n11, 253n74
arthavyavastha (practice of economy), 259n21
Asian values, 8
association. *See* civic association
"Autobiography of a Joint-Stock Company, The" (Oliphant), 33
autonomy. *See* sovereignty

badni transactions, 153, 173–74, 179, 181
Bagchi, Amiya Kumar, 38, 258n18
Baij Nath, Lala Rai Bahadur, 143
Bajaj, Jamnalal, 214–15
Banerji, Surendranath, 162–63, 287n74, 289n93
banias, 17–18, 202
bankruptcy law, 41–43, 48, 260nn39–40
Bansilal Abirchand, 271n75
Barua, Rishi Jamini Kaushik, 276n15, 301n35
Basu, Bhupendra Nath, 210, 303n71, 304n73
Bayly, C. A., 153, 244n25, 251n64
bazaar, 9–10, 243n24, 252n72, 254n83; *dharmada* collections in, 88–89; personal and private classification of, 139
beneficiary, 81; diety as, 85–86, 270n63; public as, 103–5, 129, 133–34
Bengal Chamber of Commerce, 51, 150–51, 192–93, 196, 206, 211
Bengal Child Marriage Prevention Bill, 220–21
Bengal Public Gambling Amendment Bill of 1913, 189–90, 192

Bengal Rain-Gambling Act, 169–73, 289n101, 290nn106–7, 294n150
betting, 149, 158. *See also* gambling
Betting and Gambling (Rowntree), 149
Bhagavad Gita, 1, 239n3
Bharat Chamber of Commerce, 189, 300n20. *See also* Marwari Chamber of Commerce
Bharat me Marwari Samaj (Kedia), 276n15
Bhatia Mitra Mandal, 183
Bhatias, 152
Bill for the Suppression of Rain-Gambling. *See* Bengal Rain-Gambling Act
Birla, G. D., 296n166, 299n10
Birla, J. K., 284n32
Birla, Radhakrishna, 285nn38–39
Bogla, Sheubux, 161–62
Bombay Act III of 1866, 154–55, 285n48
Bombay Chamber of Commerce, 206–7
Bombay Cotton Contracts Act of 1922, 296n174
Bombay Native Piece-Goods Merchants' Association, 206–8
Bombay Prevention of Gambling Act (IV of 1887), 154–60, 170
Bombay Securities Control Act of 1925, 296n174
Bose, Bhupendra Nath, 163–64
Bose, Sugata, 242n17
Bourdieu, Pierre, 266n15, 268n48
boys. *See* child marriage
British Charitable Trusts Act of 1853, 69
British Charitable Trusts Act of 1887, 69–70
British Companies Acts of 1844 and 1856, 40
British Indian Association, 47, 58, 164, 287n79

British Mortmain Act of 1736, 69
British Mortmain and Charitable Uses Act of 1888, 69–71, 266n8
British Partnership Act of 1890, 50–51, 261n49
British Trustee Act of 1888, 266n13
British Trustee Act of 1893, 266n13
British Trust Investment Act of 1889, 266n13
"Bubble Act" of 1720, 35, 40, 257n7
burlap. *See* jute speculation
Burrabazar area of Calcutta, 160–72, 188–90, 192, 213, 286nn64–66, 288n86
business education, 151

Calcutta. *See* Burrabazar area of Calcutta
Calcutta Improvement Trust, 286n64
Calcutta Municipal Corporation, 190, 295n162
Calcutta Trades Association, 260n40, 278n39
Calcutta Vaishya Sabha, 213
caste-based market practices. *See* kinship- and caste-based practices
certificate taxes, 55
Chakrabarty, Dipesh, 241n10, 254n83, 299n12
Chamaria, Hardutai, 284n32
Charitable Endowments Acts of 1890, 28
charity. *See* social welfare practices; trusts
Charlu, Ananda, 129
Charter Act of 1813, 22, 252n71
Chatterjee, Partha, 26–27, 242n16, 245nn27–29, 255n85, 257n94, 299n12
Chaudhuri, Arindham, 239n3
Chaudhuri, K. N., 242n17, 245n33

Chettiars, 18, 74, 98–99, 244n25, 249n47
Chetty, Ramaswamy Diwan Bahadur, 131
child marriage, 202–3, 216–22, 227–31, 304n82, 305n94, 305n96
Child Marriage Restraint Act of 1929, 203, 219, 227–31, 304n82, 305n94, 305n96
chittis (letters of credit or debt), 61
Choudhuri, K. C. Roy, 297n182
Chowdury, Hukmi Chand, 172
citizenship, 48. *See also* sovereignty
civic association, 37, 48–53, 119, 199–200; consolidation of, 212–16; of Marwaris, 171–72, 189–90, 211–16, 290nn102–5, 295n162, 297n179, 301n30, 301n35, 302n42; reformist journals of, 213–14; regulations of, 37, 48–53. *See also* public charitable trusts
civil marriage, 215–16, 224–27, 230, 303n71, 304n73
civil society: as arrangement of economic men (Foucault), 8, 26, 199–200, 243n20; Marx's view of, 25–26; public sphere and (Habermas), 26, 256nn89–90; the social and (Arendt), 256n89. *See also* civic association; corporate life
Code of Gentoo Laws, or Ordinances of the Pundits (Halhead), 247n39
Cohn, Bernard, 14, 247n41
Colebrooke, H. T., 90–91, 247n39
colonial governance: commercial castes, 17; Company Raj, 11–12, 245n33; contract law, 21, 24, 30, 35–36, 254–55nn80–81, 258n9; disembedding of the market, 24, 33–37; economic development discourses of, 4–9, 20–23, 240nn8–9; hegemony of, 7; market governance, 7–8, 13–15, 242–43nn19–20; noninterference policies, 3–4, 63, 66, 73; as political economy, 22–23, 252–53nn69–74; rule of law, 1–2, 15, 37–38, 239nn1–2. *See also* East India Company; sovereignty
colonial subject, 6–7, 234, 241n13; as bearer of capital, 8; as complicit, 6, 242n15; as subject of interest and of law/rights, 21–22, 234, 251n65
Colvin, Auckland, 56
commercial and tax regulation: on bankruptcy, 41–43, 48, 260nn39–40; on civic association, 37, 48–53; consonance with British law of, 40; creation of public and private arenas by, 38–39, 258n18; creation of the legal subject by, 36; disembedding of the market by, 33–39; on family firms, 49–53, 60, 204–12, 260n44, 261n46, 263n70; Ilbert's opinion on, 262n66; Indian Companies Act of 1882, 28, 34, 39–48; Indian Income Tax Act of 1886, 36, 53–60, 262nn54–55, 262n63; Land Revenue and Agriculture department, 36–37; on limited liability, 39–48; Negotiable Instruments Act of 1881, 60–66; on partnership, 263n70; Super-Tax Act of 1917, 209–11. *See also* market governance
Commercial Intelligence Department, 106–7
community and capital, 6–7, 9–10, 24–27, 105, 237, 241n11
Community and Civil Society (Tönnies), 241n11
Company Raj, 11–12, 245n33
conduct of conduct, 9, 23–24, 65, 243n23, 254nn78–83

INDEX 331

contract law, 30; conduct of conduct in, 9, 23–24, 65, 243n23, 254nn78–83; ethical context of, 24, 46, 254nn80–81; gifts for dharma and, 75–78; impact on marriage of, 215–16, 223–27, 230, 303n71, 304n73; Indian Contract Act of 1872, 258n9; intentionality and, 24, 65, 70, 72, 81, 84, 86–87, 120, 191; joint contracts, 111–15, 276n18; standardization of, 35–36, 60–66, 264n83. *See also* trusts

coparcenors, 17, 48, 57–58, 91–92. *See also* Hindu Undivided Family

co-residence, 16–17

corporate governance, 8, 243n22, 251n63

corporate life, 24–27, 105; as fictitious persons, 67; Hindu Undivided Family and, 209. *See also* community and capital

Cotton, C. W. E., 107

cotton markets, 40–41

cotton speculation, 184–90, 294n150, 294n153, 295nn156–58

Criminal Jurisdiction Bill of 1883, 56, 262n66

cultural value-coding, 298n2

culture. *See* ethnicity and cultural contexts; kinship- and caste-based practices; personal law

customary law. See *lex mercatoria*; *logos/nomos* categories; personal law

customs duties, 36, 53

Daga, Kastur Chand Seth, 114, 271n75

Dakor Temple case, 85–87, 96, 108, 273n109

Das, Premsook, 169–70

Davis, Natalie Zemon, 10–11

dead hand. *See* mortmain and perpetuity

Deccan riots of 1875, 94, 272n91

deities: household management of, 85–87, 270n67; as infant heirs, 84–85, 96–97; as juristic entities, 85–87, 93–94, 96, 101, 108, 270n63, 273n109; in mortmain practices, 92–93, 96; as proprietors of property, 80–85, 96, 269n51, 270n63; taxation of, 96–99

Deleuze, Gilles, 242n15

democracy's fixed costs, 1

Department of Commerce and Industry, 106, 151

Derrett, J. D. M.: on gifting practices, 76, 83, 86–87, 269n51; on inheritance practices, 91; on standardization of personal law, 247n41

Derrida, Jacques, 242n15, 268n48

dharma gifts: in charitable practices, 71, 74–76, 79, 86, 267n37; classification of, as illegitimate, 119–21, 278n44; commercial approaches to, 87–89

Dharmashastras, 204

Dharmashastra Smriti (Colebrooke), 247n39

dharmshala (*dharmsala*) centers, 74; legal debates on, 106, 109–10, 119–28; Marwari endowment practices, 88–89, 139, 271n75

Dhayabhaga system of Hindu law, 17, 247n39, 249n50; discussion of perpetuities in, 90–91; patriarchal authority in, 17, 249n50

Didu Maheshwari Panchayat, 213

Dirks, Nicholas, 246n37, 252n71

Discovery of India, The (Nehru), 300n13

disembedded market, 4, 9, 33–39, 236, 240n9, 283n25; as abstrac-

tion of market exchange, 120–21, 144, 150; creation of legal subjects and, 24, 36; fiscal system and, 36; as the public, 4, 26, 39, 104; standardization of contract law and, 35–36, 60–66, 264n83; standardization of information and, 37, 147, 149–50. *See also* market governance; sovereignty; virtual capital
Diwali, 87–89
donors, 81
Dufferin, viceroy of 1886, 115
Dutt, R. C., 251n63
dyarchy, 281n81

East India Company, 3, 233–34; Company Raj of, 11–12, 104, 245n33; free-trade practices of, 22, 34; monopoly practices of, 252n71; public/private boundaries of, 22, 252n72; theories of political economy of, 22–24, 254n80; tributes paid by, 77
Economic and Philosophical Manuscripts (Marx), 255n86
Economic Man, 12, 233–35, 237; gendered readings of, 200–201; Indian Economic Man, 2, 8, 18, 240n4; Marx on, 8, 234, 306n7; trustees as, 71, 103–4
economy, as object: in economic science, 20–23, 250n57, 250n59, 251–53nn62–73; economy as practice of governing vs., 7–8, 21–24, 39, 242n19, 250n59, 251–52nn64–68, 253n74; economy/culture distinction, 3–4, 8–10, 68, 200, 231. *See also* Foucault, Michel; market governance; political economy
Economy and Society (Weber), 241n11, 259n20
Elliot, Charles, 162, 168

Empress v. Narotamdas Motiram, 159, 294n150
Encyclopédie (Rousseau), 253n74
endowments. *See* social welfare practices; trusts
ethnicity and cultural contexts, 8, 243n22; anthropological readings of, 10–11, 245–46nn30–34; dis-embedding of culture, 24; personal law as cultural formation, 5–6, 13, 21, 251n63; of public religious trusts, 135–38; Spivak's "culture alive," 24, 254n83. *See also* kinship- and caste-based practices; personal law
Ewan, R. S. T., 60
"Excepts from James Mill's *Elements of Political Economy*" (Marx), 255n86

fakta transactions, 190, 284n36
family firms, 5–6, 268n48; coparcenary status of, 17, 48, 57–58, 225; criminal investigations of, 29–30; de-legitimation of, 48–53, 110–11, 260n44, 261n46; excess-profits of, 208–11; Indian Partnership Act of 1935, 261n49; inheritance and property in, 111–15; joint contracts, 111–15, 276n18; legal infrastructure of, 15–17, 27–29, 248–49nn44–50; legitimation of, 60; property relations in, 16–17, 248n48, 249n50; reform and regulation of, 203–12; registration of, 206–8; risk management methods of, 151; social welfare practices of, 59, 88–89, 108; taxation of, 54–60, 208–11, 223, 263n70; unlimited liability of, 49–53, 204. *See also* gender contexts; Hindu Undivided Family

INDEX 333

Federation of Indian Chambers of Commerce and Industry (FICCI), 200, 298n1, 305n96
feminist political theory. *See* gender contexts
financial legislation. *See* commercial and tax regulation
fiscal system expansion, 36
forward trade transactions, 153
Foucault, Michel: on conduct of conduct, 9, 23–24, 243n23, 254n79; on the economic subject, 234–35; on governmentality and political economy, 7–8, 21–24, 39, 242n19, 250n59, 251–52nn64–68, 253n74, 259n19, 263n78; on liberalism, 8, 243n20; on rights and the law, 253n77; on sovereignty, 258n10; on the subject of interest and of law/rights, 251n65
free trade, 5; East India Company, 22, 34, 252n71; invisible hand and (Smith), 22, 69, 89, 234; nationalist critiques of, 150–51. *See also* the disembedded market
futures contracts, 147–48
Futures Market Bill, 195–96
futures markets, 178–81, 282n4; in agricultural products, 146; forward trading, 152–53; illegitimate forms of, 149; in jute, 190–98; legitimate forms of, 193–98, 297n176. *See also* speculative practices

gambling, 29; as distinguished from speculation, 154–60, 286n55; Euro-American contexts of, 146–50, 282n7, 283n19, 290n107; as wagering and public betting, 149, 157–60. *See also* rain gambling; speculative practices

Gandhi, Mohandas K. (Mahatma), 1, 12, 103–4, 203, 239n3, 268n38, 274n1, 298n1
Geertz, Clifford, 243n24, 245n30
gemeinschaft and gesellschaft, 6–7, 24, 27, 105, 237, 241n11
gender contexts, 13; of age-of-consent and child marriage debates, 201–3, 215–22, 227–31, 304n82, 305n94, 305n96; of civil marriage, 223–27, 230, 303n71, 304n73; in discourses on public morality, 30; of education of women, 202–3; of families, households, and tradition, 14, 16–17, 30, 202–3, 243n50, 248n42, 259n22; historiography of, 201, 298n6, 298n8; of inheritance and property rights, 201, 298n8; of nationalist discourses, 202, 299n12; public/private distinction in, 14, 25–26; in readings of economic development, 243n22; in social reform discourses, 200–203, 216–31; in widow remarriage conflicts, 201–2
General Family and Bengal Christian Family Pension Funds, 116
General Family Pension Fund, 116
general public utility criteria, 29, 68–70, 78–79, 98, 103–10, 115, 236
General Theory of Employment, Interest and Money, The (Keynes), 282n4
Ghose, Rash Behari, 129
Ghosh, Protap Chandra, 46
Gift, The (Mauss), 268n48
gifting. *See* religio-cultural contexts of indigenous charity; social welfare practices; trusts
girls. *See* child marriage
Given Time (Derrida), 268n48
globalization, 254n83

G. M. Tagore v. U. M. Tagore, 93–95, 272n88
"God Not Beyond IT Act," 96
Goenka, Rai Bahadur Hariram, 217–20
Gokul Dass, Seth Rai Bahadur, 113–14
Gold Bricks of Speculation (Hill), 148–49, 283n17, 283n19
Goondas Act of 1926, 288n86
gotres clans, 16
Gour, Hari Singh, 135–39, 219–20, 224, 227, 303n58
governmentality, 7–8, 20–24, 39, 242n19, 250n59, 251–52nn64–68, 253n74. *See also* market governance
"Governmentality" (Foucault), 21–22, 251–52nn64–68, 253n74
Government of India Act of 1858, 245n33
grain speculation, 173–74, 177–83
Great Transformation, The (Polanyi), 240n9, 241n11, 268n48
Guha, Ranajit, 22, 242n18, 252n69
Gujaratis, 18, 207; charitable gift practices of, 74; social reform movements of, 202; speculative practices of, 152

Habermas, Jürgen, 256nn89–91
Halhead, N. B., 247n39
Hamilton, Charles, 247n39
Handbook of Commercial Information for India (Cotton), 107
Haridas, Anandji, 199
Harishchandra, 301n35
Hastings, Warren, 40, 247n39
Haynes, Douglas, 74, 244n25
Hedaya (Hamilton), 247n39
hedging. *See* futures markets
Hegel, G. W. F., 255n85
Hill, John, 148–49, 283n17, 283n19
Himatsingka, P. D., 195–96

Hindu Disposition of Property Act of 1921, 94
Hindu Family Annuity Fund, 116
Hindu gifting practices. *See* social welfare practices
Hindu Joint Family, The (Cornish), 249n45
Hindu law. *See* personal law
Hindu Law of Religious and Charitable Trust, The (Mukherjea), 270nn58–59, 272n87
Hindu rate of growth, 8, 243n22
Hindu Religious and Charitable Trusts Bill, 135–39
Hindu Undivided Family (HUF), 27, 49–51, 236, 248–49nn44–45; charitable gifting practices of, 72, 89–95, 105, 107–8; coparcenary status of, 17, 48, 57–58, 225; delegitimation of, 48, 52–53, 110–11; feminist discourses of, 30; inheritance and property practices of, 13–17, 72, 80, 89–95, 105, 111–15, 204, 272n93; reform and regulation of, 203–12, 216–31; taxation of, 54–60, 208–11, 223, 263n71; unlimited liability of, 50. *See also* family firms; gender contexts; personal law; vernacular capitalism
Hindu Wills Act of 1870, 92, 94
historiography of indigenous capitalism, 5–6, 241nn10–11, 244n26; anthropological approach to, 10–11, 245–46nn30–34; on the bazaar, 9–10, 243n24, 254n83; on charitable trusts, 73–75; functional approach to, 10, 245nn27–29; on market governance, 12–15, 246–47nn37–43; on Marwaris, 244n25, 250n52; nationalist contexts of, 11–12, 246n35, 251n63; on negotiations with sovereignty, 11–12, 14, 246n36

INDEX 335

history of capital: hegemony and, 6–7, 242nn16–18; localized challenges to master narratives of, 7–8, 242–43nn19–20. *See also* vernacular capitalism
Home Charges, 36, 258n12
horse racing, 183–84
Hukumchand, Sarupchand, 284n32, 296n166
Human Condition, The (Arendt), 256n89
hundis (bills of exchange), 61–64, 66, 264n82

idols, 269n51
Ilbert, C. P., 56, 112, 262n66
imaginary goods. *See* speculative practices; virtual capital
Income Tax Act of 1961, 96–97
Indian Chamber of Commerce, 196–97, 199–200, 211
Indian Charitable and Religious Trusts Act of 1920, 72–73, 98, 106, 133; on contracts and accountability, 128–34; Marwari responses to, 138–39; nationalist contexts of, 134–35; on public religious trusts, 98–99, 108–10, 123; on trustees and sovereignty, 134–39
Indian Charitable Endowments Act of 1890, 72–73, 80, 99–102; general public utility framework of, 103–10, 115, 121; on pension funds, 115–19; on public religious trusts, 109–33; reforms of, 106–10, 274n5, 281n81; on role of contract law, 114–15; on sovereign role of trusts, 103–10
Indian Companies Act of 1866, 39–40, 42–48
Indian Companies Act of 1882, 28, 34, 39–48; abolition of customs duties by, 36, 53; bankruptcy amendments to, 41–42, 48, 260nn39–40; on charity, 78–79, 98, 267n37; on companies as "public legal persons," 55; delegitimation of family firms by, 48–53, 110–11, 260n44, 261n46; on not-for-profit corporations, 78–79, 267n35; opinions on, 44–48, 259–60nn31–42; partnership registration requirements of, 51–52, 130; public association framework of, 48–53
Indian Contract Act of 1872, 35–36, 112, 206, 258n9
Indian Councils Acts of 1861 and 1892, 37, 106
Indian Economic Man, 2, 8, 18, 103–4, 201, 233–35, 237, 240n4
Indian Evidence Act of 1872, 35–36, 258n9
Indian Income Tax Act of 1860, 54–55
Indian Income Tax Act of 1886, 28, 34, 36, 53; charitable exemptions under, 54–56, 79, 95–99, 262n63, 267n37; on coparcenary (family) units, 57–59; definition of charity of, 78–79, 97; income thresholds of, 57; legitimation of family firms by, 57–60; mercantile and professional targets of, 56–57, 262n67; on pension funds, 116; precedents for, 54–55, 262nn54–55, 262n63
Indian Income Tax Act of 1922, 97–99, 273n101
Indian Industrial Conference of 1905, 150
Indian Industrial Conference of 1912, 233
Indian Jute Mills Association (IMJA), 190–92
Indian Merchants' Chamber, 207, 211

336 INDEX

Indian National Congress, 12, 37, 89, 203
Indian Partnership Act of 1932, 276n18
Indian Partnership Act of 1935, 261n49, 263n70
Indian Religious Endowments Act of 1863, 78, 131
Indian Securities Act, 112
Indian Societies Registration Act of 1860, 78, 116–18
Indian Succession Act of 1965, 92
Indian Trusts Act of 1882, 81–82
Indian Union, 57–58
indigenous capitalism. *See* vernacular capitalism
information exchange: expansion and standardization of, 37, 147, 149–50; for police work, 184–85; vernacular networks of, 145, 156–57, 161
inheritance. *See* mortmain and perpetuity; trusts
Inland Customs hedge, 36
Islamic law. *See* Muslim law; personal law
Ismailis, 15, 152, 249n45
Iyer, Govindharagava, 130–31
Iyer, Seshagiri, 130–31

Jagat Mohini Dossee v. Sokheemony Dossee, 92
Jains, 15, 19, 76, 202
Jajodia, Rang Lal, 220–22, 229
Jammya v. Diwan, 249n45
Jardine (Bombay High Court justice), 158–59
Jinnah, M. A., 136
joint contracts, 111–15, 276n18
joint families, 5–6, 15–17, 30, 200–231. *See also* family firms; gender contexts; Hindu Undivided Family
joint-stock corporations, 25, 33–35; bankruptcy law governing, 41–43, 48, 260nn39–40; citizenship implications of, 48; directorship of, 223; fraudulent practices of, 42–48; limited liability concept of, 39–48, 204; managing agency system of, 60, 264n79; memorandums of association of, 47; as public (civic) associations, 37, 48–53, 119; tax status of, 55. *See also* trusteeship
Juden und das Wirtschaftslieben, Die (Sombart), 245n30
jute markets, 152
jute speculation, 190–98, 284n33, 284n36, 296nn163–66, 303n64

Karachi Chamber of Commerce, 206–7
Kedia, Bhimsen, 276n15
Keynes, John Maynard, 282n4
Khaitan, Debi Prosad, 193–94, 211, 220–22, 224–25, 229, 303n64
Khandelwal kinship group, 19
Khattris, 18
Khimji, Hemraj, 156–58
kinship- and caste-based practices, 7, 12, 237; basis in trust of, 16, 51; codification of, 216–31; coparceners, 17, 48, 57–58; coresidence and property relationships of, 16–17, 248n48, 249n50; divisions of profession by, 284n28; historiography of, 10, 244n25; information networks of, 145; joint families, 5–6, 15–17, 30, 200; *mahajans*, 15; risk management, 151. *See also* family firms; Hindu Undivided Family; symbolic economies; vernacular capitalism

Lachiram, Nasiram, 235–36
Lachmichand Lalji Mal *dharmshala*, 127

Lal, Bajrang, 124–27
Lambert, John, 160
Land Revenue and Agriculture Department, 36–37
Laximichand Dossabhai and Bros., 107
layered sovereignty, 256n87
legal infrastructure. *See* contract law; joint-stock corporations; market governance; personal law; social reform; trusts
legal rights: of the public, 134; of shareholders, 48, 138
legal subjects, 6, 85–86
lex mercatoria (mercantile law), 14, 34, 66. *See also* market governance
liberalism, 8
license taxes, 55
limited liability, 33–35, 39–48; bankruptcy and, 41–43, 48, 260nn39–40; exclusion of family firms from, 49–53, 204; expansion of speculative practices of, 149; fraudulent practices of, 42–48; not-for-profit corporations, 78–79, 267n35; public nature of, 48–53
lineage, 16. *See also* kinship- and caste-based practices
logos/nomos categories, 24, 38–39, 61, 236, 259n20
London Stock Exchange, 35
Ludden, David, 240n8

Macaulay, Thomas, 6, 233–34, 241n13
Mackenzie, Alexander, 287n71
Madan Gopal, Rai Bahadur, 172–73
Madras Chamber of Commerce, 206–7
mahajans (merchant caste councils), 15
Maharani Shibessouree v. Mothooranath Acharjo, 82–83, 96, 270n59
Maheshwari journal, 213
Maheshwaris, 18, 212–13, 299n9
Maheswari Kul Chandrika (Malu), 301n35
Maheswari Mahasabha, 213
Maheswari Mahasabha Amrit Vallri (Barua), 301n35
Maine, Henry Sumner, 25, 62, 224, 241n11, 247n40
Maitland, F. W., 25, 35, 67–68, 70, 103–4, 257n7
Mal, Suraj, 124–27
Malaviya, Madan Mohan, 137, 209–10
Malu, Sukanand, 301n35
managing agency system, 60, 264n79
Mandlik, Viswanath Narayan, 262n67
Manohar Ganesh Tambekar v. Lakhmiram Govindram, 85–87, 270n63, 273n109
market, 3, 23. *See also* disembedded market
market ethics, 46, 72, 200. *See also* conduct of conduct
market governance, 12–13, 35–36, 253nn75–77; of charitable trusts, 67–79, 267n37; conduct of conduct in, 9, 23–24, 65, 243n23, 254nn78–83; contractual basis of, 21, 24, 30, 254–55nn80–81; as governmentality and political economy, 7–8, 20–24, 39, 242n19, 250n59, 251–52nn64–68, 253n74; by merchant caste councils, 15; public/private divide in, 14–17, 24–27, 38, 247–48nn39–43, 255–57nn85–94, 258n18; sovereignty of the market in, 21–25, 29, 251n65, 253n73, 256n87; subject-making of, 7–8, 36, 242–

43nn19–20, 251n65. *See also* commercial and tax regulation; disembedded market

marriage reforms, 201–3; on age of consent and child marriage, 216–22, 227–31, 304n82, 305n94, 305n96; on civil marriage, 223–27, 230, 303n71, 304n73

Marwari Agarwal journal, 213

Marwari Agarwal Mahasabha, 213, 214, 301n39

Marwari Association of Calcutta, 138, 189–93, 211–13, 220, 224–29, 290n102, 295n162

Marwari Chamber of Commerce, 189–93, 206–7, 211, 227–29, 300n20

Marwari Hitkarak journal, 213, 301n35

Marwari journal, 213

Marwari Relief Society, 213

Marwaris, 6, 17–20, 250nn53–54; on age of consent and child marriage reforms, 214–22, 227–31, 299n10, 304n82; in Burrabazar area of Calcutta, 160–72, 188–90, 192–93, 286nn64–66, 288n86; civic association and participation of, 171–72, 189–90, 211–16, 290nn102–5, 295n162, 297n179, 299n10, 301n30, 301n35, 302n42; on civil marriage reforms, 214–16, 223–27, 230, 299n10, 303n71, 304n73; cotton speculation of, 188–90; *dharmshala* centers of, 74, 88–89, 106, 109–10, 119–28, 139; endowment practices of, 109–10, 275n13, 276n15; exploitation of labor by, 19–20; futures trading of, 151–53; historiography of, 244n25, 250n52, 275n13, 276n15; homes of, 120; inheritance practices of, 113–15, 235–36; jute trade and speculation of, 152, 190–98, 284n33, 284n36, 296n166; migration patterns of, 152, 160, 284n31; opium trade of, 152, 284nn31–32, 290n107; patriarchal authority in, 30; promotion of Indian Culture by, 203; on public and private trusts, 138–39; rain gambling and, 29, 155–57, 160–73, 287nn71–75, 287n80, 288nn84–86, 289n101, 290n106, 292n120; social respectability focus of, 20, 193–98, 297n176, 297n187; social welfare practices of, 73–74, 88–89, 94–95, 106, 109–10; speculative profits of, 180, 303n64

Marwari Sudhar journal, 213

Marwari Trades Association, 193, 211, 293n138, 297n179

Marx, Karl: on bourgeois liberalism, 25, 255nn85–86; on Economic Man, 8, 234, 306n7; on gemeinschaft and gesellschaft, 241n11; on market sovereignty, 25–26; on political economy, 250n59, 255n86, 256n92; on purchase of labor-power, 271n77

Mauss, Marcel, 268n48

Me Apni Marwari Jati ko Pyar Karta Hun (Barua), 276n15

mimamsa system, 83–85

"Minute on Education" speech (Macaulay), 6, 233–34, 241n13

Mitakshara system of Hindu law, 247n39, 271n79; on family firms, 49–53; on inheritance at birth, 91–92, 272n82; on joint families, 204; patriarchal authority in, 17, 249n50; translation of, 90. *See also* mortmain and perpetuity

Mitchell, Timothy, 20–21, 240n9, 250n59, 251n62, 252n68

Mittal, Laxmi, 232–33

INDEX 339

modernity and economic development, 240nn8–9; exceptions for vernacular capitalism, 5; Hindu rate of growth, 8, 243n22; of Indian Economic Man, 2, 8, 18, 103–4, 201, 233–35, 237, 240n4; legal infrastructure of, 4–8, 20–23; stages of, 8–9, 243n22
Montague-Chelmsford reforms of 1919, 106–10, 274n5, 281n81
Morle-Minto reforms of 1909, 274n5
mortmain and perpetuity, 28, 68–72, 80, 265nn5–6; British Mortmain and Charitable Uses Act of 1888, 69–71; classification of, as private, 92–93, 272n87; customary endowments in, 90–91; of debt, 272n93; deities as proprietors of property in, 92–94; extracommercial space of, 89–90; Hindu Disposition of Property Act of 1921, 94; Hindu Undivided Family and, 89–96; Hindu Wills Act of 1870, 92, 94; Indian Succession Act of 1965, 92; survivorship and inheritance in, 91–92, 111–15, 272n93; symbolic economies of, 89, 271n77; taxation of, 95–96; Transfer of Property Act of 1882, 93–94
Motiram, Narotamdas, 156–58
Mukherjea, B. K., 81, 268n43, 270nn58–59, 272n87
Muslim law, 15–16, 249n45; on private trusts, 135, 137; on *waqfs* (charitable gifts), 75. *See also* personal law
Mussulman Waqf Act of 1913, 135, 137, 267n22
Mussulman Waqf Act of 1923, 135

Nagpur *dharmshala*, 110
Naroji, Dadabhai, 251n63

national debt, 35
nationalist contexts: of charitable and civic associations, 134–38; free-trade policies and, 150–51, 284n28; of historiography of indigenous capitalism, 11 12, 246n35, 251n63; promotion of vernacular capitalism in, 200–201; of social reform movements, 202–3, 299n12
native commerce. *See* vernacular capitalism
Nattukottai Chettiars, 38, 244n25, 249n47
Nawab of Bengal, 11
Negotiable Instruments Act of 1881, 28, 34, 37, 49, 60; assimilation of local usage by, 65–66; precedents and rationale for, 61–65; standardized policies of, 63–66, 110–11, 264n83
Nehru, Jawaharlal, 300n13
Nehru, Motilal, 136
Newatia, K. D., 302n40
not-for-profit corporations, 78–79, 267n35

objectification of the economy. *See* economy, as object
oikonomia, 23, 39, 253n74, 259n21
Oliphant, Laurence, 33
"On the Jewish Question" (Marx), 255nn85–86
opium gambling: Punjab surveys of, 172–77, 291n115, 291n117; United Provinces surveys and regulation of, 177–83, 292n126, 293n138
opium markets, 152, 284nn31–32, 290n107
options contracts, 146–48
Orientalism, 9–10, 243n24
Outline of a Theory of Practice (Bourdieu), 268n48

340 INDEX

Pal, Kristodas, 47, 164
Parsis, 152, 207
partnerships, 51–52, 261n49, 263n70
Peile, J. B., 42
pension funds, 115–19
personal law, 3–4; age of consent and child marriage and, 202–3, 216–22, 227–31, 304n82, 305n94, 305n96; charitable and private trusts and, 68–73, 80–89, 107–8, 268n38; as cultural formation, 5–6, 13, 21, 251n63; family firms and, 15–17, 27–30, 49–53, 110–11, 204–5, 248–49nn44–50; institutionalized orthodoxy of, 201–3; in jurisprudence on mortmain and perpetual endowments, 90–96, 111–15, 235–36, 272n93; patriarchal consensus in, 14, 30, 248n42; trade and finance and, 61, 264nn81–82; universalized application of, 13–15, 205, 247–48nn39–43, 249n45. *See also* kinship- and caste-based practices; social reform; vernacular capitalism
personal liability, 41
philanthropy. *See* trusts
Philosophy of Right (Hegel), 255n85
Poddar, H. P., 297n187
Poddar *Dharmshala* of Nagpur, 110
Polanyi, Karl: critical readings on, 244n26; on the disembedded market, 4, 240n9; on the economy, 250n59, 253n74; on embedded economies, 268n48; gemeinschaft and gesellschaft and, 241n11
political economy: colonial law on, 22–23, 252–63nn69–73; conduct of conduct and, 9, 23–24, 65, 243n23, 254nn78–83; cultural politics of, 11; of the East India Company, 22–24, 254n80; governmentality, 7–8, 20–24, 39, 242n19, 250n59, 251–52nn64–68, 253n74; Marx's critique of, 250n59; in nationalist contexts, 150–51, 251n63; as public household, 60. *See also* market governance
Politics, The (Aristotle), 253n74
Poovey, Mary, 33–35, 257n8
postal system, 37
postcolonial approaches: Chakrabarty on capital, 241n10, 254n83; Chatterjee on the anticolonial nation-state, 26–27; to gender and nationalism, 299n12; to market governance, 13–15; Spivak on subjectivity and agency, 241–42nn13–14, 243n22
Prahalad, C. K., 239n3
Prakash, Gyan, 250n57
Prasad, Rai Jyoti, 122–23
Presidency College, 151
princely states, 57
private trusts, 28–29, 58, 70–72, 98–102, 273n101, 275n11
Prosonna Kumari Debya and another v. Golab Chand Babu, 84
Protestant Ethic and the Spirit of Capitalism, The (Weber), 245n30
public charitable trusts, 103–39, 275n11; classifications of, 109, 119–23, 132; codification of, 129–34; contractual accountability of, 128–34; mercantile gifting to, 109–10; official trustees of, 108–9, 111, 114–15; registration of, 129–32; *Sarais* Act of 1867, 123–28; tax status of, 108, 115–19. *See also* public religious trusts
public/private domains, 3–7, 20; of family trusts, 68–73, 75; gendered discourses of tradition in,

INDEX 341

public/private domains (*continued*) 14, 25–26; of gifts to sovereigns, 101–2; historiography of, 9–12, 14–15, 247–48nn39–43; legal parameters of, 15, 38–39, 48–53; of local markets, 22, 252n72; in market governance, 4–5, 24–27, 38, 58–59, 200, 255–57nn85–94, 258n18; marriage exchange and, 201–12, 216–31; of religious trusts, 98–110; in speculative practices, 151, 158, 171–77, 197–98; in tax policy, 54–60. *See also* family firms; gender contexts; personal law; sovereignty; vernacular capitalism

public religious trusts, 98–105, 275n11; classifications of, 134; deities as, 101, 273n109; *dharmshala* centers, 88–89, 109–10, 119–28, 139, 271n75; orthodox views on, 131–32, 135–38, 267n22, 280n72

Punjab Land Alienation Act of 1901, 94

Punjab Public Gambling Act of 1867, 172–74, 291n117

purdah, 302n40

Race-Course Licensing Act of 1912, 184

Rahimtoola, Ibrahim, 129–30

rain gambling (*barsat ka satta*), 29, 155–57, 160–73, 287nn71–75, 287n80, 288nn84–86, 289n101, 290n106, 292n120

Raj. *See* colonial governance

Ram Pretap Nemani and Another v. King Emperor, 186–87

Ram Temple of Nagpur, 110

Rangoon Chamber of Commerce, 206–7

Rao, Srinivasa, 129

rape, 217–22

Ray, Rajat, 243n24, 299n12

rebellions of 1857, 3, 22, 36

religio-cultural contexts of indigenous charity, 71–74, 268n43, 268n48; "colorable" gifts, 79, 96, 267n37; in commercial activity, 87–89; deities as proprietors of property, 80–87, 92–94, 101, 269n51, 270n63, 273n109; dharma gifts, 71, 74–76, 79, 86–89, 267n37, 278n44; Diwali rituals, 87–88; Indian Trusts Act of 1882, 81–82; *mimamsa* system, 83–85; tax status of, 55, 95–102, 107–8, 262n63; temples, 73, 78–80, 85–89. *See also* public religious trusts

Religious Endowments Conference of 1914, 131–32

respectability, 20; in social reform contexts, 203; of speculative practices, 193–98, 297n176, 297n187

Rousseau, Jean-Jacques, 253n74

Roy, Sreenath, 49–51, 299n12

Royal Commission on Currency and Finance, 211

Rudner, David, 38, 74, 244n25, 249n47

rule limiting perpetuities, 90

rule of law, 1–2, 15, 37–38, 239nn1–2

Rup Chand Chowdhry v. Latu Chowdhry, 249n45

Sarais Act of 1867, 106, 123–28

Saraswati, Prannath, 86

Sarda, Har Bilas, 203, 219, 227–30, 286n66, 302n55

Sarda Bill. *See* Child Marriage Restraint Act of 1929

satta transactions, 153, 179, 190, 284n36, 285n39

secular private trusts, 275n11

342 INDEX

Sen, Amartya, 243n22
Sen, Sudipta, 22, 252nn71–72
Seth, Jagat, 11–12
sevaks ("those who serve"), 85–87, 270n67
shared sovereignty, 106–10, 274n5
share trading, 35
silver gambling, 177–83
Sindhis, 18, 244n25
Sind Mutual Family Relief Fund, 116–18
Singh, Babu Dhela, 124
Sinha, Mrinalini, 230, 248n42, 299n12, 304n82
Smith, Adam, 22, 36, 253n74, 258n10, 263n78
social, 105, 256n89
social reform, 299n10; of age of consent and child marriage, 216–22, 227–31, 304n82, 305n94, 305n96; of civil marriage, 215–16, 223–27, 230, 303n71, 304n73; historiography of, 201, 298n6, 298n8; of the joint family firm, 203–12; by Marwari civic organizations, 211–16, 301n30, 301n35, 302n42; public/private domains and, 230–31
social welfare practices, 28; dharma gifts, 71, 74–76, 79, 86–89, 267n37, 278n44; *mimamsa* system, 83–85; participation in sovereignty through, 77–78; of private family trusts, 29, 58, 71–72, 119–23; religious domain of, 72–73, 78–89, 92–94; taxation, 54–56. *See also* public religious trusts; trusts
Sohan Lal, Rai Bahadur Bakshi, 216–17
Sombart, Werner, 245n30
sovereignty: the market and, 22–23, 25; Marx's critique of bourgeois sovereignty, 25–26; merchant charitable gifting and, 29, 77–78, 101–2, 127–28, 133–39; merchants' claims to, 12, 200; merchants' negotiations with, 6, 11–12; nationalist reform of trusts and, 134–39; negotiable or layered sovereignty, 77–78, 105–10, 256n87; non-negotiable modern sovereignty, 25, 105, 236, 274nn3–4; personal law and, 4, 13–15; as public trust relation, 100–110, 129–39, 274n5; shared, vs. shares in, 106–10. *See also* disembedded market
sowda transactions, 152–53, 215, 285nn38–40
spatial readings of stages of capital, 8–9, 237
Special Marriage Act of 1872, 224
Special Marriage Amendment Bill of 1911, 224–27, 303n71, 304n73
speculative practices: betting, 149, 158; in common gaming houses, 154–60; cotton speculation, 184–90, 294n150, 294n153, 295nn156–58; ethical debates over, 144–45, 150–51, 168–69, 177–79, 183–84, 284n28, 287n72, 287n80, 288–89nn92–93, 295nn156–58; Euro-American contexts of, 145–50, 282n7, 283n19, 290n107; futures contracts, 147–48; futures trading, 145–46, 149, 151–53, 178–81, 282n4; gambling, 144, 146–50, 154–60, 286n55; grain speculation, 173–74, 177–83; horse racing, 183–84; information exchange in, 145, 147, 149–50, 156–57, 184–85; jute speculation, 190–98, 284n33, 284n36, 296nn163–66, 303n64; legitimate methods of, 182–84, 193–98, 297n176; opium gambling, 174–

INDEX 343

speculative practices (*continued*) 83, 291n115, 291n117, 292n126, 293n138; options contracts, 146–48; policing of, 184–85, 197, 285n48, 294n153; profits from, 180; public/private domains in, 149, 151, 158, 171–77, 197–98; rain gambling, 29, 155–57, 160–73, 287nn71–75, 287n80, 288nn84–86, 289n101, 290n106, 292n120; regulation of, 144–45, 154–60, 169–72, 182–84, 189–97, 287nn71–74, 289n101, 290nn106–7, 291n117, 296n174; respectability and reputation in, 183–89, 193–98, 297n176, 297n187; silver gambling, 177–83; United Provinces survey of, 177–84; wagering, 157–60

Spivak, Gayatri Chakravorty: on "culture alive," 24, 254n83; postcolonial readings by, 233–34, 241–42nn13–14, 243n22; on subaltern studies, 249n48, 256n92, 299n12; on worlding, 274n4

Sri Ranchodrai Temple, 85–87

State, Trust and Corporation (Maitland), 67

Stephen, James Fitzjames, 62

"Stock Exchange Gambling" (Wilson), 149–50

stridan (marriage portion), 17

Structural Transformation of the Public Sphere (Habermas), 256nn89–91

subaltern studies, 249n48, 256n92, 257n93, 299n12

subject formation, 13; of cultural subjects, 230–31; Macaulay's economic subjects, 6, 233–34, 241n13; as making of Economic Man, 8, 12, 71, 103–4, 201, 233–35, 237, 240n4; through market governance, 7–8, 36, 242–43nn19–20; Spivak's postcolonial readings of, 233–34, 241–42nn13–14, 243n22; of the trustee, 71, 100–110, 129–39

Subrahmanyam, Sanjay, 244nn25–26, 245n33

superstitious trusts, 69, 266n8

Super-Tax Act of 1917, 208–11

survivorship. *See* mortmain and perpetuity

Swadeshi movement, 150–51, 206

symbolic economies, 10, 72, 266n15; extensive negotiability of, 21, 61, 89, 101, 233; gift exchange and, 268n48

Tagore v. Tagore, 93–95, 272n88

Tata, Jamshedji, 110

tax policies, 275n11; on agricultural income, 53, 55; on charities, 54–56, 78–79, 95–102; on coparceners, 57–58; on customs revenue, 262n54; on deities, 96–99; on earned income, 53, 56–57, 59, 262n67; on joint family firms, 54–60, 208–11, 223, 263nn70–71; on land revenue, 262n54; license and certificate taxes, 55, 262n60; on pension funds, 116; on private trusts, 98–102, 273n101; public/private distinctions in, 54–60; on public religious trusts, 108, 115–19; religious exemptions, 55, 79, 96–99, 108, 115–19, 262n63, 267n37

teji mundi transactions, 153, 173–75, 181, 285n40

telegraph communication, 147, 150

temples, 73, 78–80; Dakor Temple case, 85–87, 96, 108, 273n109; donations to, 88–89; public oversight of, 109–10. *See also* public religious trusts; religio-cultural contexts of indigenous charity

temporal readings of stages of capital, 8–9, 237
Tewary, Shivanunda, 163, 167, 169–70
Thakurdas, Purshotamdas, 136–37
Timberg, Thomas, 244n25, 250n52, 275n13, 284nn31–32
Tönnies, Ferdinand, 241n11
Transfer of Property Act of 1882, 93–94
transportation networks, 150, 283n25
"Trust and Corporation" (Maitland), 104
trust contracts, 28–29
trusteeship, 71, 81, 223; contractual accountability of, 129–34; Gandhi's concept of, 103–4, 268n38, 274n1; government's roles in, 100–102, 111, 114–15; of public religious trusts, 108, 114–15; as sovereignty, 103–10, 134–39
trusts: family trusts, 28–29, 58, 71–72, 119–23; general public utility framework of, 29, 68–70, 78–79, 98, 103–10, 119, 236, 267n37; government's role in, 100–102, 111, 114–15; historiography of, 73–75; Income Tax Act of 1961, 96–97; Indian Charitable and Religious Trusts Act of 1920, 72–73; Indian Charitable Endowments Act of 1890, 72–73, 80, 99–102; Indian Religious Endowments Act of 1863, 78; Indian Trusts Act of 1882, 81–82; as joint contracts, 111–15, 276n18; legal actors in, 81–85; as mortmain, 68–70, 72, 80, 89–96, 265nn5–6; under Muslim law, 135, 137; not-for-profit corporations, 78–79, 267n35; pension funds, 115–19; precedents for, 77–89; private trusts, 28–29, 58, 70–72, 98–102, 273n101, 275n11; public charitable trusts, 103–34; public/private domains of, 68–72, 75, 99–102; public religious trusts, 98–102, 134–39; registration of, 78, 116–19, 129–31; religious domains of, 71–74, 78–89, 92–94, 98–102; secular civic function of, 89, 106–7; secular private trusts, 275n11; sovereign status of, 103–10, 134–39; taxation of, 54–56, 95–102, 273n101. *See also* social welfare practices
Tudor, Owen Davies, 265n6

Uncovenanted Service Family Pension Fund, 116
United Provinces Public Gambling Amendment Act of 1917, 182–83
United Provinces survey of speculative practices, 177–84
Upper Burma, 56, 262n55
Upper India Chamber of Commerce, 181, 206–7
UP Public Gambling Act, 179

Vagrant Act of 1868, 144–45
Vedas, 204
vernacular capitalism, 2–12, 237; British noninterference in, 3–4, 63, 66, 73; as corporate body and national economic experts, 199–200; as cultural actor, 200; disembedding of markets in, 5–6, 34–39, 58–59, 241nn10–11; extensive negotiability in, 11–12, 14, 21, 25, 37–38, 49, 89, 105; family firms, 15–17, 27–30, 49–53, 248–49nn44–50; family trusts, 28–29, 58, 71–72, 119–23; historiography of, 9–12, 243–44nn24–26; information net-

INDEX   345

vernacular capitalism (*continued*) works in, 145, 161; inheritance practices in, 111–15; kinship basis of, 5–7, 12; legal exceptions for, 5–7; in local markets and bazaars, 9–10, 22, 252n72, 254n83; pension funds, 115; personal law of, 61, 264nn81–82; as premodern gemeinschaft, 6–7, 24, 27, 105, 241n11; public expressions of, 106–8; risk management in, 151; social welfare practices of, 28–29, 54–56, 58; standardization of, 12, 25, 27–29, 60–66, 264n83; taxation of, 53–60; unlimited liability in, 49–53, 204. *See also* Hindu Undivided Family; Marwaris; personal law; social reform; speculative practices

Victoria Acts 16–19 of 1853–1854, 144–45

Village Communities in East and West (Maine), 241n11

virtual capital, 30, 35–36, 144, 257n99

Wagering Associations Bill, 193–95, 297n176
wagers, 157–60
Wallerstein, Immanuel, 242n17
waqfs (Islamic endowments), 75, 135, 137, 267n22
Washbrook, David, 37, 240n7
Wealth of Nations (Smith), 253n74
Weber, Max, 25; on custom, 24; on gemeinschaft and gesellschaft, 241n11; *logos/nomos* distinction and, 259n20; on rationality, 245n30
Weinberger, Caspar, 239n2
women. *See* gender contexts
Working, Holbrook, 282n4
World Bank, 243n22
world-systems theory, 242n17

Yang, Anand, 243n24
Young Marwari Sabha, Karachi, 227

Zemon Davis, Natalie, 244n26, 245n30

RITU BIRLA
is an associate professor of history at
the University of Toronto.

Library of Congress Cataloging-in-Publication Data
Birla, Ritu
Stages of capital : law, culture, and market governance in
late colonial India / Ritu Birla.
p. cm.
Includes bibliographical references and index.
ISBN 978-0-8223-4245-8 (cloth : alk. paper)
ISBN 978-0-8223-4268-7 (pbk. : alk. paper)
1. India—Politics and government—1857–1919. 2. India—
Politics and government—1919–1947. 3. India—Economic
policy. 4. Great Britain—Colonies—Economic policy.
5. Rule of law—India. I. Title.
HC435.B57 2009
330.954′035—dc22
2008041778